Supply Chain Analytics

Kurt Y. Liu

Supply Chain Analytics

Concepts, Techniques and Applications

Kurt Y. Liu
Adam Smith Business School
University of Glasgow
Glasgow, UK

ISBN 978-3-030-92223-8   ISBN 978-3-030-92224-5   (eBook)
https://doi.org/10.1007/978-3-030-92224-5

This Palgrave Macmillan imprint is published by the registered company Springer Nature Switzerland AG
The registered company address is: Gewerbestrasse 11, 6330 Cham, Switzerland

To my family, who have always encircled me with love, patience, and support—my parents, my wife, and my sons.

—K.Y.L

Preface

Supply chain analytics is an emerging topic in both academia and industries as using data to get useful insights into effective decision making in supply chain and logistics management field is gaining strong momentum in recent years. However, there is a lack of textbooks that specifically focus on applying data analytics in supply chain management, while majority of available texts on the market are written for subjects such as business analytics and marketing analytics.

The main objective of this book is to introduce how data analytics and machines learning can be applied in the supply chain management field to provide meaningful insights for supply chain and logistics managers in their daily decision making. To achieve this objective, the book is structured in such a way that the readers can learn not only the fundamental concepts of supply chain management, but also the relevant data analytics techniques and the applicable machine learning algorithms for solving practical problems.

A particular focus of this book is on *application* rather than developing the various data analytics and machine learning algorithms in that the intended audience of this book is within the business management domain. Though having a computer science or mathematics background may have an advantage in understanding the content covered in this book, it is not essentially required for readers to follow through the book.

When writing this book, I have also tried to draw a clear line between supply chain analytics and operations research (OR) although these two subjects have many overlaps. However, OR is a well-established research domain which primarily involves the construction of mathematical models for optimization problems; whereas supply chain analytics focuses on the use of massive data and learning from them to improve decision making for effective supply chain management. We have only slightly touched upon linear programming for solving optimization problems in warehousing, logistics network design, and route optimization; other than that, no further topics from OR are included in the book.

This book is aimed at introductory level of supply chain analytics for those who have limited background in supply chain management, data analytics, and machine learning. It does not contain advanced machine learning algorithms and deep learning techniques and should be appropriate for postgraduate students in business and management subjects, MBA students, and senior undergraduate students, who have interests in both supply chain management and data analytics. The book could also be useful as a reference book for practitioners in relevant industries looking for learning analytics and digital transformation in their supply chain and logistics operations.

Each chapter in this book generally contains key learning outcomes, concepts, techniques, and algorithms as well as practical examples, followed by discussion questions and keyboard exercise in the end. All the practical examples and analytics models introduced in this book are developed with Python; however, it does not prevent interested learners from applying alternative programming languages to solve these problems. A detailed structure of the data analytics introduced in this book is revealed in the diagram given below:

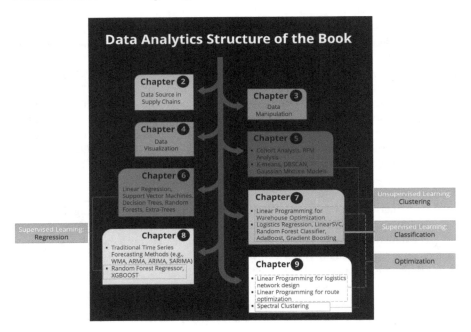

For Instructors

All the instructor resources can be found at Palgrave Macmillan's resource centre. The additional Python Jupyter notebooks, exercises, and solutions for each related chapter can be found at our online GitHub repository: https://github.com/pysca/SCA.

For Students

This book can be used by students who have no programming background; however, it does not intend to cover all Python basics in programming. Students are highly recommended to use complementary textbooks while studying this book to gain a better understanding of Python and its various libraries and packages. In addition to the online GitHub repository provided above, where students can find all the Jupyter notebooks, exercises, and solutions for each chapter, there are numerous free online resources available (e.g., GitHub and Kaggle) for students to practise their coding and programming skills.

Glasgow, UK

Kurt Y. Liu

Acknowledgements

I would like to thank the reviewers whose suggestions significantly helped shape the structure and contents of the book. I would also like to thank the editors and the publisher for their efforts and support throughout the process. I am forever grateful to my former professor and friend at ASU, Prof. Sue P. Siferd, who has always believed in me and encouraged me to reach higher in my career. She will be deeply missed.

"The textbook *Supply Chain Analytics* by Kurt Liu provides an excellent hands-on introduction to supply chain management and logistics and associated quantitative methods from a data-science perspective using Python. The book first covers supply chain management basics and how to get started in data science using Python including data handling, pre-processing and visualization. Fundamental supply chain activities, data analysis, forecasting and decision making on the customer and supplier side, in inventory management, and for location and routing in logistics are introduced. The didactical concept to integrate topical basics and to present fundamental data analysis and decision support methods with examples coded in Python gives students a unique introduction to both important areas and the required knowledge and skills in supply chain analytics. I highly recommend this book for class adoption."

—**Professor Dr Stefan Minner** *Chair of Logistics and Supply Chain Management, TUM School of Management, Technical University of Munich, Germany*

"*Supply Chain Analytics* by Kurt Liu combines the essence of supply chain strategy with decisions taken at strategic, tactical, and operational levels and how data can support these decisions. Dr Liu makes this title appealing to supply chain students and researchers by integrating analytics themes with their execution in Python, which is among the top preferred data science languages. The treatment of data manipulation before any modelling exercise is commendable since the data from the real world are hardly ever ready to use. It is exciting to find the state-of-the-art prediction algorithms applied to supply chain problems. This book will join the reading lists of many supply chain programmes."

—**Prof Dr Emel Aktas** *Chair of Supply Chain Analytics, Cranfield School of Management, Cranfield University, United Kingdom*

"Data analytics is transforming the practice of supply chain management. This excellent primer provides an essential introduction of supply chain analytics that can benefit all interested learners, from novices to experienced ones. It offers an insightful synthesis of supply chain management and data analytics.

A truly impressive book on the topic that is well developed, very readable, and full of real-life examples that illuminate the underlying principles and emerging trends. Worth reading and highly recommended."

—**Benjamin B. M. Shao** *Professor of Information Systems, Director of the Digital Society Initiative, W. P. Carey School of Business, Arizona State University, United States of America*

Contents

About the Author

Kurt Y. Liu is an Associate Professor of Supply Chain Analytics at the Adam Smith Business School, University of Glasgow. He teaches Executive, MBA, graduate, and undergraduate students on supply chain, logistics, and operations management. His research focuses on supply chain analytics, supply network configuration, and sustainable supply chain management. He studied at Waikato Management School, University of Waikato, New Zealand, and W.P. Carey School of Business, Arizona State University, USA, for his bachelor's degree in Supply Chain Management. He has Master's in Logistics Management and Master's in Transport Management from the Institute of Transport and Logistics Studies (ITLS), University of Sydney, Australia, and a PhD in Engineering from the University of Cambridge, UK. He is a Fellow of the Higher Education Academy (FHEA) and a Chartered Member of The Chartered Institute of Logistics and Transport (CILT), UK.

Introduction

1

Contents

Learning Objectives
- Understand the supply chain structures and its major components.
- Describe the three supply chain flows and explain their importance.
- Explain why there is a supply chain and why we should manage it.
- Understand the concepts of business analytics and explain its four major types.
- Explain what supply chain analytics is, its main benefits, and SMART goals.

1.1 What Is a Supply Chain?

The term **supply chain** has been widely used today to represent the complex networks and links of businesses entities to make and deliver products and/or services to customers. Similar terms exist, for example, demand chain (from the customer

© The Author(s), under exclusive license to Springer Nature
Switzerland AG 2022
K. Y. Liu, *Supply Chain Analytics*, https://doi.org/10.1007/978-3-030-92224-5_1

perspective), supply network, value chain or value network, whilst the latter focuses more on value-adding/creating activities. Despite having different emphases, they basically mean the same thing, i.e., supply chain. In reality, a supply chain is a very complex system consisting of multiple suppliers, distribution centres, warehouses, and retailers, etc. Thus, a supply chain is not a simple chain but rather a **supply network**. In this book, we use the terms supply chain and supply network interchangeably.

Within a supply chain, there must be a focal firm, who is the key product and/or service provider, albeit it may not actually make any physical goods or delivery service itself. For instance, iPhone is designed by Apple Inc., however the company itself does not actually manufacture the product. As a focal firm, Apple Inc. outsources the manufacturing activity to its suppliers such as Foxconn, which makes iPhones in China and then ships the finished products to the US market or other places around the world where there is customer demand. In other words, the focal firm is the initializer of a supply chain, with the aim of making and delivering products and/or services to customers. Without the focal firm, the supply chain would not exist.

1.1.1   Why Do We Need a Supply Chain?

Let us consider the case of making a car. A typical car consists about 30,000 parts made from different raw materials and various manufacturing processes. Imagine that if a car maker could produce everything in-house itself, from raw material extraction, refinery, parts and components making, to painting, assembly, and final products delivery to customers, then it may not need any suppliers, distributors, and dealers, etc. In reality, this is not possible! The car maker would have to focus on its core competences (e.g., car design and final assembly), and outsource non-competent and/or non-value activities (e.g., making car stereos, delivery, etc.) to other manufacturers who are specialized in certain processes and activities. By outsourcing, car makers can substantially reduce costs and maximize profits.

In short, if we can produce everything by ourselves, supply chain would not exist. However, there is no such magic in the world. Every business, no matter big or small, would need a supply chain to delivery products and/or services (directly or indirectly) to customers. A sole service provider may have a very simple and short supply chain, but once there exists a buyer–supplier relationship, there is a supply chain.

1.1.2   Structure of a Supply Chain

A typical supply chain may include all the parties who are, directly or indirectly, involved in the making and delivering of products and/or services to the end customers. For example, an automotive supply chain may consist of hundreds of suppliers and service providers, who supply the automakers, and once cars are produced, they will be shipped to downstream wholesalers and car dealers, and finally sold to customers. Figure 1.1 represents a simplified supply chain structure.

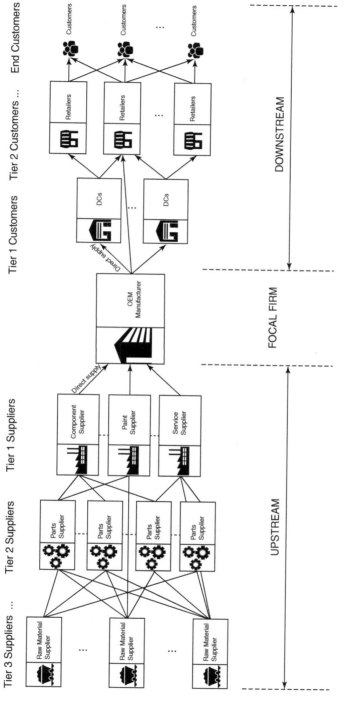

Fig. 1.1 Structure of a supply chain

There are several terms that are commonly used in a supply chain. From a focal firm's point of view, a supply chain has the **upstream**, which are mainly comprised of all the suppliers. In the upstream, there are first-tier suppliers, who directly supply products and/or services to the focal firm. The first-tier suppliers also have their own suppliers (i.e., suppliers' suppliers), who are often referred to second-tier suppliers of the focal firm. A supply chain can have multi-tier suppliers in the upstream, depending on the business types or sectors, i.e., from first tier, second tier, third tier, etc., all the way up to the original raw material suppliers.

The **downstream** of a supply chain is often regarded as the customers of the focal firm. Likewise, it can have first-tier customers, second-tier customers, and all the way down to the end customers. Customers can be both internal and external ones. For instance, when a finished car comes off its production line, it can be shipped to a regional distribution centre (DC) before being sent off to a specific car dealer. In this case, the DC can be called a first-tier customer, though it may be owned and operated by the car maker itself. The car dealer can be named second-tier customers, and an individual car buyer from the car dealer is the third-tier customer or the end customer.

1.1.3 Supply Chain Processes

Another useful perspective to look at supply chain is through the process angle. A supply chain can be viewed as inter-connected processes wherein various involved members work together to acquire resources (e.g., raw materials, information, parts and components), convert them into finished products and/or services through specific transformation processes, and delivery the products and/or services to fulfil customer expectations (see Fig. 1.2).

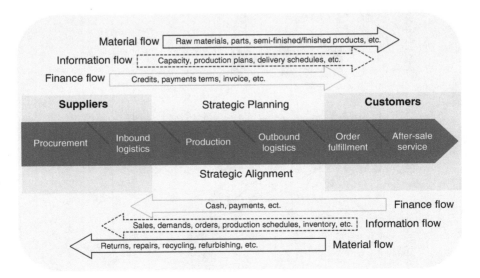

Fig. 1.2 Supply chain as processes to fulfil customer demand

These key supply chain processes include **procurement** (e.g., contract negotiation, supplier selection and evaluation), **logistics** (inbound and outbound), internal **production** (i.e., transformation process), **order fulfilment** (e.g., demand management, order processing, and order delivery), and **after-sale service** (e.g., warranty, repairs, returns, and recalls).

> *A supply chain can be viewed as inter-connected processes wherein various involved members work together to fulfil customer expectations.*

Each supply chain process contains a variety of activities, which are summarized in Table 1.1. Note that there are different views on the definitions of logistics and supply chain. In this book we treat logistics as a part of supply chain processes, which mainly deals with the physical movement and distribution of goods and services.

Supply chain processes are not isolated but are rather **boundary-spanning activities** across various business functions within an organization, for instance, research and development (R&D), product design, accounting and finance, sales and marketing, etc. Supply chain excellence cannot be achieved without strong collaboration and coordination among internal departments. The active involvement of supply chain department in strategic decision making can bring enormous

Table 1.1 Examples of supply chain activities

Procurement	Inbound logistics	Production	Outbound logistics	Order fulfilment	After-sale service
• Make purchasing decisions • Select and evaluate suppliers • Negotiate contracts and form partnerships with suppliers • Develop strategic alliance with suppliers • Monitor and evaluate suppliers' performances, etc.	• Materials receiving from suppliers to a focal firm's factory/plants • Route selection • Transport mode selection • Fleet management • Warehousing and storage • Inventory management, etc.	• Internal operations management • Production planning and scheduling • Quality improvement and control • Business process engineering • Cost control, etc.	• Deliver finished goods to customers • Packaging • Route and transport mode selection • Warehousing and storage • Inventory management, etc.	• Order receiving and recording • Order processing • Order picking • Order checking and packing • Ship orders to end customers • Customer account management • Demand management	• Warranty and repairs • Installation • Product returns and recalls • Spare parts • On-site support • Maintenance • User training • Recycle and reuse

benefits to the focal firm. For example, effective production planning and scheduling requires accurate demand forecasting, which can only be realized if there is strong collaboration between internal operations and the sales and marketing team to share timely demand information. When launching new products to the market, actively involving the procurement team in the product design process can assist in searching for competent and reliable suppliers who are capable of delivering required components for making the new products.

When a focal firm initially designs and configures its supply chain, it needs to decide carefully on the types of supply chains that align well with its competitive strategies and core competences. For instance, a cost leadership focused business may choose to adopt an efficient supply chain design in order to drive cost down in its supply chain processes. **Strategic planning** and **alignment** of supply chain processes with a firm's competitive strategies can ensure effective supply chain configurations for realizing business objectives and sustained competitive advantages.

For example, when there are stable, high volume, low variety, and less uncertainties in demand, a **lean supply chain** configuration that focuses on efficiency and waste reduction might work best, whereas an **agile supply chain** may excel in a less predictable environment where there are high variety, less stable, and high uncertainties in demand (Christopher and Towill 2000). In some sectors, a *'leagile'* supply chain configuration (see Fig. 1.3), combining the lean process and agile process with a decoupling point in the supply chain is often used to improve efficiency, responsiveness, and flexibility to satisfy various customer demands, such as in the automotive industry.

1.1.4 Supply Chain Flows

Within a supply chain, there are three critical flows that underpinning the success of a supply chain management, namely **materials flow**—the physical movement of raw materials, parts and components, semi-finished and finished products; **information flow**—all the relevant data and information communicated and shared among supply chain members including, for example, sales and demand data, production plans and schedules, delivery date, inventory levels, and available production capacities; **financial flow**—the related transactions about money payment, credit, cash, and invoice among supply chain members.

As illustrated in Fig. 1.2, all three flows can go bi-directional in the supply chain. The vital task of achieving supply chain excellence is to ensure the smooth, accurate,

Fig. 1.3 A leagile supply chain configuration

and timely movement of the three supply chain flows. In addition, although which might not be so visible and formally recognized, the inter-firm **power** can be another important supply chain element. Careful exertion and manipulation of supply chain power can play a critical role in establishing effective and integrated buyer–supplier relationships for achieving high performance in a supply chain (Benton and Maloni 2005).

1.2   Supply Chain Management

In previous section, we have introduced the basics of a supply chain, including its concepts, key components, processes, and flows. However, what is supply chain management (SCM) and why do we need to manage the supply chain? These are important questions to address.

Supply Chain Process at Starbucks

Consider yourself walking into a Starbucks and ordering a cup of coffee. The supply chain process starts with a staff taking your order and payment. Starbucks then prepares your order, using stored coffee beans, fresh milk, and other ingredients, through its unique coffee making process at the shop, and finally hands over the gourmet coffee to you in a timely manner.

The whole process may seem to be a very simple and straightforward process. However, to delivery your order, Starbucks needs to make sure they have enough coffee beans and other ingredients in stock to meet daily customer demands. At the background of its operations, each store sends point-of-sales data and replenishment orders to regional warehouses or distributors, who deliver the replenishment orders to the store. Starbucks supply chain team must accurately forecast the demands, source the right amount and premium quality of coffee beans, make timely production in its roasting centres, and then rapidly deliver the beans to each of its branch stores.

Starbucks also needs to establish a good relationship with coffee farmers and key suppliers, which can not only help the firm to secure high-quality supplies of coffee beans and other ingredients, but also drive the cost down. Considering its over 25,000 stores in six continents, supply chain management at Starbucks is not an easy task at all. It has a massive supply network, riddled with complexities and uncertainties. For the operator of a small commercial enterprise, Starbucks may have a lot of more urgent business priorities than its supply chain management. However, it must ensure an affordable movement of ingredients, materials, products, and services to make Starbucks offerings spectacularly unforgettable to its customers (Leblanc 2018). ◄

▶ **Supply chain management** is defined as the systematic and strategic integration and coordination of various business functions and processes across the supply chain to create value for the ultimate customers in an effective and efficient manner.

It encompasses the management of internal and external supply chain processes, the involved supply chain flows, the buyer–supplier relationships, and the structures of the networks of inter-connected businesses as well as making strategic planning and alignment of supply chain strategies with the overall business objectives.

Supply chain management (SCM) aims to deliver enhanced customer service and experience through synchronized management of the flow of physical goods, associated information and finance, from point of origin to point of consumption. A simpler way to put it, SCM aims to make the **right** products and services to the **right** customers, at the **right** cost, **right** quantity, **right** quality, **right** time, and **right** place (i.e., **7Rs** of SCM). Effective SCM should align closely with a firm's overall business strategy (e.g., cost leadership vs. differentiation) and improve a firm's competitive advantage and profitability by enhancing overall customer satisfaction (Fig. 1.4).

The management philosophy of SCM extends traditional internal business functions and processes by bringing supply chain partners together with the common goal of optimization and efficiency (Tan et al. 1998). In today's highly competitive environment, the increasing reliance on supply network relationships, shifting channel power, and globalization necessitate the use of SCM for enhanced competitiveness.

Supply chain offers a rich venue for businesses to seek strategic access to complementary resources, knowledge, and technologies from supply chain partners and

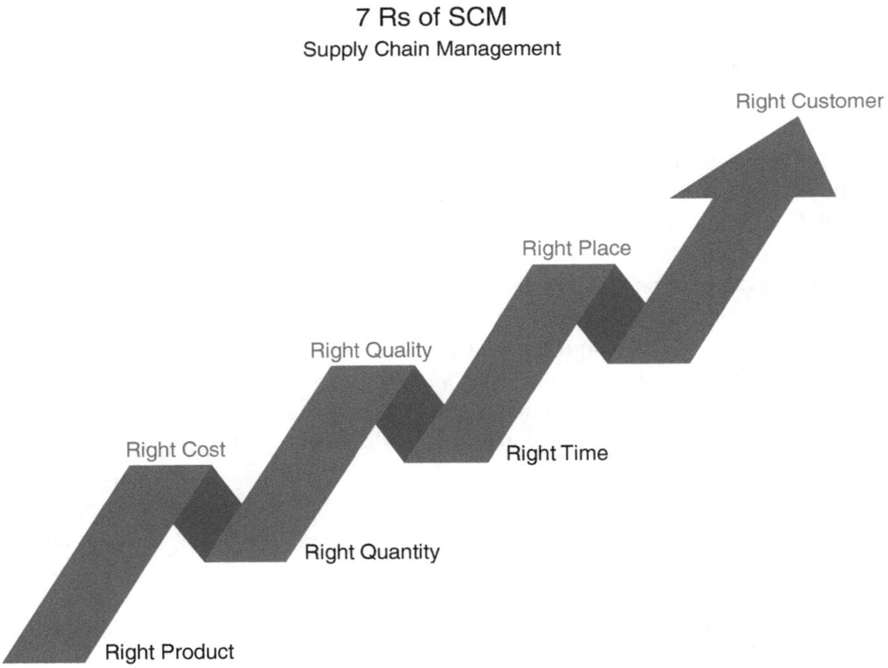

Fig. 1.4 7Rs of SCM

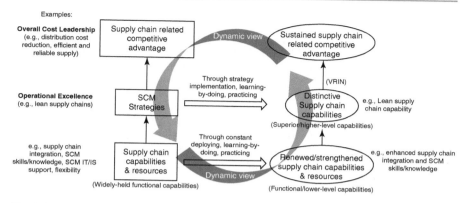

Fig. 1.5 Developing supply chain capabilities for competitive advantage

thus developing unique **capabilities** that are extremely valuable, rare, inimitable, and non-substitutable (VRIN), i.e., the resource-based view of the firm (Barney 1991). Organizations should focus on continuously developing their specific **supply chain capabilities** that can support their SCM strategies for achieving sustained competitive advantages in the fast-changing and dynamic business environment (Fig. 1.5).

1.3   Business Analytics

When surfing on the internet for some products that you want to buy, you probably have seen the 'recommended for you' advertisements, popping up somewhere at the bottom of an article or on either side of a social media page. When searching for your favourite videos on YouTube, you are more likely to get similar recommended contents for you. Likewise, when shopping on eBay, you might get 'items for you' ads directly sent to your email address, which are most likely to interest you based on your previous search or purchase history.

Sometimes, these marketing efforts can get it right and you are tempted to buy the recommended items; while sometimes you are not bothered at all, because the recommendations are not relevant. This is one of the most widespread forms of advertising on the internet, and you probably experience it every day. You might wonder how these companies know what you want and are able to identify relevant content for each individual customer? The answer lies in the algorithms that are developed by content recommendation platforms for marketing analytics.

As the advancement of computing power, businesses today have the opportunity to gain better understandings of their customers by applying advanced analytical methods into their daily operations. The surging adoption of smart technologies in many areas around our daily lives and in the manufacturing sectors has boosted the availability of massive data source. For instance, consumer data generated from point-of-sales, online orders, payments through smart devices, search engines, and social media, can be used to better understand customers' shopping behaviour and make future predictions. Well-developed analytics on the consumer data can therefore lead to improved product design, better advertising and pricing strategies as well as more accurate demand forecasting, which can subsequently result in enhanced operation efficiency, increased customer satisfaction and profitability.

Example

The story of Amazon against Walmart in e-commerce wars (Dastin 2017) can be an excellent example of how giant retailers use advanced analytics in determining pricing strategies. Amazon.com itself gathers enormous amount of data on purchases made by its customers every day. The company analyses customers' purchases, shopping patterns, browsing history and demographics information, etc., and uses some advanced algorithm to come up better product recommendations to its customers.

In early 2017, the programme developed by Walmart engineers to track prices on Amazon.com several million times a day suddenly stopped working. This was because Amazon had developed a new tactic to block these programmes, commonly known as 'bots'. Losing access to Amazon's data was not a small issue, as Walmart relies on the data to determine its listings accordingly. A tiny difference in pricing can mean losing a sale. Whether or not Walmart eventually got back on track to retrieve Amazon's data is out of our interest, but what we can learn from the case is that big retailers can use smart and advanced analytics to track what their rivals are doing and determine better pricing strategies in the competition. ◄

▶ **Business analytics** is the application of statistical techniques and programming in the process of *capturing*, *storing*, *sorting* and *transforming* data into insightful knowledge and information for effective business decision making.

Business data analysts can use advanced computing methods and tools to build analytics models to understand current business situations, predict future states, and offer best possible business solutions and recommendations. Business analytics can be categorized into four basic types as described in Fig. 1.6 below.

1. **Descriptive analytics**. Typically use a real-time dashboard to visualize, present, and report what is going on based on collected data. Examples include sales performance for various product categories, financial performance for past months, and customer categories based on their shopping patterns and styles.
2. **Diagnostic analytics**. The use of data to explore, determine, and explain what has happened and why something happened. Examples include quality monitoring with statistical process control and maintenance engineers using diagnostics data to identify the cause for a jet engine failure.
3. **Predictive analytics**. The use of data to discover and identify patterns and trends to predict what will happen in the future. Examples include aggregate demand forecasting based on historical sales data and specific products purchase prediction based on customers' previous shopping history and patterns.

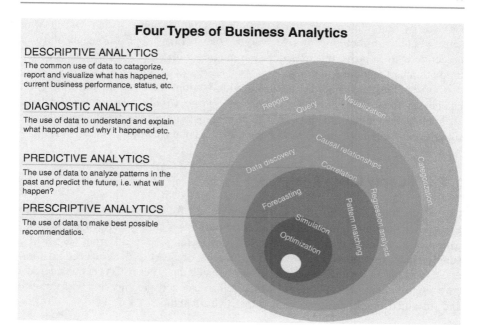

Four Types of Business Analytics

DESCRIPTIVE ANALYTICS

The common use of data to catagorize, report and visualize what has happened, current business performance, status, etc.

DIAGNOSTIC ANALYTICS

The use of data to understand and explain what happened and why it happened etc.

PREDICTIVE ANALYTICS

The use of data to analyze patterns in the past and predict the future, i.e. what will happen?

PRESCRIPTIVE ANALYTICS

The use of data to make best possible recommendatios.

Reports Query Visualization

Data discovery Causal relationships Correlation Categorization

Forecasting Simulation Pattern matching Regression analysis

Optimization

Fig. 1.6 Four basic types of business analytics

4. **Prescriptive analytics**. The use of data to reveal what actions should be taken and make best possible recommendations for next steps. Examples include the use of social media data, types of communications, reviews, comments to determine the best marketing campaign strategies, pricing optimization, and best product design features; delivery route optimization based on customer locations, traffic information, road works, etc.; safety stock and inventory level recommendations for different stock keeping units (SKUs).

In practice, different business analytics types are not mutually exclusive, but can be used simultaneously or in sequence to provide best insights for effective decision making. For example, recent data from an express courier reveal that the company's on-time delivery rate has significantly dropped (descriptive analytics). Data analysts at the company have explored that the main cause of the delays is because of the dramatic surge in demand during holiday seasons (diagnostic analytics). It is also predicted that the delays could get even worse if no immediate actions are taken (predictive analytics). To ensure the delivery of all parcels within the promised time window, the analysts suggest that the company hire 30 extra part-time truck drivers in the festive season to cope with the increasing demand (prescriptive analytics).

More advanced business analytics applies human-like intelligence, combining machine learning and artificial intelligence (AI) techniques to learn from data and progressively improve performance on a specific task and then drive insights over time based on hypothesis engines, i.e., **cognitive learning** or **cognitive analytics.** Cognitive analytics is capable of providing real-time answers and personalized services by searching and learning through massive amounts of data and making sense of context. Though cognitive analytics has its many applications, its ultimate objective is to improve business decision making with more reliable and accurate prediction and recommendations.

In short, business analytics has been widely adopted in various industries and businesses. Companies like *Nike, Coca-Cola, Haier, Alibaba.com,* and *PayPal* have all applied businesses analytics in different areas within their business to deliver superior performances and achieve competitive advantages.

1.4   Supply Chain Analytics

One of the most important and fast-growing areas for the application of business analytics is the supply chain. **Supply chain analytics** is simply defined as the application of machine learning and data analytics techniques in different stages of a supply chain to improve the overall performance of SCM to meet/exceed customers' expectations. The effective use of supply chain analytics (SCA) is considered a core supply chain capability, with which a firm can achieve superior performance and sustained supply chain related competitive advantages.

- *"To improve the efficiency of the entire supply chain, we want to take the emotion out of strategic decision-making and let data do the talking."*
  —Homarjun Agrahari, Chief Data Officer, MODE Transportation

Example

For example, Hanesbrands Inc. is an apparel manufacturer and marketer based in the USA, which includes iconic brands such as Champion and Bali. The company has adopted supply chain analytics to determine the likelihood of stockout at a particular time, using supply chain data from external and internal sources. If an inventory stockout is predicted, prescribed actions will be triggered, for example, resequencing manufacturing and purchase orders and changing transport mode to make quicker deliveries. With the effective support from its SCA capability, Hanesbrands Inc. is able to react quickly to supply chain signals and balance mitigation cost with the benefits to the company (Bowers et al. 2017). ◀

▶   A survey of more than 1000 supply chain leaders was recently administered by Logility, a supply chain solution company and APICS[1] to uncover the priorities and challenges firms face as they embrace analytics, big data, and

---

[1] APICS is the Association for Supply Chain Management, www.apics.org.

machine learning (Logility 2018). The results identify that faster, more accurate, and unique fulfilment is a top supply chain priority moving forward; however, to achieve that, companies must have the ability to access the right supply chain information when and where they want it, and the ability to derive quick insights from the data. Also, among the highlights:

- 36% believe that a top driver for their analytics initiatives is the opportunity to optimize inventory to balance supply and demand.
- 30% identify a top business priority moving forward is the need to respond to customer mandates for faster, more accurate, and unique fulfilment.
- 28% see a key benefit of adopting advanced analytics initiatives is the ability to blend data from multi-systems for complete supply chain visibility.
- 19% say they want to leverage machine learning to improve forecast accuracy.

There are increasing amounts of available data sources in today's supply chains. If organizations can capture the value hidden in those data with effective SCA and provide real-time insights for daily operations, certainly they can expect to reduce uncertainties and complexities in their SCM with enhanced supply chain traceability and visibility. As a result, those organizations that have strong SCA capabilities can realize superior supply chain performance and a sustained competitive advantage can be expected.

The areas of where SCA can be applied are many along the supply chain. For example, we can use SCA to understand how customers interact through various channels and offer more personalized product designs. We can use SCA to optimize inventory and deliver products based on real-time actual demand. Also, SCA can be applied to determine the locations of warehouses and optimize delivery routes to satisfy customers at the best place possible, in the shortest time possible and at the lowest cost possible.

With the aid of SCA, better insights, visibility, and transparency can be attained in all the key supply chain processes. The associated benefits of applying SCA include:

- Enhance understanding of customer requirements
- Improve efficiency and reduce operational costs
- Minimize lead time
- Improve product/service quality
- Optimize distribution networks

1.4.1 SMART Goals of SCA

To achieve a highly effective and efficient level of SCA capability, supply chain managers should always keep in mind that SCA should be SMART (see Fig. 1.7).

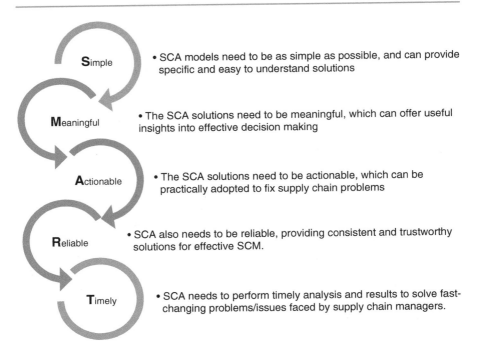

Fig. 1.7 SMART goals of SCA

- *SCA needs to be as simple as possible and can provide specific and easy-to-understand solutions.* As Richard Daigle, group director for Automation and Analytics at Coca-Cola, stated that 'analytics supply chain models must be simple and transparent, yet effective' (Bowers et al. 2017). If the SCA models get too complicated and solutions are difficult to understand, it is more likely that supply chain managers will not use it. In other words, the simpler the model and the more understandable the specific solutions it provides, the greater the likelihood that it will be adopted.
- *SCA needs to create meaningful solutions, which can offer useful insights into effective decision making in SCM.* SCA analysts should have a deep and thorough understanding of supply chain processes in order to build the right models to tackle the specific problems in SCM. Otherwise, one 'can end up with nothing more than fun and interesting facts', observed Ben Martin, chief officer, advanced analytics and global planning at Hanesbrands (Bowers et al. 2017).
- *The SCA solutions need to be actionable, which can be practically adopted* to fix specific supply chain problems. To achieve this, again SCA professionals should develop a complete and comprehensive knowledge of supply chain processes. Otherwise, the SCA solutions may become irrelevant, more problems than actionable solutions will result.
- *SCA needs to be reliable, which can provide consistent and trustworthy solutions for effective SCM.* SCA should not only create simple, easy-to-understand, meaningful, and actionable solutions, but also produce something that is reliable,

accurate, and consistent over time. No matter how the business environment changes, the analytics models developed by SCA professional should be resilient, robust, and adaptable to the uncertainties, and provide insights that can be trusted by the managers.

- *SCA needs to generate timely results and solutions.* To cope with the fast-changing environment, problems, and issues faced by modern supply chain managers, SCA must be able to generate effective solutions and insights in a timely fashion. Moreover, effective SCA should take a more proactive stance to prevent problems, rather than being reactive to fix problems.

The SMART goals set the foundation for effect SCA in supporting superior supply chain performance. In addition, achieving effect SCA requires top management team commitment and support. Without the support from senior executives, it would be very difficult for organizations to achieve a higher level of SCA capabilities. There also should be a supportive culture created both within an organization and with its supply chain partners, in which users fully trust and embrace supply chain analytics in their daily operations and planning, as well as strategic decision making.

1.4.2   SCA

The subject of supply chain analytics has overlapped with other domains such as Management Science, Operations Research, and Decision Science. In particular, **management science (MS)** focuses on the application of scientific methods, data and math to the study of management, with strong intersections with business, economics, engineering, and other fields. When management science is used to solve specific problems in the context of production and manufacturing (i.e., operations management), or provide solutions for supply chain management, it becomes the subject of **operations research (OR)**. OR involves the construction of mathematical models, and through the application of optimization, simulation, queueing theory, and other stochastic models, to make better decisions. OR also has strong links to computer science and analytics. **Decision science (DS)** draws upon the methods and techniques from both management science and analytics as well as design thinking and behavioural science to help organizations make better decisions.

Often it is hard to draw clear lines between supply chain analytics (SCA) and the other two subjects (i.e., OR and DS), depending on the business context and the specific problems to be solved. However, one may note that OR places strong emphases on mathematical modelling and optimization, whilst SCA explores and learns from data to find answers to specific supply chain related problems. The Venn diagram below displays the relations of these subject domains (Fig. 1.8).

In this book, we focus on the application of SCA on some of the key supply chain processes and activities, including customer management (in Chap. 5), supply management (in Chap. 6), warehouse and inventory management (in Chap. 7), demand management (in Chap. 8), and logistics management (in Chap. 9). We will also touch upon some OR optimization techniques such as linear programming in

Fig. 1.8 Intersections
between SCA and other
domains

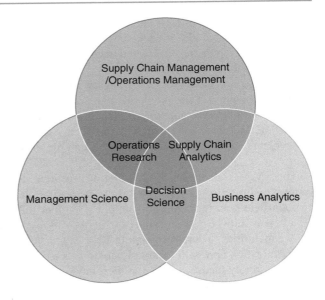

later chapters, however they are not the primary focus of this book and will only be introduced briefly. Other areas such as sales and marketing, product development, and internal factory operations (i.e., operations management) are not considered key supply chain processes, and thus are excluded in this book.

Summary of Learning Objectives
1. **Understand the supply chain structures and its major components.**
    Supply chain is the term that we use to describe the inter-connected business networks and links in the making and delivering products and/or services to customers. A supply chain or supply network typically involves a focal firm which is the key products and/or services provider. We use the term 'upstream' to describe the suppliers who directly or indirectly supply to the focal firm. It may have multiple tiers/echelons in the upstream. Similarly, we use the term 'downstream' to describe the customers of the focal firm, which may also involve multi-tier structures (i.e., tier-1, tier-2…) The key components of a supply chain involve the various processes from procurement to after-sale service as well as the supply chain flows.
2. **Describe the four supply chain flows and explain their importance.**
    The commonly known three flows within a supply chain (i.e., materials flow, information flow, and financial flow) are regarded as supply chain flows. We described the meaning of each as well as their flow directions. 'Power' can be another important supply chain element, which can constantly change, influence and govern the buyer–supplier relationship. To achieve effective and efficient SCM, organizations must ensure the smooth, accurate, and timely movement of supply chain flows as well as a careful exertion of 'power' in fostering a good and effective buyer–supplier relationship.

3. **Explain why there is a supply chain and why we should manage it.**

   We used the automotive supply chain as an example to illustrate why we need a supply chain. This is because in reality we cannot make everything in house. Even if it is possible, it might not be the best option, considering the time, cost, technological constraints, etc. Therefore, we should look for business partners who can make and supply parts/services to us more efficiently and effectively. A supply chain can be very short and simple, but also can be very long and complex, depending on business types. The reason why we need to manage a supply chain is because we need to maintain a smooth supply of goods and/or services to satisfy our customers, with the 7Rs of SCM objectives, i.e., make and deliver the right product and service to the right customers, at the right cost, right quantity, right quality, right time, and right place. In addition, different organizations may have different business objectives and strategies (e.g., cost leadership and differentiation), therefore they will need to manage and design the best supply chains that can align closely with their business objectives.

4. **Understand the concepts of business analytics and explain its four major types.**

   The use of data analytics is getting strong momentum in today's businesses. Business analytics is defined as the application of statistical techniques and programming in the process of capturing, sorting, sorting and transforming data into insightful knowledge and information for effective business decision making. With the support of business analytics, organizations can expect to better understand their customers, design and make products or services that attract the customers most and improve operation efficiency, customer satisfaction, and profitability. There are four major types of business analytics, including descriptive analytics, diagnostic analytics, predictive analytics, and prescriptive analytics. They can be used either separately or simultaneously, but the ultimate aim of their application is to provide solutions and meaningful insights for effective decision making.

5. **Explain what supply chain analytics is, its main benefits, and SMART goals.**

   An important and fast-growing area for the application of business analytics is the supply chain. Supply chain analytics is defined as the application of data analytics techniques in different stages of a supply chain to improve the overall performance of SCM. To manage the supply and demand more effectively, with enhanced traceability, transparency, and visibility in a supply chain, SCA plays a critical enabling role. Companies that have strong SCA capabilities can expect to achieve superior supply chain performance and a sustained competitive advantage. Nevertheless, a strong SCA capability does not necessarily mean a complex model or algorithm to be developed but SMART. The SMART objectives suggest that SCA be simple, meaningful, actionable, reliable, and timely.

Discussion Questions

1. What is a supply chain? Why is there a supply chain? Can you think of a business which does not have a supply chain?
2. Can you give examples of supply chain flows and explain why they are important to achieving supply chain excellence?
3. Explain what supply chain management should involve and discuss why are the 7Rs objectives important to successful supply chain management?
4. Can you give any examples of business analytics in practice? How can different types of business analytics be used to support effective decision making in business?
5. Discuss the possible applications of SCA in different stages of a supply chain and why are the SMART objectives are important?

Case Study: Amazon's Anticipatory Shipping

From 2-day shipping, to next day, the same day, and even within next hour, Amazon fulfilment has been at an uncatchable pace to win customers, bestowing the company a massive advantage over its rivals in the online retail business. Speed is everything in today's e-commerce as customers will not tolerate on your delays anymore. On the Christmas eve of 2013, Amazon made one step ahead further by successfully obtaining the patent, officially known as 'method and system for anticipatory package shipping'.

Photo by David Ballew on Unsplash

Amazon describes it as a way of shipping products to the destination geographical area without completely specifying the delivery address at time of shipment. The packages could wait at depots or on trucks until a customer order arrives. If implemented well, the system could help the company to boost sales and potentially reduce shipping, inventory, and logistics costs. However, this is all reliant on the accurate and timely prediction of customers' orders.

But how? According to Amazon, a well-defined forecasting model is bound to provide decision support for speculative shipping of items, using data from

Amazon customers' previous shopping histories, links clicked, searched items, wish lists, etc. Amazon collects troves of data about its customers, which can be sued to predict what its customers want, when and where they want the products, and then ship the items automatically.

Convenience and speed are the best attractions of Amazon's anticipatory shipping, but they are not all of it. Imagine you are too busy to notice your laundry powder or toilet tissues almost run out. Unexpectedly, you open your door and receive an Amazon package which contains exactly what you need for household replenishment. Wouldn't it feel delightful and exciting? Even if Amazon got it wrong, you might still feel quite excited to open a box when you don't know what's inside. You might be tempted to keep it, especially if Amazon offers certain discounts or even as outright gifts. In its patent, 'Delivering the package to the given customer as a promotional gift may be used to build goodwill', said Amazon (Kopalle 2014).

Further reading:
Mitchell, C. (2015), "Amazon patents "anticipatory shipping" of items their data says you'll buy", Harvard Business School Digital Initiative.
Questions:

1. Why does Amazon come up the idea of anticipatory shipping and what are the benefits?
2. How could Amazon achieve it? What sort of data can be used in predicting customer orders?
3. What options does Amazon have if its anticipation of customer orders was wrong?
4. Do you think Amazon's anticipatory shipping will succeed? How can its rivals compete with Amazon.

References

Barney, J. 1991. "Firm resources and sustained competitive advantage", Journal of Management, Vol. 17 No. 1, pp. 99–120.

Benton, W.C. & Maloni, M. 2005. "The influence of power-driven buyer/seller relationships on supply chain satisfaction", Journal of Operations Management, Vol. 23 No. 1, pp. 1–22.

Bowers, M.R., Petrie, A.G. & Holcomb, M.C. 2017. "Unleashing the Potential of Supply Chain Analytics", MIT Sloan Management Review, Vol. 59 No. 1, pp. 14–16.

Christopher, M. & Towill, D.R. 2000. "Supply chain migration from lean and functional to agile and customised", Supply Chain Management: An International Journal, Vol. 5 No. 4, pp. 206–213.

Dastin, J. 2017. "Amazon trounces rivals in battle of the shopping 'bots'", Reuters, Retrieved 15 Oct, 2018, from https://www.reuters.com/article/us-amazon-com-bots-insight-idUSKBN1860FK.

Kopalle, P. 2014. "Why Amazon's Anticipator Pure Genius", Forbes, Retrieved 1 Nov, 2018, from https://www.forbes.com/sites/onmarketing/2014/01/28/why-amazons-anticipatory-shipping-is-pure-genius/?sh=588e61564605

Leblanc, R. 2018. "How Starbucks changed supply chain management from coffee bean to cup". The Balance Small Business.

Logility, 2018. "Logility Survey Reveals the Top Supply Chain Priorities for Advanced Analytics", Retrieved 20 Oct, 2018, from https://www.logility.com/press-release/logility-survey-reveals-the-top-supply-chain-priorities-for-advanced-analytics/

Tan, K.C., Kannan, V.R. & Handfield, R.B. 1998. "Supply chain management: supplier performance and firm performance", International Journal of Purchasing and Materials Management, Vol. 34, pp. 2–9.

Data-Driven Supply Chains and Intro to Python

2

Contents

Learning Objectives
- Explain why data is important for effective supply chain management.
- Discuss the various data sources and related IT adoption in supply chains.
- Describe what big data is, its characteristics and the 5Vs of big data.
- Understand how to download and install Python and the essential Python libraries.

2.1 Data and Its Value in SCM

▶ **Data** is defined as 'information, especially facts or numbers, collected to be examined and considered and used to help decision making, or information in an electronic form that can be stored and used by a computer' in Cambridge Dictionary.

Some have described data as the 'new oil' of the digital economy. In fact, data can be anything and can come from anywhere; however, getting the true value of data depends on whether an organization can capture the data, store the data, interpret the data, and most importantly, derive meaningful insights from the data for effective decision making. In other words, the ability to find the data, see the value of the data, and mine the 'gold' out of the data varies significantly among different organizations.

Example

Data plays an increasingly important role in today's business operations. For example, Coca-Cola is a well-loved brand by people from all walks of life. In 2015, the company initiated a digital-led loyalty programme, with which Coca-Cola was able to connect with its customers better and collect valuable data through social authentication. In particular, the super beverage brand collects customers' reviews and opinions through apps or social networks and uses the data to develop their products and create tailored advertisements to different audiences. In Japan, a similar app called Coke On has been developed. With the data from the app users, Coca-Cola can optimize where to supply and how their vending machines are placed to ensure they are meeting customer demand. The data strategy has proven to work well, not only in terms of sales but also cutting down costs and satisfying customers at the right place and the right time. ◄

As discussed in the previous chapter, achieving supply chain excelltence, especially the 7Rs objectives, requires organizations to effectively manage and coordinate supply chain processes. However, the effective management and coordination of supply chain processes would need smooth, timely and accurate information and data exchange throughout the supply chain. For instance, without critical data on customer demand and sales, current inventory level, and available capacities, it can be very difficult for manufacturers to make effective decisions for their production planning and scheduling. In addition, inaccurate information and data exchange such as slight demand forecasting errors in the downstream can cause significant bullwhip effect in the upstream (see Fig. 2.1), which subsequently affect supply chain efficiency—disturbing supplies and potentially creating waste and high cost in inventory (Lee et al. 1997).

Many organizations have realized the importance of data for their supply chain management, and thus implementing various software packages to capture and exchange essential data in their supply chains, such as ERP (enterprise resource planning) and CRM (customer relationship management) systems. Managers, however, must decide carefully which systems to use, as the selected ones must align well with their business types, objectives, existing processes, etc. Otherwise, serious problems can occur in the supply chain, which can cause production interruption, severe delays in supplies, and loss of customers.

For instance, in 2000, Nike decided to do better demand forecasting to improve its supply chain management according to customer requirements. The company spent US$400 million on the new software I2, hoping to remove unwanted products from its production schedule and inventory as well as maintenance cost. But the new

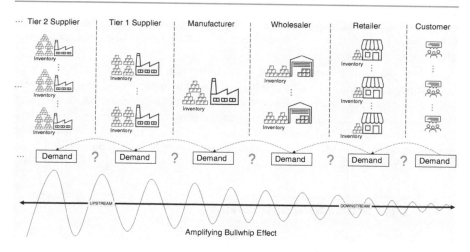

Fig. 2.1 Bullwhip effect in the supply chain

software was unable to provide the accurate data on the complete market requirements because it had some bugs, did not integrate well, and was too slow. Besides,
Nike's employees were inadequately trained to use the system. As a result, the
designers and planners at Nike could not interpret the demand of the market to make
timely production plans and unique production process to meet the customer
requirements. Due to this ERP failure, Nike had an estimated US$100 million lost
in sales, a 20% stock price dip and several class action lawsuits (Bosari 2012).

In addition to using incompetent software packages that fail to address business
objectives and problems, what other factors could affect data and information sharing in supply chains? There can be many reasons, but some of major ones are as
follows:

- Lack of trust among supply chain members
- Unwilling to disclose sensitive data and information (e.g., sales data and customer account)
- Incompatibility of systems in the supply chain (e.g., different systems are being
  used by suppliers).
- Lack of collaboration and coordination both intra- and inter-firms (e.g., departments work in silos), creating barriers for effective data sharing.

Therefore, to overcome these barriers for effective information and data sharing,
organizations need to build partnerships with supply chain members, and to foster
trust with them so that they are willing to share critical and timely data with the
focal firms as well as with other members in the network. Certainly, establishing
partnership and trust may take very long time but is worth the effort. Internally,
organizations should try to simplify data sharing procedures and improve cross-
functional collaborations. Sometimes this may require a change of organizational
structure, business process re-engineering or even creating a new collaborative

organizational culture. Top management support and commitment also plays a vital role in ensuring effective and smooth data and information sharing across internal and external boundaries.

In short, data is extremely valuable for effective supply chain management. From procurement, inbound and outbound logistics, internal production, order fulfilment to after-sale services, data is at the central heart of ensuring the smooth running and synchronization of these processes to increase customer responsiveness and reduce costs. Without meaningful data and effective data sharing in supply chains, supply chain management would fail, which could consequently lead to detrimental business performance.

2.2   Data Source in Supply Chains

There are many available data sources in supply chains, not only within a focal firm but also across firm boundaries. Information and data exchange among supply chain members are essential for effective supply chain coordination and collaboration. If each tier members within a supply chain share appropriate and important information and data with other tier members, then fast and appropriate supply chain responsiveness can be realized.

For example, a car dealer promptly shares timely sales data with a car manufacturer. The car maker then uses the sales data to adjust production plans at its plants. The critical production plans must be rapidly communicated with suppliers as well, who then strive to adjust their own production plans and achieve just-in-time (JIT) deliveries to the car maker's plants.

The fast adoption of information technology (IT) has enabled organizations to streamline their supply chain processes, improve visibility in the supply chain, and facilitate better decision-making. Technology evolvement, especially the advent of smart technologies, has greatly improved data capture, data storage, and data sharing within the supply chain. Some of the examples include:

Electronic Data Interchange (EDI) EDI replaces traditional paper-based orders, invoices, postal mail, fax, and email with standard electronic format to exchange business documents through computer-to-computer network between companies. EDI eliminates the errors and waiting time caused by human handling. Examples of documents exchanged via EDI include purchase orders, invoices and shipping status documents, inventory documents, and bill of lading.

Barcoding System The system usually consists of barcoding hardware (e.g., handheld scanners, mobile computers, and printers) to scan and capture product information and a supporting software to read, decode, interpret, and transmit data to a central database. We can see today that the barcoding system has been widely adopted in many areas of businesses, from, for example, checking out items when shopping at a supermarket, to using the QR (Quick Response) code scanner on your smartphones to check a product price and make purchase.

The benefit of using a barcoding system is that it can automatically collect data, provide real-time and very accurate information transferring, and essentially reduce the risk of human error. In a supply chain, barcoding system can be used to handle incoming and outgoing goods in a warehouse, automatically record inventory levels, track shipment details and status in transportation and distribution of products and services.

Radio-frequency Identification (RFID)   RFID, as revealed by its name, uses radio-frequency waves to automatically transfer data, allowing users to identify and locate items and assets quickly and uniquely. The technology adopts RFID tags or smart labels, whereby digital data and information are encoded. RFID tags are attached to items in order to track them using an RFID reader and antenna. These tags typically do not have a battery but receive energy from the radio waves generated by the reader. Data can be transmitted through radio waves to the reader/antenna combination, and then transferred to a host computer system and stored in a database for further analysis.

Unlike the barcoding system, data from the RFID tags can be read without line of sight, making it more favourable for a range of applications, including, for example, inventory tracking, logistics (materials management) and vehicle tracking, tolling and real-time location system.

Enterprise Resource Planning (ERP)   ERP system integrates different business processes and multiple stages of the supply chain with a common database to enable the smooth, real-time, and accurate data flows between them. ERP system consists of various ERP modules such as Finance and Accounting, Human Resource Management (HRM), Sales and Marketing, Inventory management, Customer Relationship Management (CRM), and Supply Chain Management (SCM) (Fig. 2.2).

ERP typically uses a common, defined data structure to create, store, and share data between these core processes, facilitating fast-track reporting, eliminating data duplication and errors as well as enhancing data integrity. Today, ERP system has evolved to embrace emerging technologies such as cloud computing (Cloud ERP) and smartphones (Mobile ERP), offering organizations more affordable, flexible, and remote access to ERP with enhanced security. Top ERP vendors on the market include SAP, Oracle, Sage, Microsoft, and Infor.

Geographic Information System (GIS)   GIS is a system that capture, store, and analyse geographical data for problem solving and effective decision making in relation to spatial analysis. GIS can be used in SCM to tack and manage resources and make location decisions. For instance, supply chain professionals can use GIS to determine facility site, trace and track trucks or ships, and visualize where goods are located.

Today, GIS has gradually evolved into more advanced **location intelligence (LI)** applications, which incorporate geo-enriched data sources (e.g., demographics, weather data, and real-time data streams) and embrace advanced location data

Fig. 2.2 ERP modules

analytics methods for optimization and prediction (Moreno 2017). For example, LI can be used by logistics managers to optimize delivery route based on real-time traffic data and customer locations.

Intelligent Transportation System (ITS) ITS is a combination of sensing, communication, control and analysis technologies to facilitate safer, smarter, more coordinated and more efficient ground transportation management. ITS has four major communication layers including vehicle-to-infrastructure (V2I), vehicle-to-vehicle (V2V), infrastructure-to-infrastructure (I2I), and vehicle-to-mobile devices (V2M). The adoption of ITS in supply chains is expected to enable real-time vehicle tracking and improve fleet management via effective monitoring, planning, and control (Veres et al. 2017) (Fig. 2.3).

Cyber Physical System (CPS) CPS is a system that links the physical world with the virtual world using embedded computers and networks. In a CPS system, the physical entities/processes are monitored, controlled, and optimized through computing algorithms, tightly integrated with sensors, actuators, communication networks, software and computers. Just as the internet revolutionized how we interact with each other, CPS radically transforms the interaction between the physical and the virtual world. The major CPS application areas include energy (e.g., smart grid), health (e.g., medical monitoring), mobility (e.g., autonomous automobile systems), and manufacturing (e.g., process control systems, robotics systems). CPS can be adopted in SCM to facilitate intelligent and efficient production systems, monitor and tracking deliveries, optimize logistics and inventory control.

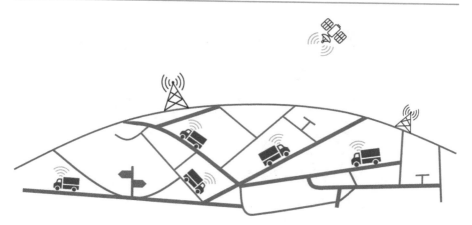

Fig. 2.3 Real-time vehicle tracking with ITS system

Internet of Things (IoT) IoT is a network of uniquely identifiable physical objects (e.g., home appliances, mechanical and digital machines, vehicles, devices, etc.) embedded with sensors, actuators, software, and computing devices, enabling them to exchange data over the internet. CPS and IoT have significant overlaps, however CPS emphasizes more on the link between computation and the physical world, whereas IoT focuses more on the internet-connected devices and embedded systems. If we consider CPS moves the first step towards vertical digital integration by connecting the physical entities to the virtual world, IoT sets the future where anything is connected over the internet, allowing them to collect data about the physical world from anywhere and share with other systems and devices.

If we extend the concept of IoT to manufacturing, the IoT becomes Industrial Internet of Things (IIoT) , which is also known as Cyber Physical Production Systems (CPPS), Industrial Internet, or Smart Factory. Similarly, if we extend the concept to our homes, it becomes smart homes with connected home appliances (e.g., television, air conditioning, kitchen, lights, security cameras, etc.). When the smart devices or machines are connected, they generate a massive amount of IoT data which can be analysed, leveraged, and acted upon in real-time without human intervention (Fig. 2.4).

In the environment of IoT and CPS, coupled with AI, machine learning, and the cloud, machines can interact with other machines as well as human beings, learn about them and adapt to their wants and needs. It has been said that the advent of IoT and CPS is driving the biggest shift in business and technology since World War II, which have set a foundation for a fourth industrial revolution, i.e., **Industry 4.0** (Carruthers 2016).

Blockchain Blockchain is a record-keeping technology behind the Bitcoin cryptocurrency, developed by an unknown person (or people) under the name of Satoshi Nakamoto in 2008. Unlike traditional database, blockchain is a specific type of database that stores information and data in blocks. Once a fresh block receives new

Fig. 2.4 Smart lock and smart lights IoT system

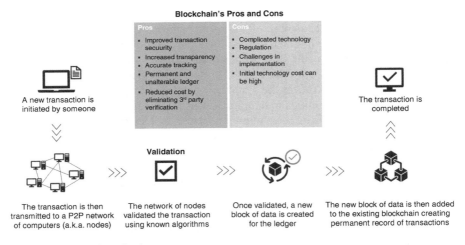

Fig. 2.5 Blockchain technology

data, it is chained together with the previous block in chronological order. One of the unique features and advantages about blockchain is that it is a decentralized ledger of all transactions across a peer-to-peer network, with each node in the decentralized system having a copy of the blockchain, and thus data entered is incorruptible and irreversible. Figure 2.5 illustrates how blockchain works and its pros and cons.

Blockchain has great potential applications beyond just bitcoin and cryptocurrency. Many companies have already adopted the technology such as Walmart, Pfizer, AIG, Siemens, Unilever, and a host of others. For instance, IBM has created its Food Trust blockchain to trace and track the journey that food products take to get to its locations (Conway 2020).

In operations and SCM, there are a number of opportunities for blockchain application to transform practices, including impacting new product development, enhancing product safety and security, improving quality management and sustainability, advancing inventory management, and reducing cost of supply chain transactions (Cole et al. 2019), to name a few.

The technology's decentralized network of computers records and timestamps every transaction in a shared ledger that is constantly and collectively updated in real-time. Therefore, it can be used to improve trust amongst supply chain members, ensure the validity of each transaction and reduce risks of fraud (Ganeriwalla et al. 2018). The potential application of blockchain in supply chain both in terms of risk and trust is summarized in Fig. 2.6 below.

- When there is high level of risks involved in transaction, and trust is critical among the involved members in the supply chain (either they do not know each other or it would be too costly to build trust), blockchain has high value of potential application because it can provide participants with secure transactions, trusted data, and self-executing contracts.
- When the level of risks is high (e.g., food safety issues), but trust is not essential in the transaction (e.g., long-term partnership already established), blockchain can be applied to track assets along the supply chain and throughout their life cycle to minimize the risk.
- When the level of risks in transaction is low (e.g., commodity products/non-critical items), but trust is still critical in the transaction (e.g., many parties involved in transaction), blockchain can be applied to create a permanent and

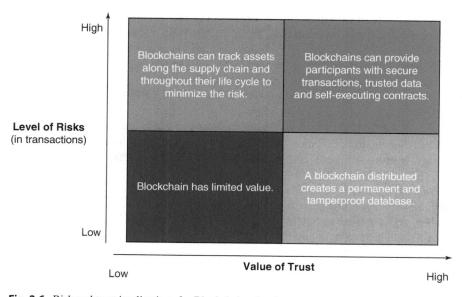

Fig. 2.6 Risk and trust implications for Blockchain adoption

unalterable database that are fully traceable an auditable, which can be accessed by different parties and facilitates reliable and secure data exchange.

• However, if both the level of risks and value of trust are low, blockchain may have limited value of adoption.

2.3 Big Data

Due to the wide adoption of IT systems and smart technologies in the supply chain, along with e-commerce, social media and more, there are a massive amount of data available for businesses to harness and act upon. The characteristics of vast volume, variety, velocity give rise to a surging popular term **Big Data**.

In the past, organizations usually have limited ability to collect large amounts of data due to storage constraint, and they were unable to process so large, complex, and fast-changing data and information in a timely manner using traditional methods. Today, with greater computing power and cheaper storage on platforms such as *data lakes* and *Hadoop*, businesses can access, store, and process much more data in real-time or near real-time for effective decision making. In addition to large volume, big data has four other important dimensions which will be explained in the following paragraphs.

In terms of **variety**, big data comes in different forms, which can be categorized into three basic types:

1. *Structured data*—refers to the data that are in a fixed format or an ordered manner, which can be readily and seamlessly stored, retrieved, and processed. It is considered the most 'traditional' form data which can be stored for example, in Excel spreadsheet or SQL database. Common examples of structured data include GPS data, sales records, financial data from stock market, etc.
2. *Unstructured data*—refers to the data that are not in a standard or fixed format. It often takes more time to process and analyse this type of data, e.g., audio recordings, videos, customer comments, or Twitter posts, etc.
3. *Semi-structured data*—there is no clear definition for this type of data, but generally it contains data with both forms (structured and unstructured) present, e.g., JSON, XML, CSV, etc. It is relatively easier to process and analyse this type of data than unstructured data as most analytics tools today have the ability to efficiently transform, read, and process the semi-structured data.

Velocity refers to the speed at which data is generated. Big data usually is generated, captured, and processed in real-time or near real-time. This is important as it enables organizations to quickly identify problems, adjust their plans, and respond to fast-changing business environment (Fig. 2.7).

Variation reflects the changes in data flows, patterns, and structures. In today's uncertain business environment, big data becomes very unpredictable and vary significantly over time. Organizations need to understand this variation and develop robust analytics tools or algorithms to cope with the uncertainty and unpredictability of big data.

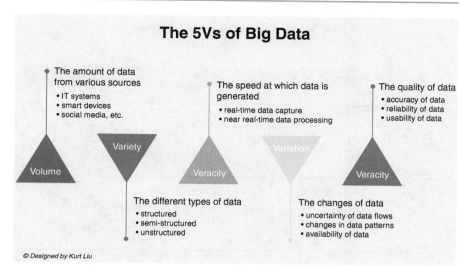

Fig. 2.7 The 5Vs of big data

Veracity means the quality of data in terms of accuracy, reliability and usability. If the collected data are inaccurate, i.e., poor-quality data, no matter how large amounts we collect, they become useless and are not trustworthy even though we have developed very sophisticated and robust analytics tools, i.e., 'garbage in, garbage out' (GIGO). The results produced would not be reliable (can be faulty) for effective decision making. Therefore, it is imperative to avoid bias in data collection and perform data cleaning before feeding the data into your analytical models.

▶ Big data has intrinsic value, but it can only become valuable when organizations can derive meaningful insights from it for accurate and effective business decision making. In order to do so, business analysts, managers, and top executives should ask the right questions, identify appropriate data, make informed assumptions, and develop robust analytics models.

It is also important to note that there is no 'one-size-fits-all' analytics models; for different types of big data, appropriate analytics techniques should be adopted, aligning with business objectives. In the supply chain context, we summarize the possible data source, big data, and SCA examples in Fig. 2.8.

2.4 Introduction to Python

In this section, we start to introduce Python, its installation, the Jupyter Notebook, and essential Python libraries, which will be used throughout the book for our analytics examples. In the following Chap. 3—Data manipulation and Chap. 4—Data visualization in Python will be introduced, respectively.

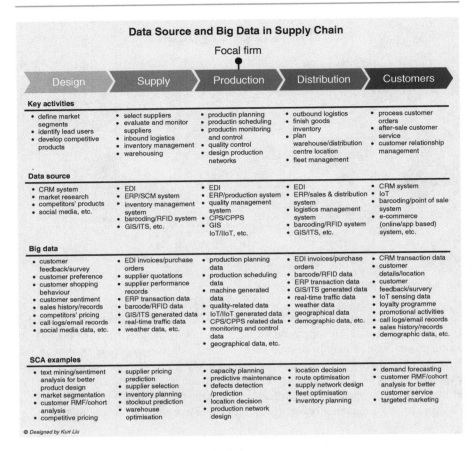

Fig. 2.8 Data source and big data in supply chain

Since its first released in 1991, Python has become one of the most popular programming languages, along with Java, C, R, MATLAB, and others. It was created by Guido van Rossum at Stichting Mathematisch Centrum in the Netherlands as a successor of a language called ABC. Python is an interpreted, object-oriented, high-level programming language with dynamic semantics (python.org).

It is simple, easy-to-learn syntax, enhance code readability and dynamic typing and binding, make it very attractive to the fast-growing scientific computing and data analytics community. In recent years, Python has developed a large and active ecosystem of third-party packages and improved support for libraries, such as NumPy, pandas, Matplotlib, and scikit-learn. Today, Python is one of the most important languages for data science, machine learning, and general software development in academia and industry.

2.4.1 Python Downloads and Installation

This book is written with the syntax of Python 3.8 version, which contains many new features and optimizations that might not be compatible with its earlier versions. You can download the latest release by visiting *www.python.org/downloads*. All Python releases are open source.

Installation of Python is simple and straightforward. However, instead of directly installing Python onto your computer, it is recommended to use Anaconda distribution (see *https://www.anaconda.com/distribution/*), which works similarly but includes a suite of pre-installed packages for data science and machine learning on Linux, Windows, and Mac OS.

2.4.2 Python IDE and Jupyter Notebook

Python can be run in many ways, but for beginners a more efficient way of using and learning it may be through a Python IDE. IDE is the short abbreviation for Integrated Development Environment. In addition to just a code editor, IDE provides testing, debugging, code suggestions, auto-completing your code and a lot more, which can significantly speed up your work. There are a lot of well-developed Python IDEs such as PyCharm and Spyder. It is your own choice of deciding which Python IDEs to use, or whether to use it at all. However, the coding and syntax explained in this book are written in Jupyter Notebook.

Project Jupyter is an open-source project, based on the IPython Project (see *IPython.org*) in 2014. It has evolved to support interactive data science and scientific computing across dozens of programming languages (see *Jupyter.org*). The **Jupyter Notebook** offers web-based server-client structure that allows users to create, analyse, and manipulate documents in the form of notebooks. **Kernel** is a program that runs and interprets the user's code. There are different kernels for different languages that Jupyter Notebook uses (Python, R, Java, etc.). However, for Python it extends the IPython kernel. The kernel executes the code in cells and returns output to the frontend interface.

▶ To install Jupyter Notebook, you need to pre-install Python as a prerequisite. The easiest way might be through Anaconda, which includes Jupyter Notebook package in its distribution. For more introduction and documentation of the Jupyter, visit its official website (see *Jupyter.org*).

Jupyter Notebook is a super-intuitive and interactive browser-based GUI, which has gained a lot of popularity in terms of coding and debugging. We will be using Jupyter Notebook throughout this book, but you can also try different Python IDEs or any other text editors.

2.4.3   Essential Python Libraries

Python library is a collection (or a package) of functions and methods that allows its users to perform many actions without writing their own code. There are many useful Python libraries made available to data scientists and business analysts. The following examples are among the most popular and frequently used ones.

For analytics, it is essential to store, process, and transform various data sources into numerical representation, for example, images and text. No matter what analytics tools or algorithms you are going to use, the first step in making data analysable would be to transform them into arrays of numbers.

NumPy, short for Numerical Python, provides a fundamental package for scientific computing with Python involving numerical data. It contains among other things:

- A powerful N-dimensional array object *ndarray*
- Sophisticated functions for element-wise computations with arrays
- An efficient multidimensional container for generic data
- Useful linear algebra, Fourier transform, and random number capabilities
- Tools for integrating C/C++ and Fortran code

(*NumPy.org*)

NumPy arrays provide much more efficient storage and data manipulations than other Python built-in data structures. Many numerical computing tools are built upon NumPy arrays, making it the foundation of nearly the entire ecosystem of data analytics tools in Python. To install NumPy, it is recommended to use scientific Python distribution such as Anaconda. There are many available online tutorials and materials on NumPy. For a quick introduction to NumPy, you can go to NumPy Tutorial (see *https://numpy.org/devdocs/user/quickstart.html*).

pandas, stands for 'Python Data Analysis Library'. It is an open source, which was originally written by Wes McKinnney in early 2008. Its name is directed from panel data, an econometrics term for multidimensional structured datasets. While NumPy is efficient handling numerical computing tasks, it lacks flexibility and capability in dealing with element-wise broadcasting (groupings, pivots, etc.). pandas, built on top of NumPy, can efficiently analyse less structured data that is commonly seen in real world, especially with pandas `Series` and `DataFrame` objects.

Series is a one-dimensional labelled array object. **DataFrame** is a tabular, column-oriented data structure with both row and column labels. pandas is powerful in handling spreadsheets and relational databases (e.g., SQL). Its sophisticated indexing functionality makes it easy to reshape, slice, aggregate, and select subsets of data. As such, pandas has become one of the most preferred and widely adopted tools in data wrangling or data manipulation.

The easiest and quickest way to install pandas is through Anaconda (see *https://pandas.pydata.org/getting_started.html*). There are also many available online tutorials on pandas. For a quick introduction, go to pandas' official site (see *https://pandas.pydata.org*).

To use pandas, you need to import the pandas library first in your Python IDE, such as Jupyter Notebook or Spyder (pre-installed in Anaconda by default).

```
import numpy as np
import pandas as pd
```

Matplotlib is the most popular Python library for visualization, which is developed by John Hunter and many other contributors. It is used to plot static, animated, and interactive high-quality graphs, charts, and figures in Python. The library is extensive and capable of working with many operating systems and graphics backends.

To install Matplotlib, it is suggested to use scientific Python distribution. Anaconda includes Matplotlib as a default package. For tutorials, you can visit the official site (see *https://matplotlib.org/tutorials/index.html*).

Seaborn is built on top of Matplotlib and closely integrated with pandas data structures, but offers more attractive features and variations in plot style and colour defaults. It aims to make visualization a central part of exploring and understanding data. Some of the key features include:

- dataset-oriented plotting for examining relationships between multiple variables
- specialized support for using categorical variables to show observations or aggregate statistics
- automatic estimation and plotting of linear regression models for different kinds dependent variables
- high-level abstractions for structuring multi-plot grids

(*seaborn.pydata.org*)

To install the latest version of seaborn, you can use pip, which is the standard package manager for Python. pip allows users to install and manage additional packages that are not part of the Python standard library.

```
pip install seaborn
```

Alternatively, you can use conda in Anaconda Prompt:

```
conda install seaborn
```

In order to use Matplotlib or seaborn, you need to import it in your Python IDE:

```
import matplotlib.pyplot as plt
import seaborn as sns
```

Table 2.1 SciPy submodules

Submodules	Description
cluster	Clustering algorithms
constants	Physical and mathematical constants
fftpack	Fast Fourier Transform routines
integrate	Integration and ordinary differential equation solvers
interpolate	Interpolation and smoothing splines
io	Input and Output
linalg	Linear algebra
ndimage	N-dimensional image processing
odr	Orthogonal distance regression
optimize	Optimization and root-finding routines
signal	Signal processing
sparse	Sparse matrices and associated routines
spatial	Spatial data structures and algorithms
special	Special functions
stats	Statistical distributions and functions

(*SciPy.org*)

You can learn seaborn tutorials via its official site (see *https://seaborn.pydata. org/tutorial.html*).

SciPy library provides many user-friendly and efficient numerical routines, such as routines for numerical integration and interpolation, optimization, linear algebra, and statistics. It is recommended to use scientific Python distribution to install SciPy. Anaconda includes SciPy as a default package.

SciPy is organized into submodules covering different aspects of scientific computing (see Table 2.1).

To use a specific module, simply import them in your Python IDE:

```
from scipy import linalg, stats
```

For tutorials, you can visit the office site (see *https://docs.scipy.org/doc/*).

statsmodels is a Python library that contains classical statistical models and econometrics. It can produce an extensive list of results statistics for each estimator, which allows hypothesis testing and data exploration. Some of the models that statsmodels includes are listed below:

- Linear regression
- Generalized linear models
- Robust linear models
- Linear mixed effects models
- ANOVA (Analysis of Variance) models
- Time series analysis: AR, VAR, ARMA, ARIMA, and other models
- Nonparametric methods: kernel density estimation, kernel regression

(*statsmodels.org*)

The easiest way to install statsmodels is through Anaconda distribution. To install the latest release however, you can use conda command:

```
conda install -c conda-forge statsmodels
```

Again, to use statsmodels, you need to import it in your Python IDE:

```
import statsmodels.api as sm
import statsmodels.formula.api as smf
```

For more information, you can visit its official site (see *https://www.statsmodels.org/*).

Last but not least, one of the most popular machine learning libraries in Python is **scikit-learn**. It is open source, which is built upon NumPy, SciPy, and Matplotlib. Scikit-learn provides a variety of simple and efficient tools for data analytics, ranging from classification to clustering. Most of the analytics models used in the book are derived from scikit-learn. Below are examples of submodules it includes (Table 2.2):

There are different ways to install scikit-learn. Anaconda includes scikit-learn as part of its free distribution. In order to use scikit-learn, you need to import it in your Python IDE:

Table 2.2 Submodules of scikit-learn

Submodules	What for?	Algorithms
Classification	Identifying which category an object belongs to	SVM (Support Vector Machines), Nearest Neighbours, Decision Trees, Random Forest, etc.
Regression	Predicting a continuous-valued attribute associated with an object	SVC (Support Vector Regression), Logistics Regression, Lasso, Ridge Regression, Random Forest, etc.
Clustering	Automatic grouping of similar objects into clusters/groups	K-Means, Mean-shift, Spectral Clustering, DBSCAN, Gaussian Mixtures, etc.
Dimensionality reduction	Reducing the number of random variables to consider	PCA (Principle Component Analysis), K-Means, Feature Selection, Non-negative Matrix Factorization, etc.
Model selection	Comparing, validating and choosing parameters and models	Cross-validation, Grid Search, Metrics and Scoring, Validation Curve, Learning Curve, etc.
Preprocessing	Feature extraction and normalization	Standardization, Normalization, Feature Extraction, Non-linear Transformation, Imputation of missing values, etc.

(*scikit-learn.org*)

```
from sklearn import svm
from sklearn import linear_model
```

For a quick introduction, you can visit the official site (see *https://scikit-learn. org/stable/getting_started.html*).

Thus far, we have introduced a few popular Python libraries. There are still many other useful open-source Python libraries (e.g., Plotly, Keras, TensorFlow) out there for you to explore at your own discretion. In the following chapters, we will introduce some of the libraries and try them out for solving our data analytics problems.

Anaconda includes several common packages already in its distribution; however, you may wish to install additional Python libraries or update some of the existing ones over time. In general, it can be done with the following command in Anaconda Prompt:

```
conda install library_name
conda update library_name
```

2.4.4   Jupyter Notebook Optimization

There are different ways to customize your Jupyter Notebook to make it better, faster, and simpler to work with. First, you can change how your notebook looks by installing a package of **Jupyter Themes**. Note that it is possible to run shell commands in a cell within the notebook by adding an exclamation mark at the beginning of the cell (see below):

```
!pip install jupyterthemes
```

Once you have installed the themes, you can check the list of all available themes by using the following command:

```
!jt -l
```

```
Available Themes:
    chesterish
    grade3
    gruvboxd
    gruvboxl
    monokai
    oceans16
    onedork
    solarizedd
    solarizedl
```

Then, you can choose a theme (e.g., oceans16) using the following command. Once it is done, refresh the page and you can see the new theme.

```
!jt -t oceans16
```

If you want to go back to the original Jupyter Notebook theme, simply run the following command and refresh your page.

```
!jt -r
```

In addition to different themes, there are useful **Jupyter Notebook Extensions** that can enhance the user experience and offer a wide range of personalization tools. *Nbextensions* is a good example, which can be installed with either `pip` or `conda`:

```
conda install -c conda-forge jupyter_contrib_nbextensions
conda install -c conda-forge jupyter_nbextensions_configurator
jupyter contrib nbextension install --user
```

Once it is installed, there will be an extra *Nbextensions* tab on your Jupyter notebook homepage. By clicking on the tab, you will find a list of available widgets (see Fig. 2.9 below).

Spend a few minutes and get yourself familiar with some of the useful extensions as well as how to enable them and disable them (Table 2.3).

Working with Jupyter Notebook can be more efficient with the use of **shortcuts**. Note that the Notebook has two different keyboard input modes. *Edit mode* allows you to type code or text into a cell and is indicated by a green cell border.

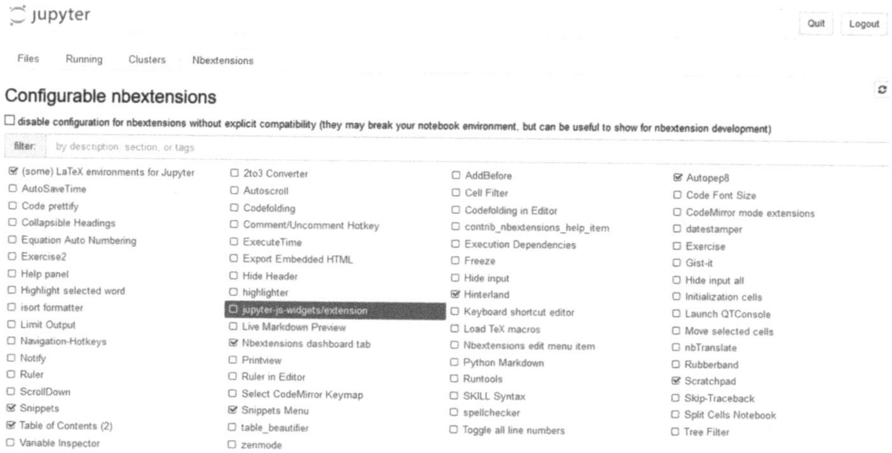

Fig. 2.9 Screenshot of Nbextensions tab

Table 2.3 Nbextensions

Extensions	Description
Snippets	Adds a drop-down menu to insert snippet cells into the current notebook
Table of contents	Auto-generate a table of contents from markdown headings
Hinterland	Enable code autocompletion menu for every keypress in a code cell, instead of only enabling it with tab
Autopep8	Use kernel-specific code to reformat/prettify the contents of code cells
Scratchpad	Adds a scratchpad cell to Jupyter notebook
LaTeX environments	Enable to use laTeX environments in Jupyter's markdown cells
Snippets menu	Add a customizable menu item to insert code and markdown snippets

Command mode binds the keyboard to notebook level commands and is indicated by a grey cell border with a blue left margin. You can enter the command mode by pressing **Esc** key.

In command mode, pressing **H** key can show all the shortcuts available in Jupyter Notebook. Some common shortcut keys are listed below:

- **Ctrl + Enter**: to run the selected cells
- **Shift + Enter**: run the current cell and move the next one
- **Ctrl + S**: save notebook
- **B**: insert a new cell below
- **A**: insert a new cell above
- Press **D** twice: delete the selected cells
- **Z**: undo the deletion of selected cells
- **X**: cut the selected cells
- **V**: paste the selected cells
- **M**: change the type of cell to Markdown
- **Y**: change the type of cell to Code

In the edit mode within a cell,

- **Tab** key: code completion suggestion or indent
- **Shift + Tab:** tooltip
- **Ctrl + Z**: undo
- **Ctrl + Y**: redo
- **Ctrl + A**: select all

Table 2.4 Magics examples

Magics	Description	Example
%load	Load code into the current frontend	%load mycode.py
%time	Time execution of a Python statement	%time 3**5
%timeit	Average time execution of a Python statement	%timeit pass
%matplotlib	Set up Matplotlib to work interactively	%matplotlib inline
%who	Print all interactive variables	%who str
%writefile	Write the contents of the cell to a file	%writefile mycode.py
%pwd	Return the current working directory path	%pwd

- **Ctrl + /**: insert comment or change selected codes to comment
- **Ctrl + Home/UP**: move cursor to cell start
- **Ctrl + End/Down**: move cursor to cell end
- **Ctrl + Left**: move cursor one word left
- **Ctrl + Right**: move cursor one word right

Magics are commands which can be used to perform specific tasks. There are two types of magic commands: line magics start with a percent character %, which apply their functionality just for one single line of a cell (where the command is placed); cell magics start with two %%, which apply their functionality for the whole cell. To view all available magics, you can run %lsmagic:

```
%lsmagic
```

Some of the useful magics are listed in Table 2.4.

For more details of the built-in magic commands, visit the official site (see *https://ipython.readthedocs.io/en/stable/interactive/magics.html*).

Summary of Learning Objectives

1. **Explain why data is important for effective supply chain management.**

    Data can be anywhere along the supply chain and is often regarded as the 'new oil' of today's digital economy. Data can be a critical source for effective SCM and decision making because the management and coordination of various supply chain processes require smooth, timely, and accurate information and data exchange, without which supply chain will not function properly, leading to delays, poor production planning and scheduling, and inaccurate demand forecasting, and potentially causing bullwhip effect, creating waste and high cost in inventory.

2. **Discuss the various data sources and related IS adoption in supply chains**

    There are many available data sources in the supply chain due to the wide adoption of IT/IS systems and smart technologies. Examples can include the use of EDI system to transmit data, the barcoding system to scan and capture product info and origins, the RFID technology to locate and track items, and ERP system that contains many modules with a shared database. The adoption of cyber physical systems and IoT, coupled with AI, smart devices, and machine learning has given rise to the fourth industrial revolution–Industry 4.0. Blockchain has also gained momentum in operations and supply chain field applications, such as supply chain tracing and tracking, quality improvement, and risk minimization as well as improving trust amongst supply chain members.

3. **Describe what big data is, its characteristics and the 5Vs of big data.**

   Big data is the term we use to describe the vast amount of data available for businesses to harness and act upon. It has the characteristics of large volume and variety including structured, semi-structured, and unstructured data types. We usually use 5Vs to define big data, i.e., Volume, Variety, Velocity, Variation, and Veracity. Big data has its intrinsic value but can only become valuable to organizations if meaningful insights can be derived from it for effective decision making. This would require data analysts, managers, and top executives to identify appropriate data for the right type of questions, make informed assumptions, and develop robust analytics models.

4. **Understand how to download and install Python and the essential Python libraries.**

   It is recommended to use Anaconda distribution to download and install Python onto your computer for the exercises included in this book, though stand-alone installation can be done by downloading Python directly from its official website. We introduced Python IDE, especially the Jupyter Notebook, which will be used in our exercises and examples in the following chapters. You can also use other Python IDEs at your discretion. The essential Python libraries introduced here include, for example, pandas, Matplotlib, Seaborn, and scikit-learn. Make sure you understand their main purposes of use, and how to install and import them into your notebook. Finally, you can try to optimize your Jupyter Notebook by installing extensions and also make sure you understand the various shortcuts available to improve the efficiency while working with it.

Discussion Questions

1. Explore a specific company's supply chain and examine what data sources are available and how different types of data might be used for the company's supply chain management.
2. What factors could affect information and data sharing in supply chains? Can you give some practical examples?

3. Discuss the potential causes of bullwhip effect in the supply chain and how could you reduce it or avoid it completely?
4. Explore the IT/IS systems that have been adopted in a supply chain of a particular organization. Discuss the associated data sources and how they can be used for effective decision making and performance improvement?
5. Discuss the potential application of blockchain technology along a specific supply chain in the sector of your choice. What can be the challenges for its application?

Keyboard Exercises
1. Download Anaconda distribution and install the essential Python libraries as discussed in the chapter.
2. Try to import different libraries and submodules into your Jupyter Notebook.
3. Install Jupyter Notebook extensions and try to optimize it using the examples demonstrated in the chapter.
4. Get familiar with different shortcuts and magic commands in Jupyter Notebook

References

Bosari, J. 2012. "Real Costs of Choosing the Wrong Software Vendor", Forbes, Retrieved 10 Nov, 2018, from https://www.forbes.com /sites/moneywisewomen/2012/10/04/real-costs-of-choosing-the-wrong-software-vendor/?sh=5a3a1bd64997

Carruthers, K. 2016. "Internet of Things and Beyond: Cyber-Physical Systems", IEEE Internet of Things.

Cole, R., Stevenson, M. & Aitken, J. 2019, "Blockchain technology: implications for operations and supply chain management", Supply Chain Management, Vol. 24 No. 4, pp. 469-483.

Conway, L. 2020. "Blockchain Explained", Invenstopedia, Retrieved 20 Nov, 2020, from https://www.investopedia.com/terms/b/blockchain.asp.

Ganeriwalla, A., Casey, M., Shrikrishna, P., Bender, J.P. & Gstettner, S. 2018, "Does your supply chain need a blockchain?" Boston Consulting Group, Retrieved 22 No, 2020, from https://www.bcg.com/en-gb/publications/2018/does-your-supply-chain-need-blockchain.

Lee, H.L., Padmanabhan, V. & Whang, S. 1997. "Information distortion in a supply chain: The bullwhip effect", Management Science, Vol. 43 No. 4, pp. 546–558.

Moreno, H. 2017. "Location Intelligence: Mapping The Opportunities In The Data Landscape", Forbes, Retrieved 12 Nov, 2018, from https://www.forbes.com/sites/forbesinsights/2017/01/19/location-intelligence-mapping-the-opportunities-in-the-data-landscape/?sh=2dd79c4a1bc6

Veres, P., Bányai, T. & Illés, B. 2017. "Intelligent Transportation Systems to Support Production Logistics" In: Jármai K., Bolló B. (eds) Vehicle and Automotive Engineering. Lecture Notes in Mechanical Engineering. Springer, Cham.

Data Manipulation

3

Contents

Learning Objectives
- Describe what data manipulation is and the basic procedures.
- Discuss the benefits of data manipulation in supply chain analytics.
- Understand the various methods for data manipulation in Python.
- Learn and grasp how to work with text data and datetime data in Python.

3.1 What Is Data Manipulation?

As discussed in Chap. 2, data can be collected in many ways and exit in many forms. When it comes to data analytics, not all data are readily actionable and precise for processing and analysing. Some data, for example, can be stored randomly in a spreadsheet with lots of mistakes and typos; others may contain categorical data that need to be transformed before feeding them into analytics models. Getting data ready for further analysis has thus become a very important task. In practice, a lot of data scientists and analysts spend more time in data cleaning preparation than training the analytics models alone.

▶ **Data manipulation**, in this book, is defined as the process of organizing and transforming data to make it appropriate, consistent, and valuable for the purpose of downstream analysis such as data analytics and machine learning.

It can involve tasks such as data cleaning, data conversion and transformation as well as feature engineering. Data manipulation is crucial for supply chain analytics because it can ensure data clarity and readability, and most importantly, the reliability and validity of the analytics results for effective supply chain decision making.

The benefits of data manipulation include:

- *Data Appropriateness*—Selecting appropriate data out of various sources for different purposes not only saves time, but also improves the accuracy of the analytics models being trained.
- *Data Consistency*—Consistency in data allows readability and efficiency. Data from various sources may not have a unified form. Thus, data manipulation can make data easy to organize and store after transformation.
- *Data Exploitation*—Data manipulation enables analysts to edit, delete, merge, and combine data. Thus, we could gain as much as possible from the available data for analytics purpose.

There are some basic steps which can be followed when performing data manipulation. Figure 3.1 illustrates a four-step procedure as a guidance; however, you do not have to strictly follow all these steps depending on real circumstances. For instance, if your data is quite clean and has no outliers or missing values, you may neglect Step 3 and directly jump onto Step 4. Sometimes, you may find your data is not adequate to train a good analytics model, and thus you would have to go back to Step 2 and figure out what additional data you could get to improve your model.

In the following sections, we will explore some data manipulation and transformation methods with pandas in Python. However, note that since the aim of this book is not to provide a comprehensive review of pandas or Python programming, you should familiarize yourself with the basics of pandas before moving onto the next sections.

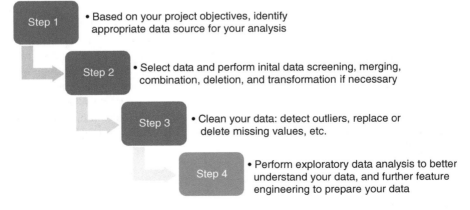

Fig. 3.1 Four-step process for data manipulation

3.2   Data Loading and Writing

pandas has built-in `reader` and `writer` functions that can read and write different types of data. For example, `pandas.read_csv()` is generally used to read a CSV file and return a pandas object. `DataFrame.to_csv()` is used to write your DataFrame objects to a CSV file. Table 3.1 contains some common `readers` and `writers` in pandas.

We will walk through an example below by loading a purchase order data. You can download the data from our online repository. First, let us import the necessary libraries by typing the following code into a cell within the Jupyter Notebook:

Ex. 3.1

```
# Import libraries
import numpy as np
import pandas as pd
```

The data is in TSV format (tab-separated values). To read this data type, we can use `pandas.read_csv()` method, with a delimiter `sep='\t'`, consider below:

Ex. 3.2

```
# Load data
df = pd.read_csv('PurchaseOrders.tsv', sep='\t')
```

After successfully loading the data, we can use the writer function to store the data into a new CSV file or any other formats of your choice:

Ex. 3.3

```
df.to_csv('PurchaseOrder.csv',index=False)
```

Table 3.1 pandas reader and writer functions

Data type	Reader	Writer
CSV	read_csv	to_csv
JSON	read_json	to_json
HTML	read_html	to_html
Local clipboard	read_clipboard	to_clipboard
MS Excel	read_excel	to_excel
HDF5 Format	read_hdf	to_hdf
Feather Format	read_feather	to_feather
Parquet Format	read_parquet	to_parquet
Msgpack	read_msgpack	to_msgpack
Stata	read_stata	to_stata
Python Pickle Format	read_pickle	to_pickle
SQL	read_sql	to_sql

The `Dataframe.info()` method prints a concise summary of a DataFrame, including the index dtype and column dtypes, non-null values, and memory usage.

Ex. 3.4

```
df.info()
```

```
<class 'pandas.core.frame.DataFrame'>
RangeIndex: 15681 entries, 0 to 15680
Data columns (total 7 columns):
Id              15681 non-null int64
Date            15681 non-null object
DeliveryDate    15681 non-null object
Quantity        15681 non-null int64
Currency        15681 non-null object
Supplier        15681 non-null object
NetAmount       15681 non-null float64
dtypes: float64(1), int64(2), object(4)
memory usage: 857.6+ KB
```

We can also use `DataFrame.head(n)` method to have a quick glimpse of the data structure and types by returning the first n rows (default 5) for the object:

Ex. 3.5

```
df.head()
```

	Id	Date	DeliveryDate	Quantity	Currency	Supplier	NetAmount
0	10206	2017-08-15	2017-08-24	26	USD	Computer & Co	289.380005
1	10206	2017-08-22	2017-08-31	27	USD	Computer & Co	300.510010
2	10206	2017-08-28	2017-09-07	36	USD	Computer & Co	400.679993
3	10206	2017-09-05	2017-09-14	19	USD	Computer & Co	211.470001
4	10206	2017-09-11	2017-09-19	13	USD	Computer & Co	144.690002

In addition, `DataFrame.describe()` method generates descriptive statistics including central tendency, dispersion, and shape of a dataset's distribution, while excluding NaN (Not a Number) values:

Ex. 3.6

```
df.describe()
```

	Id	Quantity	NetAmount
count	15681.000000	15681.000000	15681.000000
mean	65755.160576	96.487150	4365.231301
std	59681.564555	145.227237	8368.975569
min	2354.000000	1.000000	4.640000
25%	13623.000000	27.000000	314.399994
50%	54234.000000	50.000000	898.880005
75%	74034.000000	104.000000	4662.939940
max	214437.000000	2277.000000	98942.429700

DataFrame objects have several `attributes` as listed in Table 3.2, which can be useful when exploring your data.

For example, `DataFrame.shape` returns the dimensionality of the DataFrame,

Ex. 3.7

```
df.shape          #shape of the dataframe, rows x columns
(15681, 7)
```

and `DataFrame.dtypes` returns a series with the data type of each column:

Table 3.2 pandas reader and writer functions

Attributes	Description
dtypes	Return the dtypes in the DataFrame
columns	The column labels of the DataFrame
index	The index (row labels) of the DataFrame
shape	Return a tuple representing the dimensionality of the DataFrame
size	Return an int representing the number of elements in this object
values	Return a NumPy representation of the DataFrame
T	Transpose index and columns

Ex. 3.8

```
df.dtypes
Id                 int64
Date               object
DeliveryDate       object
Quantity           int64
Currency           object
Supplier           object
NetAmount          float64
dtype: object
```

3.3   Data Indexing and Selection

pandas offers various methods for accessing and modifying values in pandas Series and DataFrame objects. The axis labelling information in pandas objects serves many purposes, including identifying data using known indicators, enabling automatic and explicit data alignment and allowing intuitive getting and setting of subsets of the dataset.

First, let us take a look at some useful properties of Index objects as listed in Table 3.3.

For instance, we can check whether the column 'Id' from our previous example has any duplicate values by using Index.is_unique method:

Ex. 3.9

```
df.Id.is_unique
False
```

Table 3.3 Index objects properties in pandas

Properties	Description
Index.values	Return an array representing the data in the Index
Index.is_unique	Return if the index has unique values
Index.hasnans	Return if I have any *NaN*s; enables various perf speedups
Index.dtype	Return the dtype object of the underlying data
Index.shape	Return a tuple of the shape of the underlying data
Index.T	Return the transpose, which is by definition self

Table 3.4 Methods of index objects

Methods	Description
Index.all()	Return whether all elements are True
Index.any()	Return whether any element is True
Index.unique()	Return unique values in the index
Index.nunique()	Return number of unique elements in the object
Index.value_counts()	Return a Series containing counts of unique values
Index.argmin()	Return a *ndarray* of the minimum argument indexer
Index.argmax()	Return a ndarray of the maximum argument indexer
Index.min()	Return the minimum value of the Index
Index.max()	Return the maximum value of the Index
Index.copy()	Make a copy of this object
Index.drop()	Make new Index with passed list of labels deleted
Index.drop_duplicates()	Return Index with duplicate values removed
Index.duplicated()	Indicate duplicate index values
Index.equals()	Determine if two Index objects contain the same elements
Index.factorize()	Encode the object as an enumerated type or categorical variable
Index.insert()	Make new Index inserting new item at location
Index.reindex()	Create index with target's values
Index.rename()	Alter Index or MultiIndex name
Index.set_names()	Set Index or MultiIndex name
Index.argsort()	Return the integer indices that would sort the index
Index.sort_values()	Return a sorted copy of the index

The index objects also have methods for modifying and computations values. Table 3.4 contains a list of some frequently used ones.

In our example, we can check how many unique products are there in the data by using `Index.nunique()` method:

Ex. 3.10

```
df.Id.nunique()
98
```

We can also check the largest ordering quantity in the data by using `Index.max()` method:

Ex. 3.11

```
df.Quantity.max()
2277
```

pandas has two major types of multi-axis indexing for more explicit object locating and selection. `.loc[]` is primarily label based (i.e., look for the explicit label of the index), for example, 7 is interpreted as a label of the index rather than an integer position along the index. `.loc[]` allows data selection based on the following labels:

- A single label: e.g., `DataFrame.loc[7]` or `DataFrame.loc['a']`.
- A list or array of labels: e.g., `DataFrame.loc[['a','b','c']]`.
- A slice object with labels: e.g., `DataFrame.loc['a':'c']`.
- A *Boolean* array (any `NA` values will be treated as `False`).
- A `callable` function with one argument (the calling Series or DataFrame) and that returns valid output for indexing.

> **Note:** DataFrame has two indexers, i.e., `df.loc[row_indexer, col-umn_indexer]`. Any of the axes accessors may be the null slice `:`. Axes omitted from specification are assumed to be a `:`, e.g., `df.loc['a']` is equivalent to `df.loc['a', :]`.

For instance, if we want to select the data where its index label is 1 in our previous example:

Ex. 3.12

```
df.loc[1]
        Id                      10206
        Date               2017-08-22
        DeliveryDate       2017-08-31
        Quantity                   27
        Currency                  USD
        Supplier        Computer & Co
        NetAmount              300.51
        Name: 1, dtype: object
```

We can also use the method to check what products we spent most money on (e.g., more than $85,000 USD):

Ex. 3.13

```
df.loc[df.NetAmount > 85000]
```

	Id	Date	DeliveryDate	Quantity	Currency	Supplier	NetAmount
12688	71437	2013-05-20	2013-05-27	753	USD	Computer & Co	88545.2734
14157	73627	2014-11-03	2014-11-13	939	USD	Computer & Co	98942.4297
14158	73627	2014-11-10	2014-11-18	897	USD	Computer & Co	94516.8906

.iloc[] is integer position based (i.e., indexed position from 0 to length-1 of the axis), for example, 7 is interpreted as the eighth position along the index. The allowed inputs are as follows:

- An integer: e.g., DataFrame.iloc[7].
- A *list* or *array* of integers: e.g., DataFrame.iloc[[1,3,5]].
- A *slice* object with integers: e.g., DataFrame.iloc[1:5].
- A *Boolean* array (any NA values will be treated as False).
- A callable function with one argument (the calling Series or DataFrame) and that returns valid output for indexing.

For instance, we can select the indexed position from second to fourth in our example with slicing [1:5], alternatively you can use list [1,2,3,4]:

Ex. 3.14

```
df.iloc[1:5]
```

	Id	Date	DeliveryDate	Quantity	Currency	Supplier	NetAmount
1	10206	2017-08-22	2017-08-31	27	USD	Computer & Co	300.510010
2	10206	2017-08-28	2017-09-07	36	USD	Computer & Co	400.679993
3	10206	2017-09-05	2017-09-14	19	USD	Computer & Co	211.470001
4	10206	2017-09-11	2017-09-19	13	USD	Computer & Co	144.690002

Both .loc and .iloc indexing can accept a callable as indexer. To illustrate, let us re-run *Ex.3.13* using lambda function though it is not the best way:

Ex. 3.15

```
df.loc[lambda df: df.NetAmount > 85000]
```

	Id	Date	DeliveryDate	Quantity	Currency	Supplier	NetAmount
12688	71437	2013-05-20	2013-05-27	753	USD	Computer & Co	88545.2734
14157	73627	2014-11-03	2014-11-13	939	USD	Computer & Co	98942.4297
14158	73627	2014-11-10	2014-11-18	897	USD	Computer & Co	94516.8906

In addition to the two methods mentioned above, there is another basic indexing and selection option using []. You can use : to slice the *rows* inside [], e.g., df[1:5] and pass a list of *columns* to [], e.g., df[['Id', 'Date', 'Quantity']]. This is a common operation and can be very useful in practice.

The `where()` method can be used to select values from a DataFrame (or Series) with a Boolean criterion while preserving input data shape. As an example, let us construct a new DataFrame `df2`, consider below:

Ex. 3.16

```
# Let's build a new datafram & work on selection
df2 = pd.DataFrame(np.arange(16).reshape((4, 4)),
index=['a', 'c', 'd', 'f'],
columns=['Cambridge', 'Oxford', 'Glasgow', 'Birmingham'])
df2
```

	Cambridge	Oxford	Glasgow	Birmingham
a	0	1	2	3
c	4	5	6	7
d	8	9	10	11
f	12	13	14	15

We can then select the values where the cities have numbers greater than three, using `df2.where(df2>3)`. Note that the code below is equivalent to `df2[df2>3]`.

Ex. 3.17

```
df2.where(df2 > 3)
```

	Cambridge	Oxford	Glasgow	Birmingham
a	NaN	NaN	NaN	NaN
c	4.0	5.0	6.0	7.0
d	8.0	9.0	10.0	11.0
f	12.0	13.0	14.0	15.0

In addition, `where()` includes an optional `other` argument. Where the Boolean condition is True, the returned copy of data will keep the original value; where False, value will be replaced with corresponding value from `other` (default NaN) (see *Ex.3.17* above). As an example, let us set `other=0` in the exercise below:

Ex. 3.18

```
df2.where(df2 > 3, 0)
```

	Cambridge	Oxford	Glasgow	Birmingham
a	0	0	0	0
c	4	5	6	7
d	8	9	10	11
f	12	13	14	15

You should notice that all the values that are less than or equal to three have been replaced with value 0 in this case.

In this section we have explored some basics for data indexing and selection with pandas, for more information on different methods and their functionality, see **'Indexing and Selecting data'** and **'MultiIndex/Advanced Indexing'** sections of the pandas documentation.

3.4   Data Merging and Combination

In many applications, data analysts may seek multiple data sources for their analysis and thus merging and combining a variety of data files or databases become a common practice. pandas provides functions and methods that make this sort of data operations fast and flexible.

The `pandas.concat()` function performs concatenation operations along one axis while performing optional set logic (union or intersection) of the indexes on the other axes. In **Edit** mode, we can check its `Signature` by pressing **Shift + Tab** keys:

```
pd.concat(objs, axis=0, join='outer', ignore_index=False, keys=None,
          levels=None, names=None, verify_integrity=False, copy=True)
```

Let us build another DataFrame `df3` and then concatenate it with `df2` from *Ex. 3.16*:

Ex. 3.19

```
df3 = pd.DataFrame(np.arange(16,32).reshape((4, 4)),
index=['g', 'h', 'i', 'j'],
columns=['Oxford', 'Glasgow', 'Birmingham', 'London'])
df3
```

	Oxford	Glasgow	Birmingham	London
g	16	17	18	19
h	20	21	22	23
i	24	25	26	27
j	28	29	30	31

In order to combine the two DataFrame objects, we set `objs=[df2, df3]` while keep other parameters as default:

Ex. 3.20

```
result = pd.concat([df2, df3], sort=False)
result
```

	Cambridge	Oxford	Glasgow	Birmingham	London
a	0.0	1	2	3	NaN
c	4.0	5	6	7	NaN
d	8.0	9	10	11	NaN
f	12.0	13	14	15	NaN
g	NaN	16	17	18	19.0
h	NaN	20	21	22	23.0
i	NaN	24	25	26	27.0
j	NaN	28	29	30	31.0

Note: The entries for which no data is available are filled with NaN values. We specified sort=**False** to opt into the new behaviour of a future version of pandas, which will change to not sort by default.

By default, the pandas.concat() method performs row-wise concatenation within the DataFrame (i.e., axis=0). However, we can specify axis along which the concatenation will take place (i.e., set axis=0/'index' or 1/'columns'). Consider the following example:

Ex. 3.21

```
result = pd.concat([df2, df3], axis=1, sort=False)
result
```

	Cambridge	Oxford	Glasgow	Birmingham	Oxford	Glasgow	Birmingham	London
a	0.0	1.0	2.0	3.0	NaN	NaN	NaN	NaN
c	4.0	5.0	6.0	7.0	NaN	NaN	NaN	NaN
d	8.0	9.0	10.0	11.0	NaN	NaN	NaN	NaN
f	12.0	13.0	14.0	15.0	NaN	NaN	NaN	NaN
g	NaN	NaN	NaN	NaN	16.0	17.0	18.0	19.0
h	NaN	NaN	NaN	NaN	20.0	21.0	22.0	23.0
i	NaN	NaN	NaN	NaN	24.0	25.0	26.0	27.0
j	NaN	NaN	NaN	NaN	28.0	29.0	30.0	31.0

The `ignore_index` parameter can be used to reset index along the concatenation axis. The `join` parameter is defaulted to 'outer', which takes *union* of the DataFrame objects being concatenated. When set to 'inner', it will take the *intersection* instead. Consider below:

Ex. 3.22

```
result = pd.concat([df2, df3], join='inner', sort=False)
result
```

	Oxford	Glasgow	Birmingham
a	1	2	3
c	5	6	7
d	9	10	11
f	13	14	15
g	16	17	18
h	20	21	22
i	24	25	26
j	28	29	30

There is a shortcut to `pandas.concat()`, i.e., `append()` instance method on Series and DataFrame, which concatenates along axis=0, namely the index. For instance, rather than calling `pd.concat([df2, df3])`, we can simply use the following code:

Ex. 3.23

```
# use append() instead of calling pd.concat()
df2.append(df3, sort=False)
```

In addition, pandas provides high-performance in-memory and database-style merge and join operations for DataFrame or named Series objects (very similar to relational databases SQL). These functions are implemented under what is known as *relational algebra*, which sets the rules and foundation for manipulating relational database. They perform significantly better than other open-source implementations such as `data.frame` in R, which is mainly due to their careful algorithmic design and the internal data structure in DataFrame.

The `pandas.merge()` method offers as the entry point for all standard database-style join operations. Let us take a look at its signature:

```
pd.merge(left, right, how='inner', on=None, left_on=None,
         right_on=None, left_index=False, right_index=False,
         sort=False, suffixes=('_x', '_y'), copy=True,
         indicator=False, validate=None)
```

You can explore the detailed explanations of these parameters yourself in Jupyter Notebook. Note that `merge()` is also available as a DataFrame instance method with the calling DataFrame (e.g., `df1`) being implicitly considered the left object in the join, e.g., `df1.merge(df2)`.

If you are familiar with relationship databases (e.g., SQL), you probably understand the terminology used to describe join operations between two SQL-table like structures. When using the `merge()` method to join DataFrame objects, there are three basic cases to consider:

- **one-to-one join**: when joining two DataFrame objects on unique keys (i.e., key columns must contain unique values).
- **many-to-one join**: when one of the two key columns contains duplicate values.
- **many-to-many join**: both key columns in the joining two DataFrame objects contain duplicates

The **one-to-one** join is similar to column-wise concatenation in many ways. As an example, let us create a sample copy of the DataFrame from *Ex.3.2* but only take two columns 'Id' and 'Supplier' from it:

Ex. 3.24

```
df4 = df.sample(6, random_state=42)[['Id', 'Supplier']]
df4
```

	Id	Supplier
3288	182934	Computer & Co
4866	20345	Digital Age
5270	214437	Office Supplies
13213	72042	Techno First
2034	13623	Office Supplies
9006	51518	Digital Age

In addition, let us build a new DataFrame object with the unique values in the 'Id' column from `df4`:

Ex. 3.25

```
df5 = pd.DataFrame({'Id': [182934, 20345, 214437, 72042, 13623, 51518],
                    'Category': ['Accessories', 'Software', 'Hardware',
                                 'Service', 'Hardware', 'Software']})
df5
```

	Id	Category
0	182934	Accessories
1	20345	Software
2	214437	Hardware
3	72042	Service
4	13623	Hardware
5	51518	Software

Now, both DataFrame objects contain the unique keys in their `'Id'` columns. We can use the `pd.merge()` method to join the two objects together:

Ex. 3.26

```
df6 = pd.merge(df4,df5)
df6
```

	Id	Supplier	Category
0	182934	Computer & Co	Accessories
1	20345	Digital Age	Software
2	214437	Office Supplies	Hardware
3	72042	Techno First	Service
4	13623	Office Supplies	Hardware
5	51518	Digital Age	Software

The `pd.merge()` function can recognize that both DataFrame objects contain an overlapping `'Id'` column and automatically join this column with the unique values. However, it is always a good practice to specify which key columns to join on (i.e., `pd.merge(df4, df5, on='Id')`) Note that the merge operations discarded the index when joining columns on columns; when joining indexes on indexes or indexes on a column or columns, the index will be passed on.

For the **many-to-one** case, the duplicate entries in one of the two key columns will be preserved in the resulting DataFrame. Consider the `'Supplier'` column in df6 above that contains some duplicate values, let us create another DataFrame object that has the same key column but without duplicates:

Ex. 3.27

```
df7 = pd.DataFrame({'Supplier': ['Computer & Co', 'Digital Age',
                                 'Office Supplies', 'Techno First'],
                    'Location': ['Cambridge', 'Oxford',
                                 'Glasgow', 'Birmingham']})
df7
```

	Supplier	Location
0	Computer & Co	Cambridge
1	Digital Age	Oxford
2	Office Supplies	Glasgow
3	Techno First	Birmingham

Let us then merge these two DataFrame objects (i.e., df7 and df8) together, but using the DataFrame instance method `merge()` instead:

Ex. 3.28

```
df8 = df6.merge(df7)
df8
```

	Id	Supplier	Category	Location
0	182934	Computer & Co	Accessories	Cambridge
1	20345	Digital Age	Software	Oxford
2	51518	Digital Age	Software	Oxford
3	214437	Office Supplies	Hardware	Glasgow
4	13623	Office Supplies	Hardware	Glasgow
5	72042	Techno First	Service	Birmingham

The **many-to-many** joins seem a little complicated. Here is a very basic example, in which we build a DataFrame that contains one or more delivery dates from each supplier:

Ex. 3.29

```
df9 = pd.DataFrame({'Supplier': ['Computer & Co','Computer & Co',
                                 'Digital Age','Office Supplies',
                                 'Techno First', 'Techno First'],
                    'DeliveryDate': ['2019-03-18','2019-03-21',
                                     '2019-03-16','2019-03-20',
                                     '2019-03-23', '2019-03-27']})
df9
```

	Supplier	DeliveryDate
0	Computer & Co	2019-03-18
1	Computer & Co	2019-03-21
2	Digital Age	2019-03-16
3	Office Supplies	2019-03-20
4	Techno First	2019-03-23
5	Techno First	2019-03-27

Let us now join the two DataFrame objects (df8 and df9) that both contain some duplicate entries:

Ex. 3.30

```
df10 = df8.merge(df9)
df10
```

	Id	Supplier	Category	Location	DeliveryDate
0	182934	Computer & Co	Accessories	Cambridge	2019-03-18
1	182934	Computer & Co	Accessories	Cambridge	2019-03-21
2	20345	Digital Age	Software	Oxford	2019-03-16
3	51518	Digital Age	Software	Oxford	2019-03-16
4	214437	Office Supplies	Hardware	Glasgow	2019-03-20
5	13623	Office Supplies	Hardware	Glasgow	2019-03-20
6	72042	Techno First	Service	Birmingham	2019-03-23
7	72042	Techno First	Service	Birmingham	2019-03-27

Table 3.5 Merge method attribute

Parameter	Explanation	Example
on	Columns names to join on. Must be found in both DataFrame objects	When df1 and df2 both have the 'Id' column `pd.merge(df1, df2, on='Id')`
left_on	Columns in left DataFrame to join on	When product ID column is labelled as 'Id.' in df1, and 'No.' in df2
right_on	Columns in right DataFrame to join on	`pd.merge(df1, df2, left_on='Id', right_on='No.')`
left_index	Row index in left DataFrame to join on	When both dfs have product ID as their index, we can join them with the index
right_index	Row index in right DataFrame to join on	`pd.merge(df1, df2, left_index=True, right_index=True)`
Note: you can also specify mixed joins: i.e., index on column or column on index		When df1 has product ID as its index, the other df2 has product ID as its column `pd.merge(df1, df2, left_index=True, right_on='Id')`
how='inner'	Use intersection of keys from both frames	This is the default setting
how='outer'	Use union of keys from both frames	Note that missing values with be filled with NaN
how='left'	Use keys from left DataFrame only	The output rows correspond to the entries in the left df
how='right'	Use keys from right DataFrame only	The output rows correspond to the entries in the right df
suffixes	Make the overlapping columns unique, defaults to ('_x', '_y')	When joining df1 and df2 on 'Id', however both dfs have overlapping 'Supplier' columns, the output columns would appear 'Supplier_x' and 'Supplier_y', unless a custom suffix is specified

With the default behaviour of `merge()` method, we have performed three basic types of joins as demonstrated above. In the end, we have created a new DataFrame object (i.e., `df10`) linking product ID, associated suppliers, product categories, the locations of suppliers, and the date when the respective deliveries were made.

However, in real practice, datasets are rarely as clean as the ones we used above. Therefore, `merge()` method includes a few parameters with which we can handle a variety of complex joins. Rather than going through all these parameters in details here, below is a table containing some of the examples (Table 3.5):

When merging internally for the index-on-index, DataFrame has another convenient `DataFrame.join()` method:

```
join(other, on=None, how='left', lsuffix='', rsuffix='', sort=False)
```

In this section, we have introduced pandas basics for data merging and combination. Sometimes different joining methods can be confusing for new analysts, especially when facing complex situations in practice. Figure 3.2 provides a guidance on the selection of these combining methods.

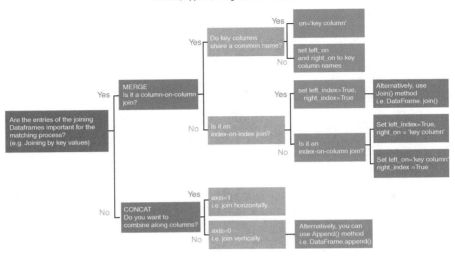

Fig. 3.2 Data merging and combination methods in Pandas

For more information on these methods and related functionality, see the '**Merge, Join, and Concatenate**' section of the pandas documentation.

3.5   Data Cleaning and Preparation

Another important task facing many data analysts is getting data cleaned before feeding them into any training models, as we often say, 'garbage in garbage out'! Data cleaning can come in many different forms, including, for example, handling missing data, deleting duplicate entries and detecting outliers. In this section, we discuss some basic data cleaning and preparation methods in pandas.

Missing data (often referred to as NA) can occur in many real applications due to lack of data availability, manual input errors and mistakes for instance. As previously mentioned, pandas uses NaN to represent missing values. The reason for using this missing value marker is largely due to convenience and computational performance. Note that pandas is built to handle both NaN and None, but automatically converts the None to a NaN value as of this writing, albeit there is an experimental pd.NA value is available to represent scalar missing values.

pandas has implemented various data manipulation methods for handling missing data (see Table 3.6).

Let us take a look at some examples. First, we modify the DataFrame df2 from *Ex. 3.16* by assigning some None values:

Table 3.6   Missing data handling methods

Method	Description
isna()	Return a Boolean same-sized object indicating which values are missing/NA
isnull()	Alias of isna()
notna()	Return a Boolean same-sized object indicating which values are not missing/NA
notnull()	Alias of notna()
fillna()	Fill missing values using the specified method (e.g., 'bfill', 'ffill', None)
dropna()	Remove missing values with specified criteria (e.g., how: 'any' 'all')

Ex. 3.31

```
df2.loc[['c','f'], ['Cambridge','Oxford']] = None
df2
```

	Cambridge	Oxford	Glasgow	Birmingham
a	0.0	1.0	2	3
c	NaN	NaN	6	7
d	8.0	9.0	10	11
f	NaN	NaN	14	15

Notice that pandas automatically converts None to NaN. Now we can use isna() method to check whether df2 has any missing values:

Ex. 3.32

```
df2.isna()
```

	Cambridge	Oxford	Glasgow	Birmingham
a	False	False	False	False
c	True	True	False	False
d	False	False	False	False
f	True	True	False	False

A straightforward way to check whether a DataFrame contains any missing values, we can use df2.isna().values.any(). To count the number of any missing values within each column in a DataFrame, consider the following code:

Ex. 3.33

```
df2.isna().sum()
Cambridge     2
Oxford        2
Glasgow       0
Birmingham    0
dtype: int64
```

We can remove the missing values by using dropna() method. However, notice that the method drops full rows or full columns that contain the null values, but cannot drop single values from DataFrame. Check the following example:

Ex. 3.34

```
df2.dropna()
```

	Cambridge	Oxford	Glasgow	Birmingham
a	0.0	1.0	2	3
d	8.0	9.0	10	11

As can be seen, the rows containing the missing values (i.e., 'c' and 'f') are removed from the frame. This is because by default, dropna() method drops all rows where there are *any* missing values (i.e., axis=0, how='any'). We can modify the default settings within the method, for instance, by specifying axis=1 will drop all columns that contain the null values. Consider the example below:

Ex. 3.35

```
df2.dropna(axis=1)
```

	Glasgow	Birmingham
a	2	3
c	6	7
d	10	11
f	14	15

In addition, setting how='all' will drop rows/columns only if they are *all* null values. Keep in mind that you might want to keep entire rows/columns if they contain at least certain number of good data, therefore there is an additional thresh parameter, which allows you to set a minimum number of non-null values for the rows/columns to be kept.

Often in practice, we would rather replace the null values than simply remove them. For example, using zero, mean, or some sort of imputation or interpolation from the good data. The fillna() method can fill in the missing values in different ways. Let us take a look at an example:

Ex. 3.36

```
df2.fillna(0)
```

	Cambridge	Oxford	Glasgow	Birmingham
a	0.0	1.0	2	3
c	0.0	0.0	6	7
d	8.0	9.0	10	11
f	0.0	0.0	14	15

Notice that the missing values have been replaced with number zero. We can also specify different values for each column:

Ex. 3.37

```
df2.fillna({'Cambridge':811, 'Oxford':924})
```

	Cambridge	Oxford	Glasgow	Birmingham
a	0.0	1.0	2	3
c	811.0	924.0	6	7
d	8.0	9.0	10	11
f	811.0	924.0	14	15

The `method` parameter can be used to either propagate last valid value forward to fill the holes or use next valid value to fill gaps backward. Consider the following example:

Ex. 3.38

```
df2.fillna(method='ffill')
```

	Cambridge	Oxford	Glasgow	Birmingham
a	0.0	1.0	2	3
c	0.0	1.0	6	7
d	8.0	9.0	10	11
f	8.0	9.0	14	15

`fillna()` has included other options which you can explore by yourself. In addition, pandas provides a `replace()` method that can be used to flexibly replace any values including missing data. Consider a simple illustration below:

Ex. 3.39

```
df2.replace(np.nan, 2020)
```

	Cambridge	Oxford	Glasgow	Birmingham
a	0.0	1.0	2	3
c	2020.0	2020.0	6	7
d	8.0	9.0	10	11
f	2020.0	2020.0	14	15

With this method, you can replace multiple values at once by passing a list (e.g., `df2.replace([2, 3, 4], 999)`) or a dictionary (e.g., `df2.replace({2:999, 3:555})`), with same or different replacement values.

Moreover, pandas offers an `interpolate()` method that performs linear interpolation at missing data points. It is a very powerful function to fill the missing values, especially when you deal with time series data. Recall that we have a `result` DataFrame from *Ex.3.22*, let us modify it by adding some null values:

Ex. 3.40

```
df12=result.reset_index(drop=True)
df12.replace([5, 10, 16,21, 24], np.nan)
```

	Oxford	Glasgow	Birmingham
0	1.0	2.0	3
1	NaN	6.0	7
2	9.0	NaN	11
3	13.0	14.0	15
4	NaN	17.0	18
5	20.0	NaN	22
6	NaN	25.0	26
7	28.0	29.0	30

Now, we can use the `interpolate()` method to interpolate new data and replace the missing values:

Ex. 3.41

```
df12.interpolate(method='linear', inplace=True)
```

	Oxford	Glasgow	Birmingham
0	1	2	3
1	5	6	7
2	9	10	11
3	13	14	15
4	16	17	18
5	20	21	22
6	24	25	26
7	28	29	30

By default, the `method` argument uses 'linear' interpolation. Setting `inplace=True` modifies the original `df12` with new values. As shown above, it has perfectly predicted the data to replace the null values in the DataFrame. There are fancier interpolation techniques that can be used, but it will depend on the type of data you are working with, for instance:

- `method='quadratic'` is appropriate for time series data with an increasing rate of growth.
- `method='pchip'` is suitable for data approximating a cumulative distribution function
- `method='akima'` can be used to fill missing values with goal of smooth plotting

In summary, we introduce different methods in this section for detecting, removing, and replacing the missing values in a DataFrame. There are still other available ways to handle missing data and perform data cleaning. It is however worth mentioning here that although data cleaning is critical for analysis, it can be more beneficial for data analysts to understand the impact of missing data and identify reasons for data missing (e.g., data collection problems) to prevent it from happening again.

For more information on how to deal with missing values, check '**Working with Missing Data**' section of the pandas documentation.

3.6   Data Computation and Aggregation

pandas offers several convenient methods for data computation and aggregation in Series and DataFrame. Table 3.7 below summarizes some common statistical functions. In this section, we will go through some of these methods.

Table 3.7 pandas common statistical method

Method	Description	cont.	
sum()	Sum of values	*var()*	Unbiased variance
mean()	Average values	*skew()*	Skewness of sample (third moment)
median()	Arithmetic median of values	*kurt()*	Kurtosis of sample (fourth moment)
max()	Maximum	*quantile()*	Sample quantile (value at %)
Min()	Minimum	*cov()*	Unbiased covariance (binary)
count()	Number of non-null observations	*corr()*	Correlation (binary)
std()	Bessel-corrected sample standard deviation	*apply()*	Generic apply
mad()	Mean absolute deviation	*prod()*	Product of all items

As a simple illustration, consider the following example:

Ex. 3.42

```
df12.quantile(0.25)
Oxford           8.0
Glasgow          9.0
Birmingham      10.0
Name: 0.25, dtype: float64
```

Using `quantile()` method, we have computed 0.25 quantile for each column in the example.

The `prod()` method returns the product of the values for the requested axis. For example, let us calculate the product of the values column-wise in `df12`:

Ex. 3.43

```
df12.prod(axis=1)
0          6
1        210
2        990
3       2730
4       4896
5       9240
6      15600
7      24360
dtype: int32
```

If you could recall that in *Ex.3.6*, we used the `describe()` method that gave us several common aggregates for each column. The method offers a convenient way to get a basic understanding of the overall statistics of a dataset.

A more powerful and flexible function for data computation and aggregation implemented in pandas is the 'GroupBy' operation, which consists of three steps:

- **Split**: separating data into different groups based on certain criteria.
- **Apply**: applying some method (e.g., aggregation, transformation, or filtration) to each group individually.
- **Combine**: combining the results into an output data structure.

The `groupby()` method can be used to group large amounts of data and perform computation on these groups. As an example, let us start by creating a new DataFrame:

Ex. 3.44

```
df13 = pd.DataFrame({'City': ['Cambridge','Oxford','Glasgow','Cardiff',
                             'London','Edinburgh','Birmingham','Swansea'],
                    'Region': ['England','England','Scotland','Wales',
                              'England','Scotland','England','Wales'],
                    'Product ID': ['S108','D256','S108','D256','S108',
                                  'D256','S108','D256'],
                    'Sales': [138,252,342,269,654,447,400,242]})
df13
```

	City	Region	Product ID	Sales
0	Cambridge	England	S108	138
1	Oxford	England	D256	252
2	Glasgow	Scotland	S108	342
3	Cardiff	Wales	D256	269
4	London	England	S108	654
5	Edinburgh	Scotland	D256	447
6	Birmingham	England	S108	400
7	Swansea	Wales	D256	242

By calling `groupby()` on a DataFrame, we can obtain a `GroupBy` object. For instance, let us group by different regions in `df13`:

Ex. 3.45

```
df13.groupby('Region')
```
```
<pandas.core.groupby.generic.DataFrameGroupBy object at 0x000002BE3ACC4160>
```

Note that the output `GroupBy` object is not a set of DataFrames, and it does not produce any computation results unless a function is applied. In the given example, if we want to know the total sales for each region, we can apply the `sum()` function, see code below:

Ex. 3.46

```
df13.groupby('Region').sum()
```

	Sales
Region	
England	1444
Scotland	789
Wales	511

In addition to grouping by one key, you can set multiple level of keys. Consider the example below, in which we check the sales of different products in each region:

Ex. 3.47

```
df13.groupby(['Region','Product ID']).sum()
```

		Sales
Region	**Product ID**	
England	**D256**	252
	S108	1192
Scotland	**D256**	447
	S108	342
Wales	**D256**	511

Instead of applying only one function, we can also pass multiple functions at once with `agg()` method. For instance, let us check the average, sum, and standard deviation of sales in each region:

Ex. 3.48

```
df13.groupby('Region').agg([np.mean, np.sum, np.std])
```

	Sales		
	mean	**sum**	**std**
Region			
England	361.0	1444	222.845238
Scotland	394.5	789	74.246212
Wales	255.5	511	19.091883

Besides, we can apply different functions on different columns by passing a dictionary mapping column names. Suppose we have another column named 'Profit' with numeric values, consider the example below,

Ex. 3.49

```
df14.groupby('Region').agg({'Sales': np.mean,
                            'Profit': np.sum})
```

	Sales	Profit
Region		
England	361.0	21360
Scotland	394.5	16280
Wales	255.5	11662

So far what we have learnt are some aggregation methods, which basically return a reduced version of the data for each group. Another useful method for `GroupBy` object is `transform()`. Instead of reducing the results, the method transforms the data and returns outputs to match the *shape* of the original input.

As a concrete example, let us find out the mean profit for each region in `df14`:

Ex. 3.50

```
df14.groupby('Region')['Profit'].transform('mean')
0    5340
1    5340
2    8140
3    5831
4    5340
5    8140
6    5340
7    5831
Name: Profit, dtype: int64
```

As you can see, we grouped by region and selected the 'Profit' column to perform the transformation. After computing the mean profit for each region, it returns a result of the same size (row-wise) as the original DataFrame. This makes recombining the output back to the original data simple.

Let us consider the following example, in which we first recombine the transformed result with `df14`, and then add an additional column that compares whether the profit from each city is better than its regional average:

Ex. 3.51

```
df14['avg_profit_region']=df14.groupby('Region')['Profit'].transform('mean')
df14['is_above_regional_avg']=df14['Profit'] > df14['avg_profit_region']
df14
```

	City	Region	Product ID	Sales	Profit	avg_profit_region	is_above_regional_avg
0	Cambridge	England	S108	138	1380	5340	False
1	Oxford	England	D256	252	5040	5340	False
2	Glasgow	Scotland	S108	342	7860	8140	False
3	Cardiff	Wales	D256	269	5420	5831	False
4	London	England	S108	654	6540	5340	True
5	Edinburgh	Scotland	D256	447	8420	8140	True
6	Birmingham	England	S108	400	8400	5340	True
7	Swansea	Wales	D256	242	6242	5831	True

Filtration is another useful operation for `GroupBy` object. The `filter()` method allows us to filter data based on some conditions and return a subset of the original object. The argument of `filter()` must be a function that is applied to the group as a whole and then returns True or False specifying whether each group passes the filtering.

Suppose we want to only take cities in regions with total regional sales greater than 800 units. From `Ex.3.46`, we already know the region is England, let us now see how the filter method works:

Ex. 3.52

```
df14.groupby('Region').filter(lambda x: x['Sales'].sum() > 800)
```

	City	Region	Product ID	Sales	Profit	avg_profit_region	is_above_regional_avg
0	Cambridge	England	S108	138	1380	5340	False
1	Oxford	England	D256	252	5040	5340	False
4	London	England	S108	654	6540	5340	True
6	Birmingham	England	S108	400	8400	5340	True

The `apply()` method offers a more flexible operation on `GroupBy` object than both `aggregate` and `transform` methods and can substitute the latter two in various standard use cases. The returned output can be either a pandas object or a scalar. Note that we can also apply a `lambda` function or a function that is defined elsewhere to a column (or a row) in the DataFrame.

Consider the following example, suppose we want to find out unit profit for each product sold in different cities:

Ex. 3.53

```
df14.groupby(['Product ID','City']).apply(lambda x: x['Profit']/x['Sales'])
Product ID  City
D256        Cardiff      3    20.148699
            Edinburgh    5    18.836689
            Oxford       1    20.000000
            Swansea      7    25.793388
S108        Birmingham   6    21.000000
            Cambridge    0    10.000000
            Glasgow      2    22.982456
            London       4    10.000000
dtype: float64
```

We can also define a new function and call it using the `apply()` method. See the example below where we defined an `avg_profit` function to compute mean profit for each group and return a new DataFrame:

Ex. 3.54

```
# Let's define a avg_profit function
def avg_profit(grouped):
    grouped['avg_profit'] = grouped['Profit'].mean()
    #return a new DataFrame with new column created
    return grouped

# Call the avg_profit function and apply it to each group
df15.groupby('Product ID').apply(avg_profit)
```

	City	Region	Product ID	Sales	Profit	avg_profit
0	Cambridge	England	S108	138	1380	6045.0
1	Oxford	England	D256	252	5040	6280.5
2	Glasgow	Scotland	S108	342	7860	6045.0
3	Cardiff	Wales	D256	269	5420	6280.5
4	London	England	S108	654	6540	6045.0
5	Edinburgh	Scotland	D256	447	8420	6280.5
6	Birmingham	England	S108	400	8400	6045.0
7	Swansea	Wales	D256	242	6242	6280.5

Note: apply() method can act as a reducer, transformer, or filter function, depending on exactly what is passed to it. Thus, the grouped column(s) may be included in the output as well as set the indices.

As demonstrated above, the GroupBy() method allows for some powerful and flexible operations for data aggregation and computation. For a full list of available functions and computation methods, see **'GroupBy'** section of pandas documentation.

In addition to GroupBy operation, pandas provide methods for creating **Pivot Table**—a spreadsheet-style pivot table as a DataFrame. The `DataFrame.pivot()` method returns reshaped DataFrame organized by given index/column values. Consider the following example:

Ex. 3.55

```
df15.pivot(index='City', columns='Product ID', values='Sales')
```

Product ID	D256	S108
City		
Birmingham	NaN	400.0
Cambridge	NaN	138.0
Cardiff	269.0	NaN
Edinburgh	447.0	NaN
Glasgow	NaN	342.0
London	NaN	654.0
Oxford	252.0	NaN
Swansea	242.0	NaN

By creating the reshaped pivot table, we can clearly observe the sales figure for each product along the city index. If values are not available after the transformation, `NaN` value will be used. However, note that when the index contains duplicate entries, `pivot()` method cannot perform reshape, and a `ValueError` will be raised. For instance, instead of using cities as index, we want to see how the sales look like for each region:

Ex. 3.56

```
df15.pivot(index='Region', columns='Product ID', values='Sales')
------------------------------------------------------------------
ValueError                              Traceback (most recent call last)
<ipython-input-205-849a7a0eb637> in <module>
----> 1 df15.pivot(index='Region', columns='Product ID', values='Sales')

D:\APPS\Conda\lib\site-packages\pandas\core\frame.py in pivot(self, index, columns, values)
   5626     def pivot(self, index=None, columns=None, values=None):
   5627         from pandas.core.reshape.pivot import pivot
-> 5628         return pivot(self, index=index, columns=columns, values=values)
```

This is because there are duplicate entries for some region and product ID combination, so that `df15` cannot be reshaped into a pivot table. In this case, we should consider using `pivot_table()` method, which contains an aggregation argument (i.e., `aggfunc`) and other useful parameters. The `aggfunc` keyword specifies what type of aggregation function is applied (default to 'mean'), for example, 'sum', 'count', 'min', 'max' or a dictionary mapping each column to a desired aggregation method.

Suppose we want to explore the mean sales figure for each product along the region index:

Ex. 3.57

```
df15.pivot_table(values='Sales', index='Region',
                 columns='Product ID', fill_value=0)
```

Product ID	D256	S108
Region		
England	252.0	397.333333
Scotland	447.0	342.000000
Wales	255.5	0.000000

There are also other pivoting methods offered by pandas such as `stack()` and `unstack()`, which are designed to work together with MultiIndex object. As a simple illustration, the above example is equivalent to the following:

Ex. 3.58

```
df15.groupby(['Region', 'Product ID'])['Sales'].mean().unstack()
```

We will not show additional examples of these pivoting methods here. For more details, check '**Reshaping and Pivot Tables**' section of pandas documentation.

3.7   Working with Text and Datetime Data

Quite often in data operations we have to work with text data, pandas provides an array of convenient string methods to make the operations easy. These methods can be accessed via the `str` attribute and generally mirror Python built-in string methods. Table 3.8 below lists some of these useful methods:

Let us consider a simple example, in which we convert column names to uppercase and strip whitespace with underscore ' _ ':

Ex. 3.59

```
df15.columns.str.upper().str.replace(' ', '_')
Index(['CITY', 'REGION', 'PRODUCT_ID', 'SALES', 'PROFIT'], dtype='object')
```

For a full list of the string methods and how to work with text data, you can refer to '**Working with text data**' section of pandas documentation.

Table 3.8 String methods

Method	Description
lower()	Convert strings to lowercase
upper()	Convert strings to uppercase
capitalize()	Capitalize first character of the string
strip()	Remove leading and trailing characters (e.g., whitespaces)
len()	Compute string lengths
split()	Split strings on delimiter
join()	Join strings in each element of the Series with passed separator
pad()	Add whitespace to left, right, or both sides of strings
contains()	Return Boolean array if each string contains pattern/regex
count()	Count occurrences of pattern
cat()	Concatenate strings
get()	Index into each element (retrieve i-th element)
replace()	Replace occurrences of pattern/regex/string with some other string or the return value of a callable given the occurrence
wrap()	Split long strings into lines with length less than a given width
get_dummies()	Split strings on the delimiter returning DataFrame of dummy variables

Now, 'put on your fancy pants, as we have a date, with time' in Python!

Very often we see data with dates and times, especially when dealing with time-series. Python has a built-in `datetime` module, which allows us to efficiently perform a variety of useful operations on dates and times. To use this module, first we need to import it:

Ex. 3.60

```
# import datetime module
import datetime as dt
```

`datetime` contains several classes, for example:

- The `datetime.date` class is for working with dates, which has `year`, `month`, and `day` attributes.
- The `datetime.time` class is for times, which has `hour`, `minute`, `second`, `microsecond`, and `tzinfo` attributes.
- The `datetime.datetime` class is a combination of both the `date` and `time` classes.
- The `datetime.timedelta` class is for a duration between two `date`, `time`, or `datetime` instances to microsecond resolution.

As an example, let us create a `datetime.date` object:

Ex. 3.61

```
ATB = dt.date(year=1912, month=6, day=23)
datetime.date(1912, 6, 23)
```

Once the object is created, we can access its attributes:

Ex. 3.62

```
print(ATB)
print(ATB.year)
print(ATB.month)
print(ATB.day)
```

```
1912-06-23
1912
6
23
```

`timedelta` is the difference between two `datetime` values. For example, if we create a `timedelta` object, and add it to ATB, it will return a new shifted `datetime`:

Ex. 3.63

```
ATL = dt.timedelta(days=15324)
ATD = ATB + ATL
print(ATD)
```

```
1954-06-07
```

Sometimes we need to change the format of a `datetime`, this is when `strftime()` method can be used. Note that `datetime.date`, `datetime.time`, and `datetime.datetime` objects all support this method. For example, we can convert the ATD `datetime.date` object to a British date format string with the following code:

Ex. 3.64

```
ATD.strftime('%d/%m/%Y')
```

```
'07/06/1954'
```

Conversely, if we want to convert a string representing a date and time to a `datetime` object, the `datetime.strptime()` can be used. Note that the method is a class method. Table 3.9 below listed the differences between `strftime()` and `strptime()` methods.

Table 3.9 Difference between strftime() and strptime()

	strftime()	strptime()
Description	Convert datetime objects to a string based on a given format	Convert (parse) a string into a datetime object given a corresponding format
Type of method	Instance method	Class method
Method of	datetime.date, datetime.time, datetime.datetime	datetime.datetime
Signature	strftime(format)	strptime(date_string, format)

As an example, let us create a date string and convert it into a `datetime` object:

Ex. 3.65

```
date_string = '1 May, 2020'
             |  |    |
dt.datetime.strptime(date_string, '%d %B, %Y')
datetime.datetime(2020, 5, 1, 0, 0)
```

The `strptime()` method takes two arguments: string (to be converted) and format code. As illustrated in *Ex.3.65*, the format code must match exactly as the string format (including, e.g., `,`, `/`, or `-`), otherwise a `ValueError` will be raised.

A list of common format codes can be found in Table 3.10. For a full list and additional information on `datetime`, see '**datetime—Basic date and time types**' section of Python documentation.

Below are a few more examples of commonly used time formats and the tokens used for parsing:

- '22 Feb 2013 at 11:50AM' ⟶ '%d %b %Y at %I:%M%p'
- '01 July, 2016, 20:50:55' ⟶ '%d %B, %Y, %H:%M:%S'
- 'Thu,13/06/19, 06:12PM' ⟶ '%a,%d/%m/%y, %I:%M%p'
- '2008-05-20, 12:13:14' ⟶ '%Y-%m-%d, %H:%M:%S'
- 'Fri, 05 August, 2005' ⟶ '%a, %d %B, %Y'

Table 3.10 Datetime format codes

Code	Description	Example
%a	Weekday as locale's abbreviated name	Sun, Mon, Tue, …, Sat
%A	Weekday as locale's full name	Sunday, …, Saturday
%w	Weekday as a decimal number, where 0 is Sunday and 6 is Saturday	0, 1, …, 6
%d	Day of the month (two digits)	01, 02, 15, …, 31
%m	Month number (two digits)	01, 02, …, 12
%b	Month as locale's abbreviated name	Jan, Feb, …, Dec
%B	Month as locale's full name	January, …, December
%y	Two-digit year (without century)	19, 20, …, 99
%Y	Four-digit year	2019, 2020, …, 2099
%H	Hour (24-h clock)	00, 01, …, 23
%I	Hour (12-h clock)	01, 02, …, 12
%M	Two-digit minute	00, 01, …, 59
%S	Two-digit second	00, 01, …, 59
%W	Week number of the year (Monday as the first day of the week)	00, 01, …, 53
%U	Week number of the year (Sunday as the first day of the week)	00, 01, …, 53
%p	Local equivalent of Am or PM	AM, PM

pandas implements a `to_datetime()` method, which makes efficient datetime parsing for data in a DataFrame. In our previous example *Ex.3.4–3.5*, we can learn that both the 'Date' and 'DeliveryDate' contain date strings, which are denoted as an `object` type in Python. We can convert them to `datetime` type with `to_datetime()` method. Consider the following:

Ex. 3.66

```
df['Date'] = pd.to_datetime(df['Date'])
df['DeliveryDate'] = pd.to_datetime(df['DeliveryDate'])
df[['Date', 'DeliveryDate']].info()
<class 'pandas.core.frame.DataFrame'>
RangeIndex: 15681 entries, 0 to 15680
Data columns (total 2 columns):
Date            15681 non-null  datetime64[ns]
DeliveryDate    15681 non-null  datetime64[ns]
dtypes: datetime64[ns](2)
memory usage: 245.1 KB
```

After running the codes, both columns have been converted to `datetime64` dtype that encodes dates as 64-bit integers. This encoding allows fast computation.

More information on this data type can be found in NumPy's `datetime64` documentation. In addition, there is a third-party `dateutil` package that can swiftly perform a variety of date and time operations. The package will be automatically installed when pandas is installed. However, we will not go through this module here. You can explore this useful third-party package at your own discretion.

Summary of Learning Objectives

1. **Describe what data manipulation is and the basic procedures.**

   Data manipulation is a term that we use to describe the process of organizing, cleaning, and transforming data into appropriate, consistent, and valuable formats for the purpose of subsequent data analytics and machine learning. Its main tasks may involve data loading, writing, cleaning, converting, and merging as well as data computation and aggregation. There are no strict procedures to follow in data manipulation, however as a general guidance, you may start from identify appropriate data source, and then select the data and perform initial data screening, merging, and transformation if necessary (e.g., dummy coding), after which further data cleaning can be conducted including, for instance, detecting outliers, replacing or deleting missing values. A final step is to perform exploratory data analysis to better understand your data and depending on data characteristics, you may conduct additional feature engineering to prepare the data before feeding it into any analytics models.

2. **Discuss the benefits of data manipulation in supply chain analytics.**

   Effective data manipulation is critical for productive supply chain analytics as it can ensure data clarity, readability, reliability, and validity of the analytics results. Inaccurate analytics models or results can certainly lead to poor decision making in supply chain management, or even severe damage to the organization's performance, thus losing customers and market shares. In particular, as we often say, 'garbage in garbage out', therefore the benefits of data manipulation include ensuring data appropriateness, data consistency, and data exploitation for developing effective supply chain analytics models.

3. **Understand the various methods for data manipulation in Python.**

   In this chapter, we have introduced various methods in Python, especially using pandas' built-in functions to perform data loading and writing, data indexing and selection, data merging and combination, data cleaning and preparation, and data computation and aggregation. Make sure you learn these methods and understand how to use them to perform different data manipulation tasks. For more details regarding each method and the related tutorials, visit their respective sections of pandas documentation.

4. **Learn and grasp how to work with text data and datetime data in Python.**

   In the final section of this chapter, we touched upon the methods to work with text data. Make sure you understand the string methods provided by pandas. We also learnt Python's built-in datetime modules, which allow us to perform various useful operations on dates and times. Again, make sure you understand the different methods that can be used to create, transform, and parse datetime objects.

Discussion Questions

1. Which simple DataFrame method should you use when trying to explore the descriptive statistics of a dataset?
2. To get the counts of unique values in an index objects, which method should you use?
3. A DataFrame is indexed with string values (e.g., 'a', 'b', 'c'), to locate and select value (s) along the index, which method(s) should you use?
4. Discuss and describe different data merging and combination methods. For merging two DataFrames on columns with a share common key, which method can you use? What if there is no shared common key?
5. What methods can you use to replace missing values in a dataset?
6. Discuss the different methods for aggregating GroupBy objects and the advantages of each method.

Keyboard Exercises

1. In your Python notebook, try to create a 6 × 6 DataFrame (i.e., 6 rows and 6 columns) that contains integer values with indexing [a, b, c, d, e, f] and column names [A1, A2, A3, A4, A5, A6] in pandas. Once created, try to save it to a CSV format file.

2. Load the DataFrame from the CSV file and see if you could perform calculations with either the pandas methods or Python operators as listed in the table below.

pandas method	Python operator
add()	+
sub(), subtract()	−
mul(), multiply()	*
mod()	%
pow()	**
div(), divide(), truediv()	/
floordiv()	//

3. Download the notebook for Data Manipulation and re-run all the exercises yourself from *Ex. 3.1* to *Ex. 3.66* as introduced in this Chapter. Pay particular attention to data merging and combination section, and see if you could apply different methods to achieve the same outcomes as described in Fig. 3.2.

Data Visualization

4

Contents

Learning Objectives
- Describe the components and elements of a Figure.
- Understand different ways of creating a Figure and Axes.
- Grasp the methods for figure formatting and customization
- Understand the purposes of each simple chart and statistical charts and be able to create these charts with Matplotlib and Seaborn
- Learn and be able to create geographic mapping using Basemap

---

4.1   Data Visualization in Python

Data visualization is an important task for almost any data analysts, either for exploratory data analysis or for results presentation. In business environment, many managers may not be interested in how data analysts develop their fancy algorithms or interpret numbers but prefer to see results with informative diagrams and figures. Thus, the ability to present and plot analytics results in a vivid and straightforward way has become a very desired skill for data analysts.

K. Y. Liu, *Supply Chain Analytics*, https://doi.org/10.1007/978-3-030-92224-5_4

Data visualization alone can be a subject that is worth writing a whole book. In this Chapter however, we mainly introduce some essential plotting methods in Python, using `Matplotlib` and `Seaborn` libraries. We will have opportunities to go through more visualization examples in subsequent chapters.

Matplotlib, as mentioned earlier, was initially developed by John Hunter in 2002 to enable interactive MATLAB-like plotting interface in Python. Matplotlib supports many graphics backends on all operating systems and a host of output graphics formats. This cross-platform ability and easy-to-plot feature make Matplotlib popular in the data science community.

In recent years, new libraries have been released (e.g., Plotly) with professional graphic styles, which makes Matplotlib look old-fashioned. However, active developers have been making effort to enhance Matplotlib features and styles, as well as developing a number of add-on toolkits such as `Seaborn`.

Seaborn is based on Matplotlib and closely integrated with pandas data structures, which provides a high-level interface for plotting more attractive and informative statistical graphics.

To use Matplotlib and Seaborn, first we need to import the packages in Jupyter notebook:

Ex. 4.1

```
import matplotlib.pyplot as plt
import seaborn as sns; sns.set()
%matplotlib inline
```

Note: plt and sns shortcuts are naming convention used in Python. sns.set() set seaborn to default darkgrid style. To change the style, you can use set_style() and axes_style() functions.

There are five preset Seaborn themes to choose including: `darkgrid`, `whitegrid`, `dark`, `white,` and `ticks`. For details on different styles and settings, see **'Controlling Figure Aesthetics'** section of Seaborn documentation.

`%matplotlib` is a magic function in IPython. `%matplotlib inline` will only plot static images in Jupyter notebook. `%matplotlib notebook` will display interactive images embedded within the notebook, where you can zoom and resize the figure.

4.2   Creating a Figure in Python

Before diving into the details of plotting with Matplotlib and Seaborn, we should learn different parts and terminologies of a figure. See Fig. 4.1 below:

As shown `Figure`, means the whole diagram, which includes the canvas and all the elements on it, such as Axes, titles, labels, markers, legends, etc. We can create an empty `Figure` (like an empty canvas) by calling `fig = plt.figure()` and add other things onto it.

Axes is what you can think of as the artistic composition (or a 'plot'). A `Figure` can contain many `Axes` (at least one to be useful), but a given Axes object can only be part of one `Figure`. For example, Fig. 4.1 contains only one Axes, i.e., one plot. You can add a title to the main `Figure` using `fig.suptitle()` method.

Note: Axes is not the plural word for Axis. The Axes contains two Axis objects (or three in the case of 3D), i.e., X-axis and Y-axis, which deal with the graph limits and generate the ticks and tick labels.

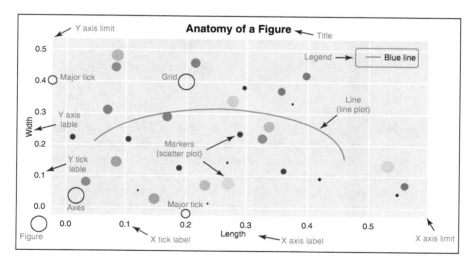

Fig. 4.1 Anatomy of a figure

The following methods can be used to adjust a few settings of the Axes:

- `set_title()`: set title for each Axes
- `set_xlim()` and `set_ylim()`: control the graph limits on *x*-axis and *y*-axis
- `set_xticks()` and `set_yticks()`: set ticks on *x*-axis and *y*-axis
- `set_xticklabels()` and `set_yticklabels()`: set tick labels
- `set_xlabel()` and `set_ylabel()`: set an *x*-label and an *y*-label

There are different ways to add Axes on a `Figure`. To create a single Axes on a `Figure`, the simplest and recommended way is via the `plt.subplots()` method. Consider the example below:

Ex. 4.2
```
x = np.linspace(0, 10, 100)

fig, ax = plt.subplots()
ax.plot(x, np.sin(x))

ax.set_title('A single plot', {'fontsize':16});
```

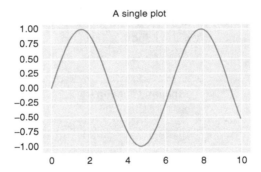

The arguments within `plt.subplots()` allow us to conveniently add Axes and create common layouts of subplots. The first two optional arguments (i.e., `nrows, ncols`) define the number of rows and columns of the subplot grid. For instance, if we want to create six subplots in a 3 × 2 grid, we can set (`nrows=3, ncols=2`), or simply (`3,2`) within the arguments. When there is only one column (i.e., `ncols=1`), we can omit the column parameter and only specify the row number. Consider the following example for vertically stacked two-row subplots:

Ex. 4.3

```
# Create vertically stacked subplots, i.e. ncols=1
fig, axs = plt.subplots(2)
axs[0].plot(x, np.sin(x))
axs[1].plot(x, -np.sin(x))

# Set titles
fig.suptitle('Main Figure Title', fontsize=12)
axs[0].set_title('Axes 0 Title', fontsize=10)
axs[1].set_title('Aces 1 Title', fontsize=10);
```

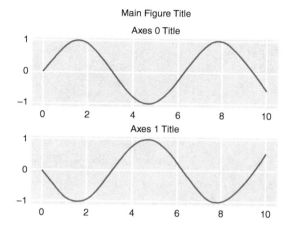

In the example above, we have just created a figure with two subplots. We have also drawn different plots and set separate titles for each subplot.

Note that when stacking in one direction, either vertically, i.e., ncols=1 or horizontally, i.e., nrows=1, the returned axs is a 1D numpy array containing the list of created Axes; when stacking in two directions, the returned axs is a 2D numpy array where each element in the array is the subplot in the corresponding location in the figure.

Because plt.subplots() method returns a tuple containing a fig and axs object(s), you can access the subplots through normal indexing (e.g., axs[0], axs[1] in the above example) or iterate over them using: for ax in axs.flat.

In the following example, we try to create four subplots in a 2D grid:

Ex. 4.4

```
# Create a 2D grid subplots
fig, axs = plt.subplots(2, 2)
fig.suptitle('Main Title', fontsize=14)

# Access each subplot using normal indexing for 2D array
axs[0, 0].plot(x, np.sin(x), 'g', linewidth=2)
axs[0, 0].set_title('Axes [0,0] Title')

axs[0, 1].plot(x, np.cos(x), '--r', linewidth=3)
axs[0, 1].set_title('Axes [0,1] Title')

axs[1, 0].plot(x, -np.sin(x), '-.b', linewidth=2)
axs[1, 0].set_title('Axes [1,0] Title')

axs[1, 1].plot(x, -np.cos(x), ':y', linewidth=3)
axs[1, 1].set_title('Axes [1,1] Title')

# Access each subplot using loop
for ax in axs.flat:
    ax.set(xlabel='x-label', ylabel='y-label')

# Hide x labels and tick labels for top plots
# and y ticks for right plots.
for ax in axs.flat:
    ax.label_outer()
```

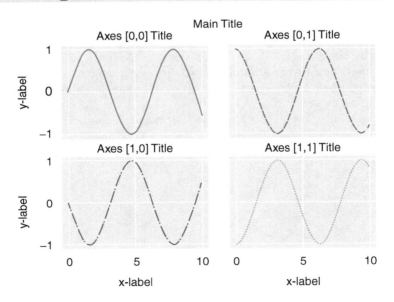

In this example, we used `label_outer()`, which is a handy method to remove ticks and labels from subplots that are not at the edge of the grid.

Sometimes we want to make the subplots neater, for instance, by removing the tick values of subplots when they share the same scale. This can be set by using `sharex` or `sharey` parameters within `plt.subplots()` to align the vertical or horizontal axis.

We can also use the parameter `gridspec_kw` to control the grid properties. For example, we can reduce the amount of height reserved for space between vertical subplots and the amount of width reserved for space between horizontal subplots to zero by setting `gridspec_kw={'hspace':0, 'wspace':0}`.

Consider the example below:

Ex. 4.5

```python
# Choose a different seaborn style
sns.set_style('ticks')

fig, axs = plt.subplots(2, 2, sharex=True, sharey=True,
                        gridspec_kw={'hspace': 0, 'wspace': 0})

# unpack the axes
(ax1, ax2), (ax3, ax4) = axs

# add a main title
fig.suptitle('Main Title', fontsize=14)

ax1.plot(x, np.sin(x), 'g', linewidth=2)
ax2.plot(x, np.cos(x), '--r', linewidth=3)
ax3.plot(x, -np.sin(x), '-.b', linewidth=2)
ax4.plot(x, -np.cos(x), ':y', linewidth=3);
```

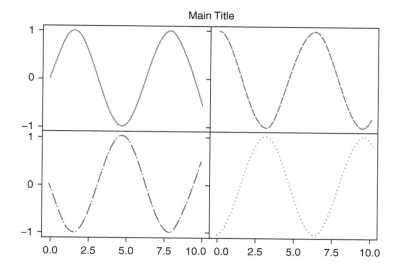

There are alternative ways of adding Axes to a `Figure`. For example, we can create a `Figure` first using `fig=plt.figure()`, and then add subplots onto it via `fig.add_subplot()` method. As an illustration, consider the following example:

Ex. 4.6

```
# reset sns to default
sns.set()
# create a figure
fig = plt.figure()
fig.suptitle('Main Title', fontsize=14)

# add subplots
ax1 = fig.add_subplot(221)
ax2 = fig.add_subplot(2,2,2)    #equivalent but more general
ax3 = fig.add_subplot(2,2,3)
ax4 = fig.add_subplot(2,2,4)

ax1.plot(x, np.sin(x), 'g', linewidth=2)
ax2.plot(x, np.cos(x), '--r', linewidth=3)
ax3.plot(x, -np.sin(x), '-.b', linewidth=2)
ax4.plot(x, -np.cos(x), ':y', linewidth=3);

for ax in fig.get_axes():
    ax.set(xlabel='x-label', ylabel='y-label')
    ax.label_outer()
```

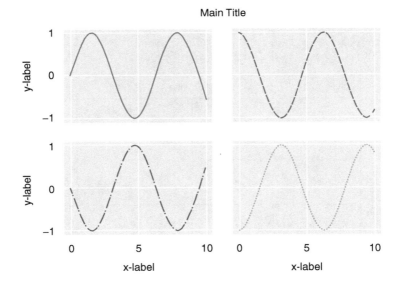

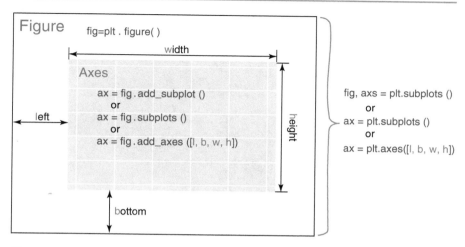

Fig. 4.2 Different ways to call axes on a figure

Additionally, you can use `plt.subplot()` which is a wrapper of `fig.add_subplot()` method. Note that `fig.add_axes()` is a more flexible approach that allows for arbitrary layouts such as subplots overlap with each other. The arguments within the method enable us to fine-tune the position and size of each subplot by its dimensions.

To give a summary of these different methods, see Fig. 4.2.

In short, these methods can be used inter changeably but have respective strengths and shortcomings. For more information on how to create a figure and add axes, see 'Matplotlib.Figure' section of Matplotlib documentation.

4.3   Formatting a Figure

In our previous examples, we used different line styles and colours. The `plot()` method contains an optional format parameter `fmt` that can be used to define marker, line style, and colour.

```
fmt = '[marker][line][color]'
```

A format string can be in combination or used separately of any markers, line styles, and colours. As an illustration, see below:

Ex. 4.7

```
fig = plt.figure(figsize=(10,5))
ax = fig.add_subplot()

# green star markers with a dashed line
ax.plot(x, np.sin(x), '*--g', label='sin(x)')

# blue circle markers with a solid line
ax.plot(x, np.sin(x+1), 'o-b', label='sin(x+1)')
# red dotted line
ax.plot(x, np.sin(x+2), ':r', label='sin(x+2)')

# magenta x markers with a dash-dot line
ax.plot(x, np.sin(x+3), 'x-.m', label='sin(x+3)')

# use ax.set() to adjust a few properties together
ax.set(xlim=(0, 11), ylim=(-1.5, 1.5),
       xlabel='x', ylabel='sin(x)',
       title='Plot Formatting')

# display legend
ax.legend();
```

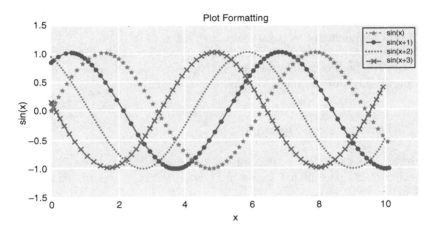

Notice that in the example above, we adjusted axis limit, labels, and title all at once with a convenient `Axes.set()` method, rather than calling each function separately.

Table 4.1 contains a sample of available format strings.

Table 4.1 Markers, colours and line styles

Markers		Colours		Line styles	
'.'	Point marker	'b'	Blue	'-'	Solid line style
','	Pixel marker	'g'	Green	'--'	Dashed line style
'o'	Circle marker	'r'	Red	'-.'	Dash-dot line style
'v'	triangle_down marker	'c'	Cyan	':'	Dotted line style
'^'	triangle_up marker	'm'	Magenta		
'<'	triangle_left marker	'y'	Yellow		
'>'	triangle_right marker	'k'	Black		
's'	Square marker	'w'	White		
'p'	Pentagon marker				
'*'	Star marker				
'h'	Hexagon1 marker				
'H'	Hexagon2 marker				
'+'	Plus marker				
'x'	x marker				
'D'	Diamond marker				
'd'	thin_diamond marker				

If colour is the only part of a format string, you can also use full colour names (e.g., `orange`) or hex strings (e.g., `#ffa500`). In addition to the format strings, Matplotlib includes default style sheets (e.g., `ggplot`). You can customize the styles by calling `style.use()` or use `rcParams`.

For more information on formatting and styles, check '**Axes.plot**' and '**Customizing Matplotlib with style sheets and rcParams**' sections of Matplotlib documentations.

4.4   Plotting Simple Charts

In this section, we first introduce simple charts plotting with Matplotlib, including scatter plot, bar chart, pie chart, histogram, pie chart, and boxplot. There are also methods in pandas for plotting these simple charts, which are introduced in later part of this section.

Scatter plot can be used to observe and display relationships between variables. A scatter plot uses dots or other markers to represent values for different variables on the horizonal and vertical axis. Matplotlib provides `Axes.scatter()` method to conveniently draw scatter plots of y vs x with varying marker size and/or colour. As an illustration, let us create a scatter plot with some random data in the example below:

Ex. 4.8

```
# Create some random data
rng = np.random.RandomState(42)

x = np.arange(50)
y = x + 10 * rng.randn(50)

colour = rng.randint(0, 50, 50)
size = np.abs(rng.randn(50)) * 100

# scatter plot
fig = plt.figure(figsize=(10,4))
ax = fig.add_subplot()
axs = ax.scatter(x, y, c=colour, s=size, alpha=0.8)
ax.set(xlabel='x', ylabel='y', title='Scatter Plot')

# show colour scale
fig.colorbar(axs);
```

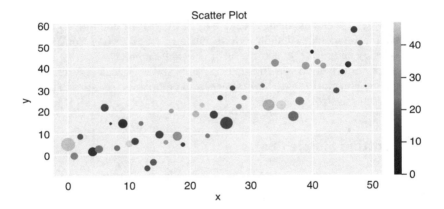

Alternatively, we can use `plt.plot()` method to create scatter plots. The `plot` function can be faster especially for large dataset; however, the resulted scatter plots contain identical markers that do not vary in size or colour.

For more information on scatter plot, including its various formatting, styling methods, and examples, see '**Matplotlib.axes.Axes.scatter**' section of Matplotlib documentation.

Bar chart is typically used to display and compare numeric values for discrete categories of data. As its name suggests, bar chat is constructed with rectangular bars with heights or lengths proportional to the values they represent. Bar chart is a very commonly used type of graph in business because they are easy to create and to interpret. In Matplotlib, `Axes.bar()` and `Axes.barh()` methods allow us to conveniently draw horizontal and vertical bar chart, respectively.

As an example, let us plot two simple bar charts to compare the cost and profit of different products:

Ex. 4.9

```
# generate some data
ID = ('a','b','c','d','e','f')
cost = (138,252,342,269,654,447)
profit = (260, 504, 786, 542, 654, 842)
x = np.arange(6)
width = 0.3

# plot bar charts
fig, (ax0,ax1) = plt.subplots(2)

ax0.bar(x, cost, width, color='m',label='cost')
ax0.bar(x, profit, width, bottom=cost, color='c',label='profit')
ax0.set(xticks=x, xticklabels=ID, title='Stacked Bar Chart')
ax0.legend(prop={'size': 10})

ax1.barh(x, cost, width, color='m', label='cost')
ax1.barh(x+width, profit, width, color='c', label='profit')
ax1.set(yticks=x+width, yticklabels=ID, title='Horizontal Bar Chart')
ax1.legend(prop={'size': 10})

fig.tight_layout();
```

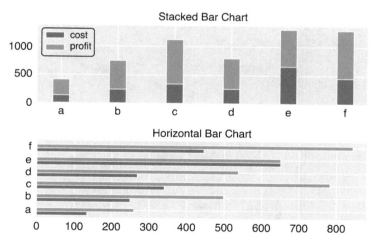

In the vertical bar chart, we stack cost and profit values together, which gives us a clear picture of profit-to-cost ratio for each product. In the horizontal bar chart, however the cost and profit values are plotted separately for each product. For more details on the functions and related examples, see '**Matplotlib.axes.Axes.bar**' section of Matplotlib documentation.

Histogram is similar to a bar chart, however it groups numbers into ranges (or bins) and shows approximate frequency distributions. The height of each bar in a histogram indicates how many data fall into each range. Histogram allows the inspection of data for its underlying distribution, skewness, outliers, etc. It can be used to check, for example, whether an output process can meet acceptable ranges for high quality production. Consider the following example, where we use `Axes.hist()` method to create different histograms:

Ex. 4.10

```
rng = np.random.RandomState(42)
x = rng.randn(1000, 3)

colors = ['green', 'red', 'blue']
n_bins = 15

# create a figure and axes
fig, axs = plt.subplots(2,2)
ax0, ax1, ax2, ax3 = axs.flatten()

ax0.hist(x, n_bins, density=True, color=colors, label=colors)
ax0.legend(prop={'size': 7})
ax0.set_title('bars with legend')

ax1.hist(x, bins=n_bins, density=True, histtype='barstacked')
ax1.set_title('stacked bar')

ax2.hist(x, n_bins, histtype='step', stacked=True)
ax2.set_title('stack step (unfilled)')

ax3.hist(x, n_bins, histtype='stepfilled', alpha=0.7, stacked=True)
ax3.set_title('stack step (filled)')

fig.tight_layout()
for ax in axs.flat:
    ax.label_outer()
```

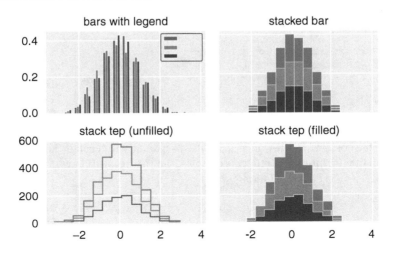

Pie chart is a circular chart that uses 'pie slices' to represent relative proportion of data. In other words, the sizes of each slice are determined by what part of the whole they represent. Matplotlib provides `Axes.pie()` method to creating simple pie charts.

Consider the following example:

Ex. 4.11

```
# create example data
product = ['webcam', 'keyboard', 'mouse', 'mic', 'PC']
pct = [20, 25, 30, 10, 15]

# only 'explode' the 3rd slice (i.e. 'mouse')
explode = (0, 0, 0.1, 0, 0)

# get some colour scheme
cmap = plt.get_cmap('Set2')
colors = cmap(np.arange(5))

# plot pie chart
fig, axs = plt.subplots(1,2)
axs[0].pie(pct, explode=explode, colors=colors, labels=product,
        autopct='%1.1f%%', shadow=True)
axs[0].set_title('Pie chart with explode',fontsize=14)

axs[1].pie(pct, colors=colors, autopct='%1.1f%%', shadow=True)
axs[1].set_title('Pie chart with legend',fontsize=14)
axs[1].legend(product, title='Products',loc='center left',
        bbox_to_anchor=(1, 0, 0.5, 1));
```

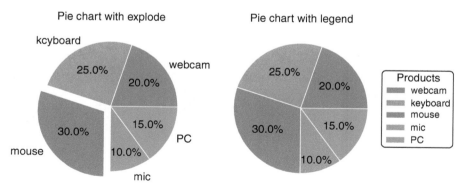

For more details on the method and related examples, see '**Matplotlib.axes.Axes. pie**' section of Matplotlib documentation.

Boxplot is a graph that shows the median and quartiles of a dataset. It is often used in exploratory data analysis to visually represent the distribution of numeric data with five-number summary: minimum, first quartile, median, third quartile, and maximum (see Fig. 4.3). Boxplot is useful for understanding whether the data is

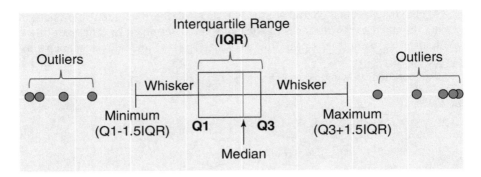

Fig. 4.3 Different parts of a boxplot

normally distributed, how the data is grouped and skewed, and can also be useful for detecting outliers in the data.

As shown above, the flier points that are outside the minimum and maximum range are considered outliers. We can use `Axes.boxplot()` method to create boxplots, consider the example below:

Ex. 4.12

```python
rng = np.random.RandomState(42)

# create some random data
spread = rng.rand(50) * 100
center = np.ones(30) * 50
flier_high = rng.rand(5) * 100 + 50
flier_low = rng.rand(5) *100 - 50
data = np.concatenate((spread, center, flier_high, flier_low))

# plot boxplots
fig, ((ax1,ax2), (ax3,ax4)) = plt.subplots(2,2, figsize=(8,4))

ax1.boxplot(data, flierprops={'markerfacecolor': 'g'})
ax1.set_title('Basic boxplot with outliers')

ax2.boxplot(data, vert=False, showfliers=False)
ax2.set_title('Horizontal boxplot w/o outliers')

ax3.boxplot(data, notch=True,           # notch shape
                  vert=True)            # vertical box alignment
ax3.set_title('Notched boxplot')

ax4.boxplot(data, notch=True,           # notch shape
                  vert=False,           # horizontal box alignment
                  patch_artist=True)    # fill with color
ax4.set_title('Notched colour box')

fig.tight_layout();
```

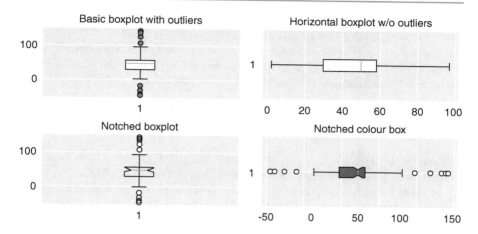

For more information on the method and related examples, see '**Matplotlib.axes.Axes.boxplot**' section of Matplotlib documentation.

Thus far, we have learnt different ways of creating figures and axes, as well as plotting several commonly used charts using Matplotlib in Python. Note that Matplotlib has two interfaces. In the plotting examples illustrated above, we basically utilized the object-oriented interface, where we used `axes.Axes` methods to render visualization on an instance of `figure.Figure`. Direct calling these methods from `Axes` gives us much more flexibility and power in customizing our plots.

The second interface is based on MATLAB, which is encapsulated in the `pyplot` module. We can call the `plt.plot()` method to plot similar charts to those created by `axes.Axes` instances. For large dataset, `plt.plot()` method can perform faster. In general, try to use the object-oriented interface over the `pyplot` interface.

In addition, pandas provides a convenient `plot()` method to easily plot decent looking charts. The method on Series and DataFrame (e.g., `df.plot()`) is a simple wrapper around `plt.plot()`. Table 4.2 below summarizes some coding examples of the method:

Instead of setting the `kind` keyword argument, DataFrame also includes `DataFrame.plot.<kind>` methods (e.g., `df.plot.bar()`) which make

Table 4.2 pandas plotting methods

Example	Description
df.plot()	Plot line chart (default) for columns with labels
df.plot(kind='bar')	Plot bar chart, set kind to 'bar' for horizontal bars
df.plot(kind='hist')	Plot histogram
df.plot(kind='box')	Plot boxplot
df.plot(kind='kde')	Create density plot, can also use 'density'
df.plot(kind='area')	Create area plot
df.plot(kind='scatter')	Create scatter plot
df.plot(kind='pie')	Plot pie chart

plotting easier. Besides, there are two additional `DataFrame.hist()` and `DataFrame.boxplot()` methods that use a separate interface.

Here we do not provide examples on these methods but will walk through some examples in the following chapters. For more information on pandas plotting methods, check '**Visualization**' section of pandas documentation.

4.5   Plotting with Seaborn

Seaborn is powerful in creating informative statistical graphics. It is based on Matplotlib and can create professional looking and complex visualization by structuring multi-plot grids. This is useful for examining relationships between multiple variables, which is essential for exploring and understanding data. As simple illustrations, we will look at two examples here.

First, let us take a look at pairplot. `seaborn.pairplot()` is used to plot pairwise relationships of numeric values in a dataset. By default, this method will create a grid of Axes, where each variable in a dataset is mapped onto a column and row. The diagonal Axes in the grid displays the univariate distribution of the data for the variable in that column.

Note that Seaborn contains a small number of sample datasets that can be used to reproduce example plots. `seaborn.load_dataset()` method provides quick access those datasets. Consider the example below:

Ex. 4.13

```
# load the iris dataset
iris = sns.load_dataset('iris')

# plot pairplot
sns.pairplot(iris, hue='species',palette='Set2');
```

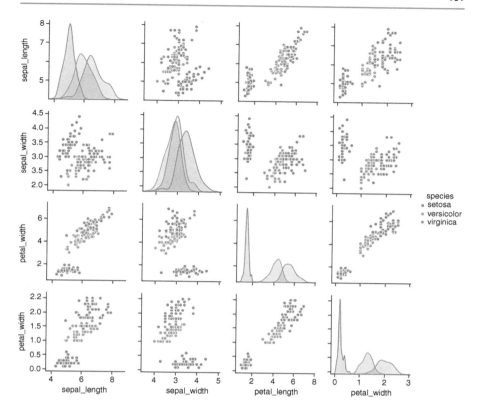

Another useful method provided by Seaborn is `seaborn.heatmap()`. The method creates a colour-encoded matrix, which is helpful for exploring the correlations between variables in a dataset. As a concrete example, see below:

Ex. 4.14

```
# set a new style
sns.set(style="white")

# generate some random data
rng = np.random.RandomState(46)
df = pd.DataFrame(data=rng.normal(size=(100, 20)),
                  columns=np.arange(20))

# Compute the correlation matrix
corr = df.corr()

# Generate a mask for the upper triangle
mask = np.triu(np.ones_like(corr, dtype=np.bool))

# Create a figure and an Axes
fig, ax = plt.subplots(figsize=(12, 8))

# Generate a custom diverging colormap
cmap = sns.diverging_palette(220, 10, as_cmap=True)

# Draw the heatmap with the mask and correct aspect ratio
sns.heatmap(corr, mask=mask, cmap=cmap, vmax=.3, center=0,
            square=True, linewidths=.5, cbar_kws={"shrink": .5});
```

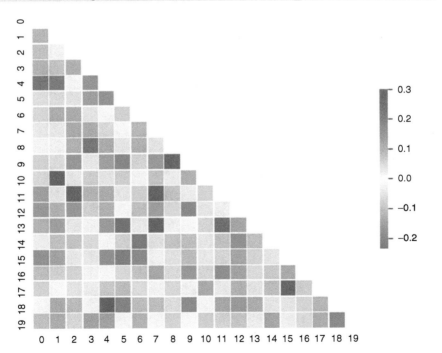

These two seaborn methods will be frequently used in our future examples. For more information on Seaborn plotting functions and related examples, check official seaborn 'User guide and tutorial'.

4.6   Geographic Mapping with Basemap

Another important type of visualization in supply chain analytics is supply chain mapping with geographic data. Such visualization can provide straightforward illustration of supply location networks, delivery routes optimization, and real-time traffic tracking, etc.

Matplotlib contains a useful Basemap toolkit under the `mpl_toolkits` namespace, which can be used to plot on map projections. There are other mapping solutions such as GeoPandas, which will be introduced in our later chapters, and the powerful Google Maps API for more intensive mapping needs, however which is beyond the scope of this book.

Since Basemap is not included as default in Anaconda distribution, to install this package, we can run the following command in conda prompt:

```
conda install -c anaconda basemap
```

Note that there are some pre-requisite packages which you will need to install before installing Basemap. For more details about its installation, check the official site of Basemap Matplotlib Toolkit.

As an illustration, let us consider the following example. First, we need to import necessary packages into our notebook:

Ex. 4.15

```
# Import libraries
import numpy as np
import pandas as pd
import matplotlib.pyplot as plt
from mpl_toolkits.basemap import Basemap
import seaborn as sns; sns.set()

%matplotlib inline
```

Next, we create an orthographic projection of the planet earth using 'bluemarble' as the map background. We can choose different projections using the `projection` parameter when creating a Basemap class instance. For a full list of supported projections, check 'Setting up the map' section of Basemap documentation.

Consider below:

Ex. 4.16

```
plt.figure(figsize=(10, 10))

# lon_0, lat_0 are the center point of the projection.
m = Basemap(projection='ortho',lat_0=5,
            lon_0=3,resolution=None)

m.bluemarble(scale=0.5)
plt.show();
```

Note here that the output map is a fully functioning Matplotlib axes which allows us to plot data on it. We can also draw coastlines, continents, countries, states, rivers, and use different map backgrounds with relevant Basemap methods. For example, we can apply the Miller Cylindrical Projection by setting `projection='mill'`, and draw coastlines, countries, and a boundary around the map, with a background filled with white colour (`fill_color='white'`). Consider below:

Ex. 4.17

```
plt.figure(figsize=(16,12))
# llcrnrlat,llcrnrlon,urcrnrlat,urcrnrlon
# are the lat/lon values of the lower left
# and upper right corners of the map.
# resolution = 'i' means intermediate resolution coastlines.
m = Basemap(projection = 'mill', llcrnrlat = -80,
            urcrnrlat = 80, llcrnrlon = -180,
            urcrnrlon = 180, resolution = 'i')

m.drawcoastlines()
m.drawcountries(color='g')
m.drawmapboundary(fill_color='white')
```

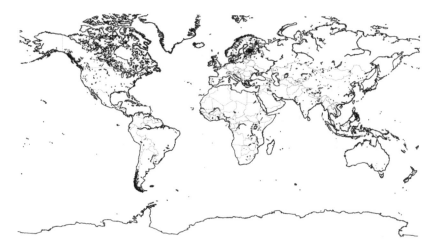

Furthermore, to plot data on a map, we can utilize Basemap instance methods (see Table 4.3).

For more details about Basemap instance methods and related examples, see the official site of Basemap documentation.

Table 4.3 Basemap methods for plotting data on a map

Example	Description
contour()	Draw contour lines
contourf()	Draw filled contours
imshow()	Draw an image
pcolor()	Draw a pseudo-colour plot
pcolormesh()	Draw a pseudo-colour plot (faster version for regular meshes)
plot()	Draw lines and/or markers
scatter()	Draw points with markers
quiver()	Draw vectors
drawgreatcircle()	Draw a great circle
barbs()	Draw wind barbs

4.7   Visualizing Starbucks Locations

Let us now move onto our Starbuck locations mapping example. The data was created by GitHub user chrismeller (github.com/chrismeller), which contains a record for every Starbucks or subsidiary store locations as of February 2017.

Our primary task is to map all Starbucks stores located in the United Kingdom. First, let us load the data and perform some exploratory data analysis.

Ex. 4.18

```
# Load data
df = pd.read_csv('Starbucks.csv')
df.head()
```

	Brand	Store Number	Store Name	Ownership Type	Street Address	City	State/Province	Country	Postcode	Phone Number	Timezone	Longitude	Latitude
0	Starbucks	47370-257954	Meritxell, 96	Licensed	Av. Meritxell, 96	Andorra la Vella	7	AD	AD500	376818720	GMT+1:00 Europe/Andorra	1.53	42.51
1	Starbucks	22331-212325	Ajman Drive Thru	Licensed	1 Street 69, Al Jarf	Ajman	AJ	AE	NaN	NaN	GMT+04:00 Asia/Dubai	55.47	25.42
2	Starbucks	47089-256771	Dana Mall	Licensed	Sheikh Khalifa Bin Zayed St.	Ajman	AJ	AE	NaN	NaN	GMT+04:00 Asia/Dubai	55.47	25.39
3	Starbucks	22126-218024	Twofour 54	Licensed	Al Salam Street	Abu Dhabi	AZ	AE	NaN	NaN	GMT+04:00 Asia/Dubai	54.38	24.48
4	Starbucks	17127-178586	Al Ain Tower	Licensed	Khaldiya Area, Abu Dhabi Island	Abu Dhabi	AZ	AE	NaN	NaN	GMT+04:00 Asia/Dubai	54.54	24.51

Ex. 4.19

```
df.info()
<class 'pandas.core.frame.DataFrame'>
RangeIndex: 25600 entries, 0 to 25599
Data columns (total 13 columns):
 #   Column          Non-Null Count  Dtype
---  ------          --------------  -----
 0   Brand           25600 non-null  object
 1   Store Number    25600 non-null  object
 2   Store Name      25600 non-null  object
 3   Ownership Type  25600 non-null  object
 4   Street Address  25598 non-null  object
 5   City            25585 non-null  object
 6   State/Province  25600 non-null  object
 7   Country         25600 non-null  object
 8   Postcode        24078 non-null  object
 9   Phone Number    18739 non-null  object
 10  Timezone        25600 non-null  object
 11  Longitude       25599 non-null  float64
 12  Latitude        25599 non-null  float64
dtypes: float64(2), object(11)
memory usage: 2.5+ MB
```

We can learn from above that the dataset contains 13 columns and 25,600 rows of entries with some missing data. Let us rank the top ten countries with the largest number of Starbucks stores. Consider below:

Ex. 4.20

```
# Rank top 10 countries with most number of stores
df.Country.value_counts().head(10)
US    13608
CN     2734
CA     1468
JP     1237
KR      993
GB      901
MX      579
TW      394
TR      326
PH      298
Name: Country, dtype: int64
```

We can then plot the ranking using Seaborn's bar plot method:

Ex. 4.21

```
# Plot top 10 countries
top10 = df.Country.value_counts().head(10)
fig, ax = plt.subplots(figsize=(10,5))
ax=sns.barplot(y=top10.index, x=top10.values,
        ax=ax, orient="h", palette = "summer")
ax.set_title('Top 10 Countries with most Starbucks stores',
        fontsize=16);
```

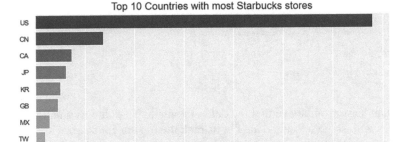

Similarly, we can observe the top ten cities in the UK with the highest number of Starbucks stores, which is omitted here.

Finally, let us attempt to plot all the Starbucks stores located in the UK using the longitude and latitude values of each store in the data. Consider below:

Ex. 4.22

```
plt.figure(figsize=(10, 20))

m = Basemap(llcrnrlon=-10.5,llcrnrlat=49.5,urcrnrlon=3.5,
        urcrnrlat=59.5,resolution='i',projection='cass',
        lon_0=-4.36,lat_0=54.7)

m.drawcountries()
m.fillcontinents(color='#0070C0')

x, y = m(list(GB["Longitude"].astype(float)),
        list(GB["Latitude"].astype(float)))
m.plot(x, y, 'o',color='#6AF6AD', markersize=2)

plt.title("Starbucks Stores UK Locations",fontsize=16)
plt.show();
```

Starbucks Stores UK Locations

Summary of Learning Objectives
1. **Describe the components and elements of a Figure.**
   As illustrated in Fig. 4.1, a Figure means the canvas and all the elements on it, including Axes, titles, labels, markers, legends, etc. Axes is the artistic composition or a plot. A Figure can have many Axes on it, but a given Axes object can only be part of one Figure.
2. **Understand different ways of creating a Figure and Axes.**
   There are different ways of creating a Figure and adding Axes to a Figure, such as using plt.subplots(), plt.figure(), fig.add_subplot(), plt.subplot(), and fig.add_axes(). Figure 4.2 summarizes these different methods. For more details regarding each method and their respective strengths and weaknesses, you can check 'Matplotlib.Figure' section of Matplotlib documentation.

3. **Grasp the methods for figure formatting and customization.**

   In addition to the methods for adjusting titles, setting graph limits, ticks, tick labels, x-axis and y-axis labels, there is a format parameter `fmt` in the plot() method. A format string can be used either in combination or separately of any markers, line styles, and colours. Table 4.1 contains a sample of available format strings that can be used to define marker, line style, and colour. Additional information can be found at 'Axes.plot' and 'Customizing Matplotlib with style sheets and rcParams' sections of Matplotlib documentations.

4. **Understand the purpose of each simple chart and statistical charts and be able to create these charts with Matplotlib & Seaborn**

   We have introduced five simple charts plotting in this chapter. Scatter plot is often used to display relationships between variables (or features in machine learning language). Bar chart is typically used to compare numeric values for discrete categories of data. Histogram is often used to show approximate frequency distributions. Pie chart can be used to represent relative proportion of data. Last but not least, boxplot is usually used in exploratory data analysis to visually examine the media and quartiles of a dataset and detect outliers. These simple charts can be plotted using either Matplotlib Axes instance methods (e.g., Axes.scatter()), or plt.plot() method. Though the latter is faster for large dataset plotting, in general, the Axes instance methods are preferred as they are more flexibility and customizable. Seaborn can also plot these simple charts with more professional looking, and is particularly useful for statistical graphics plotting. As introduced in this chapter, pairplot displays pairwise relationships of numeric values in a dataset. The heatmap is useful for exploring correlations between variables in a colour-encoded matrix.

5. **Learn and be able to create geographic mapping using Basemap.**

   In the final part of this chapter, we introduced geographic plotting with Basemap, a sub toolkit of Matplotlib under mpl_tookits namespace. Basemap contains different projection methods and instance methods for plotting data on a map. Geographic mapping is very important part of supply chain analytics and has many applications such as location networks mapping, route optimization, real-time traffic tracking, etc. We used a Starbucks data as a simple illustrative example to show how we can visualize its store locations in the UK. You should be able to plot similar mapping exercises following through the example. For more guidance and examples, see the official site of Basemap documentation.

Discussion Questions

1. If you want to display interactive images in your notebook, which magic function would you use?
2. To create a 2 × 2 subplots in a figure, what method(s) can you use?
3. How to access each subplot of a 2D grid in a figure?
4. Describe different ways to adjust properties in a figure such as title, x-label, y-label, x-limit, and y-limit.
5. Outliers often bring many issues for effective data analytics, how can we detect outliers?

Keyboard Exercises

1. In your notebook, import necessary plotting packages, re-run all the exercises in this chapter. You can adjust figure formatting, styles, and colours at your discretion.
2. Download Starbucks data, rank top ten cities in the UK with the largest number of Starbucks stores and plot the result with a vertical bar chart.
3. Further, rank top ten cities worldwide with the largest number of Starbucks stores and plot it using a horizontal bar chart.
4. Count the number of stores in terms of ownership types and plot it using a pie chart.
5. Map Starbucks locations worldwide

Customer Management

5

Contents

© The Author(s), under exclusive license to Springer Nature
Switzerland AG 2022
K. Y. Liu, *Supply Chain Analytics*, https://doi.org/10.1007/978-3-030-92224-5_5

5.1 Customers in Supply Chains

Who are the customers in a supply chain? We know that when we go shopping in a supermarket, we are considered customers. If we bought a car from a car dealer, we are considered customers. From a focal firm's perspective, an OEM develops a supply chain in order to deliver products and services to its customers and make profits.

For instance, a car maker produces cars and then sells them to the individual car buyers through its supply chain (see Fig. 5.1). The car maker (OEM) can have its first-tier customers such as the car dealers who directly purchase from the OEM. The final car buyers are regarded as second-tier customers who make direct purchase from those car dealers of the OEM. If you could recall, we call this part of supply chain as 'downstream'. The 'upstream' of a supply chain consists of suppliers. In this example, the OEM has its first-tier tyres suppliers and all the way to the third-tier crude oil suppliers.

In fact, each node (or entity) in a supply chain can be either a supplier or a customer where there is a buyer–supplier relationship, except for both ends of a supply chain (i.e., raw material suppliers and end customers). For instance, in the example above, first-tier suppliers can treat the OEM as their customer, and second-tier suppliers can treat first-tier suppliers as their customers, and so on and so forth.

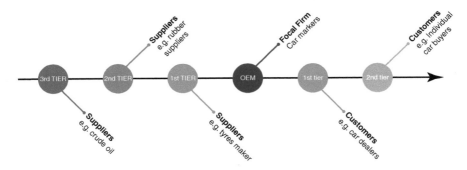

Fig. 5.1 Customers in a supply chain—a focal firm's perspective

Moreover, even within an organization, there can be internal customers who receive products or services from previous processes. The whole supply chain is connected with these supplier-customer links. If any link in the chain is broken, it can impact the next customers and possibly affect the end customers. Similarly, if any members in the supply chain cause delays or fail to meet performance target, it could potentially impact the rest of the supply chain.

However, when we talk about supply chain management, often we use a focal firm's perspective. This is because it can help us better understand questions like who is the 'owner' or 'initiator' of a supply chain? who should hold major responsibilities for the supply chain? and who are the end customers? In theory, all members of a supply chain should maintain an emphasis on the end customers as they are the buyers of the final products and the original source of revenues. In other words, managers should hold a holistic view on their supply chains and direct their attention to the final customers. This is a key to effective supply chain collaboration for successful supply chain management.

5.2 Understanding Customers

Customers play a central role in a supply chain, as the ultimate objective of managing a supply chain is to meet and exceed customer expectations. Without customers, a supply chain would not exit and thus supply chain management would have no meanings. Any type of businesses should strive to deliver excellent customer service to its customers, otherwise the business would not survive in the long run.

Organizations that are successful normally understand their customers better than their competitors. They would design a supply chain that is highly responsive, efficient, and cost-effective to maximize value offering to their customers; they would search for the most innovative and quality partners in order to provide their customers with best products and services; they would also configure a supply chain that is more resilient to risks and disruptions to ensure consistent and reliable service to their customers.

A better understanding of customers undoubtedly brings many advantages to a firm. Most successful companies regularly invest a large amount of money into market research to understand their customers in terms of what products they should offer, what value proposition they should have, and at which market segments they should target, etc.

Example

For example, the world's largest clothing retailer Zara has been thriving in the past decade. The company lays a strategic emphasis on its customers and delivers exceptional customer experience with right products, at right time, right price, and right place. Every day, Zara analyses its sales data from stores across the world to determine what items sell fast and what items do not sell well, and makes quick changes in designs to appeal to its customers. Besides, Zara listens and reacts quickly to customer feedback. They employ advanced sentiment analytics on customer feedback and comments (Uberoi 2017) (e.g., 'I don't like the collar' or 'wish there were more colour choices') to understand what customers really want and come up better fashion designs. With this data-driven approach, Zara is also able to gain a real understanding of regional or local customers' preferences, thus tailoring its collections based on the demographics that a given store serves (Danziger 2018). ◄

Imagine that you are trying to order a new webcam from an online computer store, after comparing different available products and placing the final order, you find out that it would take a week for the item to arrive. In such a scenario, you are more likely to be put off by the long waiting time and go elsewhere for a quicker delivery. In today's highly competitive market, every business should by all means understand and satisfy their customers in order to compete with their rivals. A greater customer experience would require a more customer-centric supply chain. A customer-centric supply chain emphasizes on what customers really desire and then strategically allocate resources, coordinate efforts, and develop capabilities to fulfil the customer expectations. Regardless of industry, size, geography, old or new, companies should all place customers in the central heart of their business and daily operations.

5.2.1 Benefits of a Customer-Centric Supply Chain

There are several benefits for firms to gain a better understanding of their customers and develop a customer-centric supply chain (SC). For example, more appealing product designs that differentiate your business and attract customers, fast delivery service that can fulfil a customer order when and where the customer need it, and a great shopping experience that is tailored to individual customer's preference based on their previous purchase patterns. Table 5.1 contains some of the benefits and their implications:

Table 5.1 Benefit of understanding customers

Benefits	Implications
Better product design	Could potentially attract more customers, differentiate your business from rivals, etc.
Tailored products/ individualization	Could also attract more customers, create great customer experience, and improve customer loyalty, etc.
Targeted pricing and promotion	More effective pricing and promotion strategies targeting specific customers at specific time and location
Improved customer relations	Could enhance customer relationship management with deeper understanding of their needs and desires
Better customer service	Likewise, could enhance customer service to better serve their needs, with fast response, personalized customer experience, etc.
Enhanced supply chain collaboration	Could build a customer-centric culture across the supply chain, improve overall supply chain efficiency and performance
Better visibility and transparency	Could enhance information sharing and timely data exchange, thus improving overall supply chain performance

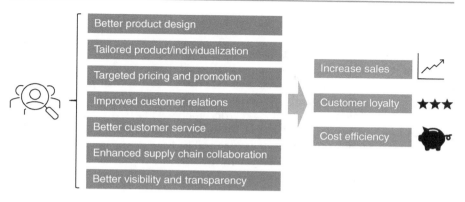

Fig. 5.2 Benefits of having a customer-centric SC

With these benefits, companies can expect to increase their sales and generate more revenues. In a longer term, customer loyalty can be fostered, and a better company image can be created. Because of the increased supply chain collaboration, greater visibility, and information transparency, issues such as bullwhip effect can be quickly identified and minimized or avoided completely. As such, companies can expect to significantly cut down their cost and achieve a larger profit margin in the long run (Fig. 5.2).

5.3   How to Build a Customer-Centric SC

Developing a customer-centric supply chain may not be as easy as it seems. Companies need to change not only the way how they traditionally interact with their customers, but also how they strategically align their supply chains to deliver what their customers really desire. In addition, all members in a supply chain should get involved, directly or indirectly, from upstream suppliers to downstream customers, to create a positive and excellent customer experience. How to design and develop a customer-centric supply chain? We summarize it into five generic steps:

5.3.1   Step One: Define Customers

First, firms should have a clear definition and understanding of who the real customers are in their supply chains. As stated earlier, all members involved in a supply chain should emphasis on end customers who purchase the final products, rather than on a fraction of the supply chain or on their internal processes. This is vitally important for developing a customer-centric supply chain. If you lose the market, you will lose the business, and consequently, the entire supply chain. Therefore, only when a clear definition of customers is realized and communicated across the whole supply chains, will every player involved devote themselves to building a truly customer-centric supply chain.

5.3.2   Step Two: Understand Customers' Real Needs

After knowing who the customers are, the next stage is to learn their real needs and desires. Firms should have a clear vision on which market segments they should target at, and what value propositions they should uphold for a particular market segment. For example, if you are a newly start-up firm developing smart activity trackers, then you might want to ask yourself (Fig. 5.3):

- What market segments should we focus on? (e.g., young people or the elderly)
- What values do we want to offer to customers? (e.g., high-quality product, multi-functions, low cost?)
- What do customers really want from the product? (e.g., accuracy of tracking, or more health tracking capabilities such as blood pressure monitoring?)

To understand customers' real needs, companies used to conduct all sorts of market research. Traditionally, organizations could ask their customers for feedbacks, administer market surveys, and use focus groups. Today, firms have more options such as using big data analytics and machine learning to learn their customers and predict future

Fig. 5.3 Why do customers buy the activity tracker?

trends. For instance, customers purchase records, sales history, customers shopping patterns, demographic information, and even weather conditions in different regions, are all useful data that can be used to analyse and understand customers' real needs.

5.3.3 Step Three: Translate Needs into Product Features

Once customers' real needs are identified, a critical step for firms is to translate those needs into product (or service) features. However, this is often a challenging task because organizations can either 'lost in translation' (e.g., unable to interpret what the real needs are and identify appropriate features in their product design), or have to comprise due to their technology and resource constraints (e.g., capital and cost matters). Competent firms might be able to successfully come up new features in their offerings, and therefore beating their competitors and winning the market. Others might have to think of different ways to address the customers' needs and compete, such as reducing cost and shifting to a different segment. Some common product features include:

- **Functionality**: different functions that a product can perform or include.
- **Appearance**: outlook design of a product (e.g., colour, shape, and texture), whether it looks stylish and appealing to customers?
- **Quality**: whether a product is made to a high-quality standard or performs as expected, e.g., is it durable? Does it use good materials?
- **Reliability**: whether a product is reliable to use and is always dependable
- **Availability**: whether customers can get hold of enough supplies.
- **Contact**: how customers are treated, whether customer service is friendly enough, etc.
- **Cost**: whether a product is offered at a customer's acceptable price, i.e., maximizing the value to customers.
- **Velocity**: whether a product is delivered to customers at acceptable speed.
- **Flexibility**: whether a product contains a mixed range of features, allowing customization or individualization, etc.

5.3.4 Step Four: Design Supply Chain Processes

After translating the needs to product features, the next and most challenging step is to design appropriate supply chain processes to make and deliver the right products to the right customers. For instance, if your customers value quality the most, then whether your supply chain processes can ensure high-quality production, from raw material sourcing, suppliers performance monitoring to internal quality assurance and final distribution to your customers. If your customers want more choices and personalization in their products, then whether your supply chain is agile and flexible enough to cope with demand variations and make fast response to various customer requests.

Different product features would imply the need for different supply chain types. In the typical automobile industry, for example, a '*leagile*' supply chain process combining *lean* and *agile* mechanisms might be most appropriate. On the one hand, the lean operations can ensure just-in-time (JIT) supplies, thereby improving efficiency and lowering cost; on the other, the agile operations ensure flexibility and fast response to different customization requests from customers.

Indeed, designing appropriate supply chain processes requires the selection and evaluation of good supply chain partners. Competent suppliers, for instance, can help ensure quality and performance targets. Building a long-term and strategic partnerships brings several benefits, including enhanced trust, cost minimization, joint problem-solving, consistent and reliable supplies. A good relationship with supply chain partners can also help focal firms to access external resource and capabilities that they internally lack, and potentially build barriers for competitors or new entrants to imitate your key competence.

In order to design appropriate supply chain processes, it would be advantageous to involve supply chain partners in the product design stage, including suppliers, supply chain managers, retailers, and even customers. By doing so, every member in the supply chain could understand clearly what their customers want, and what product features they should aim to deliver, and what preparations they should make at a very early stage. Of course, this effort should be on an on-going basis, and information and data sharing should be timely communicated throughout the supply chain (Fig. 5.4).

5.3.5   Step Five: Build Efficient Logistics Systems

Last but not least, although logistics operations can be an integral part of supply chain process, it would be beneficial to consider it separately if it is not your organization's core business. Today, most firms outsource their distribution and logistics service to a third-party logistics (3PL) provider. Developing an efficient distribution network can help improve delivery performance, cut down customers' waiting

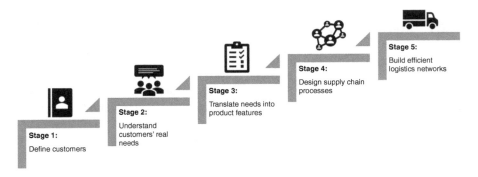

Fig. 5.4 Stages of designing a customer-centric supply chain

time, and eventually make your customer happy. For instance, using analytics and machine learning, firms can optimize their delivery routes, achieve efficient fleet management, and track real-time products locations, etc. With AI and IoTs, firms could monitor how their products are handled, stored, transported, and delivered to their customers' doorstep.

In summary, designing and developing a customer-centric supply chain can be a challenging task. It can involve a complete re-engineering of the existing supply chain processes of an organization. However, meeting customer expectations today is not just about fulfilling customers' orders, but rather it is about delivering exceptional customer experiences, which will eventually fall onto a firm's supply chain. A customer-centric supply chain can deliver much better experience for the customers and give a business a competitive advantage.

In the following sections, we introduce some useful ways to understand and manage customers.

5.4   Cohort Analysis

Cohort analysis has been used in social science in the past few decades to study demography, psychology, epidemiology, political science, and sociology, etc. (Glenn 2005). Broadly speaking, it is a quantitative research method to studying groups of people with similar characteristics and their effect on some outcome variable(s). In recent years, the method has become increasingly popular in business-related subjects such as marketing to understand customer's behaviour by categorizing them into related cohorts or groups for analysis.

5.4.1   What Is a Cohort?

A cohort refers to individuals who share similar characteristics (e.g., gender, age, or culture) or a common experience during a specified period of time (e.g., a graduation cohort). For companies, cohort is usually referred to customer groups clustered with a certain timespan such as day, week, or month when they first make a purchase from the companies.

5.4.2   What Is Cohort Analysis?

Cohort analysis is often used to compare the behaviour of different groups of people. As there is an abundance of data available to businesses today, cohort analysis has emerged as a useful analytical technique to analysing the behaviour of groups of customers over time. For example, customer groups' retention and engagement rates against each other over a specified period. It enables organizations to carefully examine their customers by groups rather than as a whole, thereby offering meaningful insights into what customers they should focus on.

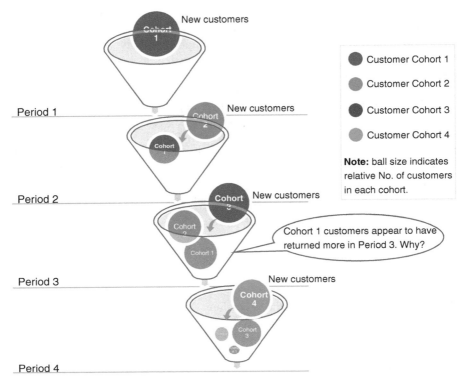

Fig. 5.5 Illustration of cohort analysis

Based on the cohort analysis results, firms can develop specific pricing and promotion strategies targeting each customer cohort. Additionally, for example, when launching new products, firms can check whether the changes or new features have a positive impact on customer acquisition and retention. With this analytical approach, firms can gain better understanding of their customers so as to come up better communication strategies, improve customers relationships, invest resources for enhanced customer experience.

For example, imagine that you are running a hair salon on a high street. After a full year of business, you want to find out who your regular customers are, how you can retain them and provide better services to them. In addition, over the year, you have offered several promotional activities and so you want to explore whether the promotions have worked well and helped you to attract and retain customers. These questions can be relevant for performing a cohort analysis (Fig. 5.5).

5.4.3 Steps for Cohort Analysis

To conduct an effective cohort analysis, there are certain steps to follow. In general, we should start by determining the right cohort types, specify the cohort size, then appropriate metrics should be selected in order to make comparison amongst cohorts. This is then followed by setting a date range for the cohort analysis. Once these are all set, we can perform the actual cohort analysis. Lastly, we can visualize and interpret the result as appropriate. See details below:

- **Determine right cohort types**—based on the specific question you want to answer, the first step is to decide what types of cohort you want to explore for the analysis. For example, grouping by age, sex, income, or times when customers made their first purchase. Note that latter one is the most common type currently being used for customer cohort analysis. In the hair salon example, you might classify customer cohorts by the time when they first visited your salon.
- **Specify cohort size**—once cohort types are determined, the next step is to define cohort size. Here by size we mean the range or intervals of data that we use to group customers. For instance, the age range for each customer cohort (e.g., 20–29, 30–39 and so on), and most commonly, customers acquired by week, month, or quarter, etc. In our example, customers by month might be relevant if we learnt that on average a customer visit the hair salon every month.
- **Select metrics**—this is the step to choose what specific value you want to compare across different groups, such as retention rate and amount spent. In general, cohort analysis examines retention rate as the default metric. In the hair salon example, we can check the monthly retention rate over a specified period of time.
- **Set date range**—this is the date range that you want to examine with cohort analysis. For instance, you can compare the cohorts for the last 12 weeks. In our example, since we have run the business for a year, we might want to check the monthly retention rate against groups over the 12-month period.
- **Perform the cohort analysis**—Once the above are all set, you can perform the cohort analysis and obtain the results.
- **Visualize and interpret the results**—It is not unusual to use data visualization to represent the cohort analysis results. Remember to focus on your initial questions that you want to address and make sure the interpretations make sense.

5.4.4 Cohort Analysis Example in Python

Let us walk through an example to understand how cohort analysis can be performed in Python. The complete code, data, and Jupyter notebooks for the example can be found at our online repository. For brevity, we only attempt to show the essential parts here.

The data has been initially cleaned and saved as Excel spreadsheet file 'Retail_init_cleaned.xlsm'. First, we need to load the data and create a DataFrame using `pandas.read_excel()`.

Ex. 5.1

```
# load data
data = pd.read_excel('Retail_init_cleaned.xlsx')
data.info()
```

```
<class 'pandas.core.frame.DataFrame'>
RangeIndex: 397924 entries, 0 to 397923
Data columns (total 9 columns):
InvoiceNo      397924 non-null int64
StockCode      397924 non-null object
Description    397924 non-null object
Quantity       397924 non-null int64
InvoiceDate    397924 non-null datetime64[ns]
UnitPrice      397924 non-null float64
CustomerID     397924 non-null int64
Country        397924 non-null object
Amount         397924 non-null float64
dtypes: datetime64[ns](1), float64(2), int64(3), object(3)
memory usage: 27.3+ MB
```

As shown above, the data contains 397,924 entries and a total of nine columns. After further data screening and cleaning, we select only the UK data to conduct our analysis. See below:

Ex. 5.2

```
df_uk = data[data.Country == 'United Kingdom']
# save it to Excel file for later use
df_uk.to_excel('UK_Data.xlsx')
df_uk.shape
```

```
(333828, 9)
```

Next, let us set index to `InvoiceDate` column and create a copy of the DataFrame.

Ex. 5.3

```
df_date = df_uk.set_index('InvoiceDate')
df_date.head().append(df_date.tail())
```

InvoiceDate	InvoiceNo	StockCode	Description	Quantity	UnitPrice	CustomerID	Country	Amount
2010-12-01 08:26:00	536365	85123A	WHITE HANGING HEART T-LIGHT HOLDER	6	2.55	17850	United Kingdom	15.30
2010-12-01 08:26:00	536365	71053	WHITE METAL LANTERN	6	3.39	17850	United Kingdom	20.34
2010-12-01 08:26:00	536365	84406B	CREAM CUPID HEARTS COAT HANGER	8	2.75	17850	United Kingdom	22.00
2010-12-01 08:26:00	536365	84029G	KNITTED UNION FLAG HOT WATER BOTTLE	6	3.39	17850	United Kingdom	20.34
2010-12-01 08:26:00	536365	84029E	RED WOOLLY HOTTIE WHITE HEART.	6	3.39	17850	United Kingdom	20.34
2011-12-09 12:31:00	581585	22466	FAIRY TALE COTTAGE NIGHT LIGHT	12	1.95	15804	United Kingdom	23.40
2011-12-09 12:49:00	581586	22061	LARGE CAKE STAND HANGING STRAWBERY	8	2.95	13113	United Kingdom	23.60
2011-12-09 12:49:00	581586	23275	SET OF 3 HANGING OWLS OLLIE BEAK	24	1.25	13113	United Kingdom	30.00
2011-12-09 12:49:00	581586	21217	RED RETROSPOT ROUND CAKE TINS	24	8.95	13113	United Kingdom	214.80
2011-12-09 12:49:00	581586	20685	DOORMAT RED RETROSPOT	10	7.08	13113	United Kingdom	70.80

   With the datetime index, we can then check aggregate monthly sales using `resample()`, which is a convenience method for frequency conversion and resampling of time series. Here we resample by month end by setting frequency to 'M' and aggregate total monthly orders. Consider below:

Ex. 5.4

```
# resample monthly order sum
df_date.Quantity.resample('M').sum()
```
```
InvoiceDate
2010-12-31    136531
2011-01-31    114839
2011-02-28    115701
2011-03-31    150471
2011-04-30    137127
2011-05-31    166845
2011-06-30    151168
2011-07-31    158254
2011-08-31    161129
2011-09-30    251192
2011-10-31    262976
2011-11-30    335931
2011-12-31     96064
Freq: M, Name: Quantity, dtype: int64
```

   Since we do not have the full-month data for December 2011, the total number of orders fall considerably in that month as shown above. Similarly, we can check the total number of unique customers in each month:

Ex. 5.5

```
# Let's check total unique customers per month.
df_date.CustomerID.resample('M').nunique()
```
```
InvoiceDate
2010-12-31     777
2011-01-31     617
2011-02-28     638
2011-03-31     842
2011-04-30     749
2011-05-31     925
2011-06-30     854
2011-07-31     824
2011-08-31     793
2011-09-30    1096
2011-10-31    1199
2011-11-30    1462
2011-12-31     539
Freq: M, Name: CustomerID, dtype: int64
```

In this exercise, assume that we try to explore the monthly retention rate of each cohort over a 12-month period. We need to remove the December 2011 data from the DataFrame since it is incomplete. There are different ways to do this, here is an example below:

Ex. 5.6

```
df_uk = df_uk[(df_uk.InvoiceDate.dt.date < dt.date(2011, 12, 1))]
```

Recall that for cohort analysis, first we need to determine the cohort type. In this example, we decide to divide customers into monthly cohort according to the date when they made their first purchase. To achieve this, we can group by `CustomerID` and find each customer's earliest invoice date, and then convert these dates to month period. See below:

Ex. 5.7

```
cohort = df_uk.groupby('CustomerID')['InvoiceDate']\
                            .min().dt.to_period('m')
cohort = cohort.to_frame()

# Rename a column
cohort.columns = ['Cohort']
cohort.head()
```

	Cohort
CustomerID	
12747	2010-12
12748	2010-12
12749	2011-05
12820	2011-01
12821	2011-05

We can see from the output that each customer has now been linked to a particular cohort. In *Ex.5.7*, we have also converted `cohort` from Series into a DataFrame to join with `df_uk`. Check the code below, where we set `CustomerID` as the joining key:

Ex. 5.8

```
df_uk_cohort = df_uk.set_index('CustomerID').join(cohort)
```

In order to calculate the retention rate of each cohort over the 12-month period, we need to find out the months in which each customer placed their orders. So, let us create an additional column `SalesPeriod` by converting `InvoiceDate` to month period:

Ex. 5.9

```
# create a new column by converting InvoiceDate to Month period
df_uk_cohort['SalesPeriod'] = df_uk_cohort['InvoiceDate']\
                                            .dt.to_period('m')
```

We can now check what cohort a unique customer belongs to and the other months in which the customer made any purchases by locating a particular customer ID. For brevity, we will not show it here.

Next, with the newly created DataFrame, we can check the number of retained customers from each cohort over the 12-month period:

Ex. 5.10

```
df_uk_cohort.reset_index(inplace=True)
# check each cohort's retention over months
df_uk_cohort.groupby(['Cohort', 'SalesPeriod'])\
                            .CustomerID.nunique()
```

```
Cohort    SalesPeriod
2010-12   2010-12        777
          2011-01        274
          2011-02        244
          2011-03        280
          2011-04        274
                         ...
2011-09   2011-10         61
          2011-11         84
2011-10   2011-10        322
          2011-11         78
2011-11   2011-11        295
Name: CustomerID, Length: 78, dtype: int64
```

To have a better illustration of the results, we can create a heatmap with Seaborn in the notebook. But before that we need to create a pivot table for plotting purpose:

Ex. 5.11

```
# create a copy of the rentention data and reset index
retention = df_uk_cohort.groupby(['Cohort', 'SalesPeriod']).\
                            CustomerID.nunique().reset_index()
# create a pivot table
retention = retention.pivot(index='SalesPeriod', columns='Cohort',
                            values='CustomerID')
```

To calculate the retention rate, we can define a simple function:

Ex. 5.12

```
# define a function to calculate the retention rate
def reten_rate (df):
    for x in range(len(df)):
        df.iloc[:,x] = df.iloc[:,x].divide(df.iloc[x,x])
    return df
```

We can then call the function and calculate the retention rate, consider below:

Ex. 5.13

```
reten_rate(retention)
```

Cohort SalesPeriod	2010-12	2011-01	2011-02	2011-03	2011-04	2011-05	2011-06	2011-07	2011-08	2011-09	2011-10	2011-11
2010-12	1.000000	NaN	NaN	NaN	NaN	NaN	NaN	NaN	NaN	NaN	NaN	NaN
2011-01	0.352638	1.000000	NaN	NaN	NaN	NaN	NaN	NaN	NaN	NaN	NaN	NaN
2011-02	0.314028	0.198251	1.000000	NaN	NaN	NaN	NaN	NaN	NaN	NaN	NaN	NaN
2011-03	0.360360	0.259475	0.177914	1.000000	NaN	NaN	NaN	NaN	NaN	NaN	NaN	NaN
2011-04	0.352638	0.230321	0.193252	0.151807	1.000000	NaN	NaN	NaN	NaN	NaN	NaN	NaN
2011-05	0.393822	0.326531	0.282209	0.260241	0.207407	1.000000	NaN	NaN	NaN	NaN	NaN	NaN
2011-06	0.353925	0.274052	0.285276	0.197590	0.200000	0.191235	1.000000	NaN	NaN	NaN	NaN	NaN
2011-07	0.328185	0.247813	0.254601	0.228916	0.207407	0.171315	0.173077	1.000000	NaN	NaN	NaN	NaN
2011-08	0.346203	0.250729	0.242331	0.163855	0.196296	0.167331	0.139423	0.163743	1.000000	NaN	NaN	NaN
2011-09	0.387387	0.303207	0.260736	0.260241	0.225926	0.215139	0.235577	0.204678	0.208633	1.000000	NaN	NaN
2011-10	0.359073	0.326531	0.266871	0.233735	0.225926	0.227092	0.245192	0.239766	0.223022	0.225926	1.000000	NaN
2011-11	0.492921	0.358601	0.309816	0.272289	0.259259	0.270916	0.317308	0.280702	0.237410	0.311111	0.242236	1.0

With this pivot table and `seaborn.heatmap()` plotting method, we can visualize the results, consider below:

Ex. 5.14

```
# visualize the result using heatmap
fig, ax = plt.subplots(figsize=(16,6))
ax = sns.heatmap(retention, annot=True, cmap='Purples',fmt='.0%')
ax.set_ylabel('Sales Period', fontsize = 14)
ax.set_xlabel('Cohort Group', fontsize = 14)
ax.set_title('Retention Rates Across Cohorts',fontsize=16);
```

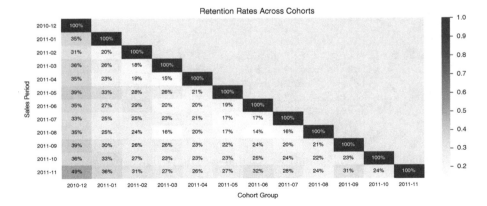

After performing the analysis, we should attempt to interpret the results reasonably based on the initial questions that we want to answer in a specific business context. For example, from the heatmap we can see that cohort 1 (i.e., 2010–12) appears to have the highest retention rate over the 12-month period than other cohorts. What is the reason for that? Obviously to answer the question, it would require certain business background information. You could build some initial propositions and validate them through further analysis.

In our example, it turns out that the retail store was opened in December 2010, and most of the first cohort customers lived locally near the store. Therefore, they visited the store more often than other cohort customers. This cohort should be our focus, and as a business owner, you can make strategies to retain them.

In addition, there are several spikes of retention rates during period 2011–05, 2011–09, 2011–10, and 2011–11. Why did more customers return during these periods? Was that due to the special events, promotional campaigns, or marketing efforts that we did in the past? After further analysis, we learnt that these spikes were closely related to the promotional campaigns and advertisements. The more significant increase in retention in 2011–11 was also associated with Christmas shopping. Therefore, the analysis and results enable us to learn whether our efforts to customer retention are effective and whether we should continue to do the same campaigns at specific times.

Overall, cohort analysis is helpful for business managers to understand the loyalty of their customers. Whilst it cannot produce direct actionable results, as indicated in our example, cohort analysis can still provide useful insights into how we can gain and retain customers. By analysing the results, you can think of effective strategies to increase customer retention after ascertaining what works and what does not, such as promotional campaigns, marketing efforts, and new product features.

5.5   RFM Analysis

RFM analysis is a useful customer segmentation technique, which has been widely adopted in marketing research. It can help categorize customers into various clusters and thus allowing businesses to target specific customer groups with tailored communications, engagement campaigns, and special treatment that are much more relevant for each group.

In this section, we introduce the basics of RFM analysis and use an example to demonstrate how we can perform the analysis in Python.

5.5.1   What Is RFM?

RFM stands for **Recency**, **Frequency**, and **Monetary**, each corresponding to some key customer values (see Fig. 5.6).

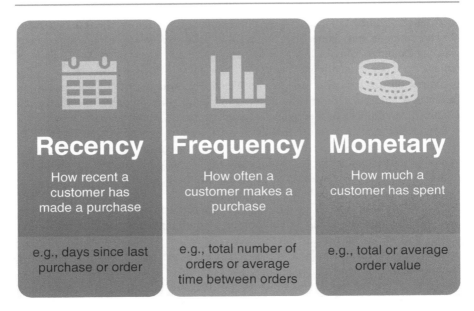

Fig. 5.6 RFM analysis for customer segmentation

The three RFM metrics are important indicators of a customer's behaviour as they can reflect customer retention, engagement, and lifetime value.

- **Recency**—refers to how recent a customer has made a purchase. It measures the time elapsed since a customer's last order or transaction with a business. A high recency score usually means that a customer has positively considered your business for a purchase decision over competitors. It might be more likely that the customer will be responsive to communications and engagement campaigns from your business.
- **Frequency**—refers to how often a customer makes a purchase. It can be measured with the total number of orders from a customer over a particular period of time or with average time between orders. A high frequency score usually means that the customer is actively engaged and loyal to your business.
- **Monetary**—refers to how much money a customer has spent in total or on average over a particular period of time. A high monetary score usually means that the customer is a big spender to whom your business should pay close attention.

5.5.2   What Is RFM Analysis?

When performing customer segmentation, evaluating customers based on a single metric is insufficient and can be biased sometimes. For instance, an overseas tourist has made a recent visit to a retail store but will never come back again. Though the customer may have a high recency score, it can be difficult to retain this type of customers and thus, they cannot be regarded as best customers for the business.

RFM analysis combines the three different customer attributes and classifies customers with a numeric ranking of the three metrics, thus leading to a more balanced view. In general, customers with the highest overall score are considered best customers, depending on business contexts.

RFM analysis is a popular method for customer segmentation because it is simple to perform, and its output can be easily interpreted and understood. In particular, RFM can help address the following questions:

- Who are the most valuable customers?
- Who has the potential to become more valuable customers?
- Which customers can be retained?
- Which customers are more likely to respond to engagement campaigns?

5.5.3 Steps for RFM Analysis

There are certain steps to follow when performing an RFM analysis:

- **Set RFM analysis scope**—this is the step to determine the period that your RFM analysis to cover, for example, you can conduct RFM analysis for the past 3 or 6 months, or even longer. Of course, this also depends on the availability of your data. This step is important as it sets a reference date point for calculating the three R, F, M scores.
- **Calculate R, F, M values**—Once the scope is determined, you can calculate the R, F, and M values, respectively. For instance, to calculate R, simply deduct a customer's most recent purchase date from today's date, the difference gives the R value (e.g., 1, 10, or 120 days). To calculate F, you can either calculate the total number of orders from a customer over a particular period of time, or use average time between orders. Obviously, for the first option, the higher the better; whereas for the second option, the smaller the better. Likewise, for M value, you can either work out the total money a customer has spent during the timeframe, or use average money spent per order (see Table 5.2).
- **Convert R, F, M values to scale scores**—this is the step in which we convert the three R, F, M values to scale scores. Different businesses may use different scales, while the most common one is 1–5 scale. To define the scales, we can set fixed ranges or work out quantiles based on the three respective R, F, M values.

Table 5.2 RFM analysis example

Customer ID	Recency (days)	Frequency (times)	Monetary (total)
205381	5	13	183.79
205382	7	26	589.45
205383	2	5	27.80
205384	15	50	561.48
205385	89	3	46.89

To give you an example, we can divide the R value distribution into five equal groups using four quantiles (i.e., [0.2, 0.4, 0.6, 0.8]), and any values below the first 0.2 quantile value will be assigned a score of 5. Note here that a smaller R value means a more recent purchase/visit from customer, thus a high R scale score of 5. Similarly, we can calculate the quantiles for F and M values and then assign the scale scores to each customer.

- **Apply RFM formula for aggregated RFM scores**—you can stop at the previous stage, and simply use the individual R, F, M scale scores for customer segmentation (e.g., 1-1-1 for a low segment, and 555 for a high segment). Alternatively, businesses can come up a formula of their own to derive an aggregated RFM score for each customer. For instance, using average of the three RFM scale scores or the sum. Depending on the nature of the business, you might introduce different weights for the three RFM variables to arrive at a more relevant RFM score to your business. For example, monetary value per transaction can be more important for a piano shop than the other two metrics, compared to a convenient store, where recency and frequency can be considered more important (Table 5.3).
- **Segment customers**—the final step is to create customer segmentations based on the RFM scores. Again, depending on the nature of the business, you can decide a most suitable way of dividing customers into different segments. See Table 5.4 for an illustrative example.

Table 5.3 Aggregating RFM score

Customer ID	R score	F score	M score	RFM score (mean)
205381	5	2	3	3.33
205382	5	3	4	4
205383	5	1	1	2.33
205384	4	4	4	4
205385	1	1	1	1

Table 5.4 Customer segmentation example

Segment label	RFM score	Characteristics
Diamond	4.5–5.0	The best customers, who bought most recently, buy most often, and are big spenders
Platinum	4.0–4.5	Second most valuable customers, who have the potential to become diamond customers
Gold	3.5–4.0	High value customers, must-keep segment, which requires continuous attention
Silver	3.0–3.5	Mid-tier customers who may be more likely to be attracted to promotions, tailored campaigns, etc. maybe price sensitive
Bronze	2.5–3.0	Shop switchers, who might be converted to a higher segment with targeted promotions and pricing, etc. high risk of losing
Standard	2.0–2.5	New customers, less engaged customers, or small spenders. Some might be potentially converted with offers/discounts

The example contains arbitrary labels and tiers, which should be tailored to suit the needs of a particular business. Using RFM segmentation, organizations can develop effective retention strategies and tactics for each segment. For instance, the top tier Diamond and Platinum segments are the most loyal customers who may be more willing to try your new products and promote your brand. The Silver and Bronze customers may be more sensitive to pricing and promotions. As such, your business can offer tailored promotions and targeted pricing strategies in order to retain them and potentially convert some of them to a higher tier segment.

5.5.4 RFM Analysis Example in Python

In this section, we go through an RFM analysis example in Python. The data for the analysis is the one exported from *Ex. 5.2* in the cohort analysis. Note that the complete code, data, and Jupyter notebooks can be found at our online repository. Here we only attempt to show the critical parts for brevity reason.

First, we need to load the data:

Ex. 5.15

```
# load the data
df_uk = pd.read_excel('UK_Data.xlsx',index_col=0)
```

If you could recall, the dataset covers invoice dates from 2010-12-01 to 2011-12-09. For simplicity, let us just take this whole period for our analysis. To calculate Recency value, we need to get a reference date. Consider the following code:

Ex. 5.16

```
# get the reference date
ref = df_uk.InvoiceDate.dt.date.max()
ref
```

```
datetime.date(2011, 12, 9)
```

Since `InvoiceDate` column contains time values, we need to convert the column to date only values:

Ex. 5.17

```
# convert InvoicdDate to date only
df_uk.InvoiceDate = df_uk.InvoiceDate.dt.date
```

We can then get Recency values for each customer by calculating the difference between the reference date (i.e., 2011-12-09) and the most recent date when a customer made a purchase. Consider below, where we groupby `CustomerID` and apply a lambda function on `InvoiceDate`:

Ex. 5.18

```
recency = df_uk.groupby('CustomerID')['InvoiceDate'].\
          apply(lambda x: (ref - x.max()).days)

recency.head()
```

```
CustomerID
12747      2
12748      0
12749      3
12820      3
12821    214
Name: InvoiceDate, dtype: int64
```

We sampled top five customers as indicated above, for example, customer ID 12748 purchased on the reference date, whereas customer ID 12821 had not made any purchase for 214 days.

To calculate Frequency values, we can use the total number of unique invoice number per customer. Consider below:

Ex. 5.19

```
freqency = df_uk.groupby('CustomerID')['InvoiceNo'].nunique()
freqency.head()
```

```
CustomerID
12747     11
12748    200
12749      5
12820      4
12821      1
Name: InvoiceNo, dtype: int64
```

For Monetary values, we can use the total amount spent by each customer over the entire period:

Ex. 5.20

```
monetary = df_uk.groupby('CustomerID')['Amount'].sum()
monetary.head()
```

```
CustomerID
12747     3073.41
12748    24891.45
12749     4032.98
12820      923.62
12821       92.72
Name: Amount, dtype: float64
```

After getting all three R, F, and M values, we can combine them into one DataFrame. There are different ways to achieve this. As an example, consider below:

Ex. 5.21

```
# Combine Recency and Frequency first
df_rf = recency.to_frame(name='Recency').\
            join(freqency.to_frame(name='Frequency'))

# then Montary
df_rfm = df_rf.join(monetary.to_frame(name='Monetary'))
df_rfm.head()
```

CustomerID	Recency	Frequency	Monetary
12747	2	11	3073.41
12748	0	200	24891.45
12749	3	5	4032.98
12820	3	4	923.62
12821	214	1	92.72

The next step is to convert the respective R, F, and M values into scale scores. As previously mentioned, we can use quantiles to determine five equal sized groups, thereby assigning R, F, and M values on a 1–5 scale. Consider below:

Ex. 5.22

```
# Get 4 quantiles values
Quantiles = df_rfm.quantile(q=[0.2, 0.4, 0.6, 0.8])
Quantiles
```

	Recency	Frequency	Monetary
0.2	12.0	1.0	197.766
0.4	32.0	2.0	393.700
0.6	70.0	3.0	734.940
0.8	178.6	5.0	1576.588

As shown above, the `quantile()` method has conveniently produced four quantile values for each metric in the columns. Based on these values, we can convert the three R, F, M values into scale scores.

First, we need to define a function for R score conversion:

Ex. 5.23

```
def Rscore(x, q, df):     # x=value, q=column, df=dataframe
    if x <= df[q][0.2]:   # if x < first quantile value
        return 5          # return 5 as it is most recent.
    elif x <= df[q][0.4]:
        return 4
    elif x <= df[q][0.6]:
        return 3
    elif x <= df[q][0.8]:
        return 2
    else:
        return 1
```

Note that since we will use `df_rfm` for other purpose later, we shall create a copy of the DataFrame and then apply the function to derive R score. Consider below:

Ex. 5.24

```
# create a copy of the dataframe.
rfm_copy = df_rfm.copy()

# convert to R score
rfm_copy['Rscore'] = rfm_copy['Recency'].\
                        apply(Rscore, args=('Recency', Quantiles))
rfm_copy.head()
```

CustomerID	Recency	Frequency	Monetary	Rscore
12747	2	11	3073.41	5
12748	0	200	24891.45	5
12749	3	5	4032.98	5
12820	3	4	923.62	5
12821	214	1	92.72	1

Likewise, we can define a function for F and M scores conversion and call it to create `Fscore` and `Mscore` columns in the `rfm_copy` DataFrame. See below:

Ex. 5.25

```
def FMscore (x, q, df):
    if x <= df[q][0.2]:
        return 1
    elif x <= df[q][0.4]:
        return 2
    elif x <= df[q][0.6]:
        return 3
    elif x <= df[q][0.8]:
        return 4
    else:
        return 5
rfm_copy['Fscore'] = rfm_copy['Frequency'].\
                apply(FMscore,args=('Frequency',Quantiles))
rfm_copy['Mscore'] = rfm_copy['Monetary'].\
                apply(FMscore,args=('Monetary',Quantiles))
rfm_copy.head()
```

CustomerID	Recency	Frequency	Monetary	Rscore	Fscore	Mscore
12747	2	11	3073.41	5	5	5
12748	0	200	24891.45	5	5	5
12749	3	5	4032.98	5	4	5
12820	3	4	923.62	5	4	4
12821	214	1	92.72	1	1	1

Alternatively, we can use pd.qcut() method to get the R, F, and M scores. For the full code, check the notebook.

For customer segmentation, we can use the aggregate RFM scores by simply taking the average of the R, F, M scores derived above. Consider below:

Ex. 5.26

```
# ve use the avavage of R,F,and M scores for RFM score
rfm_copy['RFMscore'] = rfm_copy[['Rscore', 'Fscore',
                        'Mscore']].mean(axis=1)

rfm_copy.head()
```

CustomerID	Recency	Frequency	Monetary	Rscore	Fscore	Mscore	RFMscore
12747	2	11	3073.41	5	5	5	5.000000
12748	0	200	24891.45	5	5	5	5.000000
12749	3	5	4032.98	5	4	5	4.666667
12820	3	4	923.62	5	4	4	4.333333
12821	214	1	92.72	1	1	1	1.000000

Finally, based on the RFM score we can segment customers into different groups. As an example, we arbitrarily divide them into six groups by defining the following function:

Ex. 5.27

```
def segment(df):
    if df.RFMscore <= 1:
        return 'Basic'
    elif df.RFMscore <= 2:
        return 'Bronze'
    elif df.RFMscore <= 3:
        return 'Silver'
    elif df.RFMscore <= 4:
        return 'Gold'
    elif df.RFMscore <= 4.5:
        return 'Platinum'
    else:
        return 'Diamond'
```

Let us apply the function to the DataFrame and get the segmentation:

Ex. 5.28

```
rfm_copy['LoyaltyGroup'] = rfm_copy.apply(segment, axis=1)
rfm_copy.head(n=10)
```

CustomerID	Recency	Frequency	Monetary	Rscore	Fscore	Mscore	RFMscore	LoyaltyGroup
12747	2	11	3073.41	5	5	5	5.000000	Diamond
12748	0	200	24891.45	5	5	5	5.000000	Diamond
12749	3	5	4032.98	5	4	5	4.666667	Diamond
12820	3	4	923.62	5	4	4	4.333333	Platinum
12821	214	1	92.72	1	1	1	1.000000	Basic
12822	70	2	806.08	3	2	4	3.000000	Silver
12824	59	1	397.12	3	1	3	2.333333	Silver
12826	2	7	1460.80	5	5	4	4.666667	Diamond
12827	5	3	430.15	5	3	3	3.666667	Gold
12828	2	6	1018.71	5	5	4	4.666667	Diamond

We can then check how many customers in each group in our example:

Ex. 5.29

```
rfm_score = rfm_copy.reset_index()
rfm_score.groupby('LoyaltyGroup')['CustomerID'].\
                count().sort_values(ascending=False)
LoyaltyGroup
Bronze      1081
Silver       911
Gold         748
Diamond      555
Basic        270
Platinum     253
Name: CustomerID, dtype: int64
```

Once a business has segmented its customers, it can then develop specific strategies to target each segment for creating better customer service and experience. For example, using promotions, offers, or discounts to retrain 'shop switchers', while providing superior customer experience to make loyal customers feel more valued.

However, it is important to realize that, while RFM analysis can help effectively segment customers into various tiers and create a quick snapshot of customers who are most valuable to your business, it does not necessarily mean that the segmentation can accurately reflect what the customers desire and the true motivations behind their behaviours. Whilst you can develop tailored engagement campaigns, marketing advertisements, prioritized nurturing, and loyalty programmes for each customer segment, they may not want to hear from you for all those kinds of efforts all the time.

Therefore, make sure you have a clever communication strategy in place and do not overwhelm your customers with excessive emails and calls to promote your products, which would certainly annoy them and eventually turn them away. Remember that a high RFM score may be a sign to further analyse those valuable customers and find their true motives behind their behaviours, rather than to try to push more products to them right away.

5.6   Clustering Algorithms

In previous sections, we have explored two useful methods to group customers. In this section, we move on to a more advanced approach for customer segmentation using clustering algorithms. Clustering algorithms can learn from the properties of data and assign (or predict) an integer label to each datapoint, indicating which cluster a particular datapoint belongs to. Scikit-learn library contains a few clustering algorithms that can be used for customer segmentation, including k-means, DBSCAN, and Gaussian Mixture, which will be briefly introduced here.

5.6.1   K-Means Algorithm

K-means is one of the most popular and simplest algorithms for clustering. K-means algorithm separates data into predetermined number k of non-overlapping clusters, in which each datapoint belongs to only one cluster. The algorithm aims to minimize the within-cluster sum of squared distance (i.e., inertia) between each datapoint and the cluster's centroid (i.e., arithmetic mean of all the datapoints within the cluster). The objective function can be expressed as:

$$\min \sum_{j=1}^{k} \sum_{i=1}^{n} \|x^{ij} - \mu_j\|^2 \qquad (5.1)$$

where k is the number of clusters, n is the number of datapoints, μ_j is the centroid of cluster j, and x^{ij} is the ith datapoint allocated cluster j.

K-means algorithm is usually referred to as Lloyd's algorithm, especially in the computer science community. K-means clustering involves an iterative refinement approach commonly known as **Expectation-Maximization**. First, the approach guesses some initial centroids. Then, the **Expectation** or 'E' step assigns each datapoint to its closest centroid, forming clusters. The **Maximization** or 'M' step involves determining new centroids by taking the mean value of the datapoints in each previous cluster. The last two steps repeat until the centroids have stabilized or do not move significantly.

Note that given enough time, the algorithm can always converge, however probably to a local minimum, rather than to a global optimum. Therefore, different initializations of the centroids may lead to different clusters. One method to address the issue is the k-means++ initialization scheme, which initializes the centroids to be distant from each other, leading to better results than random initialization (Arthur and Vassilvitskii 2007).

The sklearn.cluster module from scikit-learn contains several clustering algorithms, including k-means. To use the algorithm, we need to import it from the module:

Ex. 5.30

```
from sklearn.cluster import KMeans
```

Let us take a look at its default parameters:

```
KMeans(n_clusters=8,init='k-means++',n_init=10,max_iter=300,
       tol=0.0001,precompute_distances='auto',verbose=0,
       random_state=None,copy_x=True,n_jobs=None,algorithm='auto')
```

By default, it selects k-means++ as the initialization method. n_init sets the number of times of running the k-means with different centroid initialization. The best result will be reported. tol is the within-cluster variation metric used to declare convergence. You can set tol to a very small value, but it is not advised to set it to 0 because otherwise convergence may never happen. The k-means model in scikit-learn contains several methods as listed below (Table 5.5):

Table 5.5 Scikit-learn K-means methods

Methods	Description
fit(self, X[, y, sample_weight])	Compute k-means clustering
fit_predict(self, X[, y, sample_weight])	Compute cluster centres and predict cluster label for each sample
predict(self, X[, sample_weight])	Predict the closest cluster each sample in X belongs to
fit_transform(self, X[, y, sample_weight])	Compute clustering and transform X to cluster-distance space
transform(self, X)	Transform X to a cluster-distance space
get_params(self[, deep])	Get parameters for this estimator
set_params(self, **params)	Set the parameters of this estimator
score(self, X[, y, sample_weight]	Opposite of the value of X on the K-means objective

As an example, let us create some synthetic two-dimensional data from scikit-learn samples generator and then cluster it with the k-means algorithm:

Ex. 5.31

```
from sklearn.datasets import make_blobs

# generate synthetic two-dimensional data
X, y = make_blobs(n_samples=500, centers=3,
                  cluster_std=1.8, random_state=42)
```

We can visualize the data using scatterplot:

Ex. 5.32

```
# plot the data
fig,ax=plt.subplots(figsize=(8,4))
sns.scatterplot(X[:,0], X[:,1], s=50);
```

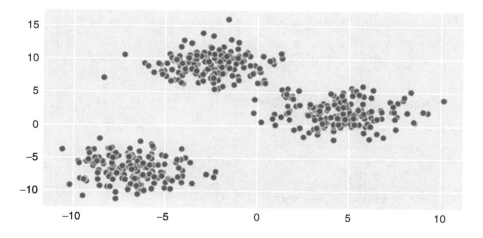

It is obvious that there are three clusters in our sample data. Next, we train the model by specifying three clusters and then use it to predict clustering labels for each datapoint.

Ex. 5.33

```
# specify number of clusters
kmeans = KMeans(n_clusters=3)

# train the model
kmeans.fit(X)

# predict clusters
y_pred = kmeans.predict(X)
```

After training the model, we can use the estimator's attributes `cluster_centers_` to check the coordinates of cluster centres and `labels_` to check labels for each datapoint:

Ex. 5.34

```
print(kmeans.cluster_centers_)
print(kmeans.labels_)
```

```
[[ 4.55690488  1.94230495]
 [-6.79245828 -6.65774811]
 [-2.56531875  9.09355876]]
[1 0 0 2 0 0 1 0 0 1 0 2 0 2 0 0 2 1 1 2 0 2 0 1 1 0 0 1 1 2 0 2 2 2 0 0 0
 0 1 1 0 2 2 2 2 0 0 0 0 1 1 2 1 1 0 2 2 1 0 1 1 2 0 1 0 1 0 1 0 1 2 0 0 0 0 1
 2 1 2 0 2 2 1 2 0 2 1 1 1 1 0 2 1 0 2 0 0 1 2 2 2 1 0 2 2 1 1 2 2 1 2 1 1
 1 1 1 1 0 2 1 0 1 2 2 0 0 1 0 2 0 1 1 1 0 0 1 0 1 1 1 0 2 1 1 0 0 1 1 1 2
 2 2 0 1 0 0 2 1 2 1 0 0 1 1 2 2 1 2 2 0 1 1 1 2 2 1 1 2 2 0 0 0 2 1 2 2 1
 1 2 0 2 1 1 1 1 1 2 0 2 2 1 1 0 2 2 1 1 0 1 2 2 1 2 1 2 0 0 2
 1 2 0 2 2 1 0 0 0 0 2 1 1 1 2 0 2 0 0 0 2 2 1 1 0 2 2 0 2 2 2 2 0 2 1 2 1
 2 2 2 1 2 0 0 0 2 0 0 2 2 0 1 2 2 2 2 1 1 2 0 2 2 1 2 0 1 0 0 1 2 2 2 1 2
 1 0 0 2 0 1 0 0 2 0 0 0 0 2 0 1 0 0 0 1 1 0 0 2 1 0 0 1 1 1 0 1 1 1 1 0
 1 2 1 2 2 1 2 0 0 2 2 0 2 0 2 0 0 0 2 0 1 1 0 1 2 0 2 0 2 0 0 1 2 0 0 2 1
 2 1 2 0 1 2 1 0 1 1 0 1 2 0 1 1 2 0 1 0 1 0 2 2 0 1 0 2 2 2 0 1 0 2 0 0 1
 1 0 0 1 2 0 1 2 0 2 2 2 0 2 2 2 1 1 0 2 0 1 2 2 0 1 0 0 1 1 0 1 2 2 1 0 1 2
 2 1 0 1 2 2 0 1 2 0 0 0 0 0 2 0 1 0 1 0 2 2 2 0 0 2 1 1 2 2 1 1 2 1 0 0 2
 2 1 1 2 0 1 1 0 1 1 2 1 0 2 1 2 0 1 0]]
```

Let us plot the results with the three centres:

Ex. 5.35

```
fig,ax=plt.subplots(figsize=(8,4))
sns.scatterplot(X[:,0], X[:,1], hue=y_pred, s=50, palette='viridis')

centers=kmeans.cluster_centers_
ax.scatter(centers[:,0], centers[:, 1], marker='^', c='red', s=80);
```

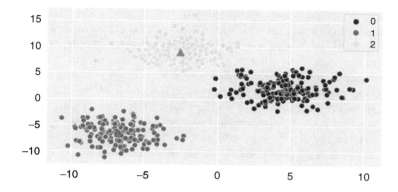

One of the challenges with k-means is that we must predetermine the number of clusters in the model, i.e., the algorithm cannot learn itself from the data. For example, if we tell the model to predict five clusters, it will proceed and try to find the best results:

Ex. 5.36

```
# specify number of clusters
kmeans = KMeans(n_clusters=5, random_state=42)

# train and predict
y_pred = kmeans.fit_predict(X)

# plot clusters
fig,ax=plt.subplots(figsize=(8,4))
sns.scatterplot(X[:,0], X[:,1], hue=y_pred, s=50, palette='viridis')

centers=kmeans.cluster_centers_
ax.scatter(centers[:,0], centers[:, 1], marker='^', c='red', s=80);
```

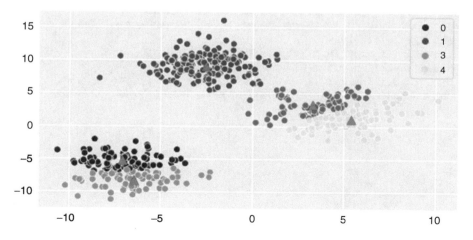

Whether or not the results are meaningful may depend upon the nature of the business and the questions to be addressed. However, note that clustering algorithms do not have a solid evaluation metric with which we can evaluate their performance. Sometimes experience and intuition may help. For example, in our example above, it is very intuitive to select three clusters than five.

Therefore, selecting the right number of clusters can be a challenging task. One intuitive approach that can be used is called **Elbow Method**. The method can help to get a rough idea on the appropriate k number of clusters. Based on the sum of squared distance (i.e., inertia), a scree plot can be created showing the number of clusters on x-axis and corresponding inertia values on y-axis. The 'elbow' of the curve can then be used as a cut-off point to determine the optimum value of k, where the inertia starts to flatten out. This is a common heuristic in mathematical optimization that selecting a point where diminishing gains are no longer worth the additional cost.

For our previous example, we can adopt the elbow method to determine the best number of clusters. Consider below, where we first create an empty list, then use a `for` loop to train k-means models that generate clusters from one to ten, and lastly append the resulted inertia in the list:

Ex. 5.37

```
inertia = []  # create an empty list
for n_clusters in range(1, 10):
    kmeans = KMeans(n_clusters=n_clusters, random_state=42)
    kmeans.fit(X)
    # append the inertia values from each model to the list
    inertia.append(kmeans.inertia_)
```

Then, we can create a scree plot using the code below:

Ex. 5.38

```
df_inertia = pd.DataFrame({'Cluster': range(1, 10),
                           'Inertia': inertia})
plt.figure(figsize=(8, 4))
plt.plot(df_inertia.Cluster, df_inertia.Inertia, '-o')
plt.xlabel('Number of Clusters')
plt.ylabel('Inertia')
plt.title('The Elbow Method', fontsize=15);
```

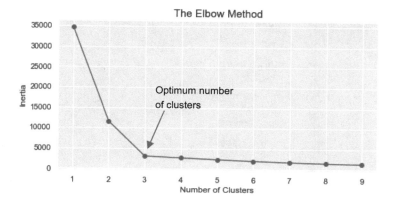

The Elbow Method

As shown above, choosing three clusters is the best option for our example.

However, the elbow method sometimes does not show a clear elbow or an obvious point where the plot starts flattening out. If that is the case, you might want to try out a different selection approach such as the **silhouette analysis**. We will not explore this method here, for details check scikit-learn documentation on '**Selecting the number of clusters with silhouette analysis on KMeans clustering**'.

Alternatively, you might use a more complicated clustering algorithm such as DBSCAN and Gaussian Mixture Models, which will be introduced shortly.

Note: Since clustering algorithms including k-means use distance-based measures to determine the similarity between datapoints, it is recommended to standardize the data before feeding it into the training model.

5.6.2   Customer Segmentation with K-Means

After understanding the basics of k-means algorithm, let us walk through a practical example using k-means to segment customers. The data is from our previous RFM analysis, which contains the Recency, Frequency, and Monetary values. See below:

Ex. 5.39

```
df_rfm.head()
```

	Recency	Frequency	Monetary
CustomerID			
12747	2	11	3073.41
12748	0	200	24891.45
12749	3	5	4032.98
12820	3	4	923.62
12821	214	1	92.72

In this example, we will use the k-means clustering algorithm to get the optimum number of clusters based on the three RFM values only. Before feeding the data into the model, let us plot the data and check its distribution with `seaborn.histplot()`:

Ex. 5.40

```
fig, axs = plt.subplots(3, figsize=(8,6))
sns.histplot(df_rfm['Recency'], ax=axs[0])
sns.histplot(df_rfm['Frequency'], ax=axs[1])
sns.histplot(df_rfm['Monetary'], ax=axs[2]);
```

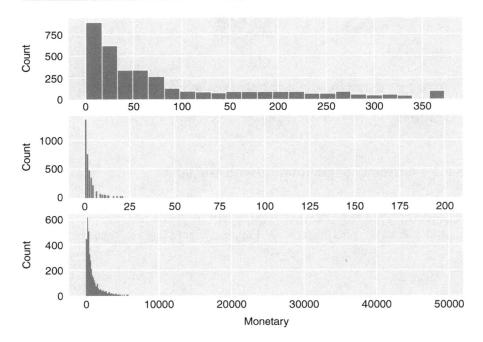

Note that k-means algorithm assumes symmetric distribution, however as shown above these RFM values clearly are right skewed. We can log-transform them by using `np.log1p()` since Recency contains zero values:

Ex. 5.41

```
df_rfm_log = np.log1p(df_rfm)
```

Next, we can use scikit-learn `StandardScaler` to standardize the data. The method standardizes features by removing the mean and scaling to unit variance. Consider below:

Ex. 5.42

```
from sklearn.preprocessing import StandardScaler
scaler = StandardScaler()

#fit and then tranform the data
df_rfm_scaled = scaler.fit_transform(df_rfm_log)

#convert output to dataframe
df_rfm_scaled = pd.DataFrame(data=df_rfm_scaled,
                             index=df_rfm.index,
                             columns=df_rfm.columns)
```

After the transformation, we shall train the model with the data. However, the question for us to consider is that how many clusters we should select to train the model. We could try the Elbow method as discussed before to determine the right number of clusters:

Ex. 5.43

```
df_inertia = pd.DataFrame({'Cluster': range(1, 10),
                           'Inertia': inertia})
plt.figure(figsize=(8, 4))
plt.plot(df_inertia.Cluster, df_inertia.Inertia, '-o')
plt.xlabel('Number of Clusters')
plt.ylabel('Inertia')
plt.title('The Elbow Method', fontsize=15);
```

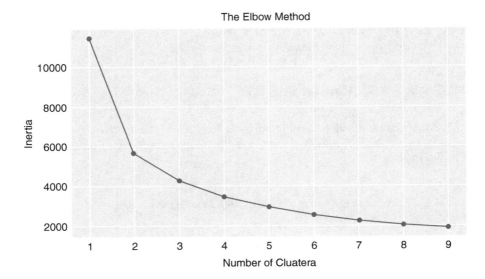

In this example, the Elbow method does not offer a clear result, however it seems that either point two or three is where the elbow starts. Let us select three clusters to train the model, and then plot a 3D figure to have a better visualization of the results. Check below:

Ex. 5.44

```
# train kmeans model
kmeans = KMeans(n_clusters=3, random_state=42)
clusters = kmeans.fit_predict(df_rfm_scaled)
cluster_lable = kmeans.labels_

# 3D scatter plot with 3 clusters
fig = plt.figure(figsize=(8, 6))
ax = Axes3D(fig)
ax.scatter(df_rfm_scaled.Recency, df_rfm_scaled.Frequency,
           df_rfm_scaled.Monetary, c=cluster_lable,
           edgecolor='k', cmap='Accent')
ax.set_xlabel('Recency')
ax.set_ylabel('Frequency')
ax.set_zlabel('Monetary')
ax.set_title('Three Clusters', fontsize=15);
```

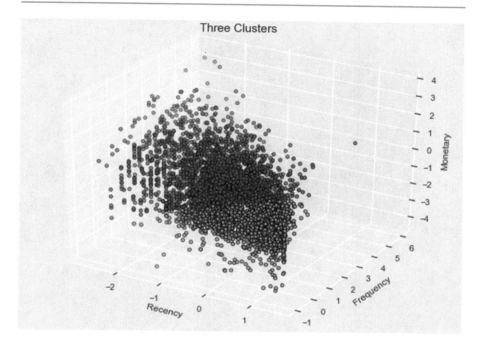

As indicated above, we have derived three clusters using the algorithm. By examining the 3D scatterplot, it seems that the lower-level cluster includes the customers with relatively higher Recency, lower Frequency and Monetary values, whereas the cluster in the middle seems to cover the full range of Recency, while having relatively lower Frequency and medium Monetary values. The top cluster seems to be the customers with relatively lower Recency, high Frequency and Monetary values.

Using k-means clustering algorithm, we can easily segment customers into predetermined number of clusters. Although the Elbow method can help us decide the optimum number k for clustering, whether the clustering makes sense and how we should interpret it may depend on the nature of your business and the questions to be addressed. For example, if we initially decided to segment customers into six different tiers as we did in the RFM analysis, we can certainly specify k to six and retrain the model to get the following:

Ex. 5.45

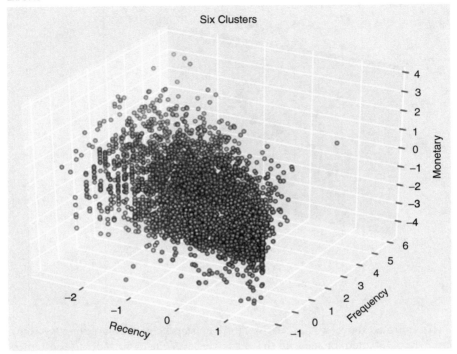

In this example, since the datapoints are not clearly differentiated, it is reasonable to argue that either three or six clusters are fine, which after all, depending on how you want to categorize your customers in line with your business context and requirements. Another thing to note here is that, we only used three RFM values to train our model in the example; however, in real practice, there can be more features in the dataset that could potentially generate more accurate and meaningful clustering results, and thereby offering much more realistic and useful business insights.

In short, k-means is a commonly used clustering algorithm owing to its efficiency and simplicity. However, it does not mean the algorithm is not without limitations. K-means usually performs well when clusters have a spherical and evenly sized shape, otherwise the clustering results may not be as accurate as those of other sophisticated clustering algorithms. In other words, the algorithm cannot handle complicated geometric shapes. Besides, k-means gives more weight to the bigger clusters and if there are overlaps between clusters, it has no intrinsic measure of probability as to which cluster label to assign to each datapoint in the overlapping region. Another challenge, as mentioned earlier, is that we need to predetermine the number of clusters in the algorithm to train the model.

Scikit-learn also includes a Mini Batch K-Means algorithm, which uses minibatches (i.e., subsets of the input data) to reduce the convergence time of k-means, thereby improving the computation efficiency, especially for very large datasets. Note that the quality of the results from `MiniBatchKmeans` can thus be comprised.

For a detailed comparison of different clustering algorithms, see scikit-learn documentation on '**Clustering**'.

5.6.3 DBSCAN

DBSCAN is the short form of Density Based Spatial Clustering of Applications with Noise (Ester et al. 1996). DBSCAN is a very useful clustering algorithm. Unlike k-means that uses distances between points as the metric to cluster, DBSCAN instead uses distances between nearest points as its metric. It views clusters as areas of high-density datapoints, separated by areas of low-density points. The advantages of this algorithm are that it can identify clusters with complex shapes and can capture noise points, and most importantly, it does not require users to pre-specify the number of clusters.

The DBSCAN algorithm is based on two parameters:

- **minPts**: the minimum number of points that can be clustered together to be considered a dense area.
- **eps** (ε): an arbitrary distance measure for locating datapoints in the neighbourhood of any datapoint.

The two parameters are used in DBSCAN to determine the minimum density areas, which are separated by lower-density areas, to form a cluster. Basically, a datapoint with at least minPts neighbours within the radius ε (including the datapoint itself) is considered a core point. All neighbouring points within the ε radius of a core point are considered to be in the same cluster as the core point (called direct density reachable). If any neighbouring points meet the same criteria and thus a core point, their neighbourhood are transitively included (called density reachable). Any non-core points in the density reachable area are called border points. All the points within the density reachable area are called density connected. Points that fall out of the density reachable areas are considered noise, meaning that they do not belong to any cluster (Schubert et al. 2017) (see Fig. 5.7).

In Fig. 5.7, the `minPts` is set to 4, and the ε radius is indicated by circles. A is the core point. Arrows indicate direct density reachability. And all the red points meet the criteria to be a core point too. B and C are considered border points as they do not meet the criteria to be a core point, but are density connected. N is a noise point as it is not density reachable (Schubert et al. 2017).

In particular, the algorithm works like this: it starts from point A and visits its neighbours (within ε radius). If these neighbouring points are core points, their neighbours are visited in turn and so on, until there are no more core points within the ε radius of the cluster. Then, the algorithm picks another point which has not yet been visited, and the same process is repeated. If there are less than `minPts`

Fig. 5.7 Illustration of the
DBSCAN cluster model
(Adapted from Schubert
et al. 2017)

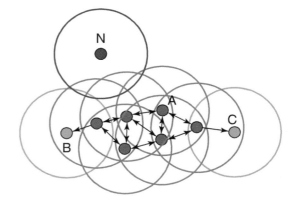

within the ε radius of the newly picked point, the point is labelled as a *noise*. The
process is like a chaining approach to determining whether a point is located within
a particular cluster.

Scikit-learn includes DBSCAN implementation in its clustering algorithms. To
use the algorithm, we need to import it, consider below:

Ex. 5.46

```
from sklearn.cluster import DBSCAN
```

Let us check its default parameters:

```
DBSCAN(eps=0.5, min_samples=5, metric='euclidean', metric_params=None,
       algorithm='auto', leaf_size=30, p=None, n_jobs=None)
```

Note that in scikit-learn implementation, by default `eps` is set to 0.5. You can
adjust this important parameter appropriately for your dataset and distance function.
`min_samples` is the same as `minPts`, which includes the point itself. You are
recommended to explore these parameters yourself.

As an example, we create some synthetic data of complex shapes and then use
the algorithm to predict clusters:

Ex. 5.47

```
# create more complex shape data
from sklearn.datasets import make_moons
X, y = make_moons(1000, noise=.05, random_state=42)
```

Before feeding the data into the training model, we shall normalize it with
`StandardScaler`:

Ex. 5.48

```
# normalize dataset
from sklearn.preprocessing import StandardScaler
X = StandardScaler().fit_transform(X)
```

Let us try k-means first and see how it performs:

Ex. 5.49

```
kmeans = KMeans(2, random_state=42)
y_pred = kmeans.fit_predict(X)

# plot the clustering results
fig,ax=plt.subplots(figsize=(8,5))
sns.scatterplot(x=X[:,0],y=X[:,1],hue=y_pred,s=30,palette='viridis')

# plot the centroids
centers=kmeans.cluster_centers_
ax.scatter(centers[:,0],centers[:, 1],marker='o',c='r',s=120);
```

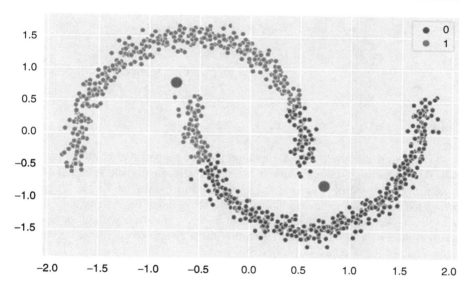

Clearly, the k-means algorithm has done a poor job in this case as it always try to construct a nice spherical shape around the centroid. Next, let us try the DBSCAN algorithm:

Ex. 5.50

```
# train the model and then predict
db = DBSCAN()
lbls = db.fit_predict(X)

# plot the results
fig,ax=plt.subplots(figsize=(8,5))
sns.scatterplot(x=X[:,0],y=X[:,1],hue=lbls,s=30,palette='viridis')
```

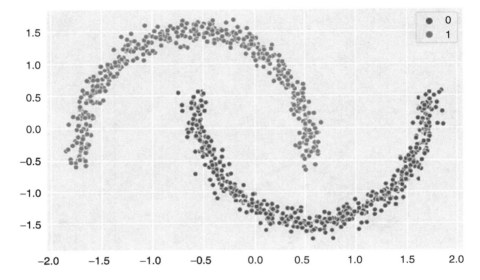

It is obvious that the DBSCAN method has done a better job in this clustering task, despite having used only default settings for all the parameters. Recall that the `eps` parameter controls the local neighbourhood of the points, i.e., it determines how 'close' a point to the core point should be in order for it to be included in the cluster. Setting `eps` too large can lead to a single cluster with all datapoints, whereas setting it too small can mean that there is no core point and all points become noise (labelled as −1 for noise).

We can specify a smaller `eps` value and see what could happen:

Ex. 5.51

```
# set a smaller eps
db = DBSCAN(eps=0.15)
lbls = db.fit_predict(X)
fig,ax=plt.subplots(figsize=(8,5))
sns.scatterplot(x=X[:,0],y=X[:,1],hue=lbls,s=30,palette='viridis')
```

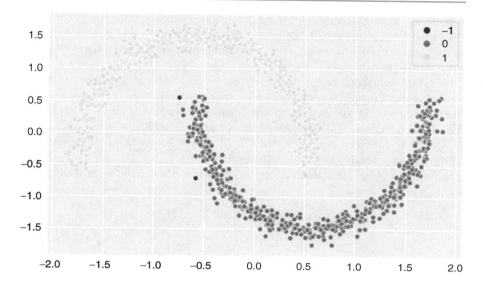

As can be seen, when setting `eps = 0.15`, it detects two clusters while getting two noise points labelled as −1.

Note: DBSCAN always generates the same clusters when given the same data in the same order. If a different data order is given, core points and nose points remain the same, but boarder points can differ in cluster membership depending on the order.

In summary, the DBSCAN algorithm has many advantages, for example, it does not require a predetermined number of clusters and can work well with very large datasets with complex shapes of clusters. However, the algorithm might not work well when there are clusters of varying densities. And setting appropriate ε and `minPts` for identifying the neighbourhood can be challenging when there are variations in density levels, especially with high dimensional data.

5.6.4 Gaussian Mixture Model

A Gaussian mixture model (GMM) is a probabilistic model that assumes that all the datapoints are from a mixture of certain number of Gaussian distributions (i.e., normal distribution), and each of these distributions forms a cluster. In general, the GMM model does not require knowing which distribution a datapoint is from but learn it automatically by identifying the probability of each datapoint belonging to each of these distributions in a given set of data.

A GMM is parameterized by two types of values, the mixture `component weights` and the `means` and `variances` (for univariate case) or `covariances` (for multivariate case) of the component. Suppose we have a dataset with K clusters (i.e., K components in GMM), cluster k has a mean of μ_k and covariance matrix Σ_k.

Similar to k-means clustering, the GMM adopts **Expectation-Maximization** (EM) technique for maximum likelihood estimations.

First, the E-step calculates the probability of each datapoint's membership in each cluster:

$$\gamma_{ik} = \frac{w_k p(x_i | \mu_k, \Sigma_k)}{\sum_{j=1}^{K} w_j p(x_i | \mu_j, \Sigma_j)} \tag{5.2}$$

where γ_{ik} is the probability that point x_i is generated by component (i.e., distribution/cluster) k, w_k is the mixture component weight for component k, and $p(x_i | \mu_k, \Sigma_k)$ is the probability density function of a Gaussian distribution.

Second, based on the values from E-step, the M-step updates the parameter values (i.e., w_k, μ_k and Σ_k) for each cluster and re-calculates the probabilities for each datapoint and updates the values iteratively. This process is repeated until convergence where this is not much variation. Just as the k-means algorithm, GMM can always converge to a local optimum but might miss the global optimum. One of the main differences between GMM and k-means is that k-means focuses on the mean to update the centroid, whereas GMM takes into account both the mean and the variance/covariance of the data.

Scikit-learn contains a `sklearn.mixutre` package that enables us to learn GMMs, sample them, and estimate them from data. The `GaussianMixture` object implements the EM technique for fitting mixture-of-Gaussian models. To use it, we first need to import it:

Ex. 5.52

```
from sklearn.mixture import GaussianMixture
```

Let us take a look at its signature:

```
GaussianMixture(n_components=1,covariance_type='full',tol=0.001,
                reg_covar=1e-06,max_iter=100,n_init=1,
                init_params='kmeans',weights_init=None,
                means_init=None,precisions_init=None,
                random_state=None,warm_start=False,
                verbose=0,verbose_interval=10)
```

`n_components` specifies the number of mixture components. `covariance_type` is defaulted to 'full' but can be set to 'tied', 'diag,' and 'spherical'. The `init_params` use 'kmeans' as default method to initial-ize the weights, the means, and the precisions. You are encouraged to explore these parameters details yourself.

Similar to k-means, we need to predetermine k number of clusters and randomly initialize the Gaussian distribution parameters. As an illustration, consider the example below in which we generate some anisotropicly distributed data with four clusters:

Ex. 5.53

```
# Generate anisotropicly distributed data
X, y = make_blobs(n_samples=1000, centers=4, random_state=42)
transform = [[0.3, -0.3], [-0.3, 0.5]]
X = np.dot(X, transform)

# Plot the data
fig,ax=plt.subplots(figsize=(8,4))
sns.scatterplot(x=X[:,0],y=X[:,1],s=40);
```

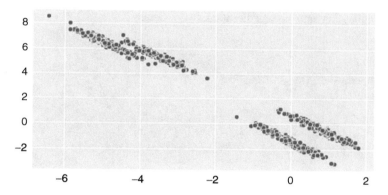

This is how the data looks like. Again, let us first try k-means clustering algo-rithm on it:

Ex. 5.54

```
# specify number of clusters
kmeans = KMeans(n_clusters=4, random_state=42)

# train & predict clusters
y_pred = kmeans.fit_predict(X)

# plot the results
fig,ax=plt.subplots(figsize=(8,4))
sns.scatterplot(x=X[:,0], y=X[:,1], hue=y_pred,
                s=40, palette='viridis')

centers=kmeans.cluster_centers_
ax.scatter(centers[:,0], centers[:, 1],
           marker='^',c='red', s=80);
```

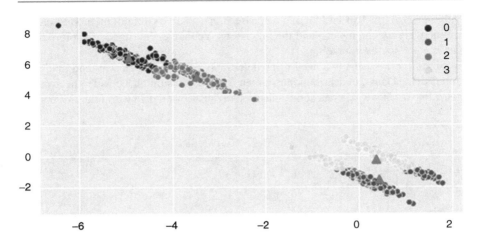

As can be seen, k-means did not identify the clusters correctly. Next, let us use GMM on the data and see whether it can work better:

Ex. 5.55

```
# train the model and then predict the labels
GM = GaussianMixture(n_components=4,random_state=42)
lbls = GM.fit_predict(X)

# plot the results
fig,ax=plt.subplots(figsize=(8,4))
sns.scatterplot(x=X[:,0],y=X[:,1],hue=lbls,
                s=50,palette='viridis');
```

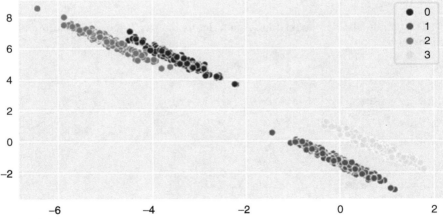

With a mixture of four Gaussians (i.e., n_components=4), the GMM worked very well in this clustering task. We can use the model's predict_prob()

method to predict posterior probability of each datapoint belonging to each component. Consider below:

Ex. 5.56

```
probs = GM.predict_proba(X)
print(probs.round(2))
[[0. 0. 1. 0.]
 [0. 1. 0. 0.]
 [0. 1. 0. 0.]
 ...
 [0. 0. 0. 1.]
 [0. 1. 0. 0.]
 [0. 0. 1. 0.]]
```

GMM is a very flexible and powerful clustering algorithm. It works in much the same way as k-means, but accounts for variance/covariance in the data and returns the probability of a datapoint belonging to each of the K clusters. As the algorithm uses probability, if a particular datapoint lies in an overlapping area of two clusters, we can define it by saying it has an $\alpha\%$ to cluster 1 and $\beta\%$ to cluster 2.

As a clustering algorithm, some of GMM's advantages include, for example, it is the fastest algorithm for learning mixture models. As the algorithm only maximizes the likelihood, it will not bias the means towards zero, or bias the cluster sizes.

However, GMM also has some drawbacks such as when there are no sufficient datapoints per mixture, estimating the covariance matrices becomes difficult. Like k-means, it requires the predetermination of number of components to use fitting the model, which can be somewhat challenging.

The GMM implementation in Scikit-learn includes two criterion that can be used for determining the optimal number of components for a given dataset: **Akaike information criterion** (AIC) or **Bayesian information criterion** (BIC). BIC, in particular, is based on the likelihood function and the lowest BIC is preferred for model selection. AIC is closely related to BIC, which estimates the relative amount of information loss and deals with the trade-off between overfitting and underfitting of a given model.

As an illustration, let us use the AIC and BIC values to select the optimal number of components for our previous example:

Ex. 5.57

```
n_components = np.arange(1, 20)
GMM = [GaussianMixture(i, random_state=42).fit(X)
       for i in n_components]

fig,ax=plt.subplots(figsize=(8,4))
ax.plot(n_components, [n.aic(X) for n in GMM], label='AIC')
ax.plot(n_components, [n.bic(X) for n in GMM], label='BIC')
plt.legend(loc=1)
plt.xlabel('No.of Components');
plt.xticks(ticks=n_components);
```

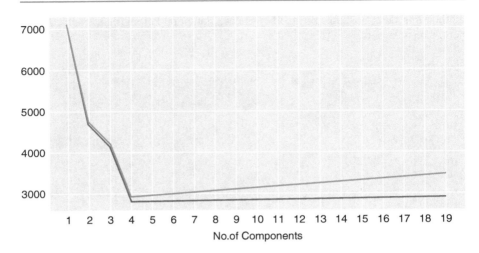

The optimal number of components should be the value that minimize the BIC or AIC. Clearly as indicated above, the number is 4 for our example. Additionally, we could use **Silhouette Score** to evaluate and select the best number of components despite its limitations, however we will not cover this method here.

Finally, note that, GMM is fundamentally an algorithm for density estimation that describes the distribution of the data. We will not go through an example here, for more details on GMMs, see '**Gaussian Mixture Models**' documentation of scikit-learn.

Summary of Learning Objectives

1. **Describe customers in supply chains and their importance for effective SCM.**

   As illustrated in Fig. 5.1, there can be many tiers of customers along a supply chain. When a buyer–supplier relationship is formed, there will be a customer. Customers can also be both internal and external. However, from a focal firm's perspective, customers are often regarded as downstream customers. Customers play a vital role in supply chains because the ultimate objective of managing a supply chain is to meet and exceed customer expectations. A better understanding of customers can enable organizations to develop products that maximize value offering to their customers and thus enhancing customers satisfaction. It can also facilitate a highly responsive, efficient, and cost-effective supply chains to meet various customer demands, as well as improving supply chain resilience and minimizing supply disruptions.

2. **Understand the benefits and steps of developing a customer-centric supply chain.**

   There are many benefits of developing a customer-centric supply chain as summarized in Table 5.1, including, for example, better product design, targeted pricing and promotion, improved customer relations and services, as well as enhanced supply chain collaboration and visibility. We summarized a five-step process of building a customer-centric supply chain, from defining customers, understanding customer's needs, to designing appropriate supply chain processes and building efficient logistics systems. Developing a customer-centric supply chain is often a challenging task, which requires both internal and external collaborations, possibly involving all important members of a supply chain. It could also mean a complete re-engineering of existing supply chain processes. However, the associated benefits often outweigh the obstacles and efforts in developing such a customer-centric supply chain.

3. **Understand cohort analysis and RFM analysis and be able to perform them in Python.**

   Cohort analysis is often used to compare the behaviours of different customer groups, based on which organization can develop specific pricing and promotion strategies targeting each customer cohort. The analysis can be useful for the focal firms to improve customer relations, retention, and engagement rates as well as enhanced customer experience. RFM is another useful technique for customer segmentation based on Recency, Frequency, and Monetary. Since the technique adopts three metrics in its classification, it provides a more balanced view, enabling organizations to gain a better understanding of their customers and come up appropriate and tailored strategies targeting each customer segment. We introduced two examples on how these two analyses can be performed in Python, you should go through these examples yourself and practise in your own notebooks.

4. **Learn and be able to use clustering algorithms to perform customer segmentation.**

   In addition to cohort analysis and RFM analysis, clustering algorithms can be very useful in customer segmentation. If we have enough data and features, clustering algorithms can learn and cluster customers from the data, and usually perform better than those traditional techniques in understanding customers characteristics. In this chapter, we mainly focused on three algorithms including k-means, DBSCAN, and Gaussian Mixture models, with each having its advantages and drawbacks. K-means usually performs well when clusters have a spherical and evenly sized shape, and DBSCAN work well with very large datasets with complex shapes of clusters, whereas Gaussian Mixture is the fastest algorithm for learning mixture models. Both k-means and Gaussian Mixture require pre-determining the number of clusters when initializing their models. There are different methods for this, such as the Elbow method for k-means and AIC/BIC for Gaussian Mixture, respectively.

Discussion Questions

1. Identify a supply chain in your chosen industry and discuss who the customers are from a focal firm's perspective.
2. What are the steps involved in a cohort analysis? Identify a business and try to develop your own cohort types, cohort size, metrics, and date range, explain your choice.
3. What type of questions is RFM analysis most useful for addressing? How can we calculate the R, F, and M values?
4. Discuss the advantages and disadvantages of each clustering algorithms introduced in this chapter.
5. What methods can we use to predetermine the number of clusters for k-means and Gaussian Mixture models?

Keyboard Exercises
1. In your notebook, import necessary packages, re-run all the exercises in this chapter.
2. Use the data from the cohort analysis example, instead of plotting the retention rate by cohorts, can you plot monthly revenue by cohorts? and total SKUs by cohorts?
3. What are the top selling products in each country? are they the same in different countries?
4. In our RFM example, we defined helper functions to calculate RFM scores, can you figure out a different way to calculate those scores?
5. Explore Silhouette Score method in scikit-learn documentation yourself and try to apply this method in determining the number of components for our Gaussian Mixture model example. How effective is this method as compared to AIC/BIC method?

References

Arthur, D. & Vassilvitskii, S. 2007. "k-means++: The advantages of careful seeding". Proceedings of the eighteenth annual ACM-SIAM symposium on Discrete algorithms. Society for Industrial and Applied Mathematics.

Danziger, P.N. 2018. "Why Zara Succeeds: It Focuses On Pulling People In, Not Pushing Product Out". Forbes.

Ester, M., Kriegel, H-P., Sander, J. & Xu, X. 1996. "A Density-Based Algorithm for Discovering Clusters in Large Spatial Databases with Noise". KDD-96 Proceedings. p. 226–231. Spatial, Text, & Multimedia.

Glenn, N.D. 2005. Cohort Analysis. 2nd ed. Sage Publication.

Schubert, E., Sander, J., Ester, M., Kriegel, H-P. & Xu, X. 2017. "DBSCAN Revisited, Revisited: Why and How You Should (Still) Use DBSCAN". ACM Trans. Database Syst. Vol. 42 3, pp. 1-21.

Uberoi, R. 2017. "ZARA: Achieving the "Fast" in Fast Fashion through Analytics". Harvard Digital Innovation and Transformation.

Supply Management

6

Contents

© The Author(s), under exclusive license to Springer Nature
Switzerland AG 2022
K. Y. Liu, *Supply Chain Analytics*, https://doi.org/10.1007/978-3-030-92224-5_6

Learning Objectives
- Describe the major activities involved in procurement and supply management.
- Understand the differences and 'fit' between vertical integration and outsourcing.
- Discuss how to select and evaluate suppliers for effective supply management.
- Understand the purpose and ways of managing supplier relationships.
- Describe the top supply chain risks and approaches to managing them.
- Learn and be able to use, evaluate and fine-tune the regression algorithms introduced.

6.1 Procurement in Supply Chains

Procurement is one of the most important processes in supply chain management. The Charted Institute of Procurement and Supply (CIPS) regards procurement and supply management as '...buying the goods and services that enable an organisation to operate in a profitable and ethical manners'. It includes activities from sourcing raw materials and services to managing contracts and relationship with suppliers. According to CIPS, procurement plays a crucial role for business success as it can account up to 70% of companies' revenue, therefore a small reduction in costs can have a huge impact on profits.

Despite various conceptualizations in the extant literature, procurement can be generally defined as the act of selecting and evaluating suppliers, negotiating and contracting with suppliers, as well as managing effective supplier relationships in order to acquire, secure and maintain smooth and quality supply of goods and services to support focal firms' daily operations. The two terms, *procurement* and *purchasing*, are sometimes used interchangeably; however, procurement is a much broader concept than purchasing. The latter mainly refers to the activity of placing and receiving orders from suppliers.

6.1.1 Vertical Integration

For any businesses, the most significant decision in their operations is the *make* or *buy* decision, i.e., whether to make the required materials, components, or services by the business itself or to source them from external suppliers. When a firm makes most of the materials or components in-house or owns most stages of a supply chain, it is commonly referred to as *vertical integration*. Vertical integration can benefit firms in many ways, such as having great controls of supply chains, effective production planning and cost controls. Vertical integration is usually desired when

Fig. 6.1 Tesla and
supercharger

organizations want to secure critical supplies of key resources or to keep core competence and capabilities in-house to avoid potential intellectual property leakage and imitation by rivals.

For example, Tesla, as a surging electric vehicle (EV) manufacturer, is about 80% vertically integrated, which is rare in the auto sector (Lambert 2016). Unlike other automakers that focuses on final assembly and engine manufacturing, Tesla owns and operates its manufacturing plants, battery pack production at its Gigafactory and global supercharger network, in addition to hardware, software development and retail. This vertical integration strategy allows Tesla to maintain key supplies of battery technologies in its own hands, ensuring high volume EV production and making it less imitable by its competitors (Fig. 6.1).

Firms can vary significantly in terms of the extent to which they are vertically integrated, however a full degree of vertical integration (i.e., making everything in-house) is literally impossible for any type of business. In addition, there are also disadvantages associated with vertical integration, such as high capital expenditure, loss of business focus and lack of flexibility, etc. Finding the right degree of vertical integration can help organizations to achieve their performance objectives and maintain a competitive edge.

6.1.2   Outsourcing

If a firm decides to purchase goods and services from external suppliers, it is commonly referred to as *outsourcing*. Outsourcing has become increasingly popular over the last few decades. It was first recognized as a competitive strategy in late 1980s and has since become an integral part of business operations. It allows companies to find the required materials, components, or services at cheaper prices and better quality than they could normally produce by themselves (or something they are unable to make in-house). For example, in the automotive industry nowadays, it is not uncommon to see that many car manufacturers outsource over 80% components and parts to external suppliers.

Whilst there has been controversy about the impact of outsourcing on economy (e.g., loss of domestic jobs), outsourcing has both its advantages and drawbacks. First, some of its benefits include:

- It can help firms to cut costs down by finding suppliers who can make things cheaper.
- It enables companies to focus on their core competencies, i.e., what they are good at doing.
- Firms can use outsourcing to access key resources and capabilities (e.g., technologies, talents, and know-how) that they lack.
- Multi-national companies can use outsourcing to access local markets and provide improved local customer service and support.
- With effective outsourcing and collaboration with suppliers and other members in a supply chain, organizations can foster a strong business eco-system that is more resilient, reliable, and difficult to imitate by competitors (Fig. 6.2).

With regard to the drawbacks, for example:

- The buying firms can become over-reliant on their suppliers, which can be risky when unexpected things occur (e.g., trade conflict).
- Companies might have little control over suppliers' operations; thus, quality and performance can be problematic sometimes (e.g., product recalls due to components failure). In addition, sustainability can be another important issue, especially for the environmental and social aspects.
- With outsourcing, supply chain visibility may be compromised, and smooth communication sometimes can be challenging, especially when dealing with distant foreign suppliers.

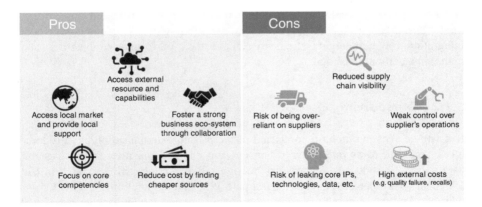

Fig. 6.2 Pros and cons of outsourcing

- External costs can be unexpectedly high, such as dealing with quality failure, recalls, supplier monitoring and auditing, etc. Company image can be damaged in some cases (e.g., poor after-sale customer service)
- There are potential risks of leaking core technologies, designs and intellectual property to external partners and issues around security and confidentiality of sensitive information and customer data.

For most organizations, deciding on what and where to outsource, and especially how to manage the associated risks with outsourcing are important questions to be addressed by top management teams. Not surprisingly, this task often falls onto the shoulders of the procurement function within an organization. For example, selecting and evaluating qualified suppliers to avoid potential future failures, fostering strong partnerships to build trust and avoid risks of supply disruptions, and so on.

As mentioned earlier, finding the right degree of vertical integration is critical for business success. To be more explicit, finding the '*fit*' or right '*balance*' between vertical integration and outsourcing can be strategically important for businesses to achieve superior performance and maintain their competitive advantages. As shown in Fig. 6.3, assuming there is a natural line of 'fit', firms can move up from current state to a higher level of vertical integration if they want to have more control of their supply chains, providing they have the required resource and capabilities to do so; or they could move down along the line to outsource some goods or services to

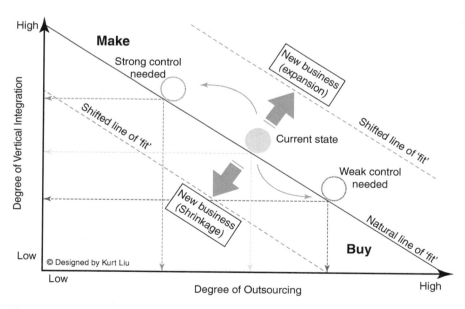

Fig. 6.3 Finding the 'fit' between vertical Integration and outsourcing

external suppliers, in which case they possess relatively weak control over their supply chains. For example, automakers today largely outsource their traditionally self-managed distribution and delivery to third-party logistics (3PL) providers because these activities are not their core businesses. Despite having a less degree of direct control, they have much more efficient logistics systems since the 3PL providers are better at distribution and delivery services.

Certainly, the line of 'fit' can be shifted when business changes, due to for instance, either expansion or shrinkage, then organizations would have to re-balance or determine a new 'fit' between vertical integration and outsourcing.

6.2   Supplier Selection

Supplier selection is the most critical initial step in procurement as it can determine the quality, reliability, flexibility and certainty of supplied goods and services to the buying firms. Developing a sophisticated supplier selection system is considered a key organizational capability because it can assist the buying firms in achieving their own business objectives and sustained competitiveness.

Effective supplier selection should be in light of an organization's competitive strategies. For example, in the mobile phone industry, some businesses are competing by offering innovative features and high-quality smartphones, while others are competing on low-cost provisions. When it comes to supplier selection, different smartphone makers must develop their own criteria in line with their competitive strategies.

As indicated in Fig. 6.4, when procurement managers develop their supplier selection systems, they must take into account their own competitive strategies and select those suppliers who can support their overall performance objectives.

Fig. 6.4 Link between supplier selection and competitive strategy

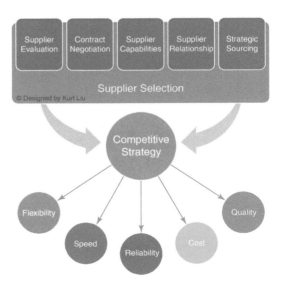

Supplier selection can be a very challenging task. In some industries (e.g., aerospace, automotive), it can take years to get suppliers eventually qualified to be part of their supply networks. There are several important activities involved in the supplier selection stage as listed below:

- **Supplier evaluation**: This evaluation can include the initial screening of new suppliers based on selection criteria, and evaluating existing suppliers for future projects, as well as continuous supplier performance monitoring and auditing.
- **Contract negotiation**: Involving pricing, auction bidding, and negotiating contract terms with pre-qualified suppliers and awarding contracts to qualified suppliers.
- **Supplier capabilities development**: Assessing current capabilities (e.g., technology, skills, know-how) of suppliers, and their potential to grow and develop future capabilities. This can be part of initial supplier evaluation but can also be a continuous improvement effort.
- **Strategic sourcing**: It can involve supplier segmentation based on their importance to a business (e.g., strategic vs. non-strategic suppliers), and supplier base rationalization (i.e., maintaining the right number of suppliers per component) for cost minimization, reliability, flexibility, and risk mitigation purposes.
- **Supplier relationship management**: Different types of relationship with suppliers exit in a supply chain. Some can be critical to the business and thus a long-term partnership is desired; others can be non-essential, and many qualified suppliers are readily available out there. Effective supplier relationship management is crucial for business success because it can help foster collaboration, trust, and joint-problem solving between suppliers and the buying firm.

When organizations select their suppliers, there may be an initial pool of candidates based on the geographical preferences, supplier's current locations and their capacities or willingness to supply to the production sites. Then, the list of potential suppliers can be shortened by using certain evaluating criteria such as supplier's quality, technological capability, and previous supply records. Besides, selecting appropriate suppliers should also take into account the external business environment including political, economic, social, technological, environmental and legal factors (i.e., PESTEL). For instance, suppliers that are located in countries where there are many unrests should be normally avoided if there are alternatives, as political uncertainties can potentially cause supply disruptions.

Supplier selection does not necessarily mean always selecting new suppliers. Established businesses often need to choose between their existing suppliers and new ones, creating a 'dilemma' for the decision makers as there can be associated advantages and disadvantages for either choice (see Table 6.1). Sometimes firms have to select and develop their existing suppliers because there are no other qualified suppliers available on the market.

Table 6.1 Supplier selection 'dilemma'

	Advantages	Disadvantages
Existing suppliers	• Long-term partnership, thus understanding each other well • Can be efficient in new project development • Close and transparent with each other due to trust • Strong collaboration for innovation and cost improvement opportunities	• Risk of being over-reliant on suppliers • Suppliers may become 'lazy' in the sense of no competition for business • 'Opportunity cost' for losing out better innovative suppliers, especially when new technology arrives
New suppliers	• Chance of getting leading technologies and innovations • Adding 'fresh blood' to the supply stream may bring up overall technological and quality levels • Stimulating existing suppliers for better performance and cost improvement	• New selection can be a long, drawn-out process • Also takes time to develop partnership and trust • Potentially high switching cost • Many risks can be involved with new partners • Adverse effects on partnerships with existing suppliers

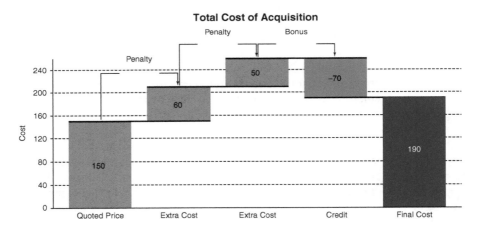

Fig. 6.5 An illustration of total cost of acquisition

Price and contract negotiation are also important processes in supplier selection, whereby firms negotiate the price with pre-qualified suppliers and determine the final suppliers to be awarded the contract. Large firms usually have a well-developed and structured negotiation approach for the pricing and bidding process. However, no matter large or small, one critical thing for organizations to consider in the negotiation process is the total cost of acquisition (TCA) than the quoted prices from suppliers (Fig. 6.5).

The TCA should cover all aspects, including both monetary and non-monetary factors. For example, outsourcing from an overseas supplier can incur additional costs such as import duties and insurance costs. Selecting a relative poor-quality supplier could mean that additional efforts are required to bring their quality up and that there can be a risk of goodwill damage if anything goes wrong due to quality failure. These factors can increase the overall TCA. There are also bonus factors such as a longer payment term from suppliers and proximity of supplier's plants to the buyer' production site, which could potentially bring TCA down. Therefore, firms should use TCA comparing different pricings from suppliers.

In the actual bidding process, approved suppliers can place their bid prices and compete for the contracts. Firms usually have their targeted prices and adopt different auction approaches (e.g., Dutch, and English auction) for selecting the final winners for the contracts.

6.3 Supplier Evaluation

Supplier evaluation can consist of three basic types depending the size and nature of the business: initial supplier qualification based on selection criteria, continuous supplier performance monitoring and auditing, as well as evaluating existing suppliers for new projects.

For initial selection criteria, organizations should consider the suppliers who can support their competitive strategies and meet their performance objectives. Examples include supplier's quality level, R&D capability, management attitudes and previous supply records, etc. The criteria enable the buying firms to have a preliminary assessment on whether the potential suppliers have the capabilities to supply high-quality products, and whether they have the capacity to supply the required volume and the potential to expand, and so on.

In terms of performance objectives, different companies have their specific focuses. For instance, some put more emphases on quality, while others are more concerned about cost reduction. Therefore, effective selection criteria can introduce a weighting system, i.e., assigning weights to different factors. See Table 6.2 for an example, in which two suppliers are evaluated by adopting the weighting score for each selection criterion and calculating the total weighted sum.

In addition to the initial supplier evaluation, to ensure consistent and reliable supplies, organizations usually conduct on-going assessment and auditing the

Table 6.2 Weighted supplier selection criteria

Criterion	Weight	Supplier A	Weighted score	Supplier B	Weighted Score
Quality level	10	9	90	7	70
Cost	10	9	90	10	100
Delivery performance	9	7	63	10	90
R&D capability	7	7	49	6	42
Management	6	8	48	5	30
Technology	6	8	48	6	36
Total weighted score			**388**		**368**

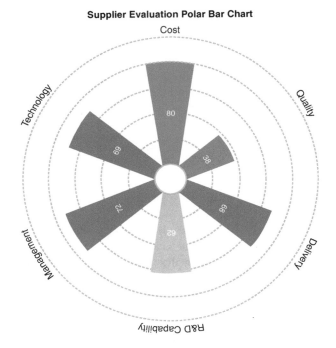

Supplier Evaluation Polar Bar Chart

Fig. 6.6 An illustration of supplier evaluation

performance of their existing suppliers. These types of assessments can include setting different performance targets that are similar to the initial evaluation criteria, and supplier capabilities assessment for technological, design, and cost improvement, etc.

Figure 6.6 is an illustrative polar bar chart to indicate the overall performance of a supplier using six evaluation criteria. Similar charts such as radar chart are being adopted by many organisations to give a straightforward view of each supplier's performance and draw comparisons between them.

In general, supplier performance should be continuously reviewed and recorded, and feedback should be promptly shared with suppliers in order for them to make necessary adjustment and improvement. Such on-going assessment can create certain pressure for suppliers to perform, but to some extent which could also bring about opportunities for process breakthrough and improvement. Suppliers are expected to meet minimum performance standard and make continuous improvement year on year.

Depending on suppliers' performances and their criticality to the business, the buying firms can choose different approaches to managing their suppliers. For example, as shown in Fig. 6.7, for those high-performance and critical suppliers, firms should try to foster a strong and strategic partnership with them. These suppliers should be prioritized when making selection for future businesses. Whilst for those who do not achieve a superior performance but still are critical to the business,

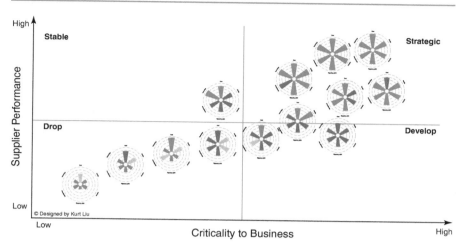

Fig. 6.7 Supplier performance-criticality matrix

the buying firms can offer as much assistance as possible to develop their capabilities and collaborate for joint problem-solving. For relatively non-critical suppliers with acceptable level of performance or above, a stable transactional relationship should suffice as there are many alternative suppliers with similar performance on the market. However, for those suppliers who cannot meet the performance requirements and are non-critical to the business, the buying firms should not consider them for future businesses or end the relationship for better alternatives.

If the existing suppliers cannot deliver what they have promised or fail to meet the performance targets, the buying firms usually give them notice for improvement. If the issues persist and cannot be resolved, organizations can choose to exit poor performers if necessary. However, it is not always the best option for organizations to arbitrarily end a supplier-buyer relationship as switching suppliers can be very costly. Therefore, new supplier selection becomes very important, and companies need to try their best to choose the right suppliers at the initial stage.

6.3.1 Supplier Capability Assessment

As an integral part of supplier evaluation, supplier capability assessment is also critical to supplier selection as it evaluates not only suppliers' current capabilities but also their potential to develop and grow future capabilities. Supplier capability assessment can include the evaluation of suppliers' fundamental quality management system, their technological skills and know-how, and flexibility to cope with changes and uncertainties.

Supply capability assessment can be conducted at supplier's manufacturing sites, focusing on their on-going performance and continuous improvement efforts. Organizations can provide support for their suppliers' capability improvement with supplier development expertise and advice as part of relationship.

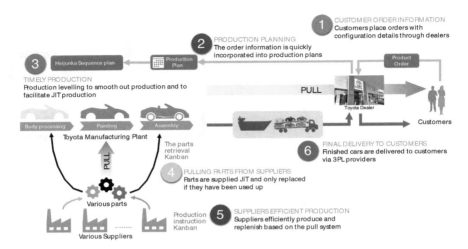

Fig. 6.8 An illustration of the Toyota production system

For example, a key success factor of Toyota's supply chain is the automaker's role in its supplier capability development. Toyota provides direct assistance to its suppliers at both individual and group level. At individual level, Toyota sends experts to the suppliers' sites to observe and suggest improvements. This type of assistance focuses on quick results.

At group level, Toyota adopts a tool called *jishuken*, which means 'self-study'. It is a tool used to develop people capabilities. Basically, the jishuken group consists of production managers from stable group of companies who jointly develop capabilities for applying the Toyota Production System (TPS) (see Fig. 6.8). Through frequent jishukens, suppliers can improve their personnel know-how and long-term capabilities (Sako 2004).

6.4   Supplier Relationship Management

Supplier relationship management plays a very important role in supply management. Effective supplier relationship management not only can guarantee high-quality supplies from suppliers, but also can help reduce uncertainties and risks involved in supply chains. However, it is not always an easy task to manage supplier relationship effectively as there are many contingent factors that might impact the relationship.

First, different types of supplier relationships exist in a supply chain. As mentioned earlier in Fig. 6.7, suppliers can be categorized into different types based on the performance-criticality matrix. There are other types of categorizations for suppliers such as by the total purchasing volumes, total expenditures, and performance records. Similar to customer segmentation, supplier segmentation can enable organizations to have a better understanding of their suppliers and develop more specific and effective supplier management strategies.

Second, for different types of suppliers, firms should adopt dissimilar approaches to managing the relationships. This is because firms usually have limited resource and capabilities and thus, they must focus on those important relationships that could possibly generate the most rents for them. It is not saying that they should neglect the less important ones, but rather create a more effective strategy for managing different types of relationships. For example, organizations should devote more resources and efforts towards developing a long-term and strategic partnership with those more critical suppliers, while maintaining a stable and efficient arm-length relationship with the non-critical ones.

In addition, fostering a long-term and strategic partnership requires time and commitment from both parties. The willingness to share critical information and be transparent with each other, sharing not only rewards but also risks are great enablers for strong collaboration. Of course, this type of trust can only be built when the true partnerships exist between buyer and supplier, which is not easy to achieve. The buying organizations should take a more proactive stance on developing such trust, by offering direct assistance and support to their suppliers for their technological innovation, cost improvement and capability development. This is because trust and partnership can bring about many benefits to the focal firm, including for instance,

- Enhanced supply chain visibility and transparency
- Shortened innovation cycle and launch of new products
- Joint problem-solving and improved productivity
- More resilient supply chains
- Creating barriers for competitors to entry and emulate core competence
- Reduced bullwhip effects and inventory levels
- Decreased defects rates and cost

In today's highly volatile market, stronger partnerships with suppliers can provide the focal firms a better chance to confront various challenges such as supply disruptions due to political unrests and trade conflict, to name a few.

6.4.1 Managing Tiered Supply Network

A supply network usually consists of suppliers that are organized into tiers, starting from tier-1 suppliers who directly supply goods and services to the focal firm, tier-2, tier-3, and all the way up to the raw material suppliers. Managing the entire supply network efficiently is a complex and challenging task, and there can be different ways of managing them. First, let us consider tier-1 suppliers:

As shown in Fig. 6.9, the focal buying firm can adopt a single sourcing strategy, whereby there is only one supplier for each component or part. This strategy is commonly used by SMEs. The benefits of single sourcing strategy are that it can bestow

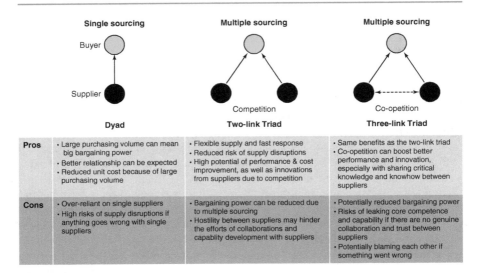

Fig. 6.9 Dyad and triad supply networks

the buying firm a relatively bigger bargaining power compared to multiple sourcing when the purchasing quantity is fixed. It could also help foster a better relationship with single suppliers. When the purchasing volume is large, there are possibilities of negotiating a better price for the purchased items. However, there are also potential drawbacks involved in single sourcing, such as the risks of experiencing supply disruption and becoming over-reliant on single suppliers.

By contrast, large organizations often adopt multiple sourcing strategy for each component or part. Depending on industries, many firms usually use two or three suppliers on average per component. This is because that with limited number of suppliers, the buying firms not only can maintain a relatively large purchasing volume for each supplier, thus having great bargaining power, but also ensure flexibility and certainty in supply, minimizing risks of supply disruption. Such an approach is often regarded as **supply base rationalization**, i.e., determining the appropriate number of suppliers.

With multiple sourcing, firms can also decide on whether allowing the same component suppliers to be completely isolated from each other, forming a sense of competition between them (i.e., two-link triad), or allowing them to both compete and collaborate at the same time, forming a sense of **coopetition** (i.e., three-link triad). The pros and cons associated with each strategy are listed in Fig. 6.9. In particular, for the two-link triad, suppliers may continuously improve their performance and cost due to competition, while for the three-link triad, suppliers can support each other with complementary knowledge and know-how, which may boost even better innovation and performance in the longer term. It might be easier for the focal buying firms to form a stronger strategic alliance with their suppliers in the three-link triad network.

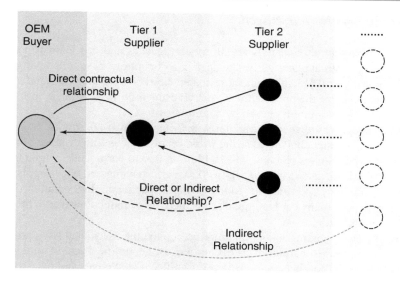

Fig. 6.10 Tiered relationship in supply network

Next, organizations should also carefully consider the way of managing their tiered supply network from tier-2 upwards (see Fig. 6.10). Some buying firms only establish direct contractual relationships with their tier-1 suppliers, who then have their autonomy to select their own suppliers; while other firms also form direct relationship with their tier-2 suppliers, i.e., designating the suppliers for tier-1 suppliers. Note that however, it is rare to see that organizations also have direct contractual relationships with tier-3 suppliers and the tiers beyond. In the automotive sector for example, OEMs often establish direct contractual relationships with tier-1 suppliers, who are normally the assemblers of systems, managing sub-tier suppliers. If there are any problems with the supplied components, these tier-1 suppliers would have to take full responsibilities.

In addition, although the buying firms do not have direct contractual relationships with tier 2 or tier 3, etc., they would normally still monitor those sub-tier suppliers' performance to ensure quality supplies and check whether the sub-tier suppliers meet certain requirements such as sustainability standards.

In some cases, however, the focal buying firms also establish direct relationships with tier-2 suppliers. This strategy may help the focal firm to maintain a great control of their supply network and ensure high-quality performance of their suppliers. However, such arrangement may create conflicts and a blaming culture between tier-1 and the designated tier-2 suppliers, as which is often the case when problems arise in the supplied components and parts. Thus, organizations should carefully determine the best strategy to managing their tiered supply network, ensuring quality, certainty, and flexibility of their supplies by forming the right type of relationships and creating clear responsibilities of their suppliers.

6.5   Supply Risk Management

In 2016, major Japanese automakers were hit by earthquakes and had to suspend much of their productions at plants across Japan due to disruptions of supplied parts (Tajitsu and Yamazaki 2016). Although those manufacturers were able to make a quick recovery and resume their productions, such an event reflects the vulnerability of supply chain to the disruptions caused by natural disasters.

According to a report published by McKinsey & Company in 2020, supply chain managers are facing greater challenges as the world seems to be getting 'riskier'. In 2019, global economic losses reached US$150 billion due to earthquakes, floods, fires, and the like (Alicke and Strigel 2020). In 2020, we also witnessed huge supply chain disruptions in many countries due to the Covid-19 pandemic. In the automotive sector in particular, many car manufacturers halted their productions due to the shortage of semiconductors.

As supply chains are getting longer and more complex, the associated risks are growing too. In addition to natural disasters and crises, geopolitical uncertainties such as Brexit and trade conflict could also pose significant challenges and risks to the global supply chains. For example, longer lead times due to border delays, additional safety stock to cover the uncertainties in supply shortages, and increased import and export tariffs.

In this fast-changing world, volatility now has become the new normality. As such, the only thing that remains unchanged is 'change' itself. The uncertainties, in combination with unpredictability, have made supply risk management especially challenging. The risks involved in supply chain can be manifold, which include not only the supply disruptions as mentioned above, but also quality issues of supplied parts, raw material price fluctuation, volatility in energy prices, and so on. According to the 2013 Global Supply Chain and Risk Management Survey conducted by *PricewaterhouseCoopers*, the top-rated supply chain risks by the supply chain professionals can be found in Fig. 6.11.

These risks can result in unwanted, sometimes unexpected supply chain disruptions, which can significantly affect organizations' operations and financial performance. To avoid and mitigate the risks in supply chains, many firms have established their own supply chain risk management systems. Large organizations usually have well-developed and systematic risk management approaches, comparing to SMEs which are relying mostly on reactive measures and have no contingency plans in place preparing for the worst scenarios.

Supply chain risk management is a rather broad topic, which itself is worth writing a whole book. In this section, however, we briefly introduce some of the key activities involved. To build an effective and proactive supply risk management system, advanced organizations often develop a risk portfolio, and constantly review and anticipate new risk challenges such as sustainability issues and cyberattacks. There are some general steps to follow, including:

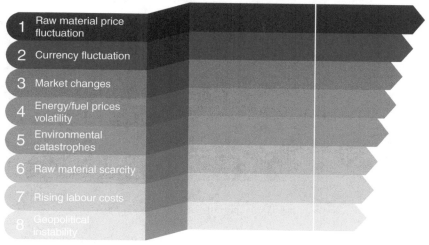

Source: PwC Global Supply Chain and Risk Management Survey 2013

Fig. 6.11 Top supply chain risks

6.5.1 Step One: Risk Identification

This is the step wherein supply chain managers identify all potential risks from their supply chains. For instance, from the supply side, examples can include suppliers' quality failure, supply shortages, and supplier factory shutdown, etc. Risk events should be identified, tracked, and monitored rigorously on an on-going basis.

6.5.2 Step Two: Risk Assessment

Once the risks have been identified, the next step is to assess and evaluate each risk to determine their severity and urgency. Risk assessment can help firms to effectively allocate their resources to manage the risks identified. A common approach for risk assessment is called risk assessment matrix, in which risks are categorized based on their likelihood to happen and the potential impact they can produce on different performance dimensions, such as supply disruption, financial, and environment (see Fig. 6.12).

As demonstrated in Fig. 6.12, very high risks are highlighted in red colour for example, which require urgent attention from the firm as they are mostly likely to happen and can produce severe impact on firm performance. By contrast, the risks

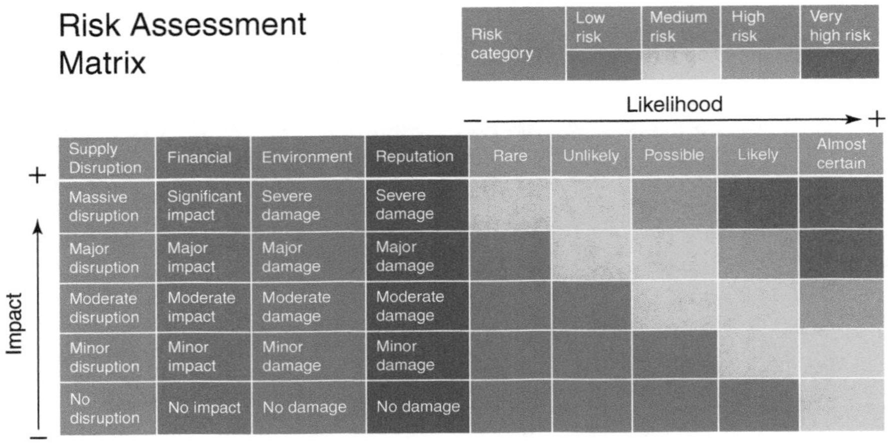

Risk Assessment Matrix

Risk category	Low risk	Medium risk	High risk	Very high risk

Likelihood − ⟶ +

Impact +↑

Supply Disruption	Financial	Environment	Reputation	Rare	Unlikely	Possible	Likely	Almost certain
Massive disruption	Significant impact	Severe damage	Severe damage					
Major disruption	Major impact	Major damage	Major damage					
Moderate disruption	Moderate impact	Moderate damage	Moderate damage					
Minor disruption	Minor impact	Minor damage	Minor damage					
No disruption	No impact	No damage	No damage					

Fig. 6.12 Risk assessment matrix example

that fall into the green zone usually mean that they require less effort and urgency to manage since they do not have a high impact and are not very likely to happen in the near future. To the make the matrix work, it is critical to develop a consistent scoring methodology and tolerance thresholds for each risk category that are fit for each organization's risk management priorities.

6.5.3 Step Three: Develop Risk Response Strategies

Depending on risk types, firms should develop specific response strategies in order to target different risks most effectively. The reason for that is twofold: first, businesses usually have limited resources and thus, they have to prioritize their efforts and take quick actions to resolve the most urgent and critical risks confronting their businesses; second, risks can vary significantly and there is no one-size-fit-all solution, therefore firms need to maintain and develop specific strategies and plans for different risk categories. For instance, to reduce the risks of supply disruptions, large organizations can use the multiple sourcing strategy. For potential quality failure from suppliers, they can constantly track and monitor the performance of suppliers, and periodically send support teams to assist suppliers in their continuous quality improvement effort.

6.5.4 Step Four: Continuous Monitoring and Regular Review

Supply risks need to be continuously monitored and controlled to avoid or mitigate their damages to an organization. Successful monitoring systems can quickly identify potential risks and alert organizations to take prompt actions. The increasing adoption of digital technologies in today's operations and supply chains has made it possible for quick identification and tracking of the risk indicators. For example, process monitoring technology may track the deviations on production lines to predict quality issues.

The risk response strategies require regular reviews as well to ensure that the risk mitigation plans and actions are comprehensive and up-to-date, especially when there are emerging risks to disrupt supplies. Organizations should periodically review their strategies and define new mitigation plans if necessary, making sure that they have adequate resources, additional support and staff with expertise to maximize the chances of avoiding, or at least mitigating, the impact from the risks in a supply chain.

In short, these four steps should be jointly performed and taken as an on-going process in order to achieve a more agile and resilient supply chain. Moreover, organizations should take a more proactive stance in their supply risk management and find new ways of reducing the risks and improving their preparedness for a wide range of expected and unexpected risks.

The most challenging and difficult thing in supply risk management is managing the unknown and unexpected risks. These risks are those that are very difficult or impossible to forecast and incorporate into the risk management routines as discussed above. Reducing their impact and increasing the response speed when they do occur can reflect the true resilience of a supply chain. Developing a strong level of resilience for unexpected risks can depend on a number of factors. However, organizations should consider at least the following:

- Build strong partnerships and collaboration with suppliers
- Use multiple sourcing for components and parts
- Use not only global but also regional sourcing strategy
- Regular supplier site visits and assessment
- Suppliers training and support
- Monitor and collaborate with suppliers' sub tiers (e.g., 2nd and 3rd tier)

Supply disruptions can cause significant financial burden and damage to a business. To sustain competitive advantage, firms should strive to create a more resilient supply chain by improving their supply chain risk management capability. Organizations with mature and strong risk management capability can be more resilient to supply disruptions. They can be less affected and can recover faster than companies with immature risk management capabilities. Top management team should also recognize that supply risk management is important for their business success, which is not merely about setting up processes and designating responsibilities, but also creating a risk-awareness culture and collaboration across functions within the whole organization as well as with external partners. By doing so, organization will increase their chances of reducing or avoiding supply risks and disruptions, while captures the full value of their supply chain strategies.

6.6   Supplier Selection Examples

In this section, we go through some examples of supplier selection and evaluation in Python. For brevity reasons, we only attempt to demonstrate the critical parts here. The complete code, data and Jupyter notebooks can be found at our online repository.

6.6.1   Coffee Quality Example

The first example is about supplier selection based on coffee quality. The data for this example contain different quality measures for coffee rating according to Coffee Quality Institute (CQI), as well as other metadata including coffee processing method, owner, country of origin, farm name, and altitude, etc. In this example, we try to achieve the following objectives with the information we have from the data:

- Coffee quality ranking by country
- Top ten high-quality coffee suppliers
- Visualize global coffee suppliers
- Important features for coffee quality prediction

To begin with, let us first import the necessary modules into the notebook:

Ex. 6.1
```
import warnings
warnings.filterwarnings("ignore")

import pandas as pd
import numpy as np
from datetime import datetime

import matplotlib.pyplot as plt
import seaborn as sns
```

Next, load the data:

Ex. 6.2
```
# Load the data
df = pd.read_csv('Coffee_data.csv', index_col=0)
```

After the initial data cleaning process, which is not demonstrated here, we derive a cleaner dataset train for further analysis:

Ex. 6.3

```
train.info()
```

```
<class 'pandas.core.frame.DataFrame'>
Int64Index: 1309 entries, 1 to 1310
Data columns (total 22 columns):
Owner.1                  1309 non-null object
Country.of.Origin        1309 non-null object
Harvest.Year             1263 non-null object
Grading.Date             1309 non-null object
Processing.Method        1159 non-null object
Aroma                    1309 non-null float64
Flavor                   1309 non-null float64
Aftertaste               1309 non-null float64
Acidity                  1309 non-null float64
Body                     1309 non-null float64
Balance                  1309 non-null float64
Uniformity               1309 non-null float64
Clean.Cup                1309 non-null float64
Sweetness                1309 non-null float64
Cupper.Points            1309 non-null float64
Total.Cup.Points         1309 non-null float64
Moisture                 1309 non-null float64
Category.One.Defects     1309 non-null int64
Category.Two.Defects     1309 non-null int64
Quakers                  1309 non-null int64
Expiration               1309 non-null object
altitude_mean_meters     1217 non-null float64
dtypes: float64(13), int64(3), object(6)
memory usage: 235.2+ KB
```

As can been seen, the data contains a total of 22 columns with 1309 samples in most cases. Note that on the column list from `Aroma` down to `Cupper.Points`, these are the ten quality measures for evaluating coffee quality. The `Total.Cup.Points`, as the indicator of coffee quality, is the sum of these ten quality measures evaluated by CQI certified reviewers for certification.

To prepare the data for later analysis, we need to perform further feature engineering on certain columns. First, let us take a look at `Grading.Date` and parse it to datetime object:

Ex. 6.4

```
train['Grading.Date'].head()
```

```
1       April 4th, 2015
2       April 4th, 2015
3        May 31st, 2010
4      March 26th, 2015
5       April 4th, 2015
Name: Grading.Date, dtype: object
```

Ex. 6.5

```
# Parse Grading date
train['GradingDate'] = pd.to_datetime(train['Grading.Date'],
                                        infer_datetime_format=True
train.GradingDate.head()
1    2015-04-04
2    2015-04-04
3    2010-05-31
4    2015-03-26
5    2015-04-04
Name: GradingDate, dtype: datetime64[ns]
```

Then, we create a new feature named 'GradingYear' using the code below:

Ex. 6.6

```
# Create new Grading Year feature
train['GradingYear'] = train.GradingDate.dt.year
```

Likewise, we create an 'ExpireYear' feature based on certificate 'Expiration' date with the same method. In addition, there are missing values in 'Harvest.Year' column, let us first check how many unique values are there in the column:

Ex. 6.7

```
train['Harvest.Year'].unique()
array(['2014', nan, '2013', '2012', '2010', '2009', '2015', '2011',
       '2016', '2017', 'mmm', 'TEST', '2018', '2008'], dtype=object
```

We notice that there are three non-year values in the data. Let us find out how many entries contain 'mmm' and 'TEST':

Ex. 6.8

```
train[train['Harvest.Year'] == 'mmm'].append(
    train[train['Harvest.Year'] == 'TEST'])
```

	Owner.1	Country.of.Origin	Harvest.Year	Grading.Date	Processing.Method	Aroma	Flavor	After
170	Daniel Friedlander	Brazil	mmm	March 23rd, 2011		NaN	7.81	7.81
171	Alexandra Katona-Carroll	Brazil	TEST	March 22nd, 2011		NaN	8.17	7.67

2 rows × 25 columns

As shown above, there are only two rows that contain the text values. We can either drop these two rows or replace the missing values with some estimates. However, if we look closely, it seems that most values in 'Harvest.Year' match the values in 'GradingYear'. Thus, we can replace all the missing values by using the year obtained from 'GradingYear'. Consider below:

Ex. 6.9

```
# Replace the missing value with 2011
train.loc[[170,171], 'Harvest.Year'] = '2011'
train.loc[train['Harvest.Year'].isnull(),'Harvest.Year']= train.loc\
            [train['Harvest.Year'].isnull(), 'GradingYear']
```

After completing this step, we can proceed to parse the values in 'Harvest. Year' to datatime.year as we did earlier (omitted here).

Next, we need to convert the text values in 'Processing.Method' into dummy variables for later analytics purpose. First, we should check how many unique processing methods are recorded in the column:

Ex. 6.10

```
train['Processing.Method'].unique()
array(['Washed / Wet', nan, 'Natural / Dry', 'Pulped natural / honey',
       'Semi-washed / Semi-pulped', 'Other'], dtype=object)
```

As can be seen, there are a total of six processing methods, including the NaN value. For simplicity, we can keep NaN as an unknown method when dummy coding it. Consider below:

Ex. 6.11

```
# Dummy coding Processing Method
dummies = pd.get_dummies(train['Processing.Method'], dummy_na=True)
dummies.head()
```

	Natural / Dry	Other	Pulped natural / honey	Semi-washed / Semi-pulped	Washed / Wet	nan
1	0	0	0	0	1	0
2	0	0	0	0	1	0
3	0	0	0	0	0	1
4	1	0	0	0	0	0
5	0	0	0	0	1	0

After creating the dummies DataFrame, we can join it with the train DataFrame using pandas.concat() method:

Ex. 6.12

```
# Join the dummy-coded process methods with train data
train = pd.concat([train, dummies], axis=1)
```

The final feature that contains missing value is 'altitude_mean_meters'. We can either replace the missing values with the overall mean altitude across all regions, or with the regional mean for each particular origin. The latter seems to be a better option.

To achieve this, we can use the `Groupby transform` method. Recall that the `transform` method returns an object that is indexed the same (same size) as the one being grouped.

Ex. 6.13

```
train.loc[train.altitude_mean_meters.isnull(),'altitude_mean_meters']=\
train.groupby('Country.of.Origin')['altitude_mean_meters'].transform('mean')
```

We can now drop all the duplicate columns and rename the remaining columns with a shorter format using the following code:

Ex. 6.14

```
# Drop the dupliate values
train.drop(columns=['Harvest.Year', 'Grading.Date', 'GradingDate',
                    'Expiration', 'Processing.Method'], inplace=True)
# Rename columns
train.rename(columns={'Owner.1': 'Owner', 'Country.of.Origin': 'Origin',
                    'Clean.Cup': 'CleanCup', 'Cupper.Points': 'CupperPoints',
                    'Total.Cup.Points': 'TCP', 'Category.One.Defects': 'C1D',
                    'Category.Two.Defects': 'C2D', 'altitude_mean_meters':
                    'AltitudeMean'}, inplace=True)
```

As mentioned earlier, 'TCP' is the sum of all the values from the ten quality measures. We can create a preliminary heatmap to check whether there are other features that are highly correlated with 'TCP'. Consider below:

Ex. 6.15

```
# Create a correlation heatmap
corr = train.corr()

# Generate a mask for the upper triangle
mask = np.zeros_like(corr, dtype=np.bool)
mask[np.triu_indices_from(mask)] = True

# Set up the matplotlib figure
sns.set(style="white")
f, ax = plt.subplots(figsize=(11, 9))

# Generate a custom diverging colormap
cmap = sns.diverging_palette(220, 10, as_cmap=True)

# Draw the heatmap with the mask and correct aspect ratio
sns.heatmap(corr, mask=mask, cmap=cmap, vmax=.9, center=0,
            square=True, linewidths=.5, cbar_kws={"shrink": .5});
```

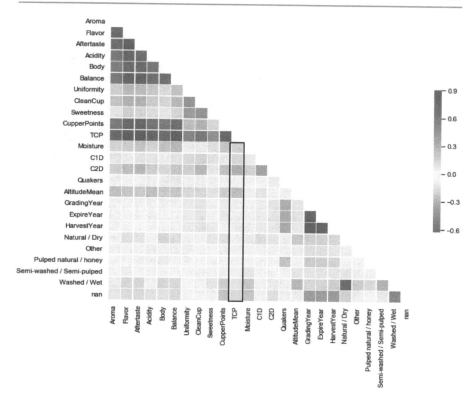

As shown above, `Moister`, `C1D` and `C2D` defects seem to have an obvious negative correlation with `TCP`, whereas the altitude and the unknown processing method (i.e., NaN) seem to be positively related to `TCP`.

Up until this point, we have obtained a training set which allows us to perform further analysis and address our initial objectives. First, to rank the coffee quality by country, we can simply use `Groupby` method and display the results with a `barplot`. See below:

Ex. 6.16

```
# Ranking by the mean of CQI index TCP
tcp_by_origin = train.groupby('Origin')['TCP'].mean().\
                    sort_values(ascending=False)

fig, ax = plt.subplots(figsize=(8,10))
ax=sns.barplot(y=tcp_by_origin.index, x=tcp_by_origin.values,
            ax=ax, orient="h", palette = "copper")
ax.set_title('Overall Coffee Quality by Country', fontsize=16);
```

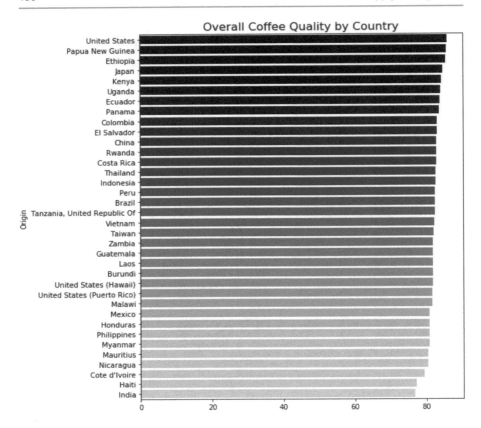

Likewise, we can rank top 20 coffee suppliers with highest average TCP points, consider below:

Ex. 6.17

```
tcp_by_owner = train.groupby('Owner')['TCP'].mean().nlargest(20)

fig, ax = plt.subplots(figsize=(8,10))
ax=sns.barplot(y=tcp_by_owner.index, x=tcp_by_owner.values,
          ax=ax, orient="h", palette = "copper")
ax.set_title('Top 20 Quality Coffee Suppliers', fontsize=16);
```

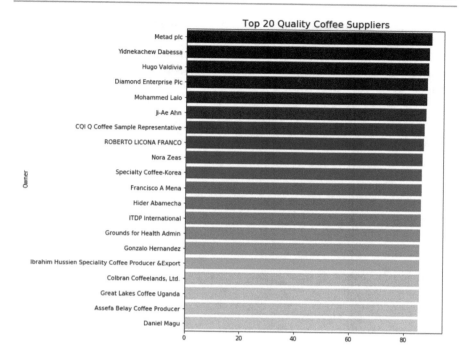

The next task is to map the coffee suppliers by origin on a world map. To do so, let us first sort out the number of suppliers by origin (results are truncated for brevity):

Ex. 6.18

```
suppliers_by_origin = train.groupby('Origin')['Owner'].\
                      nunique().sort_values(ascending=False)
suppliers_by_origin
Origin
Mexico                            112
Tanzania, United Republic Of       30
Ethiopia                           21
Colombia                           20
Costa Rica                         19
Brazil                             18
Kenya                              13
Uganda                             13
Honduras                           12
Nicaragua                          11
Guatemala                          11
Indonesia                          11
Myanmar                             8
Peru                                6
El Salvador                         6
Thailand                            5
Philippines                         4
China                               4
United States (Hawaii)              3
Panama                              3
United States                       3
Taiwan                              3
Vietnam                             2    ...
```

Geospatial visualization is useful in many business applications, for example, to display locations of suppliers, delivery routes, customers hotspots, traffic information and demographics. In this exercise, we use a simple but effective geo-plotting tool called GeoPandas that makes working with geospatial data in Python easier. For more details, see GeoPandas documentation (geopandas.org).

The quickest way to install the package is through Anaconda Distribution with `conda` package manager. Once installed, we can import and use it in the notebook:

Ex. 6.19

```
import geopandas as gpd
```

The `gpd.read_file()` method can read almost any vector-based spatial data format and return a GeoDataFrame object. Let us load some example data from `gpd.datasets`:

Ex. 6.20

```
world = gpd.read_file(gpd.datasets.get_path('naturalearth_lowres'))
world.head()
```

	pop_est	continent	name	iso_a3	gdp_md_est	geometry
0	28400000.0	Asia	Afghanistan	AFG	22270.0	POLYGON ((61.21081709172574 35.65007233330923,...
1	12799293.0	Africa	Angola	AGO	110300.0	(POLYGON ((16.32652835456705 -5.87747039146621...
2	3639453.0	Europe	Albania	ALB	21810.0	POLYGON ((20.59024743010491 41.85540416113361,...
3	4798491.0	Asia	United Arab Emirates	ARE	184300.0	POLYGON ((51.57951867046327 24.24549713795111,...
4	40913584.0	South America	Argentina	ARG	573900.0	(POLYGON ((-65.50000000000003 -55.199999999999...

We can then simply plot the world map with the following code:

Ex. 6.21

```
world.plot();
```

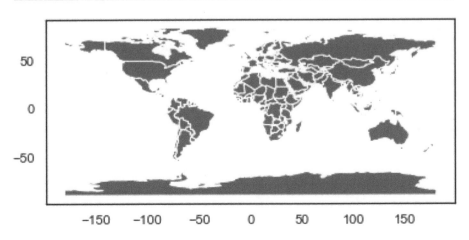

Going back to our original task, in order to plot suppliers by their origins on the world map, we need to merge the world geodata with suppliers by origin data. After performing several transformations (omitted here for brevity), we can obtain a dataset that contains the origin, geometry and suppliers information for plotting purpose. Consider below:

Ex. 6.22

```
fig, ax = plt.subplots(1, 1, figsize=(15,8))

world_coffee.plot(column='Owner', ax=ax,
                  cmap="Paired", legend=True)
ax.axis('off');
ax.set_title("World Major Coffee Suppliers Map", fontsize=16);
```

We can see from the map that most suppliers are located around the Equator. Mexico that has the most coffee suppliers is highlighted with brown colour on the map. Similarly, we can plot a coffee quality world map using the TCP values by region (coding is omitted here):

6.7   Regression Algorithms

Regression analysis is a very common statistical method for estimating the relationships between a depend variable (often called 'outcome' variable or 'target' and denoted by y) and one or more independent variables (often called 'input' variable or 'features' and denoted by x). It can help analyse the strength of the relationships, answering questions such as whether those features indeed have an impact? what features matter most and which can we neglect? In supply chain analytics, the machine learning models that borrow or 'steal' algorithms from statistics are primarily concerned with minimizing the error of a model and making the most accurate predictions possible.

6.7.1   Linear Regression

Linear regression, or *ordinary least squares* (OLS), is the simplest and most widely used technique for regression tasks. You might have been familiar with the simplest form of a linear regression model, i.e.,

$$y = ax + b \tag{6.1}$$

where,

- a is commonly known as the *slope*, or *coefficient*
- b is commonly known as the *intercept*.

When there are more features, (i.e., multiple x values), the equation can be expressed as:

Fig. 6.13 The residuals

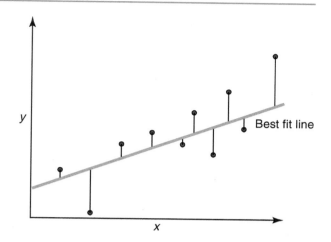

$$y = \beta_0 + \beta_1 x_1 + \beta_2 x_2 + \cdots + \beta_n x_n + \varepsilon \tag{6.2}$$

where, ε is commonly known as the *error term*, or sometimes *residual*.

The objective of the OLS is to minimize the sum of the squared errors. The errors or residuals, as indicated in Fig. 6.13, are the vertical lines showing the difference between the datapoint (actual value) and the best-fit line (predicted value).

We can use the OLS model to estimate the coefficients values when there are more than one input variables. The approach treats the data as a matrix and uses linear algebra operations to estimate the optimal values for the coefficients.

In Python, scikit-learn includes `LinearRegression` estimator with which we can fit the data and construct the best-fit line. As an example, let us train an OLS model and use it to predict the coffee quality in our previous example. Recall that the TCP value is the sum of the ten quality measures. Thus, we will not select these measures but the other features to predict the TCP values. Consider below:

Ex. 6.23

```
train_reg = train [['TCP', 'Moisture', 'C1D', 'C2D', 'Quakers',
                    'AltitudeMean', 'HarvestYear', 'Natural / Dry',
                    'Other', 'Pulped natural / honey', np.nan,
                    'Semi-washed / Semi-pulped','Washed / Wet']]
```

Next, we import necessary models from scikit-learn to train the data. Specifically, the `train_test_split` function can quickly split data into random train and test subsets. The train subset is for training the model, while the test subset is for evaluating the performance of the model.

Ex. 6.24

```
# Split the data
X = train_reg.drop(columns=['TCP'])
y = train_reg.TCP

X_train, X_test, y_train, y_test = train_test_split(
    X, y, test_size=0.2, random_state=42)
```

We will use X_train and y_train subsets to train the model, and use X_test and y_test to evaluate the model performance. The training process is very simple, as illustrated below:

Ex. 6.25

```
# train the model
ols = LinearRegression(fit_intercept=True)
ols.fit(X_train, y_train)
```
```
LinearRegression(copy_X=True, fit_intercept=True, n_jobs=None, normal
ize=False)
```

Once the OLS model is trained, the *intercept* is stored in the intercept_ attribute of the model, while the *coefficients* are stored in the coef_ attribute.

Ex. 6.26

```
print("Model intercept:", ols.intercept_)
print("Model coefficients:", ols.coef_)
```
```
Model intercept: 109.28884013563865
Model coefficients: [-6.53429830e+00 -4.57837911e-02 -1.21188055e-01  1.85885034e-01
  1.54143940e-03 -1.38603777e-02  2.78141044e-01 -1.08138637e+00
  4.10811642e-01  3.05374745e-01  5.72219477e-01 -4.85160541e-01]
```

We can then use the trained model to make predictions on the test set, consider below:

Ex. 6.27

```
# make prediction
y_pred = ols.predict(X_test)
```

To evaluate the performance of the model, here we use Root Mean Square Error (RMSE), i.e., the standard deviation of the residuals. In addition, we can use R-squared value (i.e., r^2), which is the coefficient of determination. The R-square normally has a value between 0 and 1, indicating how much of the variance in y (target variable) can be explained by independent variable x. When $r^2 = 1$, it means that the model can explain full variability in y, while $r^2 = 0$ indicates that the fitted model cannot explain any variability in the target variable.

To calculate these RMSE and R-square values, we can import the following functions from `sklearn.metrics`. Consider below:

Ex. 6.28

```
from sklearn.metrics import mean_squared_error, r2_score

mse = mean_squared_error(y_test, y_pred)
rmse = np.sqrt(mse)
r2 = r2_score(y_test, y_pred)

print('RMSE score: %.4f' % rmse)
print('R-Square score: %.2f' % r2)
RMSE score: 2.3539
R-Square score: 0.18
```

Alternately, to get R-square value, you can simply use the `score` method of the trained model, i.e., `ols.score()`. It is clear that 0.18 is not a good R-square score in this example. With regard to RMSE, in general, there is no absolute good or bad threshold for it. However, let us, take a look at the statistics of the target variable `y_test`:

Ex. 6.29

```
y_test.describe()
count     262.000000
mean       82.082290
std         2.607192
min        70.670000
25%        81.020000
50%        82.625000
75%        83.670000
max        87.080000
Name: TCP, dtype: float64
```

The values of TCP in the test set range between 70.67 and 87.08. An estimation error of 2.35 is not great but not too bad either. However, a further examination of the R-square value on the train set returns a similar low score ($r^2 = 0.15$), which may reveal that the trained model is underfitting the data. This usually happens when the included features cannot fully explain the variance in the target variable, or the model is not powerful enough.

There are different ways to fix the underfitting problem, including training the same model with better or more useful features, or using a different model. In this example, we will try different regression models to see how they perform. In the notebook however, we cover two additional regularized linear regression models for demonstration purpose, i.e., **Ridge Regression** and **Lasso Regression**. These two regression models are often useful when there are collinearity issues in the data and OLS overfits the training data.

6.7.2   Support Vector Machines

Support Vector Machines (SVMs) are simple yet powerful supervised learning models that can be used for classification and regression analysis as well as outliers detection. Since its introduction in 1990s by Vladimir Vapnik and his colleagues (Vapnik 1995), SVM has gained popularity and been successfully applied in many fields. The way that an SVM algorithm works is to define a hyperplane (or set of hyperplanes) in a high-dimensional feature space, which separates the training data in the feature space so that all the points with the same label are on the same side of the hyperplane(s) (Cortes and Vapnik 1995).

As illustrated in Fig. 6.14, *support vectors* are the datapoints that define the margin of largest separation between the two classes. The *hyperplane* can be defined here as the linear decision function with maximal margin between the vectors of the two classes. Assume the linearly separable case (hard margin), in a 2-dimensional feature space as shown in Fig. 6.14, the hyperplane can be a linear straight line (while in a 3D feature space, the hyperplane becomes a 2-dimensioanl plane). For a set of training data, x_i ($i = 1, 2, ..., N$), the hyperplane can be defined as:

$$w^T x + b = 0 \qquad (6.3)$$

where, w is an N-dimensional weight vector, and b is a bias term.

The datapoints of each class can only be $y = 1$ (i.e., Class 1 in Fig. 6.14), or $y = -1$ (i.e., Class 2) on either side of the hyperplane. Two margins that control the separability of the data can then be defined as:

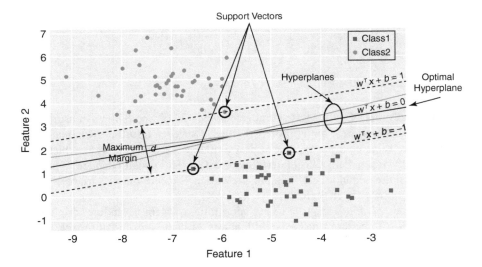

Fig. 6.14 A separable problem in a 2-dimensional feature space with SVM

$$w^T x + b \begin{cases} \geq 1 & \text{for } y_i = 1 \\ \leq -1 & \text{for } y_i = -1 \end{cases} \tag{6.4}$$

In general, there are many possible solutions of hyperplanes, but SVMs construct the optimal hyperplane by taking into account a small amount of the training data, i.e., support vectors. You can think of SVMs as maximizing the margin (i.e., finding the widest possible 'street') between the classes, a.k.a. large margin classification. Hence, it becomes an optimization problem to find the best hyperplane whereby the margin of separation d is maximized, which can be represented by the following equation:

$$d(w, b; x) = \frac{\left|\left(w^T x + b + 1\right) - \left(w^T x + b - 1\right)\right|}{\|w\|} = \frac{2}{\|w\|} \tag{6.5}$$

Thus, in order to maximize the margin, we need to minimize the dimensional vector $\|w\|$, which can be also written as $\frac{1}{2} w^T w$. The optimization problem of finding the optimal hyperplane can be then expressed as:

$$\text{Min}_{w,b} = \frac{1}{2} w^T w \tag{6.6}$$

$$s.t. \quad y_i \left(w^T x + b\right) \geq 1$$

which is subject to the constraint of the margins of two classes.

It can be solved by the Lagrange multiplier method. However, we will not go further on the mathematics behind the algorithms here, as it is beyond the scope of this book. For interested readers, see **Support Vector Machines** section of scikit-learn documentation.

There are also occasions in which data are linearly non-separable (soft margin). Nevertheless, a linear SVM might still be able to solve the problem by introducing a penalty function:

$$f(x) = \sum_{i=1}^{N} \xi_i \tag{6.7}$$

where ξ_i is the distance between the misclassified data of each class and the margin of that class. Then, the optimization function can be rewritten as:

$$\text{Min}_{w,b} = \frac{1}{2} w^T w + C \sum_{i=1}^{N} \xi_i \tag{6.8}$$

$$s.t. \quad y_i \left(w^T x + b\right) \geq 1 - \xi_i$$

$$\xi_i \geq 0, \quad i = 1, \ldots, N$$

where C is the 'trade-off' parameter used to control the strength of the penalty, and thus, acts as an inverse regularization parameter.

For non-linear case, an SVM might not have a good generalization ability even though an optimal hyperplane might be found. To solve the problem, the training data can be mapped onto a higher dimensional feature space so that a linear support vector classifier (SVC) can be created to separate them. Different kernel functions can be used for non-linear data classifications. We will leave SVCs until when we face classification problems in later chapters.

SVMs can also be extended to solve regression problems. This method is called Support Vector Regression (SVR) (Drucker et al. 1997). Similar to support vector classification, the SVR model depends only on a subset of the training data. However, instead of finding the widest possible 'street' between two classes while limiting margin violations as in SVC, SVR tries to include as many datapoints as possible **on** the street while limiting margin violations. The margin of the street is controlled by an insensitivity parameter ε, thereby the decision function is chosen so that it has the minimum deviation from the parameter. It is called insensitivity parameter because adding more training datapoints within the margin would not affect the prediction outcome. The SVR model considers the rest datapoints outside the margins for finding the optimal hyperplane with the help of slack variables ξ_i (see Fig. 6.15).

Specifically, the SVR model solves the following primal problem:

$$\text{M in}_{w,b,\xi,\xi'} = \frac{1}{2}w^T w + C\sum_{i=1}^{N}\left(\xi_i + \xi'_i\right) \tag{6.9}$$

$$s.t. \quad y_i - w^T\phi\left(x_i\right) - b \le \varepsilon + \xi_i,$$

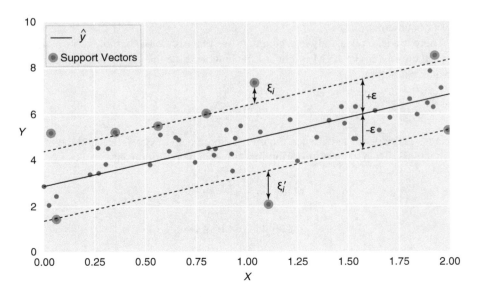

Fig. 6.15 Linear support vector regression

$$w^T \phi(x_i) + b - y_i \leq \varepsilon + \xi'_i,$$

$$\xi_i, \xi'_i \geq 0, \ i = 1, \ldots, N$$

where ξ_i or ξ'_i is zero if the datapoint is within the margins. ϕ is the identity function. Likewise, the optimization problem can be solved using Lagrange multiplier method, which will not be discussed further here.

The idea behind the development of non-linear SVR is the basically same but would require mapping data onto a high-dimensional space in certain cases. Again, different kernel functions can be used to formulate the algorithm of the SVR for non-linear data analysis; however, we will not dive into the details of these kernel types here. The scikit-learn implementation of SVR includes `linear`, `polynomial`, the Radial Basis Function (RBF), `sigmoid` and `precomputed`. In Fig. 6.16, a comparison

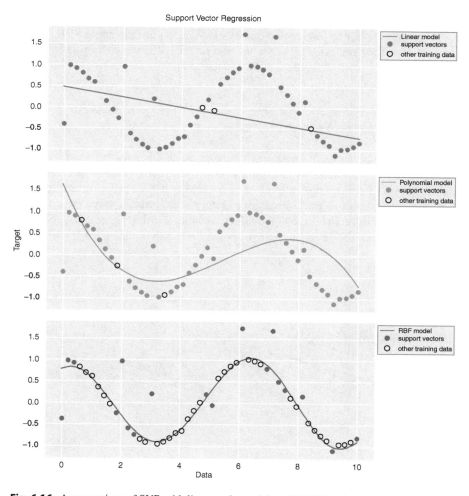

Fig. 6.16 A comparison of SVR with linear, polynomial and RBF Kernels

is drawn using linear, polynomial and RBF kernels. As can be seen, the RBF kernel out-performs the other two in the example.

> **Note:** Selecting appropriate kernel functions is largely contingent on the nature of the data; however, as a rule of thumb, the RBF (Gaussian) kernel function generally works well and can be used as a first choice when the training set is not very large. For large datasets, consider using sklearn.svm.LinearSVR.

Returning to our previous coffee quality example, let us train some SVR models and see how they perform. First, we use the linear SVR, which can be imported from `sklearn.svm.LinearSVR`, consider below:

Ex. 6.30

```
# Linear SV regression
from sklearn.svm import LinearSVR
```

This class supports both dense and sparse input, and has more flexibility in the selection of penalties and loss functions. It also works better with large datasets. In particular, `epsilon` (*default=0.0*) is the ε parameter in the epsilon-insensitive loss function, which controls the ε-insensitive margin as described earlier. Note that the value of ε depends on the scale of the target variable, and the bigger ε, the wider the 'street', and hence the fewer support vectors are selected (see Fig. 6.17).

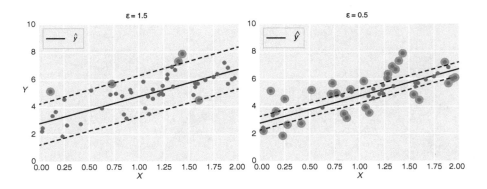

Fig. 6.17 ε and support vectors

C (*default=1.0*) is the regularization parameter, which controls the trade-off between the margin and the size of the slack variables. The strength of the regularization is inversely proportional to C. A small value will increase the number of training errors, whereas a large C value (e.g., C = ∞) will lead to hard margin SVM. You are recommended to go through its parameters, attributes, methods and examples on scikit-learn documentation of **LinearSVR** yourself.

Now, let us train a LinearSVR model with the coffee data. Notice that SVMs are sensitive to feature scales. The data that we are going to use have already been standardized with the `StandardScaler` tool of scikit-learn for training the previous Ridge and Lasso Regressions models. The transformation process however is omitted here, for details on the feature scaling check the notebook. Consider below:

Ex. 6.31

```
lsvr = LinearSVR(fit_intercept=False, epsilon=0.7,
                 random_state=42, max_iter=4000)

lsvr.fit(X_train_std, y_train_std)
y_pred_lsvr = lsvr.predict(X_test_std)
```

We have trained a LinearSVR estimator and used it for predicting the target variables. Likewise, we can use the RMSE and *R*-square values to evaluate the performance of estimator. Since we have standardized the data, we need to inversely transform the data back to the original representation for RMSE calculation:

Ex. 6.32

```
# Scale back the data to the original representation
y_pred_lsvr_inverse = y_scaler.inverse_transform(y_pred_lsvr)

# Accuracy
rmse_lsvr = np.sqrt(mean_squared_error(y_test, y_pred_lsvr_inverse))
print('LinearSVR RMSE Score: %.4f' % rmse_lsvr)
print('Variance score: %.4f' % lsvr.score(X_test_std, y_test_std))
LinearSVR RMSE Score: 2.3498
Variance score: 0.1846
```

The results are slightly better than those of the OLS estimator. With some calibrations on the values of the parameters, you could possibly get even better results. However, instead of making such an attempt, let us try to use the kernel functions in the `sklearn.svm.SVR` implementation (note that the kernel parameter is defaulted to '*rbf*'). Consider below:

Ex. 6.33

```
# Non-linear SVR
from sklearn.svm import SVR

svr = SVR(kernel='rbf', degree=2, C=3, epsilon=0.6)
svr.fit(X_train_std, y_train_std)
y_pred_svr = svr.predict(X_test_std)

y_pred_svr_inverse = y_scaler.inverse_transform(y_pred_svr)
rmse_svr = np.sqrt(mean_squared_error(y_test, y_pred_svr_inverse))

print('SVR RMSE Score: %.4f' % rmse_svr)
print('Variance score: %.4f' % svr.score(X_test_std, y_test_std))
```
```
SVR RMSE Score: 2.2848
Variance score: 0.2291
```

The SVR model using the RBF kernel has made better improvement on the performance. With a bit of twist on the hyperparameters, we could get even better results. We will come back to this point when we introduce the Grid Search method for searching best parameters for an estimator.

6.7.3 Decision Trees

Decision Trees are versatile and popular methods for decision analysis. A decision tree, as its name suggests, uses a tree-like model of decisions and their possible outcomes in which it starts with a root node at the top, and then splits into branches, internal nodes and leaves. As shown in Fig. 6.18, a decision tree mainly consists of the following components:

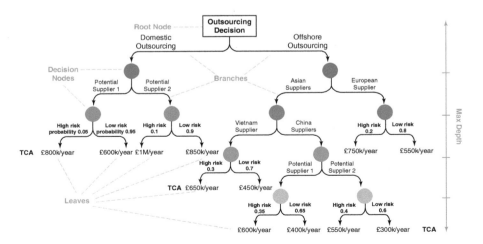

Fig. 6.18 An illustration of a decision tree

- **Root Node**: The starting point of a decision tree, which represents the entire population or sample, and then further splits into two or more homogeneous sets. In our case, Outsourcing Decision.
- **Branches**: They are the splits out of a node, which represent the outcome of the node splitting, e.g., Domestic Outsourcing and Offshore Outsourcing.
- **Decision nodes**: The nodes that can be further split into sub-nodes. Here for example, if we decided to go ahead with domestic outsourcing, we have two options, i.e., Supplier 1 and Supplier 2.
- **Leaves** (or Terminal Nodes): These are the nodes that have no further splits. Here we have, for example, TCA £800 k/year for Supplier 1 if it was a high-risk probability.

Decision tree algorithms are among the most popular machine learning methods used for classification and regression. The objective of tree learning is to predict the value of a target variable by learning simple decision rules inferred from data features. When the target variables are a discrete set of values, the decision tree models are called **Classification Trees** (i.e., leaves represent class labels), whereas when the target variables are continuous values, the tree models are called **Regression Trees.** There are other decision tree algorithms however in this book we mainly focus on classifications and regression trees (i.e., **CART**). For different tree algorithms and more details regarding the advantages and disadvantages of each, see **Decision Trees** section of scikit-learn documentation.

The Decision Trees algorithms work as the following steps:

1. Place the best feature of the dataset with the highest predictive power at the root node.
2. Split the dataset into subsets based on the feature. Subsets should contain data with the same value for a feature.
3. Continue tree building by repeating step 1 and step 2 until there are only leaves in all the branches of the tree.

Different tree algorithms use different metrics for choosing the 'best' feature (e.g., Information Gain, Gini Index or Gain Ratio). The CART models create binary splits with the feature and threshold that yield the largest information gain at each node. In particular, Gini impurity is used by CART for classification trees. It is a measure of the probability of incorrectly labelling a randomly chosen element according to the distribution of labels in the dataset. Suppose we have K classes, then the Gini Impurity can be calculated as:

$$\text{Gini} = \sum_{i=1}^{K} p_i \left(1 - p_i\right) \tag{6.10}$$

where, $i \in \{1, 2, ..., K\}$, and p_i is the probability of a datapoint labelled with class i in the set.

When training a classification tree, the best split is chosen by maximizing the Gini Gain, which is calculated by subtracting the weighted Gini score of the branches from the original Gini score. The tree keeps splitting and stops until it detects no further gain can be made, or some pre-set stopping rules are met (e.g., not enough samples to make another split).

For regression problems, CART uses different splitting criteria to determine the splitting points. When the target variable of regression tree is a continuous value, two common criteria, i.e., Mean Squared Error (MSE), which minimizes the $L2$ error using mean values at leaves (or terminal nodes), and Mean Absolute Error (MAE), which minimizes the $L1$ error using median values at leaves, are used for determining locations for splits. Note that $L1$ (i.e., Least Absolute Deviations) and $L2$ (i.e., Least Square Errors) are two loss functions in machine learning which are used to minimize the error.

Decision Trees are simple to understand and to interpret. They require little data preparation. However, in practice, Decision Trees tend to overfit on data with a large number of features, and thus getting the right ratio of samples to features is important. There are different techniques to control overfitting. For example, in scikit-learn implementation, limiting the `max_depth` (i.e., the maximum depth of the tree) to control the size of the tree, setting `min_samples_split` (i.e., the minimum number of samples an internal node must have before it can be split) or `min_samples_leaf` (i.e., the minimum number of samples a leaf node must have), to ensure that multiple samples inform every decision in the tree, by controlling which splits will be considered.

In addition, to improve the performance of a decision tree, pruning can be used to remove the branches that make use of features with low importance. Minimal Cost-Complexity Pruning is a popular algorithm used to control the size of a tree, thereby reducing its complexity and increasing its predictive power by reducing overfitting. This pruning technique adopts a learning parameter (alpha) to weigh whether nodes should be removed based on the size of the sub-tree. Greater alpha values increase the number of nodes pruned.

In scikit-learn implementation, it uses an optimized version of the CART algorithm; however, the implementation does not support categorical variables at the point when the book is written. In this section, we mainly focus on solving regression problems with the `DecisionTreeRegressor` class of scikit-learn. In later chapters where we perform classification tasks, `DecisionTreeClassifier` will be introduced.

The `DecisionTreeRegressor` model is capable of finding complex non-linear relationships in the data. It is useful not only in making predictions, but also in selecting important features. You are recommended to go through the **User Guide** of the regressor on scikit-learn documentation to learn its various parameters, methods, attributes, and examples yourself.

As an example, let us consider our coffee suppliers example. First, we need to import the estimator from `sklearn.tree.DecisionTreeRegressor`.

Ex. 6.34

```
from sklearn.tree import DecisionTreeRegressor
```

Now, let us use the model to predict the coffee quality TCQ values. To initialize the model, we keep most default settings in the parameters, and set `max_depth=4`. Recall that the `max_depth` is used to control the size of the tree to prevent over-fitting. In practice, you can start with a small value (e.g., 3 or 4) as initial tree depth and see how the tree is fitting to your data, and then gradually increase the depth.

Ex. 6.35

```
tree = DecisionTreeRegressor(max_depth=4, random_state=42)
tree.fit(X_train_std, y_train_std)
y_pred_tree = tree.predict(X_test_std)
```

Note: Decision Trees require little data preparation, i.e., they do not require feature scaling, data normalization or centring at all. However, missing values are not supported in the tree models.

Likewise, we can use the RMSE value to check the accuracy of estimator. Recall that we need to inversely transform the data back to the original representation for RMSE calculation since the data have been standardized. Consider below:

Ex. 6.36

```
# Scale back the data to the original representation
y_pred_tree_inverse = y_scaler.inverse_transform(y_pred_tree)

rmse_tree = np.sqrt(mean_squared_error(y_test, y_pred_tree_inverse))
print('Tree RMSE Score: %.3f' % rmse_tree)
Tree RMSE Score: 2.292
```

To get R-square value, we can use the `score` method of the estimator:

Ex. 6.37

```
print("R2 on training set: {:.3f}".format(
    tree.score(X_train_std, y_train_std)))
print("R2 on test set: {:.3f}".format(
    tree.score(X_test_std, y_test_std)))
R2 on training set: 0.248
R2 on test set: 0.224
```

It can be seen that this Decision Tree estimator performs better than the initial OLS model but is not as good as the RBF SVR estimator. You can try out different parameter settings and see if you could get even better outcome.

6.7.4 Cross-Validation

Another way to evaluate an estimator's performance is to use **cross-validation**. A prediction model can learn well on the training data but might perform poorly on yet-unseen data (i.e., overfitting on the training data). Therefore, we hold out part of the data as a *test set* using scikit-learn's `train_test_split` helper function. After training the models on the *training set* as in our previous examples, we used them to make predictions and then compared the results to the withheld target values of the test set. This allows us to calculate performance measures for the models on the test dataset (e.g., RSME and *R*-square) and get an estimate of the ability of the trained models on unseen data.

However, when adjusting different parameters settings for estimators (e.g., C in SVR), there is still a risk of knowledge about the test set 'leaking' into the estimator and thus, the evaluation metrics no longer report on generalization performance. To avoid this, we can hold out another so-called *validation set* to evaluate the performance and use the test set for final evaluation. Unless we have a lot of data to split however, partitioning the available data into three sets significantly reduces the size of the training set for training the model and the results can be uncertain depending on a particular random choice for the pair of the training and validation sets.

To solve the problem, we can use *k*-fold cross-validation instead, whereby the training set is split into smaller *k* sets (see Fig. 6.19). An estimator can be trained using $(k-1)$ folds as training data and validated on the remaining fold as validation

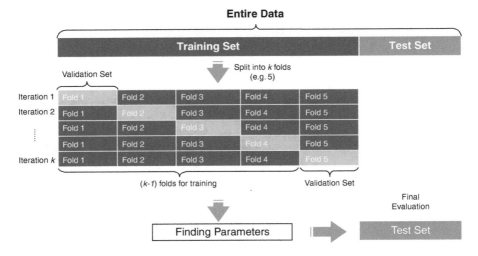

Fig. 6.19 *k*-fold cross-validation

set. The performance scores (e.g., accuracy) of the trained estimator are reported by
k-fold cross-validation (i.e., k iterations) and the average of the values can be used
as an estimate of the ability of the trained estimator.

Although this approach can be computationally expensive, the main advantages
of it are that it does not reduce the size of training data and that there is no risk of
'leaking' knowledge about the test set into the trained model as the test set is hold
out for final evaluation only.

Scikit-learn implements a few cross-validation helper functions that especially useful in certain situations. The most efficient and convenient one is the
cross_val_score helper function. As an example, let us use it to compute
the cross-validated metrics for our trained Decision Tree model and SVR model.
Consider below:

Ex. 6.38

```
# Evaluate models using cross-validation
from sklearn.model_selection import cross_val_score
```

One important parameter in this function is scoring, which by default is set to
the score method of the estimator. However, we can change the scoring parameter
to other scorer objects for specific estimator evaluation. Some of the common scorer
objects are listed below (Table 6.3). For a full list of all available values, check '**The
scoring parameter: defining model evaluation rules**' section of scikit-learn
documentation.

Note that all scorer objects follow the convention that higher return values are
better than lower return values. Thus, you can find 'neg_' sign at the beginning of
some scorer objects (e.g., 'neg_mean_absolute_error'). In our example, we will set
scoring to 'neg_root_mean_squared_error'. Consider below where we first evaluate the Decision Tree model using fivefolds cross-validation:

Table 6.3 Common scoring values

Scoring	Function
'accuracy'	metrics.accuracy_score
'f1'	metrics.f1_score
'precision' etc.	metrics.precision_score
'recall' etc.	metrics.recall_score
'roc_auc'	metrics.roc_auc_score
'explained_variance'	metrics.explained_variance_score
'neg_mean_absolute_error'	metrics.mean_absolute_error
'neg_mean_squared_error'	metrics.mean_squared_error
'neg_root_mean_squared_error'	metrics.mean_squared_error

Ex. 6.39

```
scores_tree = cross_val_score(tree, X_train_std, y_train_std,
                    scoring='neg_root_mean_squared_error', cv=5)


rmse_scores = -scores_tree

print("RMSE:", rmse_scores)
print("Mean:", rmse_scores.mean())
print("Standard deviation:", rmse_scores.std())
```
```
RMSE: [0.84100199 0.99031401 0.87922704 1.06653465 1.05783672]
Mean: 0.9669828836059144
Standard deviation: 0.0919582395734389
```

The cross-validation gives not only an estimate of the performance of the trained model, but also a measure of how precise the estimate is. The Decision Tree model has a mean RMSE of about 0.967 and a standard deviation of approx. 0.092. Next, let us evaluate our previous SVR model:

Ex. 6.40

```
# Evaluate SVR model
scores_svr = cross_val_score(svr, X_train_std, y_train_std,
                    scoring='neg_root_mean_squared_error', cv=5)


rmse_scores = -scores_svr

print("RMSE:", rmse_scores)
print("Mean:", rmse_scores.mean())
print("Standard deviation:", rmse_scores.std())
```
```
RMSE: [0.80018634 0.94529355 0.87496314 1.06466885 0.97362561]
Mean: 0.9317474993759699
Standard deviation: 0.08959705340677672
```

The SVR model has a mean RMSE of approx. 0.932 and a standard deviation of about 0.089. Overall, the SVR model performs better than the Decision Tree model. Note that the RMSE values from the cross-validations are much lower than on the test set, indicating that the estimators are overfitting the training set. Possible ways of fixing overfitting problem include, for example using regularizations or get more training data. However, before tweaking the hyperparameters (note that hyperparameters are parameters that are not directly learnt within estimators, e.g., C) and optimizing the estimators, you should try different algorithms and shortlist the most promising ones. For more discussion on cross-validation, see '**Cross-validation: evaluating estimator performance**' section of scikit-learn documentation.

6.7.5 Random Forests

Quite often better predictions come from a group of estimators than from a single predictor. This is analogous to having an expert group that offers better advice than with only one expert when making business decisions. In machine learning, using a group of estimators is called **Ensemble Learning**. Random Forests are an ensemble learning method, which consist of several Decision Trees for classification, regression, and other purposes. The idea of Random Forests prediction was first proposed by Tin Kam Ho (1995) in 1995, and later was extended by other scholars such as Breiman (2001) and Amit and Geman (1997).

As shown in Fig. 6.20, the Decision Trees are trained on various sub-samples of the dataset. Once they are trained, the predictions of all the trees are aggregated in the ensemble learning to improve the predictive accuracy and control overfitting. The aggregation function is typically the *mode* (i.e., majority vote) for classification or the *mean* for regression.

Random Forests are generally based on the bagging method (i.e., bootstrap aggregating), but adopt a modified tree learning algorithm that selects a random subset of the features (sometimes referred to as 'feature bagging') at each candidate split in the learning process. Instead of searching for the best features when splitting a node, the Random Forest algorithm searches for the best feature among a random subset of features. For a detailed explanation of different methods for constructing the ensemble (e.g., bagging, boosting and randomization), see the original papers by Ho (1995) and Dietterich (2000).

In scikit-learn, Random Forests can be imported from `sklearn.ensemble` module. We will skip the Random Forest classifier for now and focus on using its regressor for our coffee quality example here. Consider below where we randomly set parameter values for the model (note that you can select different values and try them out yourself):

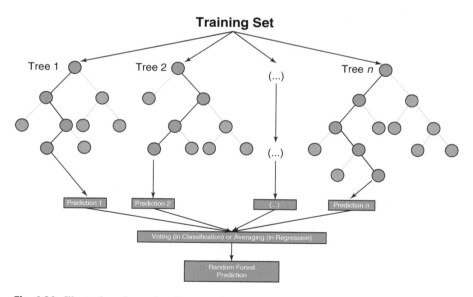

Fig. 6.20 Illustration of a random forests estimator

Ex. 6.41

```
from sklearn.ensemble import RandomForestRegressor

rfr = RandomForestRegressor(n_estimators=500, max_depth=5,
                            min_samples_split=2, min_samples_leaf=6,
                            n_jobs=-1, random_state=42)

rfr.fit(X_train_std, y_train_std)
y_pred_rfr = rfr.predict(X_test_std)

y_pred_rfr_inverse = y_scaler.inverse_transform(y_pred_rfr)

rmse_rfr = np.sqrt(mean_squared_error(y_test, y_pred_rfr_inverse))

print('RF RMSE Score: %.4f' % rmse_rfr)
print('Variance score: %.4f' % rfr.score(X_test_std, y_test_std))
RF RMSE Score: 2.2682
Variance score: 0.2403
```

As can be seen, with some random parameter settings we could get some very prom-ising results. In the scikit-learn implementation, the parameter `max_samples` (*default=None*) controls the number of samples to draw from the training set if the `bootstrap` parameter is set to `True` (*default*), otherwise the whole training set will be used to build each tree. The `n_estimators` parameter (*default=100*) defines the number of trees in the forest. `n_jobs` sets the number of jobs to run in parallel. `n_jobs=-1` means using all CPU processors. Else, the `RandomForestRegressor` basically has all the hyperparameters of a `DecisionTreeRegressor` to control how trees grow, plus all the hyperparameters of a `BaggingRegressor` to control the ensemble itself. You are recommended to go through the User Guide of the model on scikit-learn documentation to learn its various parameters, methods, attributes, and examples yourself.

6.7.6   Model Fine-Tuning

After training different regression models and evaluating their performance using cross-validation, it seems that the Random Forest Regressor outperforms all other estimators in our example. However, we did not conduct a thorough search for the optimal hyperparameter values for our estimators, but randomly set the values for these hyperparameters. In general, however, this would not truly reflect the ability of an estimator because one may perform better than the other with different set of parameters.

Therefore, instead of randomly initializing the values for the hyperparameters, a better approach that can automatically find the optimal parameters should be adopted for improving the shortlisted model's generalization performance. The most commonly used algorithm is **Grid Search,** which conducts an exhaustive search over specified parameter values for an estimator.

Scikit-learn implements Grid Search with Cross-Validation (i.e., `GridSearchCV`) to evaluate the performance of each parameter combination for an estimator. To use the grid search, we first need to import `GridSearchCV` class from the `sklearn.model_selection` module. Next, we need to create a dictionary of parameters and their corresponding list of values. `GridSearchCV` then exhaustively generates candidates from a grid of parameter values with the `param_grid` parameter.

As an example, let us create a dictionary of parameters and a list of corresponding values for our Random Forest Regressor:

Ex. 6.42

```
# create a dictionary of parameters and list of values
params = {'n_estimators': [600, 800, 1000],
          'max_depth': [None, 5, 10],
          'min_samples_leaf': [4, 6, 8],
          'min_samples_split': [2, 4, 6],
          'bootstrap': [True, False]}

rfr = RandomForestRegressor(random_state=42, n_jobs=-1)
GS = GridSearchCV(rfr, param_grid=params, cv=5,
                  scoring='neg_root_mean_squared_error')
GS.fit(X_train_std, y_train_std)
```

Note that `GridSearchCV` implements a `fit()` and a `score()` method. When trained on a dataset using its `fit()` method, all possible combinations of parameters values provided in the dictionary are evaluated and the best combination is returned. The best parameters can be accessed using the `best_params_` attribute. `best_estimator_` gives the estimator chosen by the search and `best_score_` returns the average cross-validated score of the best estimator. For a full list of its parameters, attributes, methods and examples, see '**GridSearchCV**' section of scikit-learn documentation.

Returning to our example, let us check the optimized parameters that we have found:

Ex. 6.43

```
GS.best_params_
```
```
{'bootstrap': True,
 'max_depth': 10,
 'min_samples_leaf': 6,
 'min_samples_split': 2,
 'n_estimators': 600}
```

We can then use the `GridSearchCV.predict()` method that calls predict on the estimator with the best fond parameters to make predictions on the hold-out test set and make final evaluation of the estimator. However, in case we might lose the best estimator settings especially when multiple grid searches are attempted, we can simply copy the values of best parameters and retrain the model. Consider below:

Ex. 6.44

```
# Instantiate with the best parameters
rfr_final = RandomForestRegressor(n_estimators=600, max_depth=10,
                        min_samples_leaf=6,min_samples_split=2,
                        random_state=42)

rfr_final.fit(X_train_std, y_train_std)
y_pred_grid = rfr_final.predict(X_test_std)
y_pred_grid_inverse = y_scaler.inverse_transform(y_pred_grid)

rmse_rfr = np.sqrt(mean_squared_error(y_test, y_pred_grid_inverse))
print('RF RMSE Score: %.4f' % rmse_rfr)
print('Variance score: %.4f' % rfr_final.score(X_test_std, y_test_std))
```
```
RF RMSE Score: 2.2342
Variance score: 0.2628
```

As can be seen, both RMSE and *R*-square values have significantly improved after performing the final evaluation of the best estimator on the hold-out test set. In *Ex.6.41* however, we created a fairly short list of parameters and their corresponding values only to demonstrate how we perform grid search for best parameters. This is because grid searches are quite computationally expensive to run and thus can be very slow. The cross-validation further increases the computation complexity and time. You could try out different parameters, create a longer list of values and see whether you could generate even better results.

The final Random Forest model is the best estimator we have trained so far, which can be used for future predictions on new datasets. One of very useful attributes that both Decision Trees and Random Forests models have is `feature_importances_` which returns the impurity-based feature importance. In our coffee quality example, we could potentially use this attribute to evaluate what features are most important for coffee quality prediction.

Let us plot the important features from the Random Forest model:

Ex. 6.45

```
# Plot feature importance
sns.set()
feature_rank = pd.Series(rfr_final.feature_importances_,
                        index=X_train.columns)

plt.figure(figsize=(8, 8))
feature_rank.nlargest(15).sort_values(ascending=True).plot(kind='barh')
plt.xlabel('Importance')
plt.title('Feature Importance', fontsize=15)
```

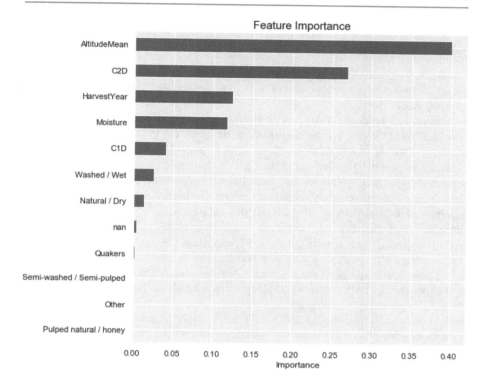

From the diagram we can see that altitude, category two defects, harvest year and moisture play a very important role in coffee quality prediction. This finding may suggest that when supply chain managers select coffee suppliers around the world, they may need to pay particular attention to these CQI criteria to determine fine quality coffee beans.

Overall, `GridSearchCV` is a flexible approach implemented by scikit-learn, which can accommodate a list of dictionaries, multiple metrics for the scoring parameter and different cross-validation strategies such as `ShuffleSplit` and `StratifiedShuttleSplit`. However, as mentioned, `GridSearchCV` performs exhaustive grid search which can be very time-consuming.

Scikit-learn also implements `RandomizedSearchCV` that performs randomized search over parameters, in which each setting is sampled from a distribution over possible parameter values. In general, this randomized search can be more efficient due to the sampling technique but might not always guarantee the optimal parameters to be found. We will apply the randomized parameter optimization algorithm in later chapters. For more details on model tuning, see '**Tuning the hyperparameters of an estimator**' section of scikit-learn documentation.

6.7.7   Extra-Trees

Another very useful model of ensembled trees is called Extra-Trees, i.e., Extremely Randomized Trees. As its name suggests, Extra-Trees uses random thresholds for each candidate feature and the best of these randomized thresholds is selected as the splitting rule.

Similar to a random forests model, the number of randomly selected features to consider when looking for the best split can be specified. In scikit-learn implementation, including `ExtraTreesClassifier` and `ExtraTreesRegressor` classes, this can be specified using the `max_features` parameter. The larger the greater the variance of the model, but also the greater the reduction in bias. By default, `max_features` is set to 'auto'; while in fact, when set to 'auto', it automatically considers all features in the dataset (i.e., `n_features`) for the regressors, but uses a random subset of size `sqrt(n_features)` for the classifiers. In general, good results can be achieved when the trees are fully developed (i.e., setting `max_depth = None` in combination with `min_samples_split = 2`), however these values are usually not optimal, and could be very computationally expensive to train the models. Keep in mind that the best parameters values should always be cross validated.

It is difficult to tell whether an Extra-Trees model performs better or worse than a Random Forest model. A good way is to try both and compare their performances using cross-validation, and then use grid search to find optimal parameters. For more explanations on the ensemble methods, see '**Ensemble method**' section of scikit-learn documentation. The application of an Extra-Trees model is not covered here; however, you will have the opportunity to apply this algorithm in the exercise project at the end of this chapter.

So far, we have introduced and trained various regression models. Each model has its own advantages and disadvantages, and sometimes it is not easy to tell which one is the best as this can depend on many factors such as *fit for purpose* and the dataset itself. In particular, we have briefly introduced the Decision Tree algorithm. Even though many researchers and data scientists believe this method is outdated and has accuracy issues, more recent development such as Random Forest (bagging method) and XGBoost (boosting method) are built upon it. Therefore, understanding the fundamental concept of the tree algorithm is essential.

In addition, we have learnt about using cross-validation to evaluate the performance of an estimator. It is always a good practice to evaluate and select models using the combinations of a training and validation set and hold out the test set for final evaluation. The overall process of evaluating and selecting best models and finding optimal parameters is illustrated in Fig. 6.21.

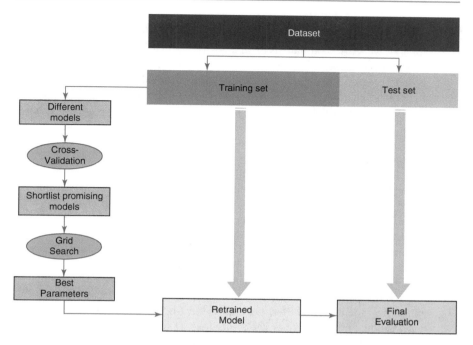

Fig. 6.21 Overview of model evaluation and selection

Summary of Learning Objectives

1. **Describe the major activities involved in procurement and supply management.**

   Procurement and supply management can involve activities such as supplier selection and evaluation, contract negotiation, supplier relationship management and supply risk management. These activities play an essential role in acquiring, securing, and maintaining smooth and quality supply of goods and services to support focal firms' daily operations to satisfy customers. The term procurement is confused with purchasing, whereas the latter is often referred to as placing and receiving orders from suppliers.

2. **Understand the differences and 'fit' between vertical integration and outsourcing.**

   Vertical integration is often achieved when a firm makes majority of parts or components in-house or owns most stages of its supply chain. By contrast, outsourcing is about purchasing goods and services from external suppliers. The degree of vertical integration varies in different organizations. In general, a higher degree of vertical integration allows firms to maintain greater control of key supplies of resources or to keep core competence and capabilities from potential leakage and imitation by competitors. However, it also has disadvantages such as high capital expenditure and lack of business focus and flexibility. Outsourcing can help firms cut cost and focus on their core competencies, but also has its own drawbacks as depicted in Fig. 6.2. Therefore, finding the 'fit' between vertical integration and outsourcing can be strategically important for businesses to achieve superior performance and objectives as described in Fig. 6.3.

3. **Discuss how to select and evaluate suppliers for effective supply management.**

   Effective supplier selection and evaluation should be in line with an organization's competitive strategies and performance objectives as indicated in Fig. 6.4. Supplier selection can be a challenging task, which can include supplier evaluation, contract negotiation, supplier capabilities development, strategic sourcing and relationship management. Organizations should develop their own supplier selection and evaluation criteria and take into account external business environment (e.g., PESTEL). The total cost of acquisition should be considered than simply the quoted prices from suppliers, such as quality costs, technical assistance, and long payment terms as shown in Fig. 6.5. Supplier evaluation can also encompass supplier capability assessment, which not only examine a supplier's current capabilities, but also their potential to develop and foster future capabilities. Supplier capability assessment can include the evaluation of suppliers' fundamental quality management system, their technological skills and know-how, and flexibility to cope with changes and uncertainties.

4. **Understand the purpose and ways of managing supplier relationships.**

   A typical supply chain can include many suppliers and different types of relationships may exist as some suppliers are critical to the business, others are not. Therefore, effective supplier relationship management not only can help the buying firms to focus on those strategically important suppliers and ensure high-quality supplies but can also help reduce uncertainties and risks involved in supply chains. There are different ways of managing supplier relationships depending on supplier types. For the critical ones, firms should devote their resources and efforts towards a long-term and strategic partnership; whereas for the non-critical ones, firms should maintain a stable and efficient arm-length relationship especially if there are many alternative suppliers out there. Figure 6.9 also discusses different ways to establishing and managing dyad and triad relationships in a supply network, as both have their own pros and cons. Determining the appropriate number of suppliers can also be critical in supplier relationship management which is often regarded as supply base rationalization.

5. **Describe the top supply chain risks and approaches to managing them.**

   There are many types of risks involved in a supply chain, which are not uncommon to supply chain managers in their daily jobs. These risks can cause significant disruptions to business operations and productions. According to the PwC report, the top-rated supply chain risks are depicted in Fig. 6.11, which include raw material price fluctuation, currency fluctuation and market changes, amongst others. To manage the risks in a supply chain, organization should develop effective supply risk management systems, and constantly review and anticipate new risk challenges. There are four basic steps to follow, including risk identification, risk assessment, risk response strategies development and continuous monitoring and review. Developing supply chain resilience for risks mitigation can depend on a number of factors such as building strong partnerships with suppliers, using multiple sourcing, and suppliers training and support.

6. **Learn and be able to use, evaluate and fine-tune the regression algorithms introduced.**

   We have covered several popular regression algorithms in this chapter, including linear regression (or ordinary least squares), support vector machines, Decision Trees, random forests and extra-trees. Each algorithm has its own advantages and drawbacks depending on the questions to be addressed and the data itself. Scikit-learn has built-in implementations of these models, which can be easily imported and trained for solving specific problems as demonstrated in the examples. To evaluate the performance of an estimator, a useful approach is using cross-validation such as k-fold cross-validation (i.e., k iterations). Scikit-learn implements Grid Search with cross-validation that can be used to evaluate and fine-tune the selected estimators.

Discussion Questions

1. Choose a manufacturing firm and a service provider, and compare and contrast which one has a higher degree of vertical integration, and which one has more outsourcing? Discuss the pros and cons of vertical integration and outsourcing with your chosen companies.
2. If you were to make a decision on outsourcing between a domestic supplier and an overseas supplier, what could be the total cost of acquisition to consider comparing between the two suppliers?
3. Develop a list of supplier selection criteria for your chosen firm by considering its competitive strategies and performance objectives.
4. Managing relationships in a multi-tier supply network can be very complex and challenging. Discuss the various relationship types in a network and

approaches to managing them. What are the pros and cons associated with each method as depicted in Figs. 6.9 and 6.10?

5. Develop a risk assessment matrix for your chosen supply chain of any businesses (e.g., a pizza store, a hotel, a car manufacturer).

Keyboard Exercises

1. In your notebook, import necessary packages, re-run all the exercises in this chapter. You can set your own parameter values and use grid search to fine turn each estimator of your choice.

2. In the coffee quality example, if your personal preference is on Aroma than other quality index, which country of origin would you choose for your next bag of coffee beans? Try to rank Aroma scores by origin and plot the results using bar chart.

3. Download the supplier pricing datasets and problem description from the repository, your primary task is to predict the price a supplier will quote for a given component. You can use any regression algorithms that may lead to the best results. However, note that exploratory data analysis, data cleaning and transformation, and feature engineering are critical for achieving a good result in this exercise project. More details can be found in this chapter's online repository.

References

Alicke, K. & Strigel, A. 2020. "Supply chain risk management is back". McKinsey & Company.

Amit, Y. & Geman, D. 1997. "Shape Quantization and Recognition with Randomized Trees". Neural Computation. Vol. 9, pp. 1545–1588.

Breiman, L. 2001. "Random Forests". Machine Learning. Vol. 45, 5-32.

Cortes, C. & Vapnik, V. 1995. "Support-Vector Networks". Machine Learning. Vol. 20, 273-297.

Dietterich, T.G. 2000. "An Experimental Comparison of Three Methods for Constructing Ensembles of Decision Trees: Bagging, Boosting, and Randomization". Machine Learning. Vol. 40, pp. 139–157.

Drucker, H., Burges, C.J., Kaufman, L., Smola, A. & Vapnik, V. 1997. "Support Vector Regression Machines". Advances in Neural Information Processing Systems. Vol. 9, 155–161.

Ho, T. K. 1995. "Random decision forests". Proceedings of 3rd International Conference on Document Analysis and Recognition. Vol 1, pp. 278–282.

Lambert, F. 2016. "Tesla is now ~80% vertically integrated, says Goldman Sachs after a Tesla Factory visit". electrek.

Sako, M. 2004. "Supplier development at Honda, Nissan and Toyota: Comparative case studies of organizational capability enhancement". Industrial and Corporate Change. 13 (2), 281–308.

Tajitsu, N. & Yamazaki, M. 2016. "Toyota, other major Japanese firms hit by quake damage, supply disruptions". Reuters.

Vapnik, V. 1995. "The Nature of Statistical Learning Theory". Springer, N.Y.

Warehouse and Inventory Management

7

Contents

Learning Objectives

- Describe the purpose and major activities of warehouse management.
- Understand WMS and its benefits as well as KPIs for warehouse performance measurement.
- Describe different inventory types and the purpose of holding them.
- Understand the key approaches to managing inventories.
- Learn warehouse optimization using linear programming and different classification algorithms and their performance evaluation methods.

K. Y. Liu, *Supply Chain Analytics*, https://doi.org/10.1007/978-3-030-92224-5_7

7.1   Warehouse Management

Businesses that sell tangible products to customers would normally have to store their goods somewhere in a warehouse along their supply chains. For example, large organizations such as a car maker usually have multi-stage warehouses for the components and finished products, either held by their upstream suppliers or by their downstream partners (e.g., car dealers). Smaller firms such as a pizza shop usually have all gradients stored in their on-site warehouses. A supermarket stores all their products on shelves and in on-site warehouses. Nonetheless, large supermarket chains such as Tesco also have regional (or national) mega warehouses, i.e., distribution centres (DCs), to distribute their goods to different local stores on a regular basis (Fig. 7.1).

7.1.1   What Is Warehouse Management?

Warehouse management is the control and coordination of the day-to-day activities within a warehouse to ensure the efficiency and effectiveness of warehouse operations. These operations include:

- Warehouse layout design and optimization.
- Receiving and recording goods coming into the facility.
- Putting-away goods.
- Tracking and locating goods.
- Picking, packing, and shipping orders.
- Optimizing internal processes and improving overall warehouse performance

Fig. 7.1 Tesco DC at Lichfield, West Midlands, United Kingdom

Warehouse layout design is essential for making sure that there is enough storage space for goods and enough working space for smooth and safe movement of goods within the warehouse. It involves the design of areas for receiving stock, staging, storing, picking, packaging, and shipping, as well as the offices within. Optimizing the layout design is a crucial process as it can determine the efficiency and productivity of a warehouse. A well-designed warehouse not only provides easy access to stored goods, but also can minimize pickup time, total travel distance, and improve order fulfilment rate (Fig. 7.2).

There are several factors to consider while designing a warehouse, including cost/budget, capacity, flow, accessibility, equipment, information technology, and safety considerations. See Table 7.1 below:

Fig. 7.2 Multi-layer layout of a warehouse

Table 7.1 Important factors to consider for warehouse layout design

Factors	Description
Cost/budget	The location, size, capacity, and layout of a warehouse should be evaluated based on the business budget, requirements, and future projection of your business growth.
Capacity utilization	Effective capacity utilization in the warehouse is crucial for operational efficiency as it can help reduce travel distance, pickup time, and inventory visibility, etc. A good layout design should consider how capacity can be utilized most effectively within a warehouse.
Flow	A good layout design should also maintain a smooth flow of goods, vehicles, personnel within a warehouse, avoiding inefficient routes, bottlenecks, and disruptions, etc.
Accessibility	A good layout design should ensure easy accessibility to all areas within a warehouse so that goods can be conveniently located and picked up without having to move other products.
Equipment	Choosing the right types of equipment for scanning, recording, sorting, lifting, conveying, storing, packing can influence productivity and efficiency of warehousing as well as the layout design.
IT	Large warehouses are often enabled with modern technologies. Different IT systems for sensing, tracking, recording, communication, etc. including warehouse management systems, can also impact a warehouse's layout design, and hence the process efficiency and productivity of a warehouse.
Safety	A good layout design should also ensure the safety of employees working in a warehouse by strictly following guidelines and industry standards.

7.1.2 Warehouse Management System

Warehouse Management System (WMS) is an IT system that helps organizations to control, automate, and optimize warehouse manual processes from the point when goods or materials enter a warehouse until they move out. A WMS can provide accurate data recording and communication as well as enhanced visibility of all warehouse operations. A WMS can be a stand-alone system but can also be a module in a complex ERP system or SCM suite, which shares a common database and can be integrated with other ERP modules such as inventory management system (IMS) and transportation management system (TMS).

Some common features that a WMS supports include warehouse design optimization, inventory tracking and locating, picking and packing goods, labelling and reporting. Modern warehouses have more advanced WMSs that integrate with smart devices and sensors, which can facilitate fully automated item picking, packing, labelling, and dispatching. For instance, Ocado is using the swarm of robots that power its new generation of automated warehouses for online grocery (see Fig. 7.3).[1]

One of the emerging technologies that have been applied in warehouse management is the Internet of Things (IoT). As previously mentioned in Chap. 2, IoT is a network of uniquely identifiable physical objects embedded with sensors, actuators, software, and computing devices, enabling them to exchange data over the internet. The data obtained via IoT can be integrated into a WMS to assist the optimization of routing of goods within a warehouse. Such integration can enable the development of a pull-based supply chain, making tailored and fast response to real-time

Fig. 7.3 Ocado automated warehouses for online grocery. Source: Copyright © Ocado 2021. Reproduced with permission

---

[1] Paul Clarke, CTO, Ocado, 2018, "How Online Grocer Ocado Is Automating Warehouses Using Swarms of Robots", Harvard Business Review.

customer demands, rather than a push-based supply chain in which stocks are pushed to downstream driven by demand forecasting.

If there are multi-stage warehouses dispersed in different regions, with IoT enabled WMS, managers can quickly identify where stock is located and how much stock is on-hand, and then effectively replenish stock, improve picking and shipping efficiency, optimize storage space and distribution routes, and reduce response time to customer requests.

7.1.3 Benefits of WMS

Implementing a WMS can bring many benefits to an organization, including those mentioned earlier, as well as timely information exchange, reduced labour costs, enhanced flexibility and responsiveness, and improved customer satisfaction, etc. Some of the main benefits of adopting a WMS are listed below:

- **Reduce paperwork and errors**: when recording data and information in warehouse, using paperwork can cause errors and delays. However, WMS can significantly reduce errors in data recording and transferring, and hence improving efficiency and accuracy of data exchange.
- **Optimize capacity utilization**: capacity can be best utilized considering the space availability (e.g., floor storage and vertical storage), stock level requirement, stock types, and the pattern of distribution.
- **Minimize picking errors**: with accurate data exchange and automated process, picking errors can be reduced and costs for correction and returns can also be avoided.
- **Optimize inventory control**: a more coordinated and balanced inventory control can be achieved, considering customers demand and capital constraints.
- **Improve efficiency and productivity**: efficient flow management and stock control, process improvement, and automation can significantly improve efficiency and productivity of a warehouse, thereby cutting waste and costs.
- **Ensure safe working conditions**: WMS not only improves workflows and optimizes layout within a warehouse, but also takes into account health and safety concerns for workers and customers. It can make appropriate risk assessments and flag up safety requirements, ensuring compliance with regulations.

Although implementing a WMS can sometimes be complex and challenging depending on business types and requirements, its benefits in the long run can outweigh the initial challenges and capital requirements. Finding the right type of WMS is a nontrivial task, given that every business has a variety of aspects unique to them and their specific warehousing requirements. In general, the major considerations for choosing a WMS include the upfront cost, desired level of integration with existing processes, degree of easy-to-use, capability to handle and integrate with other systems, and reporting and measuring performance.

7.1.4   Warehouse Management Performance Measurement

Measuring and tracking warehouse management performance is essential for continuous improvement in a warehouse. Different organizations might set their own key performance index (KPI) and targets; however, in general, the following three objectives are the primary foci:

- Accuracy of order fulfilment
- Speed of order fulfilment
- Cost of order fulfilment

Accordingly, some of the common KPIs to measure the success of a warehouse management include:

1. **Receiving efficiency**: which measures the elapsed time between the point when a stock arrives and the point when the stock is put away.
2. **Picking accuracy**: which is used to reflect the rate of incorrectly picked orders against total orders over a certain period.
3. **Holding cost**: the total costs associated carrying its stock in a warehouse over a certain period (e.g., storage costs, cost of capital, equipment, insurance, etc.)
4. **Inventory turnover**: which measures how quickly stock sells in a warehouse. It can be calculated by using cost of goods sold against average inventory.
5. **Order lead time**: which is the average time taken from when customers place orders to when they receive orders.
6. **Ontime Delivery (OTD)**: which is the ratio of goods delivered on time to customers versus total items shipped over a certain period.
7. **Rate of return**: which measures units returned versus total orders over a certain period.
8. **Stockout rate**: which measures the rate of items not available versus total orders during a certain period.

Certainly, there are many other useful KPIs to measure warehouse management performance. Organizations might develop more specific KPIs for managing their own warehouses based on their unique business requirements and circumstances. However, these are eight of the most commonly used ones amongst industries.

Note: Some KPIs are not unique to warehouse management, for example, holding cost, inventory turnover, OTD, order lead time can be useful KPIs for inventory management and the overall supply chain performance.

7.2 Inventory Management

7.2.1 What Is Inventory?

Inventories are commonly referred to as the goods held in a warehouse. Along a supply chain, inventory can exist in various forms at different stages, including, for example, raw materials, components, parts, work in progress (WIP) or semi-finished products, and finished products. Inventory can also be customers, information, and data, especially in the service industry. For instance, commuters queueing for public transport, patients in a hospital waiting for diagnosis and treatment, and information stored in a database to be analysed by a data scientist, all of which can be considered inventory to be processed (Fig. 7.4).

Table 7.2 contains examples of different types of inventories involved in various operations. These inventories can be broadly categorized into tangible goods (e.g., raw materials), intangible goods (e.g., data/information), and people (e.g., customers).

Inventories are usually considered costly to buy and keep regardless of their forms and types. For example, automakers spend a lot of money on the components and parts required to compose a vehicle. Customer data stored in the banking IT systems need constantly backup and the security of those data are vital, which also have significant cost implications.

Specifically, there are *direct* costs associated with inventory, including, for example, initial capital investment, cost for shipping, storage, running a warehouse, and insurance. When inventories become obsolete, damaged, or stolen, organizations will expose to the risk of losing their initial investments. Additionally, there are *indirect* costs associated with inventory, including, for example, opportunity costs for the capital spent on inventories, unhappy long-waiting customers who might complain and never come back again. Of course, there are exceptions that inventories can be held to gain values such as fine wines and scarce resources. However, in general, holding excessive inventories can be costly, sometimes very risky. Therefore, organizations should seek best ways to reduce their inventories where possible without interrupting their daily operations and performance.

Fig. 7.4 Commuters queueing for public transport service

Table 7.2 Example of inventories

Operations	Inventory examples
Fast food restaurant	• Ingredients for burgers, food, etc. • Customers waiting for placing orders • Order information recorded in the ordering system
University	• Current students studying a course • New student applications to be processed • Students attending degree congregations each year
Car manufacturer	• Components, parts, materials, etc. • Customer order information with configuration requirements • Finished cars waiting to be shipped
Bank	• Customer queueing for banking services • Mortgage applications to be processed • Cash notes stored in a bank
Cinema	• Audience waiting to enter cinema theatres • Films in stock to be played • Audience watching movies
Airport	• Passengers • Flights that are arriving, landed, and departing • Flights information, passenger details, etc.
Newspaper publisher	• News/stories to be edited for publishing • Papers stocked for newspaper printing • Printed newspapers to be distributed

7.2.2   The Purpose of Holding Inventory

Since inventories can be costly to buy and keep, why companies still need to hold inventories? In theory, if everything can be made and delivered instantly, there is no need to hold any inventories at all. Imagine when customers order some fish and chips in a restaurant, the chef there simultaneously cooks the food and hands it over to the customers. In such a scenario, the restaurant does not need to stock any prepared fish and chips because when customers come in and place the order, these stocks can magically arrive from suppliers or farmers at the same time. While this might happen in a magical world, however, in reality, it is impossible because products take time to make and deliver. In other words, potatoes will not instantaneously come out of the earth after planting, and fish will not automatically jump onto a dining table from a river. They all need to go through the entire supply chain process from farming, harvesting, processing, delivering, storing, and eventually being cooked and served to the customers.

> *"If everything can be made and delivered instantly, there is no need to hold any inventories at all."*

Inventories can therefore act like a 'buffer' between where/when the goods are produced and where/when they are needed. In other words, inventories are held to satisfy customers within their tolerable waiting time for their orders. Basically, businesses should place inventories somewhere along their supply chains to shorten their customers' waiting time, whilst maintaining adequate supplies and minimizing inventory related costs. For example, customers shopping in a supermarket expect to pick items from the shelves and check out quickly. Because their tolerable waiting time (TWT) is relatively short, supermarkets must store those finished products (i.e., inventories) on shelves waiting for customers to pick up (see Fig. 7.5).

By contrast, Amazon shoppers have a relatively higher waiting-time tolerance; instead of building physical retail stores, Amazon maintains fewer distribution centres (called *Amazon fulfilment centres*) across the nation to store and deliver products to its customers. Even though its customers can wait relatively longer for receiving their orders, Amazon understands that rapid delivery is essential for its success. In order to attract and retain customers, the giant e-tailer has been improving its logistics service to speed up the delivery process from next day, to the same day, and to even shorter times.

In addition to using inventory as a 'buffer', there are other reasons to carry physical inventories. The following are some of the general ones:

- **Inventory as an insurance against supply disruptions**—uncertainties and risks from the supply side are not uncommon, which can lead to disruptions of supplies. Inventories can then be used to cover the delays and disruptions in supplies.

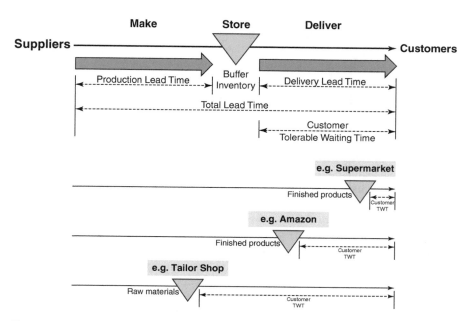

Fig. 7.5 Inventory as a buffer in supply chain

- **Economies of scale**—when demand is relatively stable, producing more finished products may cut down cost by realizing economies of scale, thereby saving greater than the cost of holding them. Likewise, when manufacturers buy a larger quantity of inventories from suppliers, they may negotiate a lower unit cost because their suppliers can achieve economies of scale as well.
- **Securing scare resources**—certain resources can be rare (e.g., rare earth minerals) or the number of capable suppliers for advanced technologies are limited; thus, organizations usually purchase and hold more inventories if they can in those circumstances.
- **Meeting future demand**—when demand for a product is expected to surge in the future, holding and accumulating enough inventory is a way to prepare for future demand increase.
- **'Buy low, sell high'**—The cost of materials and goods can fluctuate all the time, organizations can buy and hold inventories when price is low as a way to reduce their costs. Also, some products have investment potentials such as scotch whisky; holding such inventories can potentially generate profits in the future.

In short, organizations in different sectors and in various sizes may have their own reasons for carrying inventories along their supply chains. However, holding excessive inventories is always associated with high costs and risks, which should not be neglected by supply chain managers. In the following section, we focus on how to manage and control inventories effectively in supply chains.

7.2.3 What Is Inventory Management?

In a complex supply chain, which is especially the case in many manufacturing sectors such as the automotive and aerospace, managing inventory can be very challenging. Inventory management is often mixed up with warehouse management. Despite the two terms overlap to some extent, inventory management is especially focused on the actual items being held within a warehouse. It usually involves the process of ordering, handling, and storing of raw materials, components, semi-finished and finished products along a company's supply chain. A key aspect of inventory management is to maintain a balance between having an adequate level of stocks in the right place at the right time, whilst trying to minimize total cost as much as possible.

To achieve the balance for inventory management, supply chain managers need to have a clear strategy on *when* to replenish inventories, *how much* to order from suppliers, and at *what price* to pay. This can be relatively easy for small firms when demand is stable and predictable, and inventory planning and control can be done manually without using any complicated IT systems. However, larger organizations will need to adopt specialized inventory management systems to handle their complex inventory management activities.

With effective inventory management, organizations can expect to receive several benefits, including:

- **Enhanced customer experience.** Although some firms might use stock scarcity as a marketing strategy to attract customers, in general, frequent stockout and backorders can lead to a negative customer experience and potentially lose market shares in the long run.
- **Optimized fulfilment.** When inventories are optimized in terms of delivering right quantity, at right place, right time, and right cost to customers, it not only satisfies customers, but also helps avoid obsolete, spoiled, or stolen inventories.
- **Reduced cost.** Optimized inventory control also can bring opportunities for improved efficiencies in operations (e.g., reduced overhead, improved capacity utilization rate), avoiding too much inventory, thus cutting costs down.
- **Improved cash flow.** Spending too much on inventory at once can freeze capital for other things. Effective inventory management can help reduce inventory level, avoid wastage, and eliminate financial risks, etc.

7.2.4 Inventory Management Methods

Businesses might adopt different approaches to managing their inventories, depending on many factors such as the industry that a business resides in, the size of an organization, the types of inventories, the nature of customer demands, and the competitive strategies that the business pursues. For example, the methods used by furniture stores to manage their inventories can be significantly different from those used by firms in the seafood business. However, different furniture stores might also adopt different inventory management methods, for instance, IKEA, which sells pre-made, compact, easy-to-install, and standardized furniture versus a traditional furniture store, which only sells tailor-made solid wood furniture.

Despite these differences, there are some fundamental concepts that underpin effective inventory management. Imagine yourself as an inventory manager, the two most important questions to address are most likely to be '*how much to order?*' each time when you place orders from your suppliers and '*when to order?*'. In this section, we will explore inventory management methods around these two key questions.

How Much to Order?

The first question is about the number of units or quantity to purchase from suppliers. For small firms, this might not be a difficult decision providing that they do not have complex stock keeping units (SKUs) to handle. Managers could easily figure out the quantity they need from suppliers based on their own experience and previous sales record. Additionally, if suppliers are located locally who can provide rapid and flexible deliveries, determining the right ordering quantity would not be a challenging task either. This is because even if you get it wrong on some occasions, *ad hoc* deliveries can be made to cope with unexpected changes in demand.

However, for large organizations where there are complex and large numbers of SKUs, determining how much to order can be a daunting task. There are many factors that could affect the reorder quantity decisions. But as a starting point, let us

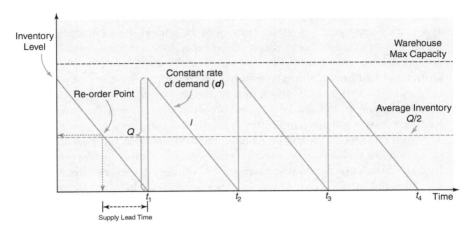

Fig. 7.6 Cycle inventory with fixed demand and supply lead time

take a look at the following diagram in which demand is assumed to be constant and supply lead time is fixed for a single item.

As shown in Fig. 7.6, there are four triangles with the same slope l, as demand d is deemed constant over time. Therefore, the inventory is depleted at the same rate over the four periods: t_1, t_2, t_3, and t_4. When inventory level goes down to zero, a new order of Q quantity will just arrive which replenishes the inventory, creating the cycle inventory.

This reorder quantity Q is what we are trying to figure out here to address the previous question. Note that the value of Q should not be set too high because it cannot exceed the maximum capacity of your warehouse; nonetheless, it should not be set too low either, considering the supply lead time. For instance, if it takes 2 days for your suppliers to deliver new stocks to you (i.e., supply lead time = 2 days), you will need to make sure that there is enough inventory to cover at least the 2-day demand before new stocks arrive to avoid stockout.

Additionally, there should be cost considerations. For example, if we keep too much inventory, the associated holding cost can be high, whereas a small Q would imply more frequent replenishment over the same period of time as compared to a bigger Q, thereby resulting in higher ordering costs.

Economic Order Quantity (EOQ)
The EOQ is the optimal order quantity in theory that a company should purchase each time from its suppliers to minimize the total costs of inventory, considering both holding costs and ordering costs. In particular, the holding costs can include storage costs such as utilities, costs of running the warehouse and salaries, financial costs such as interests and opportunity cost, and inventory related costs such as insurance, obsolescence, and shrinkage. Notice that the holding cost is often calculated as a percentage of product unit cost.

The ordering costs can include costs for handling transportation and shipping, clerical costs such as invoice processing and communication costs, import and export related charges if relevant. However, note that the ordering costs are fixed costs per order, regardless of the number of units ordered. They are not the costs of goods.

As an example, let us assume the annual demand for our product is D, the holding cost per unit, per year is H_c, and the ordering cost per order is O_c. If we order quantity Q each time, the total number of orders over a year would be D/Q times. In addition, as shown in Fig. 7.6, the average inventory being held in warehouse is $Q/2$, thus the total holding costs and total ordering costs can be calculated as follows:

$$\text{Total holding costs} = H_c \times Q / 2$$

$$\text{Total ordering costs} = O_c \times D / Q$$

Thus, the total costs of inventory C_i can be expressed as follows:

$$C_i = \frac{H_c Q}{2} + \frac{O_c D}{Q} \tag{7.1}$$

As shown in Fig. 7.7, as the order quantity increases, the total ordering costs decrease while the total holding costs go up, which forms a valley curve of the total costs of inventory. In order to minimize the total costs C_i, we need to find an optimal order quantity Q that actually pinpoints to the bottom of the valley curve. As can be seen from the diagram, it is the intersection point where the two lines of total

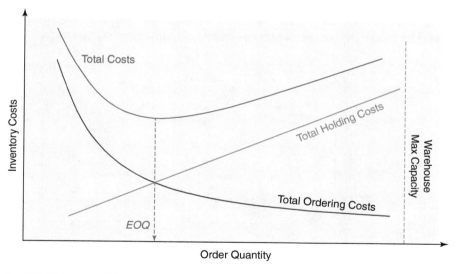

Fig. 7.7 Total costs of inventory

holding costs and total ordering cost lie across each other, i.e., when the total holding costs equalize the total ordering costs:

$$\frac{H_c Q}{2} = \frac{O_c D}{Q} \tag{7.2}$$

Thus, to get the optimal Q, i.e., the EOQ:

$$EOQ = Q = \sqrt{\frac{2O_c D}{H_c}} \tag{7.3}$$

In many organizations, inventory can be the largest asset that ties strongly with capital spending. The EOQ is thus supposed to help minimize the inventory level whilst satisfying customer demand as well as lowering the total costs. However, note that the EOQ formula is best suitable in situations where demand remains relatively stable and predictable over time. The model also assumes that both holding costs and ordering cost remain constant. If customer demand is highly volatile and unpredictable, or when there are significant supply uncertainties especially in the case of resource scarcity and shortage, then the EOQ formula might not work effectively without incorporating these uncertainty considerations in its algorithm.

Safety Stock

The EOQ model can be used to determine the optimal order quantity based on several assumptions such as stable demand and fixed costs. However, in reality, these assumptions barely hold true. For example, as illustrated in Fig. 7.8, the actual demand can change over time, resulting in varying inventory depletion rates. Sometimes inventory level can go down slowly due to lack of demand, other times it can go down much quicker than expected as demand picks up, resulting in stockouts. The uncertainties in demand pose challenges in inventory management.

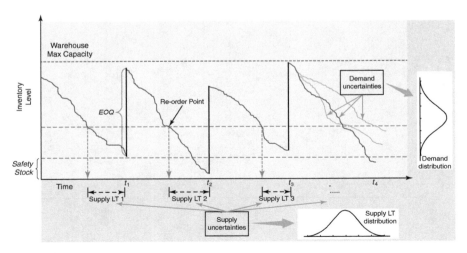

Fig. 7.8 Inventory levels with uncertainties in supply and demand sides

In addition, there can be uncertainties from the supply side as well. Suppliers cannot make on time deliveries every time due to reasons such as delays in customs, accidents and natural disasters, and even defects in products. If we record the variability in both demand and supply over time, they are likely to form a normal distribution, i.e., a *bell curve*, as demonstrated in Fig. 7.8.

The safety stock is thus used to cover the uncertainties to prevent stockouts. Operations managers from small firms might simply use their experience to set safety stock levels when their managed SKUs are not too complex. However, in large-size organizations, a better approach should be adopted to balance the needs of maintaining desired level of customer satisfaction and minimizing inventory cost. In other words, we should keep an adequate level of safety stock to meet unexpected customer demand but not overstock due to cost considerations.

The safety stock formula should take into account the variability in both supply and demand sides, which can be expressed as follows (King 2011):

$$\text{Safety stock} = Z \times \sqrt{\left(\text{LT}_{\text{avg}} \times \sigma_{\text{D}}^2\right) + \left(\sigma_{\text{LT}} \times D_{\text{avg}}\right)^2} \qquad (7.4)$$

where

Z is the Z-score (i.e., standard score),
LT_{avg} is the average lead time from the supply side,
σ_{D} is the standard deviation of demand distribution,
σ_{LT} is the standard deviation of lead time,
D_{avg} is the average demand per lead-time unit (e.g., per day).

To understand Z-score, let us take a look at the standard normal distribution as shown in Fig. 7.9. Statistically, a Z-score measures how far a data point is deviated from the mean. For example, at $+1\sigma$, the Z-score is 1 (see Fig. 7.9). Recall that the

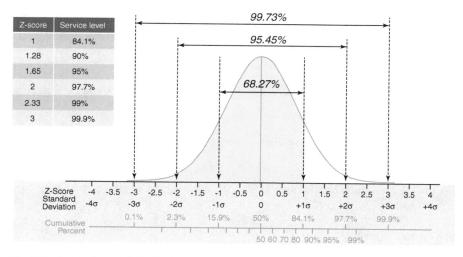

Fig. 7.9 Standard normal distribution and Z-score

standard deviation σ is a measure of how spread out the data are. Roughly, 68.27% of all data values fall within 1σ of the mean, 95.45% of values are within 2σ range, and 99.73% fall within 3σ range. Accumulatively, if the Z-score is 1, it covers about 84.1% of all the data values, and if the Z-score is 3, it can cover about 99.9% of the values, i.e., the higher the Z-score, the larger range of data values it covers. So, let us say if you have a normally distributed demand data, to potentially satisfy 90% of the demand, you will need to have a Z-score about 1.28. This is the reason why there is a Z-score in the safety stock formula. Basically, if we want to achieve a higher level of customer service (i.e., reduced possibility of having stockouts), then we need to have a larger Z-score and thus more safety stocks, and vice versa.

Now, consider the following example, where

LT_{avg} = 4 days, the average lead time is 4 days
σ_D = 20, the standard deviation of demand is 20,
σ_{LT} = 2, the standard deviation of lead time is 2,
D_{avg} = 100 units/day

Assume that we want to achieve a 99% service level, then

$$\text{Safety stock} = 2.33 \times \sqrt{\left(4 \times 20^2\right) + \left(2 \times 100\right)^2}$$
$$= 475.23$$
$$\approx 476 \text{ units}$$

Thus, we would need to keep 476 units as safety stock if we would like to achieve a 99% service level. The figure will, however, drop to 261 units if only a 90% service level is desired.

The safety stock equation is useful for predicting the extra inventory needed to cover uncertainties from both the supply and demand sides. However, if there is no variability in lead time, in other words, suppliers can always make on-time deliveries, then the standard deviation of lead time will be zero, i.e., $\sigma_{LT} = 0$, the safety stock equation will change to

$$\text{Safety stock} = Z \times \sqrt{\left(LT_{avg} \times \sigma_D^2\right)} \qquad (7.5)$$

Likewise, if the demand is always certain and stable, then $\sigma_D = 0$, and the equation will change to

$$\text{Safety stock} = Z \times \sqrt{\left(\sigma_{LT} \times D_{avg}\right)^2} \qquad (7.6)$$
$$= Z \times \sigma_{LT} \times D_{avg}$$

Finally, if there is no variability from both sides, there is no need to keep any safety stock.

When to Order?

The safety stock calculation and the EOQ model help to address 'how much to order' question in inventory management. Another important question to ask is '*when to order?*' There are two basic approaches to answering this question. First, if the inventory is continuously monitored, and when the inventory level drops to certain point, replenishment will be triggered so that new stocks can arrive before inventory hits zero. This triggering point for inventory replenishment is called **Re-order Point** (ROP) (see Fig. 7.8). To calculate ROP, we need to take into account the uncertainties from both supply and demand sides, as well as the total demand during the average supply lead-time period, see below:

$$ROP = D_{avg} \times LT_{avg} + \text{Safety stock} \qquad (7.7)$$

In Eq. 7.7, $D_{avg} \times LT_{avg}$ gives the total demand during the average supply lead time, and the safety stock covers the uncertainties. Consider our previous example, where the average lead time is 4 days, and the daily average demand is 100 units, then,

$$ROP = 100 \times 4 + 476$$
$$= 876 \, \text{units}$$

Thus, in this case, when the inventory level drops to 876 units, the replenishment process should be triggered.

Another approach to restocking inventories is using **periodic reviews**. Instead of constantly monitoring inventory levels enabled by effective IT systems, one may check inventory levels at fix time intervals (T) and re-order new stocks. Managers may set a maximum stock level Q_{max} based on the warehouse capacity or from her/his prediction on future demand. The re-order quantity Q at each review point is the gap between the current stock level and Q_{max}, as illustrated in Fig. 7.10.

In practice, there are still uncertainties from both supply and demand sides. Thus, safety stock is still required to cover these uncertainties. The Q_{max} value can also be adjusted based on demand trend and volatility accordingly. The same applies to the review time intervals T. Comparing to continuous monitoring of stock levels, this

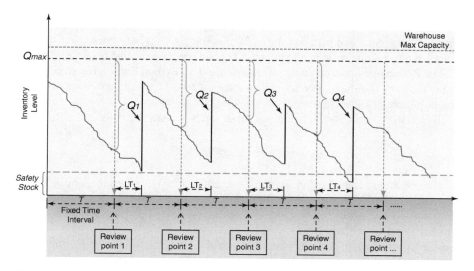

Fig. 7.10 Periodic inventory review

approach may be less responsive and resilient in managing inventories in high volatile market. Imagine there is a sudden surge in demand for your product in the middle of your review period, which could deplete you inventory faster than you would normally think, you are more likely to experience stockout if the replenishment is not automatically triggered.

In this section, we have introduced the basic techniques and approaches in inventory management. The EOQ model and safety stock calculation can help to address the question of *how much to order* by solving the optimal number of quantities to order and to keep as a backup. The re-order point (ROP) is useful for continuous cycle stock monitoring as it can help inventory managers to decide *when to order* so that new stock can arrive on time, thereby avoiding stockouts. By contrast, the periodic review method adopts regular review intervals and only orders the quantity that is needed to fill the gap between current stock level at review point and the pre-set maximum order quantities.

However, there are critics on the EOQ formula for it only takes the total cost perspective. In practice, there can be many other considerations when adjusting the order quantity. For instance, when suppliers are offering seasonal discounts for their products or there is a speculation that material price is going to go up dramatically, one may want to take the chance to purchase more inventories. Also, the EOQ only gives a 'theoretical' optimum, if a few more items can make up a full container shipping, for instance, you might want to just order a bit more to fill the gaps. Despite the critics, the EOQ model is still a useful method in inventory management by offering useful insights into the optimal order quantity.

7.3   Warehouse Optimization

7.3.1   Introduction to PuLP

In this section, we will go through some examples with Python. A linear optimization package named PuLP written in Python will be used to solve a simple warehouse optimization problem. Note here that the topic of optimization is very broad, and we only intend to cover some basic methods as it is beyond the scope of this book.

PuLP is an open-source linear programming (LP) Python library that comes with many industry-standard solvers and also integrates well with a range of open-source and commercial LP solvers.

To install the package, you can use either pip or conda, see below:

```
pip install pulp
```

For a detailed introduction, including examples and user guides, check **PuLP Documentation** at https://coin-or.github.io/pulp/.

Linear Programming
Linear programming (LP) involves the maximization or minimization of linear objective function, subject to linear equality and linear inequality constraints. LP has been widely applied in many subject areas, including operations research (OR).

Problems that can be solved by LP include resource allocation, scheduling, transportation, blending problems, and Sudoku, to name a few.

Basically, in LP, there are three components:

- **Decision Variables**—what we can control
- **Objective Function**—the equation that uses variables to express objective
- **Constraints**—the mathematical representation that sets the limits of a solution

Consider the example below:

$$Maximize : Z = 5x + 7y \tag{7.8}$$

This equation is considered as our objective function. x and y in this equation are decision variables. In this example, the objective function is subject to the following constraints:

$$s.t. x \geq 30$$

$$4y \leq 1 \ + 0$$

$$2y + 3x \leq 200$$

To solve this problem using PuLP, first we need to import it in the notebook:

Ex. 7.1

```
# Import PuLP modeler functions
from pulp import *
```

Then, we instantiate a problem class and name it 'prob' (though you could choose any names) using the `LpProblem` function. The function contains two parameters: the arbitrary name of this problem (as a string), and `LpMinimize` or `LpMaximize` depending on the type of LP to be solved. Since this is a maximization problem, we will use `LpMaximize`:

Ex. 7.2

```
# Initialize class
prob = LpProblem("LPexample", LpMaximize)
```

Next, we use `LpVariable` class to create our decision variables. The class contains four parameters, including the arbitrary name of what the variable represents, lower bound and upper bound on the variable, and the type of data (discrete or continuous). In our example, x has a lower bound of 30 and y has no bound (i.e., positive or negative infinity). Consider below:

Ex. 7.3

```
# Define variables
x = LpVariable('x', lowBound=30, cat='Continuous')
y = LpVariable('y', None, cat='Continuous')
```

The objective function is added with the '+=' operator, with a comma ',' at the end of the statement and a short string explaining what this objective function is

Ex. 7.4

```
# Define Objective Function
prob += 5*x + 7*y, "Z"
```

The constraints are entered with the '+=' operator again since we are adding more data to the 'prob' variable. See below:

Ex. 7.5

```
# Define Constraints
prob += 4*y <= 10 + x
prob += 2*y + 3*x <= 200
```

We have now created our problem with PuLP, and can have a look at it by simply run 'prob' in the notebook:

Ex. 7.6

```
# Check the newly created problem
prob
```

```
LPexample:
MAXIMIZE
5*x + 7*y + 0
SUBJECT TO
_C1: - x + 4 y <= 10

_C2: 3 x + 2 y <= 200

VARIABLES
30 <= x Continuous
y free Continuous
```

To solve the LP problem, we can use the `solve()` method. The input brackets are usually left empty; however, they can be used to specify which solver to use (e.g., `prob.solve(CPLEX())`). Consider below:

Ex. 7.7

```
# The problem is solved using PuLP's choice of Solver
prob.solve()
# The status of the solution
LpStatus[prob.status]
'Optimal'
```

The status of the solution can be requested by using the LpStatus dictionary. As shown above, the LP problem has been successfully solved, with an 'Optimal' solution found.

There are five status codes from the solver as listed in Table 7.3, with each having its own meaning.

Table 7.3 Return status from solver

Status codes	Numerical value	Explanation
'Optimal'	1	An optimal solution has been found
'Not Solved'	0	Status prior to solving the problem
'Infeasible'	−1	No feasible solutions have been found
'Unbounded'	−2	The constraints are not bounded
'Undefined'	−3	The optimal solution may exist but may not have been found

We can also view the values of variables x and y using the `varValue` method and the maximum value of the objective function with the `pulp.value` function. Consider below:

Ex. 7.8

```
# Each of the variables is printed with it's resolved optimum value
for v in prob.variables():
    print(v.name, "=", v.varValue)
x = 55.714286
y = 16.428571
```

Ex. 7.9

```
# Print the optimized solution
print("The maximized value can be =", value(prob.objective))
The maximized value can be = 393.571427
```

From the example above, we can learn the procedures to formulating an LP problem with PuLP, which include the following:

1. Initialize the problem model using `LpProblem` function.
2. Define the decision variables using `LpVariable`.
3. Define the objective function with the '+=' operator.
4. Define the constraints with the '+=' operator.
5. Solve the model with `solve()` method.

Next, we will look at a practical warehouse optimization problem.

7.3.2 Warehouse Optimization with PuLP

After understanding the basics of LP and how it can be solved with PuLP, let us now move onto a more practical problem of warehousing. Consider the example below,

Example 7.1

You are managing a small warehouse with a total effective storage size of 900 m^3. You have the option to sell eight different products online, A, B, C, D, E, F, G, and H, each with unique size and profit as is detailed in the table below. Your task is to maximize your profit while considering what to stock and how many to stock for each item.

(Note: for simplicity reason, ignore the demand pattern for each item.)

Item	Size (m^3)	Profit (£)
A	3	240
B	3	245
C	4	250
D	5	410
E	3.5	300
F	4	150
G	2	140
H	1	100

Conditions:

- Product A and B are similar with minor variations, you should at least store either item A or item B to satisfy your long-term loyal customers.
- Product G and H are sold in pairs, i.e., if Product G is selected, then product H must also be selected.

This is a profit maximization problem with warehouse capacity constraints. Specifically, we want to maximize profit such that:

$$Maximize \quad \text{Profit} = \sum \text{Profitability}_i X_i$$

where X_i is the item, and subject to the following total capacity constraint:

$$\sum \text{Size}_i X_i \leq 900$$

Additionally, we need to satisfy the conditions set out in the example. First, we must at least store either item A or item B, and second, we must store the same number of item G and item H if either is selected. These constraints can be expressed with the following,

$$X_A + X_B \geq 1$$

$$X_G - X_H = 0$$

Next, we formulate the problem with PuLP in the notebook. We start by creating a list of product items from A to H, a dictionary of the size of each item and a dictionary of the profit that each item can make, consider below:

Ex. 7.10

```
# Create a list of items
item = ['A', 'B', 'C', 'D', 'E', 'F', 'G', 'H']

# Create a dictionary of the size of each item
size = {'A':3, 'B':3, 'C':4,'D':5, 'E':3.5, 'F':4, 'G':2, 'H':1}

# Creat a dictionary of the profit of each item
prof = {'A':240, 'B':245, 'C':250,'D':410,
        'E':300, 'F':150, 'G':140, 'H':100}
```

Then, we initialize the problem model by giving it a name 'warehousing', and selecting `LpMaximize` since it is a maximization problem:

Ex. 7.11

```
# Initialize the problem model
model = LpProblem("warehousing", LpMaximize)
```

A dictionary *x* is created which contains the decision variables with an arbitrary prefix 'stock_' using `LpVariable.dicts()`. Unlike our previous example, the decision variables in this case will not be continuous, therefore we use 'integer' category. In addition, their defined lower bound is zero as negative product quantity does not make sense.

Ex. 7.12

```
# Define Decision Variables
x = LpVariable.dicts('stock_', item, lowBound=0, cat='Integer')
x
{'A': stock__A,
 'B': stock__B,
 'C': stock__C,
 'D': stock__D,
 'E': stock__E,
 'F': stock__F,
 'G': stock__G,
 'H': stock__H}
```

The next step is to create the objective function of the warehousing example. Remember the objective of this case is to maximize profit by selecting the right number of items to sell, subject to certain constraints. Instead of summing up the product of each item and its profit, we can define the objective function using a convenient `lpSum()` method, which sums a list of linear expressions. Often `lpSum` is used with Python's list comprehension. See below:

Ex. 7.13

```
# Define Objective Function
model += lpSum([prof[i]*x[i] for i in item])
```

Further list comprehension is used to define our capacity constraint. Additionally, we create two other constraints to satisfy the conditions set out in the example, consider below:

Ex. 7.14

```
# Define Constraints
model += lpSum([size[i]*x[i] for i in item]) <= 900,'Capacity Cons'
model += x['A'] + x['B'] >= 1, 'A or B'
model += x['G'] - x['H'] == 0, 'G=H'
```

Finally, let us solve the problem and print out the results:

Ex. 7.15

```
# Solve Model
model.solve()

for i in item:
    print("{} stock {}".format(i, x[i].varValue))

print("The maxmized profit could be £{}".\
                format(value(model.objective)))
A stock 0.0
B stock 2.0
C stock 0.0
D stock 1.0
E stock 254.0
F stock 0.0
G stock 0.0
H stock 0.0
The maxmized profit could be £77100.0
```

Therefore, as resolved by the model, the maximized profit could be £77,100, by stocking 254 units of item E, 1 unit of item D and 2 units of item B.

In this section, we have illustrated how to formulate and solve a simple warehouse optimization problem with linear and integer programming using PuLP. We will use PuLP again in our future examples of the following chapters. It is noteworthy that there are many open-source optimization packages in Python available on the market (e.g., SciPy, Google OR-Tools), which you can explore and try by yourself. For more details and examples on PuLP, you are encouraged to go through its documentation (see https://coin-or.github.io/pulp/).

7.4 Classification Algorithms

Classification, as its name suggests, is the process of understanding and grouping objects into pre-defined categories or 'sub-populations'. In machine learning, classification algorithms learn from input training data by recognizing certain 'patterns' in the data and predict a class (or target) label for future sets of data. In general, classification is considered an instance of supervised learning, and can be differentiated into *binary classification* (i.e., two classes only) and *multiclass classification* (i.e., more than two classes). Examples include:

- **Binary classification**: spam or non-spam emails, Yes or No, Panda or Bear, Pass or Fail, etc.
- **Multiclass classification**: e.g., sentiment analysis by polarity of opinion (e.g., negative, neural, positive, etc.).

In the sections below, we will learn different types of classification algorithms and how they work in practice to solve an inventory problem.

7.4.1 Logistic Regression

Logistic regression is a well-known algorithm for binary classification. Although it is called 'regression', it is in fact a linear model for predicting the categorical dependent variable using a given set of independent variables. Instead of fitting a regression line (e.g., OLS), logistic regression gives the probabilities (P) of describing the possible outcomes, using an 'S' shaped logistic function (sigmoid curve), which predicts values between 0 and 1 (see Fig. 7.11 below). It can be expressed as $P(y = 1|X)$ or $P(y = 0|X)$. The linear model can be written in the following mathematical form:

Fig. 7.11 Logistic regression

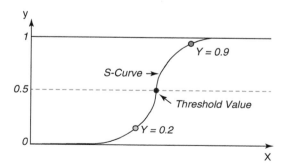

$$\ln\frac{p(x)}{1-p(x)} = \beta_0 + x\beta \tag{7.9}$$

Thus, after simple transformation, the probability can be expressed as:

$$p(x) = \frac{1}{1 + e^{-(\beta_0 + x\beta)}} \tag{7.10}$$

The logistic regression algorithm can be used to classify the observations using different types of data (e.g., continuous and discrete) and can easily determine the most important variables used for the classification.

As shown in Fig. 7.11, the value of the logistic regression must be between 0 and 1, and cannot go beyond this limit. Any values above the threshold value tend to 1, and any values below the threshold tend to 0.

In Python, scikit-learn implements `LogisticRegression` classifier. The implementation can be used to fit binary, One-vs-Rest, or multinomial logistic regression with regularization as the default setting to improve numerical stability.

To use the classifier, we need to import it from scikit-learn first. Consider below:

Ex. 7.16

```
from sklearn.linear_model import LogisticRegression
```

You are encouraged to go through its parameters, attributes, methods, and examples on **scikit-learn documentation** of `LogisticRegression` yourself.

Next, we will move onto an example and use the classifier to predict the probabilities of inventory stockout for each of the SKUs. For brevity reasons, we only attempt to demonstrate important steps here. The complete code, data, and Jupyter notebooks can be found at our online repository.

To start with, let us first import the necessary module packages into the notebook:

Ex. 7.17

```
# Import packages
import pandas as pd
import numpy as np
import matplotlib.pyplot as plt
import seaborn as sns; sns.set()
```

There are two datasets (training and test) available, however we will be using the training set in this example only. Consider below:

Ex. 7.18

```
# Load data
train = pd.read_csv('train_set.csv')
```

After initial data cleaning and transformation (omitted here), we have obtained a better and cleaner training set for later use. However, by plotting the distribution of the main features, it is obvious that the data are skewed and contain outliers. Instead of deleting some problematic SKU data, we will use `RobustScaler` to transform the data. The scaler removes the median and scales features using statistics that are robust to outliers.

Besides, since the training set contains categorial data (which has been dummy coded), we will define a function to transform only the features with datatype 'float32'. See below:

Ex. 7.19

```
from sklearn.preprocessing import RobustScaler
rscaler = RobustScaler()

def transformer (df):
    data = df.select_dtypes(include = ['float32'])
    data= rscaler.fit_transform(data)
    data = pd.DataFrame(data, columns=df.select_dtypes(
                        include = ['float32']).columns)
    df = data.join(df.select_dtypes(exclude = ['float32']))

    return df

train = transformer(train)
train.info()
```

```
RangeIndex: 1687860 entries, 0 to 1687859
Data columns (total 22 columns):
national_inv       1687860 non-null float32
lead_time          1687860 non-null float32
in_transit_qty     1687860 non-null float32
forecast_3_month   1687860 non-null float32
forecast_6_month   1687860 non-null float32
forecast_9_month   1687860 non-null float32
sales_1_month      1687860 non-null float32
sales_3_month      1687860 non-null float32
sales_6_month      1687860 non-null float32
sales_9_month      1687860 non-null float32
min_bank           1687860 non-null float32
pieces_past_due    1687860 non-null float32
perf_6_month_avg   1687860 non-null float32
perf_12_month_avg  1687860 non-null float32
local_bo_qty       1687860 non-null float32
potential_issue    1687860 non-null int32
deck_risk          1687860 non-null int32
oe_constraint      1687860 non-null int32
ppap_risk          1687860 non-null int32
stop_auto_buy      1687860 non-null int32
rev_stop           1687860 non-null int32
stockout           1687860 non-null int32
```

As shown above, the final training set contains 1,687,860 entries, and a total of 22 columns in which 'stockout' is our target variable. We can check the stockout percentage by plotting a pie chart:

Ex. 7.20

```
fig, axes = plt.subplots(figsize=(12,6))
plt.rc('font', size=12)
labels = 'Non-stockout', 'Stockout'
explode = (0.05, 0)

axes.pie(train.stockout.value_counts(), explode=explode,
        labels=labels, autopct='%1.2f%%', shadow=True, startangle=10)
axes.set_title('Stockout Pie Chart', fontsize=14)

plt.legend(loc=4,bbox_to_anchor=(1.3, 0.7)); # locating legends
```

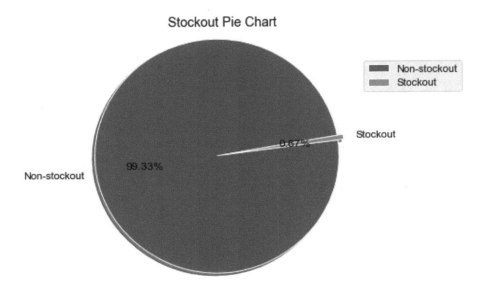

It is obvious that the stockout and non-stockout data are imbalanced in the training set. This imbalance can cause problem in class prediction, which will be discussed in later section. However, for now, let us further split the training set into training and validation sets. We will use the `StratifiedShuffleSplit` cross-validator in scikit-learn to perform this split, since it can preserve the percentage of samples for each class. Consider below:

Ex. 7.21

```
# Prepare data for training
from sklearn.model_selection import StratifiedShuffleSplit

# Use stratified split
sss = StratifiedShuffleSplit(n_splits=10, test_size=0.1,
                             random_state=42)
X, y = train.drop(columns='stockout',axis=1), train.stockout

for train_index, valid_index in sss.split(X, y):
    X_train, X_valid = X.iloc[train_index], X.iloc[valid_index]
    y_train, y_valid = y.iloc[train_index], y.iloc[valid_index]
```

Next, let us train a logistic regression model with the newly split training set. The default `solver` parameter in `LogisticRegression` classifier is set to 'lbfgs', however you can choose other solvers (see scikit-learn documentation for details). 'C' parameter determines the regularization strength. Like in Support Vector Machines (SVMs), smaller values specify stronger regularization. Consider below:

Ex. 7.22

```
from sklearn.linear_model import LogisticRegression

# Train model
lr = LogisticRegression(C=0.5, max_iter=5000, random_state=42)
lr.fit(X_train, y_train)
```

After training the model, we can use it to make predictions on our validation set. The classifier's `score()` method can return the mean accuracy on the given test data and labels. See below:

Ex. 7.23

```
y_pred = lr.predict(X_valid)
print(lr.score(X_valid, y_valid))
0.9932932826182266
```

Wow, over 99% accuracy (ratio of correct predictions) on the validation set! However, recall that our data are very imbalanced, with over 99% of data are non-stockout. Thus, even if the classifier labels all the validation set as non-stockout, it can still achieve 99% accuracy. Classification accuracy alone cannot be a good measure for evaluating the performance of a classifier. We should consider using other performance measures, especially when dealing with imbalanced datasets.

7.4.2   Classification Performance Measurement

Confusion Matrix

A better and unambiguous way to evaluate the performance of a classifier is to use a confusion matrix. A confusion matrix often uses a table to describe the performance of a classification model (i.e., a classifier) on a test set for which the true values are known. As shown in Table 7.4, the confusion matrix itself is relatively straightforward to understand. Across the tops are the predicted class labels and down the side are the actual class labels. The number of predicted class labels by the classifier are grouped into the cells accordingly.

A good classifier should be able to predict more True Positives (TP) and True Negatives (TN) than False Positives (FP) and False Negatives (FN). Specifically, there are three useful measures that can be used to evaluate the performance of a classifier:

- **Precision**: is the number of TP divided by the sum number of TP and FP (i.e., total number of predicted positives), which can be expressed as:

$$\frac{TP}{TP + FP}$$

- **Recall**: is the number of TP divided by the sum number of TP and FN (i.e., total number of actual positives), which can be expressed as:

$$\frac{TP}{TP + FN}$$

- **F1 Score**: is the harmonic mean of Precision and Recall, which can be expressed as:

$$\frac{2}{\dfrac{1}{Precision} + \dfrac{1}{Recall}} = \frac{TP}{TP + \dfrac{FN + FP}{2}}$$

As such, F1 score is high when both *Precision* and *Recall* are high.

We can regard *precision* as a measure of ***exactness*** of a classifier. A high precision can indicate a small number of false positives (FP). And recall can be regarded as a measure of ***completeness*** of a classifier. A high recall can indicate few false negatives (FN).

Table 7.4 Confusion matrix

	PREDICTED Positive	PREDICTED Negative
ACTUAL Positive	*TRUE* Positive (TP)	*FALSE* Negative (FN)
ACTUAL Negative	*FALSE* Positive (FP)	*TRUE* Negative (TN)

Table 7.5 Precision/recall in pandas vs. bears classification example

n = 250	PREDICTED Pandas		PREDICTED Bears		
	Classifier 1	Classifier 2	Classifier 1	Classifier 2	
ACTUAL Pandas	100	80	50	70	**150**
ACTUAL Bears	30	20	70	80	**100**

As an example, imagine we try to predict and classify pandas by learning the features from a dataset containing both pandas and bears (see Table 7.5).

The precision can be thought of as, out of the predicted positives (which consists of both correctly predicted pandas and incorrectly predicted pandas, i.e., bears), how many of them are correctly predicted (i.e., true pandas) by the classifier. In the example above, the precision score for classifier 1 is 76.9%, and classifier 2 is 80%.

The recall, however, can be thought of as, out of all the actual positives (all actual pandas in the data), how many of them are correctly predicted by the classifier. In the case below, the recall score for classifier 1 is 66.7%, and classifier 2 is 53.3%.

The F1 score for classifier 1 is 0.71, and for classifier 2 is 0.64.

In this classification example, if our goal is to correctly predict as many pandas as we can (high recall), classifier 1 obviously outperforms classifier 2; however, if our goal is to ensure a high accuracy of identified pandas out of the predicted samples (high precision), then classifier 2 is better than classifier 1.

Note that F1 score favours classifiers that have similar precision and recall values. Thus, overall, it seems that classifier 1 performs better than classifier 2. Whilst this might be true in our example, in some practical contexts you might favour more about precision, and in other contexts, you might care more about recall.

Unfortunately, we cannot have it both ways. Where there is a perfectly separable data, both precision and recall can reach a maximum value of 1. However, in practice, increasing precision could reduce recall, and vice versa. This is called the **precision/recall trade-off**.

In most practical cases, a dataset often contains noise which make perfect separation impossible. This is because some positive and negative classes are too close to separate. Shifting the decision boundary can either increase the precision value or the recall value but not both. In other words, there can always be misclassification by a classifier, which will lead to compromising precision or recall scores.

Precision-Recall Curve

Precision-recall is a useful performance measure for a classifier when the classes are very imbalanced, such as in our previous stockout prediction example. The **precision-recall curve** displays the trade-off between precision and recall at different threshold and is typically used in binary classification to evaluate the performance of a classifier.

Most of classifiers uses a threshold equal to 0. In scikit-learn, we cannot set the threshold directly, but can have access to the decision scores that a classifier uses to make predictions. If the decision score for each instance is equal to or greater than the threshold value, then instance belongs to a positive class (or target); if the decision score is smaller than the threshold, then instance belongs to the negative class (or target). We can use `decision_function()` method to access the decision score for each instance, and then make predictions based on those scores with any threshold of our choice.

Now, let us go back to our stockout prediction example. To evaluate the logistic regression model, we can use scikit-learn confusion matrix implementation under `sklearn.metrics`. Consider below, where we try to plot the confusion matrix:

Ex. 7.24

```
from sklearn.metrics import confusion_matrix

cm = confusion_matrix(y_valid, y_pred)

fig, ax = plt.subplots()
sns.heatmap(cm, annot=True, cmap='Blues')
ax.set(title='Confusion Matrix',
          ylabel='True label',
          xlabel='Predicted label');
```

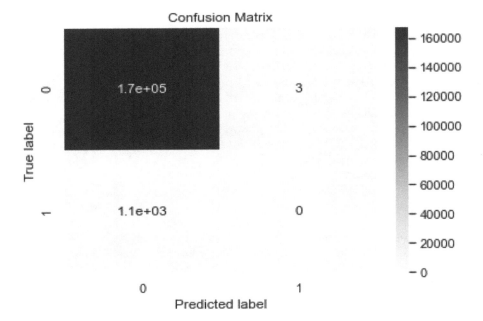

As shown above, the classifier's performance is not as good as we might have thought, despite achieving over 99% accuracy. From the confusion matrix however, we can see that the classifier predicted the number of TPs (i.e., true stockout) to be zero, indicating a rather poor performance of the logistic regression classifier in this imbalanced example. Recall that our goal in this example is to predict stockout but the classifier has failed to predict any of it correctly.

Scikit-learn has also implemented `precision_recall_curve` and `average_precision_score` under `sklearn.metrics`. Here, we first define a simple PR curve function for use later:

Ex. 7.25

```
# Define a PR curve function for later use
def plot_pr_curve (y_true, y_score, label='', linestyle = ''):
    p, r, threshold = precision_recall_curve(y_true, y_score)
    avg_p = average_precision_score(y_true, y_score, average='micro')

    fig, ax = plt.subplots(figsize=(8,5))
    ax.plot(r, p, linewidth=1, linestyle = linestyle,
            label='%s (precision = %.3f)'%(label,avg_p))
    ax.set_xlabel('Recall')
    ax.set_ylabel('Precision')
    ax.legend(loc=1)
    ax.grid(True)
    ax.set_xlim([0, 1])
    ax.set_ylim([0, 1])
    ax.set_title('Precision-Recall Curve')
```

Let us now plot the precision-recall (PR) curve of our logistic regression classifier, see below:

Ex. 7.26

```
plot_pr_curve(y_valid, lr.decision_function(X_valid),
              label='Logistic', linestyle='-')
```

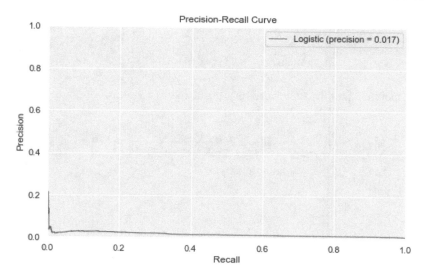

As clearly shown above, the PR curve does not look great either, with an average precision score of 0.017, indicating a poor performance of the logistic regression model.

ROC Curve

Another useful performance visualization tool is called the ROC (**Receiver Operating Characteristic**) curve. The ROC curve shows how the recall vs precision relationship changes as *threshold* changes for identifying a positive class. In particular, the ROC curve plots the true positive rate (another name for recall) on the *y*-axis against the false positive rate (FPR) on the *x*-axis. FPR is the probability of a false alarm, i.e., the ratio of negative instances that are incorrectly classified as positive.

When evaluating the performance of classifiers, we can measure the area under the curve (AUC). A ROC AUC equal or close to 1 would indicate a perfect classifier, whereas a poorly performed classifier will have a ROC AUC equal to 0.5.

Scikit-learn has both ROC curve and AUC implementations under `sklearn.metrics`. Likewise, let us first define a ROC curve function for later use. Consider below:

Ex. 7.27

```
from sklearn.metrics import roc_curve,auc

# Let's define a ROC plot function for later use
def plot_roc_curve (y_true, y_score, label='', linestyle=''):
    fpr, tpr, threshold = roc_curve(y_true, y_score)
    roc_auc = auc(fpr, tpr)

    fig, ax = plt.subplots(figsize=(8,5))
    ax.plot(fpr, tpr, linewidth=2, linestyle=linestyle,
            label = '%s AUC = %0.3f' % (label, roc_auc))

    ax.plot([0,1], [0,1], color='k', linewidth=0.5, linestyle='--')
    ax.legend(loc=4)
    ax.set_xlabel('False Positive Rate')
    ax.set_ylabel('True Positive Rate')
    ax.set_xlim([0, 1])
    ax.set_ylim([0, 1.1])
    ax.set_title('ROC Curve', fontsize=15);
```

We can then plot the ROC curve and check the AUC score:

Ex. 7.28

```
plot_roc_curve(y_valid, lr.decision_function(X_valid),
               label='Logistic', linestyle='-')
```

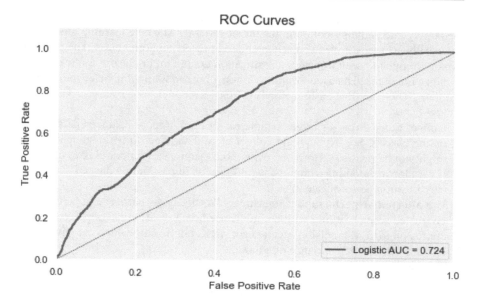

As mentioned earlier, a ROC AUC close to 1 is an indication of well performed classifier. However, what we got here is a ROC AUC score of 0.724, which is not good enough.

In summary, to evaluate a classifier's performance, solely relying on accuracy score is sufficient, especially when the dataset is extremely imbalanced. The confusion matrix, PR curve, ROC curve, and ROC AUC offer better and more reliable performance measures for the evaluation of a classifier.

Note: As a rule of thumb, PR curve is preferred when the positive class is rare or when you care more about FP than FN, otherwise ROC curve is a preferred measure.

7.4.3   Dealing with Imbalanced Dataset

Imbalanced data is not uncommon in real life. For instance, in our previous stockout example, we have a very imbalanced dataset. This is because the chance of experiencing stockout in a real business should only take a small portion of all the inventories held by the business, otherwise the business would suffer from losing customers and profits in the long run.

Imbalanced classification can lead to reduction in accuracy of a classifier due to the largely unequal distribution in the target variable. Machine learning algorithms are usually accuracy driven and can get biased towards majority class. The problem is more frequently seen in binary classification than in multi-class classification.

Since imbalanced dataset is quite common, how can we fix it if we encounter this problem? There are five basic methods to consider:

- **Collect more data**—A larger sample might bring a more balanced perspective on the classes. So, if you could collect more data, then do it! In some cases, it might not be possible. However, even more examples of minor classes can help if we adopt resampling technique to mitigate the impact of imbalanced dataset on classification performance.
- **Use alternative performance measures**—As discussed earlier, accuracy cannot be trusted when working with an imbalanced dataset. Alternatively, we can use confusion matrix, precision-recall curve, ROC curve, etc., which can give more insights into the performance of a model.
- **Resample your dataset**—Resampling techniques can be used to even-up the classes when training your predictive models. There are two basic methods, either adding copies of under-represented class (i.e., over-sampling), or deleting instances from over-represented class (i.e., under-sampling).
- **Use synthetic sampling**—Another useful approach to resampling is generating synthetic samples. There are different algorithms that can perform this synthetic sampling. A popular one is called SMOTE (i.e., Synthetic Minority Over-sampling Technique). The algorithm generates synthetic samples by randomly drawing the features from instances in the minority class (Chawla et al. 2002), instead of creating copies.
- **Try different algorithms**—Last but not least, you should always try to apply different algorithms to solve the classification problems. Some algorithms may perform better than others, especially when dealing with imbalanced datasets.

Since we are unable to collect more data for our previous example (even if we could, the data will be more likely to be imbalanced as explained earlier), we will use the synthetic sampling technique SMOTE instead. In Python, there is an `imbalanced-learn` implementation, which is an open-source python toolbox for solving the problem of imbalanced dataset in machine learning (Lemaître et al. 2017).

To install the package, we can use either `pip` or `conda`, see below:

```
conda install -c conda-forge imbalanced-learn
```

Once the package is installed, we can import it into the Jupyter notebook. The implementation includes the SMOTE algorithm as well as its variants and combinations. For a comparison of the various sampling algorithms, check **imbalanced-learn** documentation for more details.

To fix our stockout dataset, we will apply a combined over- and under-sampling method called SMOTETomek. SMOTE algorithm can generate noisy samples by interpolating new points between marginal outliers and inliers. This problem can be solved by using Tomek's link method that can clean the space resulting from over-sampling. Consider below:

Ex. 7.29

```
from imblearn.combine import SMOTETomek

smt = SMOTETomek(random_state=42)

X_train_resampled, y_train_resampled = smt.fit_resample(X_train, y_train)

# Save the new samples to file for quick re-use later on
pd.DataFrame(X_train_resampled, columns=X_train.columns).\
                        to_csv('X_train_resampled.csv',index=False)
pd.DataFrame(y_train_resampled).to_csv('y_train_resampled.csv',index=False)
```

Since the dataset is very large, it can take quite long time to train depending on your PC configuration. Once trained, we should save the resampled data into files for later use. Now, let us take a look at the target variable distribution in our resampled dataset:

Ex. 7.30

```
# Plot resampled y_train data distribution
plt.figure(figsize=(8, 4))
y_train_new.value_counts().sort_index().plot(kind='bar')
plt.ylabel("Count")
plt.title('Went on Stockout? (0=No, 1=Yes)', fontsize=15);
```

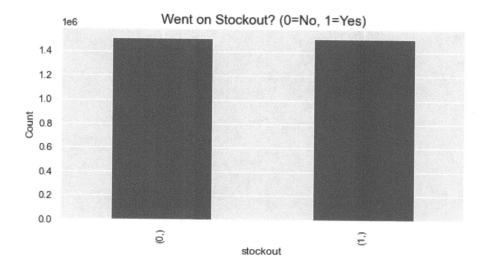

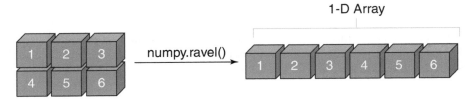

Fig. 7.12 Numpy.ravel() transformation

Obviously, the resampled dataset is balanced now. We can then retrain our logistic regression model with the new data. Here we need to apply `numpy.ravel()` function to our `y_train_new` data so as to create a contiguous flattened 1D array for training purpose, as illustrated in Fig. 7.12.

Consider the code below:

Ex. 7.31

```
# Flatten the target data for training purpose
y_train_new = y_train_new.values.ravel()
```

We will use the same parameter settings as before to train the logistic regression model with the new data and see whether the performance can be improved:

Ex. 7.32

```
# Train the logistic regression model with new data
lr.fit(X_train_new, y_train_new)
LogisticRegression(C=0.5, max_iter=5000, random_state=42)
```

After training, we can then use the two functions that were defined previously, i.e., `plot_pr_curve` and `plot_roc_curve`, to evaluate the performance of the classifier. First, the PR curve:

Ex. 7.33

```
plot_pr_curve(y_valid, lr.decision_function(X_valid),
              label='Logistic', linestyle='-')
```

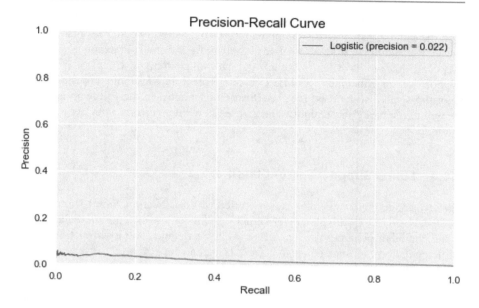

Next, the ROC curve:

Ex. 7.34

```
plot_roc_curve(y_valid, lr.decision_function(X_valid),
               label='Logistic', linestyle='-')
```

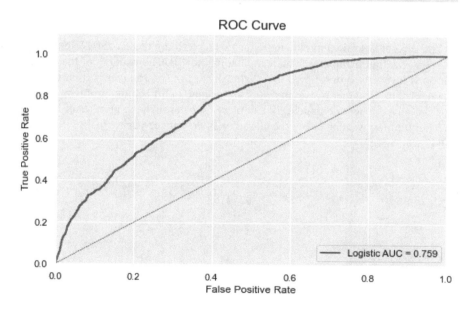

As can be seen from the two output diagrams, training on the resampled dataset with the same logistic regression model returns only slightly better results. In such a case, we should consider alternative classifiers for the stockout example.

Recall that we have learnt some regression algorithms in Chap. 6, including Support Vector Machines (SVM), Decision Trees, and Random Forests. These algorithms can also be used for classification problems. In the following section, we will use some of these algorithms and see how they perform with our stockout example.

7.4.4   Linear Support Vector Classifier

First, we are going to apply a linear support vector classification. Scikit-learn implements `LinearSVC` with parameter kernel=`'linear'`, which has more flexibility in the choice of penalties (i.e., `'l1'` or `'l2'` as default) and loss functions. The implementation can scale better to large dataset, and support both dense and sparse input. It can also handle multiclass classification using a one-vs-the-rest scheme.

Let us import `LinearSVC` from scikit-learn and train it with our resampled dataset, consider below:

Ex. 7.35

```
from sklearn.svm import LinearSVC

lsvc = LinearSVC(C=100,max_iter=5000,dual=False,random_state=42)
lsvc.fit(X_train_new, y_train_new)
LinearSVC(C=100, dual=False, max_iter=5000, random_state=42)
```

You can set your own parameter values when training the model. Note that `C` is the regularization parameter, which is defaulted to 1.0. The strength of the regularization is inversely proportional to C value. The `dual` parameter is used to select the algorithm to either solve the dual or primal optimization problem. We set `dual=False` when the number of samples is greater than the number of features.

After training, we can check the classifier's performance using the PR curve and ROC curve again:

Ex. 7.36

```
plot_pr_curve(y_valid, lsvc.decision_function(X_valid),
              label='LinearSVC', linestyle='-.')
```

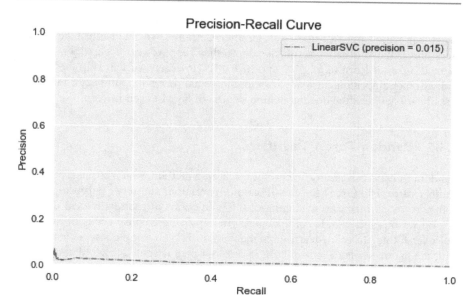

Ex. 7.37

```
plot_roc_curve(y_valid, lsvc.decision_function(X_valid),
               label='LinearSVC', linestyle='-.')
```

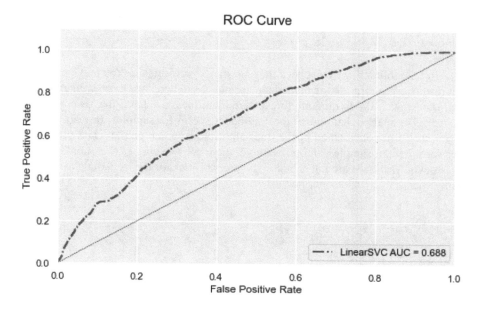

As shown above, the trained `LinearSVC` classifier does not perform any better than the previous logistic regression classifier. Certainly, we could adjust the parameters and achieve a better result or adopt other support vector classifiers implemented in scikit-learn (e.g., `SVC` and `NuSVC`). However, we will skip these steps and try other algorithms instead. For more information on support vector machines classification, check the documentation section of **SVM** in scikit-learn.

7.4.5 Random Forest Classifier

Random forest is essentially an ensemble learning method, which consists of a large number of decision trees for classification, regression, and other purposes. A random forest classifier uses averaging of the predictions of each individual decision tree on various sub-samples of the dataset to improve predictive accuracy and control over-fitting. In scikit-learn implementation, the sub-sample size is controlled with the parameter `max_samples`, if `bootstrap` is set to `True` (default), otherwise the whole dataset is used to build each tree.

Let us train a random forest classifier on our stockout example. Consider below:

Ex. 7.38

```
from sklearn.ensemble import RandomForestClassifier

rfc = RandomForestClassifier(n_estimators=1000, n_jobs=-1,
                             random_state=42)
rfc.fit(X_train_new, y_train_new)
RandomForestClassifier(n_estimators=1000, n_jobs=-1, random_state=42
```

After the training, we can check the classifier's performance. You may get different results by calibrating the parameter settings. Note here, however, unlike logistic regression and SVM, random forest classifier does not have the `decision_function` method that returns the confidence scores for samples. Instead, there is a `predict_prob` method of the trees algorithms, which predict class probabilities for the input samples. In our example, there are two classes (i.e., non-stockout vs. stockout), and we are interested in the probabilities for the stockout class, hence using slice `[:,1]`. Consider below:

Ex. 7.39

```
plot_pr_curve(y_valid, rfc.predict_proba(X_valid)[:,1],
              label='Random Forest', linestyle='--')
```

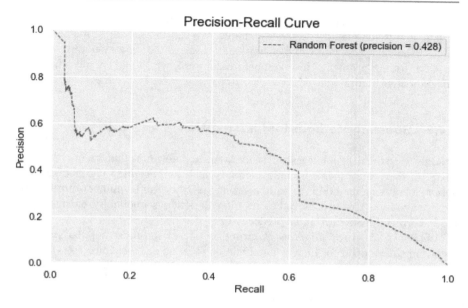

Ex. 7.40

```
plot_roc_curve(y_valid, rfc.predict_proba(X_valid)[:,1],
               label='Random Forest',linestyle='--')
```

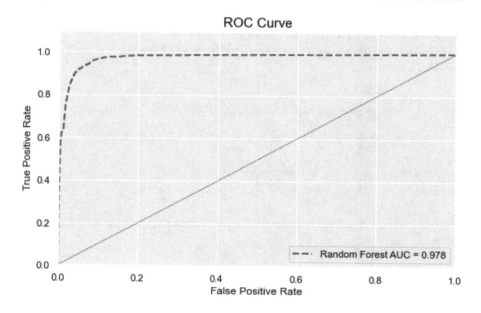

As shown above, the random forest classifier performs much better than the logistic regression classifier for our example. We can further adjust the parameter values to achieve a better result by using `GridSearchCV,` if we decide to use this classifier for our problem. However, before doing so, we should try out other classification algorithms.

7.4.6   Boosting Methods for Classification

In addition to the decision trees and random forest algorithms that are introduced in Chap. 6, there are other ensemble methods such as *boosting*. The general idea behind a boosting method is to build a strong classifier from a number of relatively weak classifiers. This is achieved by training classifiers sequentially, each attempting to correct the errors from its predecessor.

AdaBoost, short for *Adaptive Boosting*, is one of the most popular Boosting algorithms developed for binary classification (Freund and Schapire 1997). It is a meta-estimator that trains a classifier on the original dataset and then trains addition copies of the classifiers on the same dataset by adjusting the relative weights of misclassified training instances from previous classifiers. In other words, the first classifier might get many instances wrong, thus their weights get boosted so that the second classifier can do a better job on these instances, and so on and so forth.

In scikit-learn, the AdaBoost classifier implements the multiclass version of AdaBoost algorithm known as *AdaBoost-SMME* (Stagewise Additive Modelling using a Multiclass Exponential loss function) (Zhu et al. 2009). For binary classification, SMMME is equivalent to AdaBoost.

To use the classifier, we need to import it from scikit-learn under `ensemble.` Consider below,

Ex. 7.41
```
from sklearn.ensemble import AdaBoostClassifier

abc = AdaBoostClassifier(n_estimators=100, learning_rate=1,
                         random_state=42)

abc.fit(X_train_new, y_train_new)
AdaBoostClassifier(learning_rate=1, n_estimators=100, random_state=42)
```

After training on our stockout dataset, we can check the classifier's performance. See below:

Ex. 7.42
```
plot_pr_curve(y_valid, abc.decision_function(X_valid),
              label='AdaBoost', linestyle='-')
```

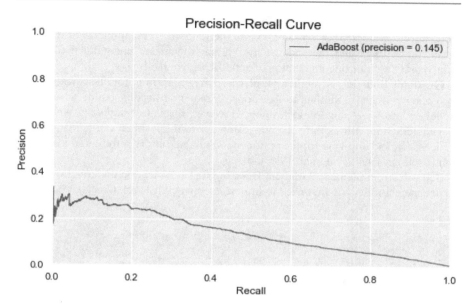

Ex. 7.43

```
plot_roc_curve(y_valid, abc.decision_function(X_valid),
               label='AdaBoost', linestyle='-')
```

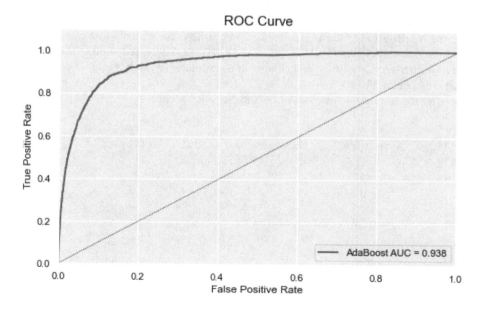

As can be seen, AdaBoost performs better than the logistic regression classifier in our example, but not as good as the random forest model. For different parameter settings and methods of the classifier, you are encouraged to check **AdaBoostClassifier** documentation of scikit-learn yourself.

Gradient Boosting is another popular Boosting algorithm for classification and regression problems. Similar to AdaBoost, Gradient Boosting builds an additive model in a forward stage-wise fashion. However, instead of adjusting weights at every interaction, it tries to fit the new estimator to the residual errors made by its predecessor, and allowing for the optimization of an arbitrary differential loss function (Breiman 1997; Friedman 1999a, b).

Scikit-learn implements Gradient Boosting for classification under ensemble. To use the classifier, we first need to import it from scikit-learn. Consider below:

Ex. 7.44

```
from sklearn.ensemble import GradientBoostingClassifier

gbc = GradientBoostingClassifier(n_estimators=500,
                                 learning_rate=0.1, random_state=42)

gbc.fit(X_train_new, y_train_new)
GradientBoostingClassifier(n_estimators=500, random_state=42)
```

Note that the loss function to be optimized is set by using the loss parameter, which is defaulted to 'deviance' (=logistic regression) for classification with probabilistic outputs. When loss = 'exponential', gradient boosting recovers the AdaBoost algorithm. The learning rate shrinks the contribution of each tree and the value (default to 0.1) is set by learning_rate parameter. There is a trade-off between learning rate and number of estimators, which is set by n_estimators (default to 100).

After the training, let us check how the classifier performs.

Ex. 7.45

```
plot_pr_curve(y_valid, gbc.decision_function(X_valid),
              label='GBC', linestyle='-')
```

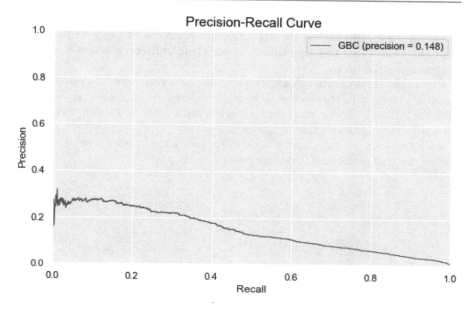

Ex. 7.46

```
plot_roc_curve(y_valid, gbc.decision_function(X_valid),
               label='GBC', linestyle='-')
```

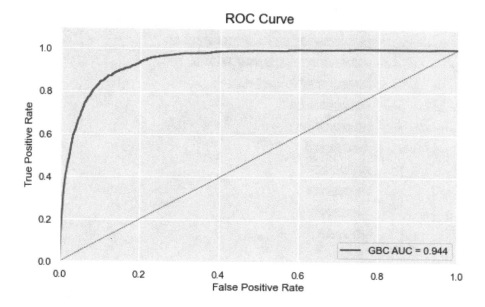

As shown above, the performance of the Gradient Boosting Classifier is similar to that of the AdaBoost classifier. For different parameter settings, methods and examples of Gradient Boosting Classifier, see **GradientBoostingClassifier** documentation of scikit-learn.

Comparing different classification algorithms, we can see that the random forest classifier outperforms the other models in our example. We can then proceed with using `GridSearchCV` to find better parameter settings for the random forest classifier. This step is omitted here.

As a final step, we can check what features play more important roles in determining stockout predictions. Consider below:

Ex. 7.47

```
# Plot feature importance
feature_rank = pd.Series(rfc.feature_importances_,
                         index=X_train.columns)

plt.figure(figsize=(8,8))
feature_rank.nlargest(15).sort_values(ascending = True).\
                              plot(kind='barh')

plt.xlabel('Importance')
plt.title('Feature Importance', fontsize =15);
```

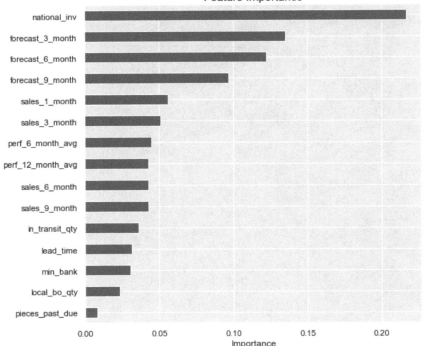

What we can observe from the feature important diagram above is that current national inventory level and the demand forecasts of an item for next 3, 6, and 9 months of play critical roles in determining the possibility of experiencing stockout. In practice, this information can be very useful for inventory managers as they may need to pay close attention to these features in order to prevent stockout from happening. Specifically, they may need to have a good inventory management system to closely monitoring their real-time inventory levels for each SKU, and well-developed algorithms for their demand forecasting, which is covered in our next chapter.

Multiclass Classification

When there are more than two classes in a classification problem, it is commonly known as multiclass classification. Multiclass classification assumes that each sample can have only one label.

Some algorithms that are used for binary classification such as Random Forest and Naive Bayes classifiers are also capable of predicting multiple classes, whilst others such as Support Vector Machine and Linear classifiers are strictly for binary classification only.

We do not cover multiclass classification in this Chapter. Scikit-learn has implemented multiclass and multioutput algorithms, please refer to **Multiclassification** section of scikit-learn documentation for more details and examples.

Summary of Learning Objectives

1. **Describe the purpose and major activities of warehouse management.**

   The purpose of managing warehouse is to ensure the efficiency and effectiveness of warehouse operations to support a smooth supply chain and production needs to satisfy customers. The major activities of warehouse management include warehouse layout design and optimization, receiving and recording incoming goods, putting-away, tracking and locating goods within a warehouse, picking, packing, and despatching orders., as well as optimizing internal processes and the overall warehouse performance.

2. **Understand WMS and its benefits as well as KPIs for warehouse performance measurement.**

   WMS is an IT system that can help improve and optimize warehouse operations, providing accurate and timely data recording, communicating and enhanced visibility of many areas within warehouses. Some common features include warehouse design optimization, inventory recording, tracking and locating. Modern warehouses equipped with more advanced WMS and smart devices and sensors can fully support automated item picking, packing, labelling, and dispatching. The associated benefits include reduced paperwork and errors, improved capacity utilization, optimized inventory control, enhanced efficiency and productivity as well as a safe working environment. When measuring the performance of a warehouse management, the accuracy, speed, and cost of order fulfilment should be the primary foci. Some key KPIs include receiving efficiency, picking accuracy, holding cost, inventory turnover, order lead time, on-time delivery, rate of return, and stockout rate.

3. **Describe different inventory types and the purpose of holding them.**

   Inventory can exist in many forms and along different stages of a supply chain, for example, raw materials, components, work in progress, and finished product. It can be tangible goods and customers, and can also be intangible things such as information and data. Table 7.2 provides a list of different types of inventories in various business operations. Inventories are usually considered costly to buy and keep. The purpose of holding inventory is mainly because goods cannot be made and delivered instantly, therefore inventories can act like a buffer between where/when good are produced and where/when they are required. In addition, there are other reasons to hold inventories such as protecting from supply disruptions, achieving economies of scale, securing scare resources, meeting future demand and the 'buy low, sell high' motives.

4. **Understand the key approaches to managing inventories.**

   In this chapter, we focus on two essential questions in inventory management, i.e., 'how much to order' and 'when to order'. In addressing the former question, the introduced approaches include determining economic order quantity (EOQ), which takes into account both holding costs and ordering costs (see Fig. 7.7), and setting the level of safety stock considering both supply and demand uncertainties. For the latter question, the discussed methods include calculating the re-order point (ROP) and using periodic reviews by setting a fixed time interval as illustrated in Fig. 7.10.

5. **Learn warehouse optimization using linear programming and different classification algorithms and their performance evaluation methods.**

   We have learnt a simple warehousing optimization problem using linear programming with PuLP. Linear programming involves the maximization or minimization of linear objective function, subject to linear equality and linear inequality constraints. Besides, we have illustrated an inventory stockout prediction example using classification algorithms. These algorithms include logistic regression, linear support vector classifier, random forest classifiers, and some boosting methods such as AdaBoost and gradient boosting. Make sure you understand these algorithms, their parameters and how to use them to solve classification problems in Python. To evaluate the performance of a classifier, confusion matrix, precision-recall curve, ROC curve, and AUC score can be useful measures. Imbalanced data often causes problems in classification, there are five basic methods to consider to improve the performance of classification as discussed in this chapter. In particular, SMOTE algorithm can be useful as it can generate synthetic samples by randomly drawing the features from instances in the minority class.

Discussion Questions

1. Choose a warehouse (e.g., a supermarket, IKEA stores) and discuss what layout designs are good and what can be improved? How could layout improve internal goods/customer flows within the warehouse?
2. Holding inventories can be costly, identify the various costs associated with inventory holding within a company of your choice.
3. Discuss why EOQ is often criticized?
4. In safety stock calculation, if there are no variations in supply lead time, what will the formula (7.4) change to? What about the demand is constant over time?
5. When the periodic reviews method is most useful and effective in restocking inventories?

Keyboard Exercises

1. In your notebook, import necessary packages, re-run all the exercises in this chapter. You can set your own parameter values and use grid search to fine-tune each estimator of your choice.
2. In the warehousing optimization Example 7.1, what would be the new solution if the condition changes to product A and B must both be stored?
3. Download the Safety Stock calculation data from the online repository and try to work out the average lead time, safety stock and re-order point for each item in Python.
4. In the inventory stockout example, download the additional 'test' dataset from the online repository and use your trained best classification model to make predictions on the test set and evaluate its performance.

References

Breiman, L. 1997. "Arcing The Edge". Technical Report 486. Statistics Department, University of California, Berkeley.

Chawla, N. V., Bowyer, K. W., Hall, L. O., & Kegelmeyer, W. P. 2002. "SMOTE: synthetic minority over-sampling technique". Journal of Artificial Intelligence Research, Vol. 16, pp. 321-357.

Freund, Y. & Schapire, R.E. 1997. "A decision-theoretic generalization of on-line learning and an application to boosting". Journal of Computer and System Sciences, Vol. 55(1), pp. 119-139.

Friedman, J. H. 1999a. "Greedy Function Approximation: A Gradient Boosting Machine". Department of Statistics and Stanford Linear Accelerator Center, Stanford University, Stanford.

Friedman, J. H. 1999b. "Stochastic Gradient Boosting". Department of Statistics and Stanford Linear Accelerator Center, Stanford University, Stanford.

King, P.L. 2011. "Understanding safety stock and mastering its equations". APICS magazine.

Lemaître, G., Nogueira, F. & Aridas, C.K. 2017. "Imbalanced-learn: A Python Toolbox to Tackle the Curse of Imbalanced Datasets in Machine Learning". Journal of Machine Learning Research, Vol. 18(17), pp. 1–5.

Zhu, J., Zou, H., Rosset, S. & Hastie, T. 2009. "Multi-class AdaBoost". Statistics and Its Interface, Vol. 2, pp. 349-360.

Demand Management

8

Contents

Learning Objectives
- Understand the purpose of demand management and the SPSS model.
- Describe different demand forecasting methods and the differences between qualitative and quantitative methods.
- Learn the components of time series and be able to use the traditional methods to perform univariate time series forecasting in Python.
- Grasp the ways of evaluating forecast accuracy.
- Learn and be able to use Random Forest Regression and XGBoost to perform multivariate time series forecasting in Python.

© The Author(s), under exclusive license to Springer Nature
Switzerland AG 2022
K. Y. Liu, *Supply Chain Analytics*, https://doi.org/10.1007/978-3-030-92224-5_8

8.1   Demand Management

Demand, in supply chain context, refers to the actual orders placed by customers. Demand is essential information for effective supply chain planning and management. Without accurate demand information, it can be challenging for companies to make production planning and control. For instance, if inaccurate demand information passes along the supply chain from downstream to upstream, significant distortion in production planning and order preparation may be created, leading to adverse bullwhip effects.

Demand management in supply chains aims to improve demand visibility, predictability, and reliability so that the focal companies can design and deliver products and services to satisfy various customers' needs in a most effective and efficient way. Demand management is considered to be a specific organizational capability, which contains a defined set of processes and routines for companies that produce goods and services.

As illustrate in Fig. 8.1, demand management can be broadly categorized into four stages, from *sense, predict, seize* to *stabilize* (SPSS), i.e., the SPSS model of demand management in supply chains.

- **Sense**—during the sensing stage, companies detect market trends, understand and capture customers' demand insights, and therefore anticipate future changes and identify demand opportunities. Examples include market research, social media sentiment analysis, and competitor analysis, etc.

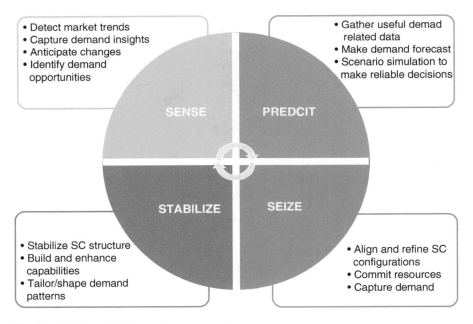

Fig. 8.1 SPSS model of demand management

- **Predict**—then companies should collect all possible demand related data and features to make demand forecast. As forecasts can be inaccurate often, scenario simulation can help decision makers to decide best plans or prepare for worst scenarios.
- **Seize**—the next step is to align and refine supply chain configurations, allocate and commit resources in order to capture demand and satisfy customers. Different companies might come up with various strategies and approaches to seizing the demands in light of their own business objectives. For instance, when customers are in favour of customizable products, the selling firm might need to align and refine its supply chains to allow a fast and flexible response.
- **Stabilize**—the final stage of the SPSS model is to stabilize and standardize supply chain structures and processes based on how the companies become successful in capturing demand. It may require firms to further develop and enhance its capabilities to cope with demand changes. For example, traditional watch makers may realign their existing capabilities and redevelop their strength in the smartwatch market because there is a tendency that customers prefer the new '*smartization*' of their wearable devices. In addition, organizations may go beyond by shaping demand patterns instead (e.g., using pricing strategies; creating product variations; modifying the timing and location of delivery) to suit their capacity constraints and performance targets.

The SPSS model is rather dynamic and should be conducted on on-going basis as external market conditions and demands change all the time. In order to capture and seize demands effectively, organizations need to continuously repeat the SPSS processes.

8.2   Demand Forecasting

Demand forecasting is a pivotal task in demand management as it underpins all production planning and control in supply chain management. There are many ways to conduct demand forecasting, however, note that the ultimate objective of performing the forecasts is to understand and predict the customer orders in the future. Demand forecasting can involve both qualitative and qualitative methods for short, medium, and long terms. Supply chain managers normally have the knowhow from experience to determining the best forecasting methods that suit their business needs.

In general, qualitative methods are based on experience and opinions. Some of the qualitative methods include:

- **Personal experience**—for small and medium enterprises (SMEs), supply chain managers can use their personal experience to estimate future demands, providing their selling products or services have relatively stable demand and supply chains are not complex. For instance, the demand for a small printing shop or a pizza store can be easy to predict with only the store managers' experience.

- **Market research**—usually uses interviews or surveys to identify customer preferences and predict future demand. This is especially useful when launching new products. However, questionnaires need to be carefully designed to avoid biased opinions.
- **The Delphi technique**—the method adopts a panel of experts to predict future demands. Each expert can make their own predictions and then all the predictions created are sent anonymously to all experts for review and re-consideration of their own forecasts. Then, a consequent prediction is made by all experts. The process is repeated until a consensus or a near consensus is reached by all the experts.
- **Scenario planning**—different scenarios can be used to predict future demands. The method also uses a panel of member to discuss potential future scenarios, from the best to the worst, in order for the focal firm to prepare for future demand changes.

Quantitative methods on the other hand use data to make predictions, including, for example, previous sales record, demographic information, seasonal pattern of demand, and weather conditions, etc. Some of these quantitative methods include:

- **Time series analysis**—this forecasting method uses historical sales data to predict future demand. It is reasonable to believe that future demand follows similar trends or patterns of previous sales. This is usually true when there is not much volatility or turbulence in market conditions.
- **Causal relational methods**—the methods identify the important features that might impact future demands such as weather conditions. For instance, during summer season, the surge of temperature can lead to significant demands for BBQ sausages. In addition to climate and seasonal variations, holidays and promotions might also be used as important features to predict customer demands in those forecasting models.
- **Machine learning**—there are also advanced machine learning algorithms that can be used to make predictions and forecast customer demands such as support vector machines and random forests. These analytics methods usually perform better than the traditional methods.
- **Simulation**—the method can be used to combine the predictions from both qualitative and quantitative methods in order to simulate the impact from various 'what-if' scenarios. It can enable supply chain managers to prepare for uncertainties in supply and demand. For example, whether we should introduce promotional activities to boost sales in the wake of declining demand in economic downturn.

Despite having various qualitative and quantitative methods available, managers should always select the most appropriate methods that fit their demand patterns and be able to provide most accurate forecasts. However, keep in mind that forecasts are rarely perfect. In general, predicting short-term demands is relatively more accurate than forecasting long-term periods. Forecasts are more accurate for aggregate data than for individual items.

In this chapter, we first explore some classical time series methods, and then we move onto more advanced analytics using machine learning algorithms.

8.3 Time Series Forecasting

8.3.1 Time Series Components

In general, time series data are recorded at regular time intervals. The methods for time series forecasting usually use time as an independent variable and the forecasted demands by those methods would be the predicted value at a specific time.

Time series data may include four main components (see Fig. 8.2) that can be explored and identified by appropriate predictive models:

- **Trend**—the upward or downward tendency in the series over a long period of time, e.g., previous sales growth or decline.
- **Seasonality**—the short-term patterns that occur during a specific period of time and repeat indefinitely, e.g., the surge of ice cream sales during summertime. However, note that seasonality does not necessarily relate to seasons. For instance, the sales of alcohols can boost every weekend, which also forms a short-term seasonal pattern.
- **Cyclical component**—long-term movements in the time series data that may take years or decades to appear. They happen due to the external economic conditions such as recession and recovery.
- **Noise** (error)—random variations in the time series due to unpredictable and unforeseen factors which happen in an irregular manner. The noise is normally the cause of the zigzag appearance in the time series diagram.

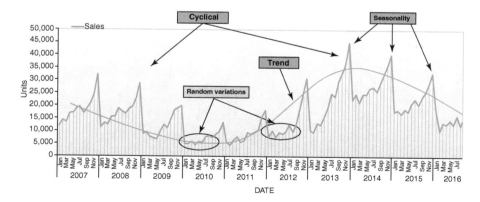

Fig. 8.2 An illustration of time series components

Time series with trends or seasonality are normally considered *non-stationary*, whereas those without trends or seasonality at which the series are observed are considered *stationary*. As an example, consider the Microsoft (MSFT) stock price example below.

As shown in Fig. 8.3, the observation of the MSFT stock price is between 2010 and 2020, in which we can see a clear trend. In such a case, the time series is considered **non-stationary**. By contrast, if the observation is between 2019-07-01 and 2019-10-01, the time series can be considered **stationary** as no clear trends or seasonality are presented during this observation period (see Fig. 8.4).

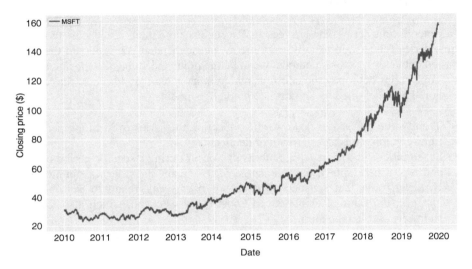

Fig. 8.3 MSFT closing stock price 2010–2020

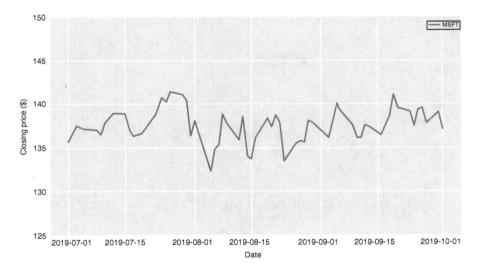

Fig. 8.4 MSFT closing stock price 1 July–1 Oct, 2019

8.3.2   Traditional Time Series Forecasting Methods

As mentioned earlier, time series analysis uses historical data to forecast. The analysis is comprised of different methods which can extract patterns and characteristics from past time series data in order to predict future demands. In this section, we look at some of the most classical and popular time series forecasting methods.

Moving Average

The moving average (MA) or rolling mean method creates a series of averages in the time series within designated periods. It assumes that observations that are close in time are similar in value and thus, the next period's forecast equals the average of the last N periods (see Eq. 8.1 below). Taking averages can eliminate the noise.

$$F_{t+1} = \frac{A_t + A_{t-1} + \ldots + A_{t-N+1}}{N} \tag{8.1}$$

where F_{t+1} denotes the next period forecast, A_t is the most recent actual demand, and N is the designated periods.

Note that a smaller N makes the forecast more *responsive* (i.e., close to the most recent actual demands), whereas a larger N makes the forecast more *stable*. For illustration, see Fig. 8.5 in which N was set to 2 and 4, respectively.

As shown in the diagram, the line shape of MA2 is relatively closer to the line shape of the actual sales (i.e., more responsive), whereas the line of MA4 tends to be flat (i.e., stable). The determination of N periods can be based on some error test, such as MAD and MSE values.

Weighted Moving Average

Another moving average method adopts weightings in its formula, i.e., the weighted moving average (WMA). The presumption is that the most recent values are more relevant for next period forecast, thus deserving a greater weighting compared to the data points in the distant past. The next period forecast is calculated by multiplying

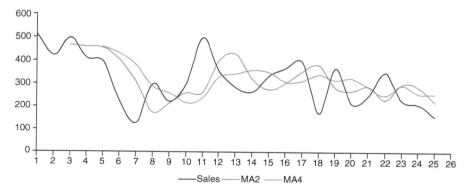

Fig. 8.5 Moving average example

each value in the last N periods by the assigned weight and summing up the total values (see Eq. 8.2 below).

$$F_{t+1} = W_1 A_t + W_2 A_{t-1} + \ldots + W_N A_{t-N+1} \tag{8.2}$$

$$s.t. W_1 + W_2 + \ldots + W_N = 1$$

The selection of weights can be arbitrary or adjusted based on the performance of the WMA model with some error test, such as MAD and MSE. By contrast, in a simple WA method, the weights for each of past N period are actually equal.

Exponential Smoothing

Another classical forecasting method is called exponential smoothing (ES). Instead of using equal weights in MA or assigned weights in WMA, the ES method assigns exponentially decreasing weights over period of time (see Eq. 8.3 below).

$$F_{t+1} = \alpha A_t + (1 - \alpha) F_t \tag{8.3}$$

where F_t denotes the previous forecast, and $F_t = A_t$ when $t = 0$. α is the smoothing constant, and $0 \leq \alpha \leq 1$. Using the smoothing constant α can help remove high-frequency noise in the data. A smaller α value makes the forecast more *stable*, whereas a larger α value makes the forecast more *responsive*.

For illustration, Fig. 8.6 compares the forecasts made by WMA ($N = 3$) with three weights and by the ES with two α values.

As shown above, when the α value is set to 0.7, the line shape of the ES2 is closer to the shape of the actual sales (i.e., more responsive); however, when α is set to 0.2, the line tends to be flattening.

The ES method has the advantage of being able to make next period forecast with just a small amount of historical data. However, note that the method would only predict one period ahead, leaving long-term forecasts 'flat'.

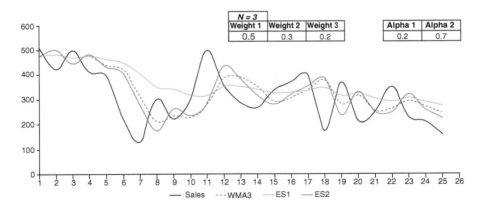

Fig. 8.6 WMA and ES example

Autoregressive Model

The autoregressive (AR) model is similar to a regression model, which learns the behavioural pattern of previous data in order to forecast future trends. In an AR model, the next time period forecast at t can be impacted by the observations at previous p period of time, *which* can be expressed as follows:

$$y_t = c + \varphi_1 y_{t-1} + \varphi_2 y_{t-2} + \ldots + \varphi_p y_{t-p} + \varepsilon_t$$
$$= c + \sum_{i=1}^{p} \varphi_i y_{t-i} + \varepsilon_t \tag{8.4}$$

where p is the order (i.e., previous time spots), c is a constant, φ is the parameter, and the random variable ε_t is the white noise.

For instance, in stock market, a current share price of any corporations can depend on all the previous share prices in the time series. The AR model calculates the regression of past values in a time series and predicts future values.

ARMA

The Autoregressive Moving Average (ARMA) model basically is the combination of the AR and the MA models.

Notice that, a MA process of order q, or MA(q) can be impacted by unexpected external factors at previous q time slots, (i.e., $t - 1, t - 2, \ldots, t - q$). Such unexpected impacts are commonly known as errors or residuals. Therefore, alternatively, a MA model can be mathematically presented as:

$$y_t = \mu + \varepsilon_t + \theta_1 \varepsilon_{t-1} + \theta_2 \varepsilon_{t-2} + \ldots + \theta_q \varepsilon_{t-q}$$
$$= \mu + \varepsilon_t + \sum_{i=1}^{q} \theta_i \varepsilon_{t-i} \tag{8.5}$$

where q is the order (i.e., previous time spots), μ is the mean of the series (often assumed to equal 0), θ is the parameter, and the random variable ε_t is the white noise.

The ARMA(p, q) model takes into account both the random noise (i.e., the MA part) and the autoregressive part, which can be expressed as follows:

$$y_t = c + \varepsilon_t + \sum_{i=1}^{p} \varphi_i y_{t-i} + \sum_{i=1}^{q} \theta_i \varepsilon_{t-i} \tag{8.6}$$

In general, when fitting the ARMA(p, q) model, the p value can be determined by plotting the **partial autocorrelation function** (PACF) and the q value can be determined by using the **autocorrelation function** (ACF) plot. To put it simply, ACF gives the autocorrelation of any time series with its lagged values, whereas PACF gives the partial correlation of the residuals with the next lagged values.

In other words, the autocorrelation of a time series at lag-1 is the coefficient of correlation between y_t and y_{t-1}. If y_t is correlated with y_{t-1}, and y_{t-1} is equally correlated with y_{t-2}, then there should be correlation between y_t and y_{t-2} too. Therefore, the correlation at lag-1 propagates to lag-2, and possibly to even more lags. The partial autocorrelation at lag-2 is thus the difference between the actual correlation at lag-2 and the propagated correlation from lag-1.

Let us simulate an ARMA (2,2) process using `statsmodels` time series analysis implementation in Python and see how the PACF and ACF plots work for the selection of *p* and *q* values. First, we need to import the necessary models into Jupyter notebook, consider below:

Ex. 8.1

```
from statsmodels.tsa.arima_process import arma_generate_sample
from statsmodels.graphics.tsaplots import plot_pacf
from statsmodels.graphics.tsaplots import plot_acf

import matplotlib.pyplot as plt
import seaborn as sns; sns.set()
import numpy as np
import pandas as pd
```

Next, we create some sample:

Ex. 8.2

```
ar2 = np.array([1, 0.5, 0.3])
ma2 = np.array([1, 0.2, 0.4])
nobs = 200
y = arma_generate_sample(ar2, ma2, nobs)
```

We can add some date range as index to the created sample, see below:

Ex. 8.3

```
# add date as index
dates = pd.date_range('2000-1-1', freq="M", periods=nobs)
y = pd.Series(y, index=dates)
y.head().append(y.tail())
2000-01-31     0.358262
2000-02-29    -0.205744
2000-03-31     0.105972
2000-04-30    -0.162135
2000-05-31    -0.396981
2016-04-30    -0.208980
2016-05-31    -0.784078
2016-06-30    -0.135264
2016-07-31    -0.264326
2016-08-31     1.405534
dtype: float64
```

Then, we can visualize the data using the code below:

Ex. 8.4

```
plt.figure(figsize=[16, 8])
plt.plot(y)
plt.title("Simulated ARMA(2,2) Process",fontsize=14)
plt.show();
```

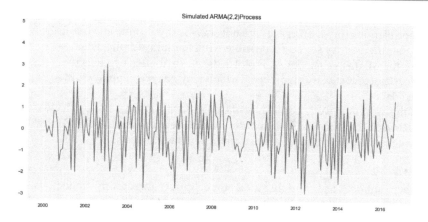

As can be seen from above, the time series seems stationary as no obvious trends or seasonality are shown. Next, we check the ACF and PACF plots:

Ex. 8.5

```
# Plot ACF and PACF
plt.figure(figsize = (10, 10))
plt.subplot(2,1,1); plot_acf(y, ax = plt.gca())
plt.subplot(2,1,2); plot_pacf(y,ax = plt.gca());
```

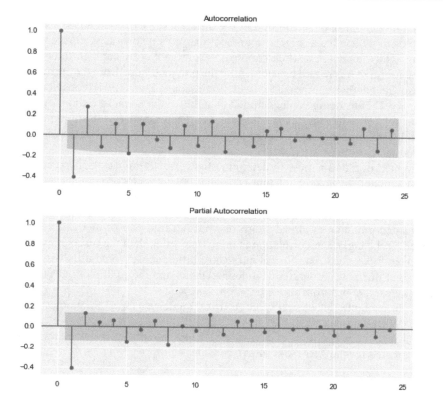

For the AR(p) value, the PACF plot indicates that after about two lags the partial autocorrelations for all other lags are not statistically significant (i.e., fall within the blue zone). This may suggest a possible AR(2) process for the data.

For the MA(q) value, the ACF plot indicates that after two lags the autocorrelations are not statistically significant, which may suggest a possible MA(2) process for the data.

In this example, we already know the correct values for p and q since we created an ARMA(2, 2) process. However, in practice, determining the right orders can be challenging. We will explore some examples in later sections.

ARIMA

Another similar and widely used time series forecasting model is called Autoregressive Integrated Moving Average (ARIMA). ARIMA models can be useful for modelling the 'non-seasonal' time series that displays patterns and is not a random white noise. If there is a seasonal pattern, then we need to add the seasonal terms to the ARIMA (i.e., SARIMA), which will be introduced shortly.

There are three terms in an ARIMA(p,d,q) model, where

- p is the order of the AR term
- q is the order of the MA term
- d is the number of differencing

Essentially, the ARIMA mathematical equation can be regarded the same as the ARMA model but with an addition of the differencing term. As introduced earlier, ARMA simply is a linear regression model that uses its own lagged values as predictors, which works best when the predictors are not correlated. Differencing can thus be useful in this regard by subtracting the previous value from the current value.

Also, recall that a time series with trends or seasonality is considered non-stationary. **Differencing** can be applied to stabilize the mean of a time series, thus eliminating (or reducing) trends or seasonality. The value of d is the minimum number of differencing required to make the time series stationary. Note that in the case of a stationary time series, $d = 0$.

The next question is how to determine the correct number of differencing d in ARIMA model? In general, if a time series has *positive* autocorrelations out to many number of lags (e.g., 10 or more), then a high order of differencing may be required.

Note that differencing tends to result in *negative* correlation. Normally, if the lag-1 autocorrelation is already zero or even negative, no further differencing is needed. If the lag-1 autocorrelation is more than -0.5, then the time series is probably over differenced. The correct number of differencing would usually get a time series that fluctuates around a well-defined mean and the ACF plot decays to zero fairly quickly, either from above or below.

As an example, let us apply the ARIMA model on the U.S. Wholesale Price Index (WPI) dataset.

As usual, let us first import necessary packages into the notebook that was previously created for the ARMA example, consider below:

Ex. 8.6

```
import statsmodels.api as sm
from datetime import datetime
import requests
from io import BytesIO
```

Next, we fetch the data from available online source:

Ex. 8.7

```
# Fetch Data
wpi1 = requests.get('https://www.stata-press.com/data/r12/wpi1.dta').content
data = pd.read_stata(BytesIO(wpi1))
data.index = data.t

# Set the frequency
data.index.freq="QS-OCT"
data.head()
```

	wpi	t	ln_wpi
t			
1960-01-01	30.700001	1960-01-01	3.424263
1960-04-01	30.799999	1960-04-01	3.427515
1960-07-01	30.700001	1960-07-01	3.424263
1960-10-01	30.700001	1960-10-01	3.424263
1961-01-01	30.799999	1961-01-01	3.427515

We can visualize the WPI data with the following:

Ex. 8.8

```
# visualize the data
plt.figure(figsize=[16, 8])
plt.plot(data.index,data['wpi'] )
plt.title("US Wholesale Price Index", fontsize=14)
plt.show();
```

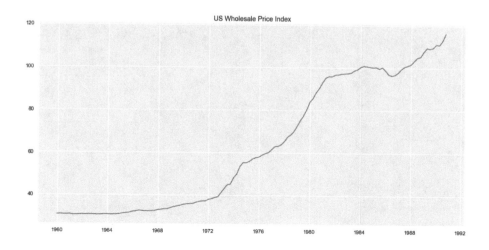

As can be seen in the figure above, there is a clear trend in the WPI data over time. We can then check the ACF and PACF plots:

Ex. 8.9

```
# Plot ACF and PACF
plt.figure(figsize = (10, 10))
plt.subplot(2,1,1); plot_acf(data['wpi'], ax = plt.gca())
plt.subplot(2,1,2); plot_pacf(data['wpi'],ax = plt.gca());
```

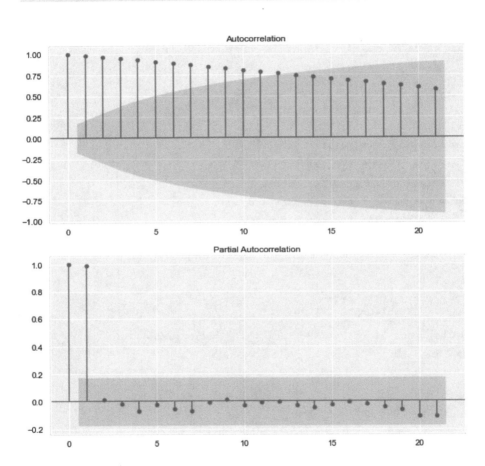

Looking at ACF plots, the autocorrelations are positively significant for a number of lags, which may signify a clear trend in the series. However, the high-order autocorrelations may be also due to the propagation of the autocorrelation at lag-1. The PACF plot displays a significant spike only at lag-1, which may indicate that the high-order autocorrelations can also be explained by the lag-1 autocorrelation.

We can then use the additional Augmented Dickey–Fuller (ADF) test to check whether a time series is stationary or not:

Ex. 8.10

```
from statsmodels.tsa.stattools import adfuller
adf = adfuller(data['wpi'])
print(f'ADF Statistic: {adf[0]}')
print(f'p-value: {adf[1]}')

ADF Statistic: 0.5872455370299964
p-value: 0.9872969979129654
```

The returned results suggest that the p value is larger than 0.05, indicating that we cannot reject the null hypothesis that the time series is non-stationary. Thus, we should apply some differencing to remove the trend.

Let us apply two differencing (i.e., $d = 2$) and compare how the differencing works on the WPI data. Consider below:

Ex. 8.11

```
# Original Series
fig, axes = plt.subplots(3, 2, figsize=(16,12))
axes[0, 0].plot(data['wpi'])
axes[0, 0].set_title('Original Series')
plot_acf(data['wpi'], ax= axes[0,1])

#1st Differencing
axes[1, 0].plot(data['wpi'].diff())
axes[1, 0].set_title('1st Order Differencing')
plot_acf(data['wpi'].diff().dropna(), ax=axes[1, 1])

#2nd Differencing
axes[2, 0].plot(data['wpi'].diff().diff())
axes[2, 0].set_title('2nd Order Differencing')
plot_acf(data['wpi'].diff().diff().dropna(), ax=axes[2, 1])

plt.show();
```

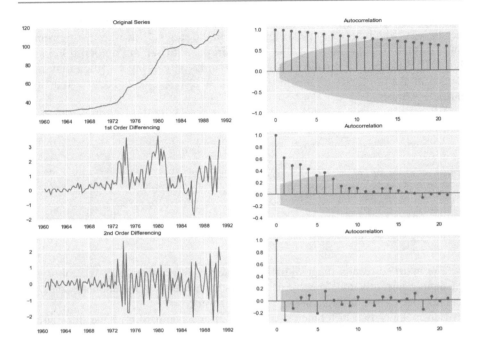

We can see that the WPI series reaches stationary with two orders of differencing. However, by checking the ACF plot for the second differencing, it is noticed that lag-1 goes into the negative zone fairly quickly, which may indicate that the series might have been overdifferenced.

Therefore, we can tentatively choose the order of differencing as 1 (i.e., $d = 1$), although the series does not seem to be perfectly stationary.

Next, we need to determine the p and q values in the ARIMA $(p, 1, q)$ model. Let us check the first order differenced series PACF and ACF plots:

Ex. 8.12

```
# Plot ACF and PACF
plt.figure(figsize = (16, 4))

plt.subplot(1,2,1);
plot_pacf(data['wpi'].diff().dropna(), ax = plt.gca())
plt.subplot(1,2,2);
plot_acf(data['wpi'].diff().dropna(),ax = plt.gca());
```

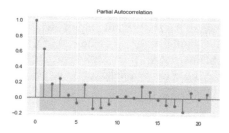 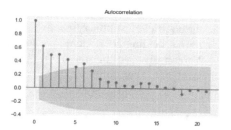

The PACF plot shows that lag-1 is the spike that is significantly above the blue zone, though lag-2 and lag-3 also seem to have crossed the significance line. Let us try to be conservative and tentatively set p to 1.

We can observe from the ACF plot that about 4 lags are well above the significance line. Let us tentatively set q to 4.

How to Build ARIMA Model in Python?

Now that we have determined the ARIMA (1, 1, 4) model for the WPI example. Next, we need to build and fit the model with the ARIMA implementation in `statsmodels` package in Python. Consider below:

Ex. 8.13

```
from statsmodels.tsa.arima_model import ARIMA

# ARIMA(1,1,4) Model
model = ARIMA(data['wpi'], order=(1,1,4))
result = model.fit(disp=0, trend='c')
print(result.summary())
```

```
                         ARIMA Model Results
==============================================================================
Dep. Variable:              D.wpi   No. Observations:                  123
Model:             ARIMA(1, 1, 4)   Log Likelihood                -133.521
Method:                   css-mle   S.D. of innovations              0.713
Date:            Sat, 20 Feb 2021   AIC                            281.042
Time:                    01:50:38   BIC                            300.727
Sample:                 04-01-1960   HQIC                           289.038
                       - 10-01-1990
==============================================================================
                 coef    std err          z      P>|z|      [0.025      0.975]
------------------------------------------------------------------------------
const          0.7454      0.275      2.708      0.007       0.206       1.285
ar.L1.D.wpi    0.8047      0.085      9.462      0.000       0.638       0.971
ma.L1.D.wpi   -0.3149      0.120     -2.618      0.009      -0.551      -0.079
ma.L2.D.wpi   -0.1797      0.126     -1.426      0.154      -0.427       0.067
ma.L3.D.wpi    0.1188      0.091      1.299      0.194      -0.060       0.298
ma.L4.D.wpi    0.2415      0.198      1.220      0.222      -0.146       0.629
                                    Roots
==============================================================================
                  Real          Imaginary           Modulus         Frequency
------------------------------------------------------------------------------
AR.1            1.2428           +0.0000j            1.2428            0.0000
MA.1            0.9957           -0.7662j            1.2564           -0.1044
MA.2            0.9957           +0.7662j            1.2564            0.1044
MA.3           -1.2418           -1.0399j            1.6197           -0.3890
MA.4           -1.2418           +1.0399j            1.6197            0.3890
------------------------------------------------------------------------------
```

The results summary output reveals a lot of information. The values under 'coef' are the coefficients of the respective terms, whereas the $P > |z|$ values signify whether the corresponding coefficients are statistically significant (i.e., p value ≤ 0.05).

We can observe that the coefficients of MA(2), MA(3), an MA(4) are highly insignificant. Therefore, we should try to drop those terms and set the q value to 1 only. Let us rebuild the model with ARIMA (1,1,1):

Ex. 8.14

```
# ARIMA(1,1,1) Model
model = ARIMA(data['wpi'], order=(1,1,1))
result = model.fit(disp=0,trend='c')
print(result.summary())
```
```
                            ARIMA Model Results
==============================================================================
Dep. Variable:                 D.wpi   No. Observations:                  123
Model:                 ARIMA(1, 1, 1)   Log Likelihood              -135.351
Method:                      css-mle   S.D. of innovations            0.725
Date:               Sun, 21 Feb 2021   AIC                          278.703
Time:                       02:10:44   BIC                          289.951
Sample:                    04-01-1960   HQIC                         283.272
                         - 10-01-1990
==============================================================================
                 coef    std err          z      P>|z|      [0.025      0.975]
------------------------------------------------------------------------------
const          0.7498      0.292      2.567      0.010       0.177       1.322
ar.L1.D.wpi    0.8742      0.064     13.707      0.000       0.749       0.999
ma.L1.D.wpi   -0.4120      0.122     -3.375      0.001      -0.651      -0.173
                                    Roots
==============================================================================
                  Real          Imaginary           Modulus         Frequency
------------------------------------------------------------------------------
AR.1            1.1439           +0.0000j            1.1439            0.0000
MA.1            2.4271           +0.0000j            2.4271            0.0000
------------------------------------------------------------------------------
```

It seems that the ARIMA (1,1,1) model has produced better results as the $P > |z|$ values of the AR(1) and MA(1) have both become highly significant. However, how can we make sure that the right order for ARIMA processes have been selected? This brings us to the next topic of Akaike's Information Criterion (AIC).

Akaike's Information Criterion (AIC)

The AIC can be used to estimate the quality of each model compared to other models. It is named after the Japanese statistician Hirotugu Akaike (Akaike 1974). The AIC can be expressed as follows:

$$\text{AIC} = -2\ln(L) + 2k \qquad (8.7)$$

where L is the maximum value of the likelihood function of the model, k is the number of estimated parameters in the model.

With the AIC test, the preferred model is the one with the minimum AIC value.

A closely related model selection criterion is called Bayesian Information Criterion (BIC) (Schwarz 1978), which can be expressed as follows:

$$BIC = -2\ln(L) + \ln(N)k \tag{8.8}$$

where L is the maximum value of the likelihood function of the model, k is the number of estimated parameters in the model, N is the sample size or the number of observations.

Likewise, the model with the lowest BIC is preferred. Both AIC and BIC reflect how well the model fits the data by introducing a penalty term for the number of parameters in the model to resolve overfitting problem.

In our previous example, the ARIMA $(1,1,1)$ is a better model since it has lower AIC and BIC values in the output results.

Note: AIC and BIC cannot be used to select the order of differencing (d). Also, the AIC and BIC values of different orders of differencing are not comparable.

PMDARIMA Library

The `Pmdarima` library in Python allows us to automatically select the best orders of (p, d, q) for ARIMA model. To install the package, we can run the following code in conda prompt:

```
conda install -c conda-forge pmdarima
```

Once installed, we can import the package into our notebook and use the `auto_arima()` method. Consider below:

Ex. 8.15

```
import pmdarima as pm

model = pm.auto_arima(data['wpi'], start_p=1, start_q=1,
                      max_p=10, max_q=10,     #maximum p and q
                      d=None,                 #let the model determine d
                      seasonal=False,         #default is True
                      D=None,
                      trace=True,
                      error_action='ignore',
                      suppress_warnings=True,
                      stepwise=True)
```

```
Performing stepwise search to minimize aic
 ARIMA(1,2,1)(0,0,0)[0] intercept   : AIC=280.732, Time=0.05 sec
 ARIMA(0,2,0)(0,0,0)[0] intercept   : AIC=299.862, Time=0.02 sec
 ARIMA(1,2,0)(0,0,0)[0] intercept   : AIC=288.831, Time=0.02 sec
 ARIMA(0,2,1)(0,0,0)[0] intercept   : AIC=279.802, Time=0.02 sec
 ARIMA(0,2,0)(0,0,0)[0]             : AIC=297.997, Time=0.01 sec
 ARIMA(0,2,2)(0,0,0)[0] intercept   : AIC=280.375, Time=0.03 sec
 ARIMA(1,2,2)(0,0,0)[0] intercept   : AIC=inf, Time=0.16 sec
 ARIMA(0,2,1)(0,0,0)[0]             : AIC=278.124, Time=0.01 sec
 ARIMA(1,2,1)(0,0,0)[0]             : AIC=279.092, Time=0.02 sec
 ARIMA(0,2,2)(0,0,0)[0]             : AIC=278.728, Time=0.02 sec
 ARIMA(1,2,0)(0,0,0)[0]             : AIC=287.049, Time=0.01 sec
 ARIMA(1,2,2)(0,0,0)[0]             : AIC=inf, Time=0.17 sec

Best model:  ARIMA(0,2,1)(0,0,0)[0]
Total fit time: 0.550 seconds
```

The model can automatically generate the output selecting the best combination of orders for *p, d,* and *q*. For details about the parameters of the method, check pmdarima documentation and tips for using auto_arima.

It can be seen from the output that the best order combination for our model is ARIMA (0,2,1) as it generates the lowest AIC value. We can then print out the model summary:

Ex. 8.16

```
print(model.summary())
```

```
                                SARIMAX Results
==============================================================================
Dep. Variable:                     y   No. Observations:                  124
Model:              SARIMAX(0, 2, 1)   Log Likelihood                -137.062
Date:              Mon, 22 Feb 2021   AIC                            278.124
Time:                      15:50:24   BIC                            283.732
Sample:                           0   HQIC                           280.402
                              - 124
Covariance Type:                opg
==============================================================================
                 coef    std err          z      P>|z|      [0.025      0.975]
------------------------------------------------------------------------------
ma.L1         -0.5105      0.072     -7.086      0.000      -0.652      -0.369
sigma2         0.5524      0.055     10.058      0.000       0.445       0.660
===================================================================================
Ljung-Box (L1) (Q):                0.21   Jarque-Bera (JB):                 9.62
Prob(Q):                           0.65   Prob(JB):                         0.01
Heteroskedasticity (H):           29.74   Skew:                            -0.13
Prob(H) (two-sided):               0.00   Kurtosis:                         4.35
===================================================================================

Warnings:
[1] Covariance matrix calculated using the outer product of gradients (complex-step)
```

The $P > |z|$ values of the MA(1) and differencing ($d = 2$) terms are highly significant in the results, indicating a good fit compared to our previous models. However, before using the refined model to make forecast, we should check the residuals to make sure there are no clear patterns (i.e., look for constant mean and variance).

We can simply use the built-in function `plot_diagnostics()`, which produces a 2×2 plot grid with the following plots (ordered clockwise from top left):

- Standardized residuals over time
- Histogram plus estimated density of standardized residuals, along with a Normal(0,1) density plotted for reference.
- Normal Q-Q plot, with Normal reference line.
- Correlogram

Consider below:

Ex. 8.17

```
model.plot_diagnostics(figsize=(12, 8))
plt.show();
```

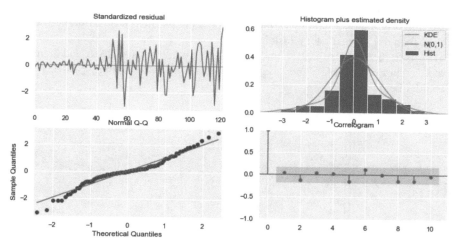

How to Interpret the Plot?
- **Top left**: The residual errors should fluctuate around a central mean of zero.
- **Top Right**: The density plot should reveal a normal distribution with a mean of zero.
- **Bottom left**: All the blue dots should fall perfectly in line with the red line. Any significant deviations would suggest a skewed distribution. In our example, majority of the dots are in line with the red line.
- **Bottom Right**: The correlogram (i.e., ACF plot) should display no autocorrelations, otherwise it would imply that there is some pattern in the residual errors which are not explained in the model.

The diagnostic plots do not signal significant issues in our model; thus, we can use the ARIMA (0,2,1) model to make some forecasts. Here, we can use the built-in `predict()` method to generate out-of-sample forecast in the future. Consider below:

Ex. 8.18

```
# predict next 10 periods
fc = model.predict(n_periods=10, return_conf_int=False)
fc
array([[118.48017369, 120.76035043, 123.04052717, 125.32070392,
        127.60088066, 129.8810574 , 132.16123414, 134.44141088,
        136.72158762, 139.00176437]])
```

Note that `pmdarima` wraps `statsmodels` under the hood. In particular, its `auto_arima` function uses the `statsmodels` SARIMAX model as can be seen from the summary results above.

However, the built-in ARIMA model in `statsmodels` has two forecasting methods. Once the model is fitted, the `ARIMAResults.predict()` method allows both in-sample and out-of-sample prediction, whereas the `ARIMAResults.forecast()` method creates out-of-sample forecast. The latter is done in the levels of the original endogenous variable. If you want prediction of differences in the levels, then use `predict()` instead.

Let us fit the ARIMA (0,2,1) model with `statsmodel`'s ARIMA and then generate some in-sample and out-of-sample forecasts using `predict()`. Consider below:

Ex. 8.19

```
# Re-run the ARIMA(0,2,1) Model
res = ARIMA(data['wpi'], order=(0,2,1)).fit()
# Predict a differenced forecast
print(res.predict(start='1989Q4', end='1992Q4'))
1989-07-01   -0.120211
1989-10-01    1.136837
1990-01-01    0.191553
1990-04-01   -0.498463
1990-07-01    0.686363
1990-10-01   -0.757584
1991-01-01   -1.087874
1991-04-01    0.018785
1991-07-01    0.018785
1991-10-01    0.018785
1992-01-01    0.018785
1992-04-01    0.018785
1992-07-01    0.018785
1992-10-01    0.018785
Freq: QS-OCT, dtype: float64
```

We can see that the `predict()` method produces the differenced forecast (i.e., difference from the actual value). If we want to predict the values in the original scale, we need to specify `typ='levels'` in the parameter setting. See below:

Ex. 8.20

```
# Predict the levels of the original endogenous variables
print(res.predict(start='1989Q4', end='1992Q4',typ='levels'))
1989-07-01    111.179792
1989-10-01    109.736836
1990-01-01    109.991556
1990-04-01    112.101535
1990-07-01    111.286369
1990-10-01    114.042419
1991-01-01    118.512117
1991-04-01    120.843022
1991-07-01    123.192711
1991-10-01    125.561185
1992-01-01    127.948444
1992-04-01    130.354488
1992-07-01    132.779317
1992-10-01    135.222930
Freq: QS-OCT, dtype: float64
```

The `ARIMAResults.plot_predict()` method allows us to visualize both the in-sample and out-of-sample forecasts. In the parameter setting, we can specify the forecast start and end dates, just like in the `predict()` method.

Ex. 8.21

```
# Plot forecasts
fig, ax = plt.subplots(figsize=(16,8))
# subsetting the data to get a better look at the forecasts
ax = data.loc['1980-01-01':]['wpi'].plot(ax=ax)
res.plot_predict(start='1980Q2',end='1992Q4',
                 ax=ax, plot_insample=False)
ax.set_xlabel('Date')
plt.show();
```

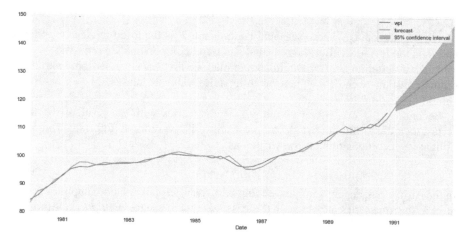

Note: Due to the nature of the ARIMA equations, out-of-sample forecasts tend to converge to the sample mean for long forecasting periods.

SARIMA

The Seasonal ARIMA (SARIMA) extends the ARIMA by incorporating the seasonal components into its model. If a time series contains seasonality, we can apply seasonal differencing in the SARIMA model. SARIMA can be expressed as follows:

$$\text{SARIMA} : \underbrace{(p, d, q)}_{\substack{\text{Non-seasonal} \\ \text{ARIMA order}}} \times \underbrace{(P, D, Q)s}_{\substack{\text{Seasonal} \\ \text{order}}}$$

where s is the number of periods in season, and often $s = 4$ is for quarterly data, $s = 12$ is for monthly data.

Before moving on the details of using the SARIMA model for predicting seasonal time series, let us first take a look at **seasonal decomposition**.

For seasonal time series, there usually are two types of decompositions (Hyndman and Athanasopoulos 2018). First, if the magnitude of the seasonality does not vary with the level of the time series, the additive decomposition would be the most appropriate model. The additive decomposition can be written as

$$y_t = S_t + T_t + R_t \tag{8.9}$$

where y_t is the data, S_t is the seasonal component, T_t is the trend-cycle component, and R_t is the residuals after the seasonal and trend components are removed.

In the Australian beer production example (see Fig. 8.7), the seasonal variation seems constant over time when the time series value increases. In this case, we should use the *additive* model.

Second, if the magnitude of the seasonality varies with the level of the time series, then the multiplicative decomposition would be more appropriate. The multiplicative decomposition can be written as

$$y_t = S_t \times T_t \times R_t \tag{8.10}$$

In the Airline passenger example (see Fig. 8.8), the seasonal variation amplifies as the level of the time series increases. In this case, we should use the *multiplicative* model.

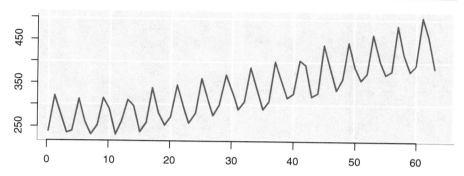

Fig. 8.7 Australia beer production data

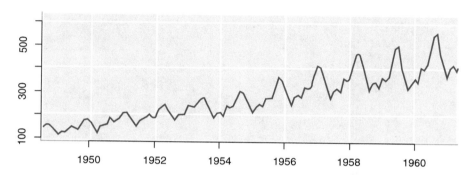

Fig. 8.8 Airline passenger data

To perform the seasonal decomposition of the time series in Python, the built-in
decompose function from pmdarima package offers a convenient way.
Alternatively, we can use the seasonal_decompose function from statsmodels.
As an example, let us first decompose the Australia beer production data with the
additive model. Consider below:

Ex. 8.22

```
# Time series analysis
from statsmodels.tsa.seasonal import seasonal_decompose

# Decompose OZ Beer Data
from pylab import rcParams
rcParams['figure.figsize'] = 10, 8
decompose_OZbeer = seasonal_decompose(OZ_data,model='additive')
decompose_OZbeer.plot();
```

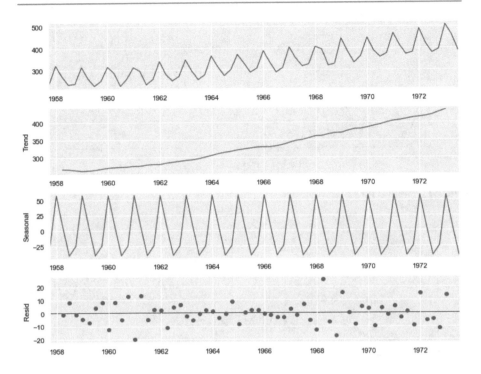

The data have quarterly `datetime` index and thus we do not need to set the `period` parameter in the `seasonal_decompose` method as it can detect the frequency automatically unless you want to override the timeseries index. The model type can be set using the `model` parameter. Here we use `'additive'`.

Next, we decompose the Airline passenger data with the multiplicative model:

Ex. 8.23

```
# Decompose AirPassengers Data
rcParams['figure.figsize'] = 10, 8
decompose_Air = seasonal_decompose(Air_data,model='multiplicative')
decompose_Air.plot();
```

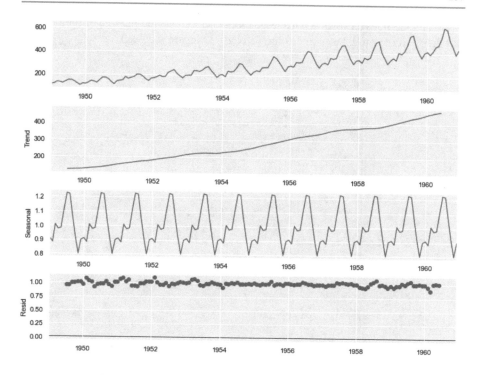

From the two examples, it can be seen that the seasonal decomposition has successfully separated the time series into three components, which allow us to have a clearer view on the trends of the two separate data examples.

After gaining a better understanding of the data with seasonal decomposition, we shall move on to using the SARIMA model to generate some forecasts. Like in the ARIMA, first we need to determine the correct order of p, d, q, and P, D, Q for the SARIMA model.

With the PACF and ACF plots, we can reasonably guess these values. Notice that attention should be paid to the seasonal lags of the ACF/PACF plots for the seasonal orders. This procedure however is omitted here.

A better way of determining these orders as mentioned previously is using the AIC/BIC criteria. We can work out the best order combinations that produce the lowest AIC/BIC values with the built-in `auto_arima` function in `pmdarima` package.

As an example, let us fit a SARIMA model on the Airline passenger data model and then use the model to make some forecast. Consider below:

Ex. 8.24

```
import pmdarima as pm
model = pm.auto_arima(Air_data, start_p=1, start_q=1,
                      start_P=1, start_Q=1,
                      error_action='ignore',
                      trace=True,
                      seasonal=True, m=12)
```

```
Performing stepwise search to minimize aic
 ARIMA(1,1,1)(1,1,1)[12]          : AIC=1022.299, Time=0.27 sec
 ARIMA(0,1,0)(0,1,0)[12]          : AIC=1031.508, Time=0.01 sec
 ARIMA(1,1,0)(1,1,0)[12]          : AIC=1020.393, Time=0.05 sec
 ARIMA(0,1,1)(0,1,1)[12]          : AIC=1021.003, Time=0.06 sec
 ARIMA(1,1,0)(0,1,0)[12]          : AIC=1020.393, Time=0.02 sec
 ARIMA(1,1,0)(2,1,0)[12]          : AIC=1019.239, Time=0.12 sec
 ARIMA(1,1,0)(2,1,1)[12]          : AIC=inf, Time=0.77 sec
 ARIMA(1,1,0)(1,1,1)[12]          : AIC=1020.493, Time=0.15 sec
 ARIMA(0,1,0)(2,1,0)[12]          : AIC=1032.120, Time=0.09 sec
 ARIMA(2,1,0)(2,1,0)[12]          : AIC=1021.120, Time=0.14 sec
 ARIMA(1,1,1)(2,1,0)[12]          : AIC=1021.032, Time=0.22 sec
 ARIMA(0,1,1)(2,1,0)[12]          : AIC=1019.178, Time=0.12 sec
 ARIMA(0,1,1)(1,1,0)[12]          : AIC=1020.425, Time=0.05 sec
 ARIMA(0,1,1)(2,1,1)[12]          : AIC=inf, Time=0.56 sec
 ARIMA(0,1,1)(1,1,1)[12]          : AIC=1020.327, Time=0.18 sec
 ARIMA(0,1,2)(2,1,0)[12]          : AIC=1021.148, Time=0.15 sec
 ARIMA(1,1,2)(2,1,0)[12]          : AIC=1022.805, Time=0.30 sec
 ARIMA(0,1,1)(2,1,0)[12] intercept : AIC=1021.017, Time=0.21 sec

Best model:  ARIMA(0,1,1)(2,1,0)[12]
Total fit time: 3.512 seconds
```

Since here we are trying to build a SARIMA model to fit the seasonal time series, we set parameter `seasonal=True`. The m parameter relates to the number of observations per seasonal cycle, and typically it will correspond to some recurrent periodicity such as $m = 7$: daily, $m = 12$: monthly, and $m = 52$: weekly. In this example, the data were record monthly, and we can see a clear monthly seasonal pattern using the seasonal decomposition from above, thus we set $m = 12$.

From the output we can see that the best combinations for the SARIMA model is $(0, 1, 1) \times (2, 1, 0)_{12}$. Using the `model.summary()` method we can have a closer look at the model results and with `model.plot_diagnostics()`, we can check the normality of the residuals, which are both omitted here.

Once the model is trained, we can use `model.predict()` method to generate some future forecasts. Let us create next 50-periods forecasts with confidence intervals, and then plot it with the actual data.

Ex. 8.25

```
# predict next 50 periods forecasts with confidence interval
forecast, conf_int = model.predict(n_periods=50,return_conf_int=True)

# create index for next 50 periods
dates = pd.date_range(Air_data.index[-1], periods=50, freq='MS')

# Plot the forecasts
fig, ax = plt.subplots(figsize=(12, 6))
ax.plot(Air_data, label='Actual Data')
ax.plot(dates, forecast, color='green', label='Forecasts')
ax.set_title('Air Passenger Demand Forecasting',size=14)
ax.set_xlabel('Dates')
ax.set_ylabel('Number')

ax.fill_between(dates, conf_int[:, 0], conf_int[:, 1],
                alpha=0.2, color='grey',
                label="Confidence Intervals")

ax.legend(loc='upper left')
plt.show();
```

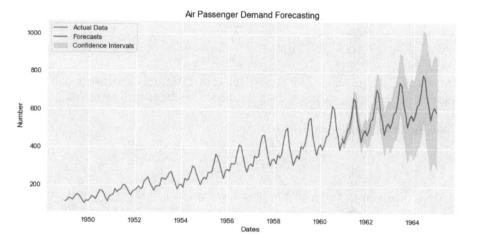

The plot shows some interesting results. The SARIMA model seems to have worked pretty well in producing similar patterns as seen in the actual data. If there is an additional dataset, we can compute error rate and test the performance of our model. Or we could split our dataset into training and test sets for evaluation. These procedures however are omitted here.

How to Evaluate Forecast Accuracy?

To evaluate the performance of a forecasting model, we can look at the forecast error. Simply, the forecast error can be expressed as follows:

$$E_t = A_t - F_t \tag{8.11}$$

where E the forecast error, A is the actual demand, and F is the forecasted demand for period t.

There are different accuracy metrics for evaluating time series forecasting. The most commonly used ones include:

- **Mean Squared Error** (MSE)

$$\text{MSE} = \frac{1}{n}\sum_{t=1}^{n}E_t^2 \tag{8.12}$$

MSE penalizes extreme errors and can be useful when the forecast error has a symmetric distribution about zero.

- **Root Mean Square Error** (RMSE)

$$\text{RMSE} = \sqrt{\frac{1}{n}\sum_{t=1}^{n}\frac{|E_t|}{A_t}} \tag{8.13}$$

RMSE is simply the square root of MSE. Note that RMSE is sensitive to outliers. It is useful for comparisons across different models on the same time series.

- **Mean Absolute Deviation** (MAD)

$$\text{MAD} = \frac{1}{n}\sum_{t=1}^{n}|E_t| \tag{8.14}$$

MAD is also known as Mean Absolute Error (MAE). It sums errors in absolute value, thereby the negative differences will not cancel out the positive differences. MAD is a good measure for the actual error in a forecast. However, since it gives the average error, it is not very useful for comparisons between different time series, especially where there is a large difference in scales.

- **Mean Absolute Percentage Error** (MAPE)

$$\text{MAPE} = \frac{1}{n}\sum_{t=1}^{n}\frac{|E_t|}{A_t} \tag{8.15}$$

MAPE is akin to MAD; however, it considers the forecast error in relation to the actual demand, and thus can be useful for comparisons between two different time series. MAPE is also a good measure when seasonality presents in a time series or demand varies significantly from one period to the next. It is probably the single most popular metric for forecast evaluation.

- **Tracking Signal** (TS)

$$TS = \frac{\sum_{t=1}^{n} E_t}{MAD} \tag{8.16}$$

TS exposes bias (positive or negative) if there are dramatic changes in demand pattern. In general, if TS is outside the range of ±6, it indicates that the forecast is biased, which may be due to either the model is flawed, or the underlying demand pattern has shifted (Chopra and Meindl 2016).

Supply chain managers can use error analysis to evaluate the performance of a forecasting model. However, remember the ultimate goal of the evaluation is to get forecast right and consistent. Albeit this might be challenging, effective forecast models can assist managers in making correct decisions in demand management. Managers should also develop well-defined contingency plans to cover unexpected changes from the demand side such as keeping an optimum level of safety stocks.

General Modelling Procedure

When using the ARMA, ARIMA, or SARIMA models to deal with time series data, there is a general procedure to follow as shown in Fig. 8.9 below:

- A good way to start with is to plot the data and observe any possible trend or seasonality patterns. Some data may display a clear pattern, others may be difficult to visually examine.

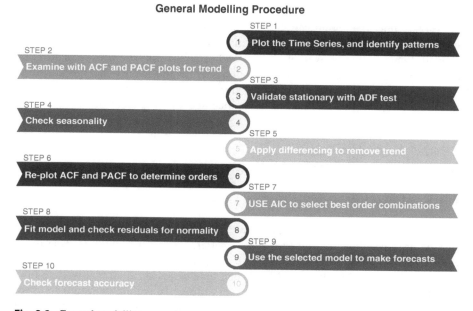

Fig. 8.9   General modelling procedure

- Second, we can further examine the autocorrelations and the number of lags that correlate with the ACF and PACF plots, to identify trend and even seasonality.
- Third, to validate the stationary of the data, the ADF test can be used to check significance level. When the *p* value is larger than 0.05, we cannot reject the null hypothesis that the time series is non-stationary.
- Fourth, to check seasonality, we can decompose the time series with some seasonal decomposition tool such as the built-in function in `statsmodels`.
- Fifth, we can then apply differencing to remove trend. The number of differencing can be determined by visually examining the ACF and PACF plots.
- Sixth, after applying differencing to the data, we can re-plot ACF and PACF plots to determine the number of orders for the AR and MA terms.
- Additionally, as described in the seventh step, we can use AIC to select the best order combinations (i.e., the one that returns the lowest AIC value). Some packages can automatically determine the best order combinations such as the `auto_arima` function in `pmdarima`.
- In the eighth step, we can fit the model with the order combinations and check the residual plots for normality to make sure it is white noise. If there are clear patterns in the residuals, it might suggest that the chosen model cannot explain some of the variance in the original data, and thus alternative models should be considered.
- Nineth, if there are no significant issues in the residuals, we can then use the model to make forecasts.
- In the final step, we can evaluate the model performance using some accuracy metrics. If the performance of model is poor, we can either adjust the model order combinations or use alternative models that can perform best.

Another important point worth mentioning here is that, before fitting a forecasting model, it is strongly recommended that the data should be cleaned and transformed if necessary. For example, real-world data may not be normally distributed and can be skewed, and a log transformation may help produce better forecasts.

So far, we have learnt some classical and commonly used forecasting methods. In the next section, we will look at some machine learning algorithms that can be very useful for demand forecasting.

8.4   Machine Learning Methods

8.4.1   Univariate vs Multivariate Time Series

All our previous examples including WPI, Australian beer production data and Airline passenger data are univariate time series, i.e., a series with a single time-dependent variable. However, in real-life, time series often have more dependent variables than only its past values, and such time series is called multivariate time series. The additional dependency can be very useful for predicting future demand.

Machine learning algorithms are capable of processing (or learning from) the additional variables (or features) that correlate with demand, therefore making the forecasting more powerful and accurate. These additional features that affect demand may include, for example, promotion activities, sports and cultural events, holidays, weather conditions, and even natural disasters.

In this section, we focus on using Random Forest Regression and XGBoost algorithms. Other very useful machine learning algorithms for time series forecasting include, for example, Neural Networks (RNNs), Long Short-Term Memory (LSTM) networks, and other sequence-based models (e.g., Seq2Seq). These algorithms are not covered here since they are deep learning algorithms which are more complex and thus beyond the scope of this book.

8.4.2 Random Forest Regression

As introduced in previous chapters, a random forest is an ensemble learning method that can be used for classification, regression, and other purposes. In this chapter, we will adopt the random forest regressor (RFR) to solve a practical demand forecasting example.

The example to be introduced here is a featured prediction competition on Rossmann store sales launched at *Kaggle.com* in 2015. Rossmann operates over 3000 drug stores in seven European countries. The task is to predict up to 6 weeks of daily sales for 1115 stores located across Germany. As instructed, the store sales can be influenced by many factors, such as promotions, competition, school and state holidays, seasonality, and locality. The data provided include both train and test sets as well as a supplemental information about the stores. For details about the data, see the Rossmann competition site on Kaggle. However, note that the *'store. csv'* dataset contains the following useful information:

- **Store**: each store has a unique ID.
- **StoreType**: four different store types: a, b, c, d.
- **Assortment**: describes an assortment level: a = basic, b = extra, c = extended.
- **CompetitionDistance**: distance in metres to the nearest competitor store.
- **CompetitionOpenSince[Month/Year]**: the month and year when the nearest competitor was opened.
- **Promo2**: a promotion for some stores: (0 = not participating, 1 = participating)
- **Promo2Since[Week/Year]**: the calendar week and year when a store started participating in Promo2.
- **PromoInterval**: the intervals of Promo2 throughout a year.

For brevity reason, the preliminary data cleaning, feature engineering and exploratory data analysis (EDA) are omitted here, while the entire coding can be found at our online repository. You are recommended to go through these procedures carefully as they are critical for ensuring the performance of your model.

First, let us take a look at some plots to gain some initial understanding about the data. We can check the monthly average sales in four different types of stores, and how promotion impacts their sales. Consider below:

Ex. 8.26

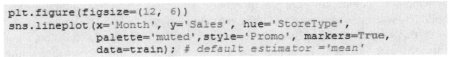

```
plt.figure(figsize=(12, 6))
sns.lineplot(x='Month', y='Sales', hue='StoreType',
             palette='muted',style='Promo', markers=True,
             data=train); # default estimator ='mean'
```

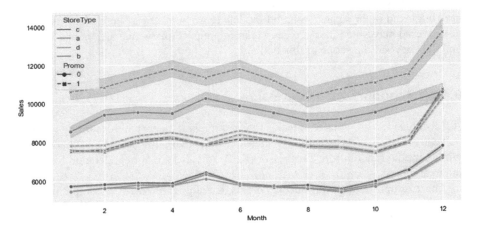

By using the `lineplot` of seaborn, we can observe the trends of sales by month in these four different types of stores. Also, it can be seen that the sales are boosted when stores run a promotion as indicated by the dashed line.

We can also check the sales trends and patterns in different **Assortment** types.

Ex. 8.27

```
plt.figure(figsize=(12, 6))
sns.lineplot(x='Month', y='Sales', hue='Assortment',
             palette='muted', style='Promo',
             markers=True, data=train);
```

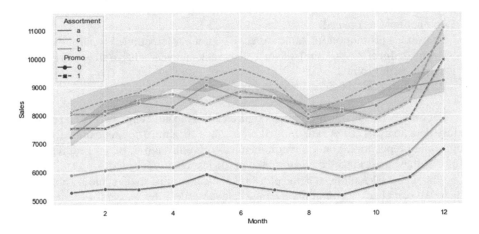

As shown above, we have the following observation:

- the sales trends are preserved in different **Assortment** types.
- promo boosts the sales in all **Assortment** types (perhaps works better in type a and c)
- **Assortment** b has more sales than the other two types (i.e., a and c), but note that we talk about average here.

Next, let us move on to model fitting and training with RFR. To use the estimator, we first need to import it from sklearn.ensemble module:

Ex. 8.28

```
# Time series analysis
from sklearn.ensemble import RandomForestRegressor
```

The cleaned and transformed training data has been further split into *train* and *valid* sets. We can fit the RFR estimator with the *train* data and then use the trained model to make predictions on the *valid* set. Consider below:

Ex. 8.29

```
# Random Forest Regressor
rfr = RandomForestRegressor(random_state=42)
rfr.fit(X_train, y_train)

# Prediction
y_pred = rfr.predict(X_valid)
```

After the model is trained, we can then evaluate the model performance using the accuracy metrics introduced earlier. However, all submissions to the competition on Kaggle are evaluated on RMSPE (i.e., Root Mean Square Percentage Error) scores, which can be written as:

$$\text{RMSPE} = \sqrt{\frac{1}{n}\sum_{t=1}^{n}\left(\frac{E_t}{A_t}\right)^2} \tag{8.17}$$

Thus, to compare our model performance with other entries in the competition, let us define a helper function that can help us calculate the RMSPE values:

Ex. 8.30

```
def rmspe(y_true, y_hat):
    loss = np.sqrt(np.mean(np.square(((y_true - y_hat)/y_true))))
    return loss
```

Then, we can call the function to get the RMSPE score for our model by comparing the predicted values to the actual values in the valid set:

Ex. 8.31

```
error = rmspe(np.exp(y_valid), np.exp(y_pred))

# Print the error:
print("Valid RMSPE: %.4f" % error)
Valid RMSPE: 0.1568
```

The RMSPE is not too bad since we have used only the default parameter settings in the RFR model. However, note that the winning score submitted to the competition on Kaggle public leaderboard is around 0.1002. Before fine tuning our model, let us visualize our predictions against the actual sales in store 1.

Ex. 8.32

```
# Creat a copy of the valid data
df_pred = valid.copy()
# Add the forecasts
df_pred['Forecast'] = np.exp(y_pred)

# Plot Actual vs. Forecast for Store 1.
plt.figure(figsize=(16, 6))
plt.plot(df_pred[df_pred.Store == 1]['Sales'],label='Actual')
plt.plot(df_pred[df_pred.Store == 1]['Forecast'],
        color='red', label='Forecast')
plt.legend();
```

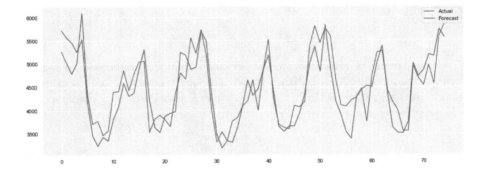

The predictions seem to be quite good. However, to further improve the model performance, we can use scikit-learn's GridSearchCV function as introduced in our previous chapters to search for best possible parameters (alternatively, you can try RandomizedSearchCV, which can be faster).

In GridSearchCV, different scoring methods can be used to evaluate the performance of a cross-validated model on the test set. For our example, we set scoring to the RMSPE value. To do this, we need to import make_scorer method from sklearn.metrics. Consider below:

Ex. 8.33

```python
from sklearn.model_selection import GridSearchCV
from sklearn.metrics import make_scorer

params = {'n_estimators': [200,400,500],
          'max_features': [10,15,20]}

"""WARNING: The following search can be very time-consuming"""
rfr = RandomForestRegressor()

GS = GridSearchCV(rfr, param_grid=params, cv=5,
            scoring=make_scorer(rmspe,greater_is_better=False))
GS.fit(X_train, y_train)
GridSearchCV(cv=5, estimator=RandomForestRegressor(),
            param_grid={'max_features': [10, 15, 20],
                        'n_estimators': [200, 400, 500]},
            scoring=make_scorer(rmspe, greater_is_better=False))
```

Given the very large size of the train data, the searching and fitting the model can be very time consuming depending on your PC configurations. As an illustration, we have limited the search scope by only selecting n_estimators and max_features parameters.

After fitting, we can use the best estimator found to make predictions on the *valid* set. Check below:

Ex. 8.34

```python
rfr_final = GS.best_estimator_
rfr_final.fit(X_train, y_train)
y_pred = rfr_final.predict(X_valid)

error = rmspe(np.exp(y_valid), np.exp(y_pred))
# Print the error:
print("Valid RMSPE: %.4f" % error)
Valid RMSPE: 0.1455
```

Not a bad result! Since we have only tried a couple of parameters, you may want to try other parameter values to possibly improve the model performance.

Lastly, based on our final RFR model, we can plot feature importance to look at what features play a vital role in determining the sales:

Ex. 8.35

```python
# Plot feature importance
feature_rank = pd.Series(rfr_final.feature_importances_,
                         index=X_train.columns)

plt.figure(figsize=(8,8))
feature_rank.nlargest(15).sort_values(ascending=True).\
                                    plot(kind='barh')
plt.xlabel('Importance')
plt.title('Feature Importance', fontsize =15);
```

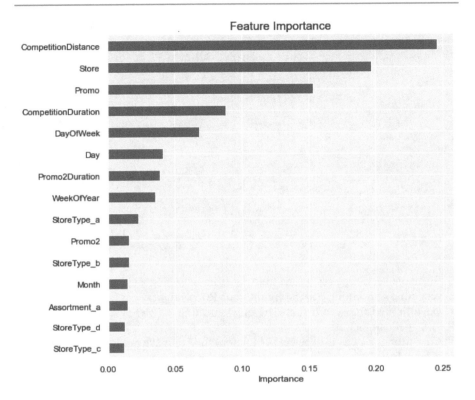

As shown above, the top four most import features derived from our RFR model are CompetitionDistance, Store, Promo, and CompetitionDuration.

In summary, our RFR model returned a RMSPE value of 0.1455 on our validation set, which is a reasonably good result. However, you might still be able to improve the forecasting accuracy by applying one of the following approaches:

- Allocate more data to the training set when splitting so that the algorithm has more data to train on.
- Adjust the hyperparameters to reach a better optimal combination (which can take even a longer time).
- Use different algorithms, e.g., XGBoost.

8.4.3 XGBoost

Another powerful decision-tree-based ensemble machine learning algorithm is XGBoost, which stands for 'Extreme Gradient Boosting'. XGBoost was initially created under the gradient boosting framework by Tianqi Chen (Chen and Guestrin 2016), and originated from research project at University of Washington. It has now

Evolution of Tree-Based Algorithms

A similar ensemble method like AdaBoost, but the method tries to build the new predictor to the residual errors of its previous predictor.

An ensemble of Decision Trees, generally trained via the bagging method but instead search for the best feature among a random subset of features.

Non-parametric supervised learning algorithm for classification and regression problems. A tree can be seen as a piecewise constant approximation by certain decision rules.

A scalable tree boosting method using parallel processing, clever penalization of trees, regularization, extra randomization to optimze model performance.

An ensemble method that combines weak learner into a strong learner by training predictors sequentially, each trying to correcy its predecessor (e.g. AdaBoost)

Bootstrap aggregating or Bagging trains multiple decision trees on different random subsets of the training set and then aggregates the results.

Fig. 8.10 Evolution of tree-based algorithms

gained much popularity and has been dominating supervised machine learning and many Kaggle competitions, especially when it comes to small-to-medium structured or tabular data.

Figure 8.10 depicts the evolution of XGBoost from Decision Trees algorithm.

Compared to Gradient Boosting, XGBoost can work faster. XGBoost uses Newton Boosting (Newton–Raphson method of approximations) which takes a more direct route to the minima than gradient descent (Nielsen 2016). XGBoost also provides more regularization options and penalization on the number of leaf nodes to prevent model from overfitting. In addition, XGBoost introduces more randomization into the learning process. The extra randomization can be effective in reducing the correlation between the trees, thus improving the performance of the ensemble of classifiers.

Worth mentioning here, any objective functions that we use to train our models consist of two main parts: *training loss* and *regularization term*:

$$obj(\vartheta) = L(\vartheta) + \Omega(\vartheta) \tag{8.18}$$

where L is the training loss function, which measures how well the model fits the training data; Ω is the regularization term, which measures the complexity of the model; and θ is the best parameters. A common choice of L is the MSE (i.e., mean squared error).

Determining the best model is often about evaluating the trade-off between underfitting and overfitting (a.k.a. bias-variance trade-off). See the diagram below (Fig. 8.11):

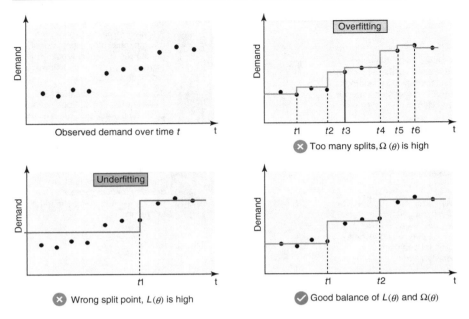

Fig. 8.11 Bias-variance trade-off

In XGBoost implementation, individual tree can be regularized by `max_depth`, `min_child_weight`, `max_delta_step` parameters as well as L1 (`alpha`) and L2 (`lambda`) penalization.

XGBoost also provides a family of parameters for subsampling of columns: `colsample_bytree`, `colsample_bylevel`, and `colsample_bynode`, thus adding more randomness into the learning process.

In essence, there are three types of parameters in XGBoost implementation which must be set before running XGBoost:

- **General parameters** relate to which booster to use, commonly tree-based models (e.g., `gbtree`) or linear model (e.g., `gblinear`).
- **Booster parameters** are those for the specific booster that you have chosen. For example, the parameters for a tree booster (when setting `booster=gbtree`), or for a linear booster (when setting `booster=gblinear`).
- **Learning task parameters** specify the learning tasks and the corresponding learning objective. For example, regression tasks may use different parameters with ranking tasks.

Specifically, Table 8.1 lists a few major parameters for tree booster and their respective meaning.

Note that some of the parameters are set automatically by XGBoost (e.g., `num_pbuffer`, `num_feature`). For more details about those various parameters, see **XGBoost Parameters** section of its documentation.

Table 8.1 XGBoost parameters for tree booster

Parameters	Value	Explanation
eta	default=0.3, range: [0,1]	alias: `learning_rate`, which shrinks the feature weights to make the boosting process more conservative, thus preventing overfitting
gamma	default=0, range: [0,∞]	Minimum loss reduction required to make a further partition on a leaf node of the tree. The larger gamma, the more conservative the model
max_depth	default=6, range: [0,∞]	Maximum depth of a tree. The larger this value, the more complex the model, and thus more likely to overfit
min_child_weight	default=1, range: [0,∞]	Minimum sum of instance weight (hessian) needed in a child. The larger this value, the more conservative the model
subsample	default=1, range: (0,1]	Subsample ratio of the training data. Setting it to 0.5 means that the XGBoost would randomly sample half of the training data, thus preventing overfitting
lambda	default=1	alias: `reg_lambda`, the L2 regularization term on weights. Increasing this value would make model more conservative
alpha	default=0	alias: `reg_alpha`, the L1 regularization term on weights. Increasing this value would make model more conservative

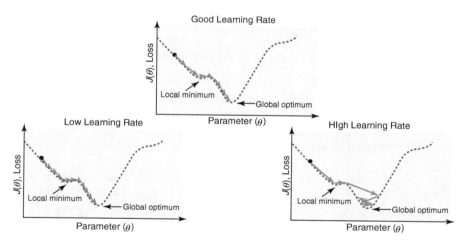

Fig. 8.12 Learning rate trade-off

8.4.4 Learning Rate

The **learning rate** is represented using the notation of the Greek letter `eta`. In optimization, the learning rate is a configurable hyperparameter used to determine the size of the step at each iteration while moving toward a minimum. There is a trade-off between the rate of convergence and overshooting when setting the learning rate. When the learning rate is too low, it can lead to extremely slow convergence, whereas when the value is set too high, it can overshoot the minimum, or it may fail to converge or even diverge (see Fig. 8.12).

In Gradient Boosting, new trees are created to correct the residual errors of its previous predictor and added sequentially. As such, there is a risk of overfitting the training data when the model is fit quickly. To slow down the learning in Gradient Boosting model, we can apply the learning rate (or shrinkage factor) for the corrections by new trees when added to the model.

In practice, the learning rates are often configured by the users based on their experience. It would be a good idea to start training the XGBoost model by initially setting a low learning rate and increasing it at each iteration. In addition, we can use the grid search function in Scikit-learn to evaluate and select best possible learning rates.

Next, let us go back to our Rossmann example and train an XGBoost model to make sales forecasts.

To install the XGBoost package, we can run the following with conda:

```
conda install -c conda-forge xgboost
```

Once installed, it can be imported into our notebook, see below:

```
import xgboost as xgb
```

Before training an XGBoost model, we need to prepare data as XGBoost adopts DMatrix data structure that is optimized for both memory efficiency and training speed. Consider below:

Ex. 8.36

```
# Preparing data
dtrain = xgb.DMatrix(X_train, label=y_train)
dvalid = xgb.DMatrix(X_valid, label=y_valid)
```

XGBoost has the capability of evaluating and reporting on how well the model is performing on both training and test sets during training. All we need to do is to specify a test set using the `evals` parameter and an evaluation metric using `eval_metric` parameter when training the model. XGBoost supports a range of evaluation metrics such as RMSE, MAE, MAPE, and AUC. For a full list, see the **"Learning Task Parameters"** section of the XGBoost parameters documentation.

Note: XGBoost does not support categorical features; if a dataset contains categorical features, load it as a NumPy array first and then perform pre-processing steps such as one-hot encoding.

Since we have previously split our train set, we can use the validation set to evaluate the model performance:

Ex. 8.37

```
# Specify validation set to watch performance
evallist = [(dtrain, 'train'), (dvalid, 'valid')]
```

The `eval_metric` parameter supports function call so that we can use our pre-defined RMSPE helper function by setting `eval_metric=rmspe_xg`.

The next important step is setting the parameters. XGBoost accepts either a list of pairs or a dictionary to set parameters. Consider the following arbitrary parameter settings for our example to start with:

Ex. 8.38

```
# Initialising parameters
params = {"booster" : "gbtree",              #tree based model
          "objective": "reg:squarederror",   #reg with squared loss
          "eta": 0.03,
          "max_depth": 8,
          "subsample": 0.95,
          "colsample_bytree": 0.75,
          "seed": 42 }


num_round = 6000            #number of boosting iterations
```

XGBoost model also supports **early stopping**, which is an approach to avoiding overfitting. It works by stopping the training procedure where performance on the test set starts to decrease while the performance on the training set continues to improve as the model tends to overfit. This can be set in the `early_stopping_rounds` parameter. In our example, we set this value to 100, which means that the RMSPE value needs to decrease at least every 100 rounds to continue training.

After setting parameters, we can start training the model. Consider below:

Ex. 8.39

```
bst = xgb.train(params=params, dtrain=dtrain,
                num_boost_round=num_round,
                evals=evallist, early_stopping_rounds=100,
                feval=rmspe_xg, verbose_eval=True)
[0] train-rmse:8.01646    train-rmspe:0.99963    valid-rmse:8.06237    valid-rmspe:0.99965
[1] train-rmse:7.77653    train-rmspe:0.99953    valid-rmse:7.82191    valid-rmspe:0.99956
[2] train-rmse:7.54381    train-rmspe:0.99941    valid-rmse:7.58951    valid-rmspe:0.99945
[3] train-rmse:7.31799    train-rmspe:0.99927    valid-rmse:7.36397    valid-rmspe:0.99931
[4] train-rmse:7.09898    train-rmspe:0.99909    valid-rmse:7.14546    valid-rmspe:0.99914
[5] train-rmse:6.88655    train-rmspe:0.99887    valid-rmse:6.93332    valid-rmspe:0.99894
[6] train-rmse:6.68055    train-rmspe:0.99862    valid-rmse:6.72708    valid-rmspe:0.99869
[7] train-rmse:6.48072    train-rmspe:0.99831    valid-rmse:6.52737    valid-rmspe:0.99840
```

Note here that if `verbose_eval` is set to `True`, then the evaluation metric on the validation set is printed at each boosting stage (truncated above for brevity). The training stopped after 4602 iterations due to early stopping. If early stopping occurs, the model will have three additional fields: `bst.best_score`, `bst.best_iteration` and `bst.best_ntree_limit`.

We can then print out these best results as follows:

Ex. 8.40

```
print("Best Score on Train set:", bst.best_score)
print("Best iteration:", bst.best_iteration)
print("Best tree limit:", bst.best_ntree_limit)
        Best Score on Train set: 0.139637
        Best iteration: 4501
        Best tree limit: 4502
```

As can be seen, the XGBoost model performs much better than the RFR model on the train set since the RMSPE has decreased from 0.1457 to 0.1396.

Once the model has been trained, it can perform predictions on the test set using `bst.predict(dtest)`. However, if early stopping occurs, you can get prediction from the best iteration with `bst.best_ntree_limit`. Let us run the prediction on our validation set instead and check the RMSPE value. We should obtain the same score as promised in the last round of training. Consider below:

Ex. 8.41

```
# Run prediction on validation set
y_pred = bst.predict(dvalid, ntree_limit=bst.best_ntree_limit)

error = rmspe(np.exp(y_valid), np.exp(y_pred))

# Print the error:
print("Valid RMSPE: %.4f" % error)
Valid RMSPE: 0.1396
```

As expected, the RMSPE is the same as 0.1396!

Additionally, XGBoost includes plotting module to plot feature importance and output tree. To plot importance, we can use `xgboost.plot_importance()`. See below:

Ex. 8.42

```
# plot feature importance, show top 15 features
fig, ax = plt.subplots(figsize=(8,8))
xgb.plot_importance(bst, max_num_features= 15, height=0.5, ax=ax);
```

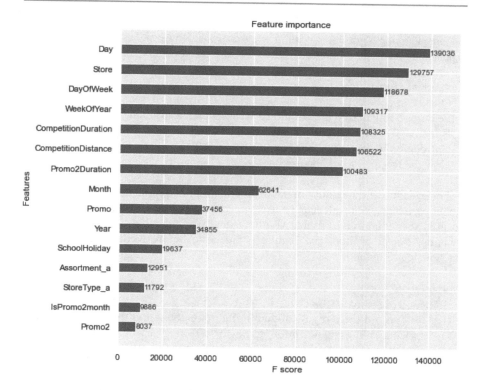

As shown above, the top important features in the XGBoost model include `Day`, `Store`, `DayOfWeek`, `CompetitionDuration`, `CompetitionDistance`, and `Promo2Duration`, which are quite different from those of the RFR model when making predictions and may explain why the XGBoost model performs better.

We can further improve the XGBoost model performance by tunning the hyperparameters. XGBoost contains the `xgboost.cv()` function which allows us to run cross-validation on our training set and the return a mean error score of our choice (e.g., RMSPE). Alternatively, we can use grid search as introduced before. However, this procedure is omitted here but you are encouraged to go through the notebook exercise yourself.

Once the best XGBoost model is found, we can save it and re-use the model on new data in the future. See below:

Ex. 8.43

```
# Save the best model
bst.save_model('my_model.model')

# Reload model
loaded_model = xgb.Booster()
loaded_model.load_model("my_model.model")

# And use it for predictions.
loaded_model.predict(dtest)
```

In summary, both Random Forest Regressor (RFR) and XGBoost are powerful machine learning algorithms for time series analysis. However, best models might not depend only on the algorithms being used, but also on other important factors including:

- Amount of historical data
- Quality of collected data
- Features being used (e.g., additional weather data if available)
- Effective feature engineering and transformation
- Correlation with explanatory features (or variables)
- How the forecast would be used

For instance, if the quality of data is poor and biased, no matter how good your model performs, the results can be useless. In other words, garbage in garbage out! So, it is very vital to ensure that you have quality data and perform effective data cleaning, transformation, and feature engineering before feeding them into any machine learning models.

Summary of Learning Objectives
1. **Understand the purpose of demand management and the SPSS model.**
     Demand is essential information for effective supply chain planning and management. Demand management aims to improve demand visibility, predictability, and reliability so that the focal companies can design and deliver products and services to satisfy various customers' needs in a most effective and efficient manner. The SPSS model is the main four stages of demand management including sense, predict, seize, and stabilize. During the *sense* stage, companies detect market trends and try to understand customer demand to identify demand opportunities. In the *predict* stage, companies collect all possible demand related data and features in order to make demand forecasts. The *seize* stage is where companies align and refine its supply chain figurations, allocate and commit resources to capture demand and satisfy customers. The final stage is *stabilize*, in which organizations stabilize and standardize supply chain structures and processes based on how they successfully capture the demand. The SPSS model is rather dynamic and should be conducted on continuous basis as market conditions and demand change all the time.
2. **Describe different demand forecasting methods and the differences between qualitative and quantitative methods.**
     There are many ways to forecast demand. In general, qualitative methods are based on experience and opinions. These methods include personal experience, market research, the Delphi technique, and scenario planning. Quantitative methods use data to make predictions such as previous sales history, demographic information, seasonal demand patterns, and weather conditions. These quantitative methods include time series analysis, causal relational

methods, machine learning, and simulation. One should remember that forecasts are rarely very accurate. Usually, short-term demand is relatively easier to predict than long-term demand. However, supply chain managers should select the most appropriate methods that fit their demand patterns.

3. **Learn the components of time series and be able to use the traditional methods to perform univariate time series forecasting in Python.**

   Time series data consist of four main components, including trend, seasonality, cyclical component, and noise (error). Time series with trends or seasonality are normally considered *non-stationary*, whereas those without trends or seasonality at which the series are observed are considered *stationary*. A series with a single time-dependent variable is considered univariate time series. The traditional forecasting methods for univariate time series include moving average (MA), weighted moving average (WMA), exponential smoothing (ES), autoregressive model (AR), autoregressive moving average (ARMA), ARIMA, and SARIMA as introduced in this chapter. One of the criteria that can be used to estimate the quality of each model is the Akaike's Information Criterion (AIC). A smaller AIC value often indicates a better model. A closely related model selection criterion is called Bayesian Information Criterion (BIC). Likewise, the model with the lowest BIC is preferred.

4. **Grasp the ways of evaluating forecast accuracy.**

   There are many ways to evaluate forecast accuracy. In this chapter, we have introduced various accuracy metrics for evaluating time series forecasting, including Mean Squared Error (MSE), Root Mean Squared Error (RMSE), Mean Absolute Deviation (MAD), Mean Absolute Percentage Error (MAPE), and Tracking Signal (TS). Each metric has its own advantage and weaknesses. Supply chain managers can use different error analysis to evaluate the performance of a forecasting model, but the ultimate goal of the evaluation is to get forecast right and consistent. Effective forecast models should assist managers in making correct decisions in demand management. Managers should also develop well-defined contingency plans to cover unexpected changes from the demand side such as keeping an optimum level of safety stocks.

5. **Learn and be able to use Random Forest Regression and XGBoost to perform multivariate time series forecasting in Python.**

   In this chapter, we introduce two useful machine learning methods for multivariate timer series demand forecasting, including Random Forest Regression and XGBoost. We have illustrated these two methods with an actual demand forecasting competition launched at Kaggle.com in 2015. Make sure you understand both algorithms, how to build the estimators in Python and calibrate their respective parameters (e.g., learning rate, boosting parameters) to achieve the best results. Also note that best forecasting models might not solely depend on the algorithms being used. It is very important to ensure data quality, and to perform effective data cleaning, transformation, and feature engineering before feeding the data into any machine learning models.

Discussion Questions

1. Of the four stages in the SPSS model, which stage do you think is most important for effective demand management? Why?
2. Can you find examples of companies using either qualitative or quantitative methods for their demand forecasting? Which method is better in your opinion?
3. When using the traditional forecasting methods MA, WMA, and ES, how can we make the forecasts more stable or responsive?
4. What is differencing? And how can we determine the order of differencing in ARIMA model?
5. Explain what is learning rate and how can we determine its value? What about early stopping?

Keyboard Exercises

1. In your notebook, import necessary packages, re-run all the exercises in this chapter. You can perform your own data cleaning and manipulation, feature engineering, use grid search to fine-tune each estimator of your choice and see if you could build a better model.
2. Download the Australian beer production data, try to build your own forecasting model and predict the following 12-month period demand. When developing your model, consider below:
   - Is the series stationary? If not, what sort of differencing is required?
   - What is the best order of your best model? (e.g., p, d, q).
   - What is the AIC of your model?
3. In the Rossmann example, we have performed some exploratory data analyses such as those in *Ex*.8.26 and *Ex*.8.27. Try to perform your own EDA, including:
   - Plot lineplots of the total monthly sales in different types of stores, and with and without promotions.
   - Plot catplots of the total sales by weekdays in different types of stores, and with and without promotions.
   - What can you tell by examining the plots?

References

Akaike, H. 1974. "A new look at the statistical model identification", IEEE Transactions on Automatic Control, 19 (6): 716–723.

Chen, T., & Guestrin, C. 2016. XGBoost: A Scalable Tree Boosting System. In 22nd SIGKDD Conference on Knowledge Discovery and Data Mining.

Chopra S., & Meindl P. 2016. Supply Chain Management. Strategy, Planning & Operation, 6th ed, Pearson, England.

Hyndman, R.J., & Athanasopoulos, G. 2018. Forecasting: principles and practice, 2nd ed, OTexts: Melbourne, Australia.

Nielsen, D. 2016. Tree Boosting With XGBoost: Why Does XGBoost Win "Every" Machine Learning Competition? Norwegian University of Science and Technology.

Schwarz, Gideon E. (1978), "Estimating the dimension of a model", Annals of Statistics, 6 (2): 461–464.

Logistics Management

Contents

Learning Objectives
- Describe the importance of logistics management and its major management activities.
- Understand different modes of transport, their respective advantages and disadvantages, and how to select appropriate transport modes.
- Learn different logistics service providers, their roles and differences in terms of the services and value-adding activities they provide.
- Grasp the meaning of commonly used INCOTERMS in global trade.
- Understand different location decisions and the approaches to making effective location selection.
- Learn different route optimization algorithms and be able to use them to solve basic routing problems.

9.1 Logistics Management

9.1.1 What Is Logistics Management?

As introduced in Chap. 1, logistics is considered a part of supply chain processes in this book, which mainly deals with the physical movement and distribution of goods and services along a company's supply chain. According to the Chartered Institute of Purchasing & Supply (CIPS), logistics management is defined as:

'Logistics Management is a component of supply chain management. It is used to meet customer demands through effective planning, control and implementation of the movement of goods'.

Logistics management plays a vital role in effective supply chain management as it ensures the smooth and timely delivery of the material flows throughout a supply chain to fulfil customer requests. In the UK, the logistics industry has become backbone of the UK economy, not only shipping goods to and from hubs and ports, but also supporting other industries such as manufacturing, retail, construction, and services. Figure 9.1 shows the number of logistics enterprises (comprising transport, storage, and postal) in different regions across the UK. According to the Logistics Report 2019 by Freight Transport Association 2019, the wider logistics sector in the UK employs over 2.7 million people and contributes £124bn to the UK economy.

From 2019 to 2020, the largest growth (10.5%) in enterprise in number is the logistics sector (see Fig. 9.2). This continues a trend of strong growth in recent years as per the Office for National Statistics (ONS).

In today's highly competitive business environment, many retailers are shifting their operations from traditional brick-and-mortar businesses to online shopping. One

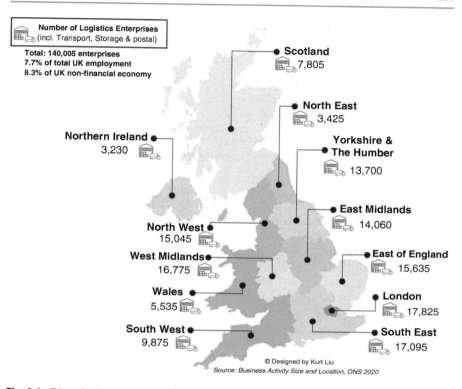

Fig. 9.1 Direct logistics enterprises in the UK

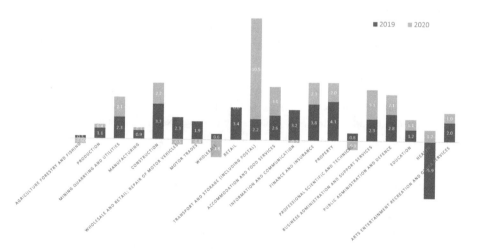

Fig. 9.2 Percentage growth by industry, UK, 2019 to 2020 *(Source: ONS 2020)*

Table 9.1 Examples of logistics as enablers for performance objectives

Objective	Logistics as enabler
Cost	Appropriate transport mode selection, and effective fleet management can help drive cost down
Quality	Fast, accurate, and on-time delivery means high quality in those customers' eyes who wait for their goods to arrive
Speed	Effective DC location and network design can help make fast order fulfilment
Flexibility	Effective logistics operations can accommodate different customer requests in terms of volume, products, and delivery window changes
Reliability	Effective DC network design and fleet management can help enhance the reliable, safe, and accurate deliveries to customers

of the critical factors underpinning the success of such transformation is the expedite and efficient logistics operations. For example, the reason that Amazon outperforms its many competitors is mainly because of its efficient logistics system that are capable of making 'next-day', 'same-day' or even quicker deliveries to its customers.

If supply chains have a significant bearing on the businesses winning against its rivals, then logistics management certainly plays an essential part in ensuring the performance objectives of a company in terms of cost, quality, speed, flexibility, and reliability. Table 9.1 gives some examples of logistics as enabler for performance objectives.

9.1.2 Main Logistics Management Activities

Within a typical supply chain, logistics management can be broadly categorized into **inbound logistics** and **outbound logistics** as depicted in Fig. 9.3 below.

More specifically, **inbound logistics** mainly handles the receiving of raw materials, goods, and components from upstream suppliers to the focal businesses, whereas **outbound logistics** covers the delivery of finished/semi-finished goods and products to downstream customers, including distribution centres (DCs), wholesalers, retailers, and the end consumers.

The main activities that both inbound and outbound logistics management involve include warehousing, storage (note that warehouse and inventory management are introduced in Chap. 7), materials handling, packaging, and transportation as well as the associated information and security.

In addition, logistics network design can be a critical task of logistics management in large organizations where there are complex supply chains involving many upstream suppliers and downstream DCs, retailers, etc. Logistics network design can be further differentiated into two broad tasks:

- **Location decision**: the selection of nodes location in a supply chain such as manufacturing base, DCs, and retail networks considering customer locations and coverage; suppliers location decision considering the lead time, cost, and other criteria. For example, just-in-time (JIT) supplies is a common logistics practice in the automotive industry, which requires suppliers (or their inventories) to be located in close range.

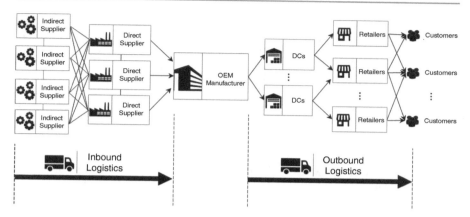

Fig. 9.3 Inbound and outbound logistics

- **Route optimization**: the selection and planning of delivery route with the objectives such as minimizing total travel distance, cost, time, etc.

9.2   Modes of Transport in Logistics

In logistics management, there are essentially five modes of transport to use:

- **Road**
- **Rail**
- **Water**
- **Air**
- **Pipeline**

Each transport mode has its own purpose of usage, and the respective advantages and disadvantages, as detailed in Table 9.2 below.

The selection of transport modes depends on many factors such as cost, service availability, speed, flexibility, risk, and security considerations. For example, road transport via trucks and vans can be most flexible for door-to-door deliveries and it has high accessibility comparing to other transport modes; however, for longer distances, this mode can be relatively slow and rather costly such as shipping goods from China to the UK. Therefore, alternative transport modes should be considered, for example, using sea cargo shipping or rail networks.

9.2.1   Chargeable Weight

In freight and cargo shipping, shipments are usually measured by both weight and volume, and logistics providers often charge for their services as a function of both weight and volume. For example, 1000 kg of stuffed toys as compared to 1000 kg

Table 9.2 Comparison of transport modes

Mode of transport	Advantages	Disadvantages	UK logistics sector facts[a]
Road	• High accessibility to customers • Most flexible for door-to-door • Rapid delivery • Low cost for short distance	• Low carrying capacity • Possible traffic jams/delays/ interrupted • Noise and air pollution	Road (including postal and courier) **£23,397** aGVA £million[b]
Rail	• High carrying capacity • Low environmental impact • Fast delivery for long distances • Ideal for heavy goods	• Reduced accessibility (non door-to-door) • Expensive for short distances • Restricted routes and networks	Rail **£395** aGVA £million
Water	• High carrying capacity • Low environmental impact • Economical for long distances • Ideal for bulky and heavy goods	• Long lead time • Inflexible routes and schedules • Low accessibility (only costal) • High risk of accidents/delays (e.g. Suez blockage in 2021)	Sea and inland waterways **£3,859** aGVA £million
Air	• Very fast • Great geographical coverage • Low risk of accidents	• Very high cost • Lack of accessibility • Limits for size and weight • Restricted items • Noise and air pollution	Air **£194** aGVA £million
Pipeline	• Fast and continuous supply • Unaffected by weather • Economical for long distances • Low environmental impact	• High fixed cost • Lack of flexibility • Only suitable for certain items (e.g. crude oil, natural gas)	Not available

[a] *Source: Logistics Report 2019, FTA*
[b] *Approximate Gross Value Added (aGVA) to the economy*

of coal, despite weighing the same, providers would charge differently as stuffed toys will occupy more space to ship.

Chargeable weight is thus an important metric being used by the logistics providers depending on the typical weight to volume capacities that constrain their resources. It can be calculated as the actual weight or the volumetric (or dimensional) weight of the shipment, whichever is the greater.

For instance, in air freight, the volumetric weight (kg) is calculated by multiplying dimensions (Length × Width × Height) in centimetres and dividing the total by 6,000.

Example 1

XYZ company is going to ship some cargo from Shenzhen, China to Glasgow, UK via air. The shipment has a gross weight of 335 kg, with dimensions 175 cm (L) × 120 cm (W) × 150 cm (H).

$$\text{Volumetric Weight}: \frac{175 \times 120 \times 150}{6,000} = 525 \text{ kg}$$

Thus, the chargeable weight for this shipment is 525 kg since the volumetric weight exceeds the gross weight of 335 kg. ◄

In sea freight, for LCL (less than container load), the volumetric weight (t) is calculated by multiplying dimensions in centimetres and dividing the total by 1,000,000.

Example 2

XYZ company is going to ship some cargo from London, UK to Sydney, Australia via sea. The shipment has a gross weight of 500 kg ($0.5t$), with dimensions 100 cm (L) × 80 cm (W) × 50 cm (H).

$$\text{Volumetric Weight}: \frac{100 \times 80 \times 50}{1,000,000} = 0.4t$$

Thus, the chargeable weight for this shipment is $0.5t$ since the gross weight exceeds the volumetric weight of $0.4t$. ◄

9.2.2   Product Value Density

From the cost perspective, one of the key factors to consider when making transport mode selection is the Product Value Density (PVD). PVD refers to the product value relative to its weight and volume, and can be expressed as follows:

$$\text{Product Value Density}(\text{PVD}) = \frac{\text{Product Value}}{\text{Chargeable Weight}} \qquad (9.1)$$

In general, for products with a low value density (i.e., low PVD), an economical and relatively slow mode of transport should be chosen. For products with a high value density (i.e., high PVD), a fast and reliable mode of transport should be considered. For example, Apple ships all iPhones and iPads by air than by sea (Worstall 2013). One of the key factors for the choice is because Apple's products PVDs are very high.

PVD has also implications for inventory management. In general, products with a high PVD should be held centrally upstream in the supply chain and use fast delivery to satisfy consumer demands. This is because high PVD is often associated with increased cost of holding inventory due to the value of the products. Using

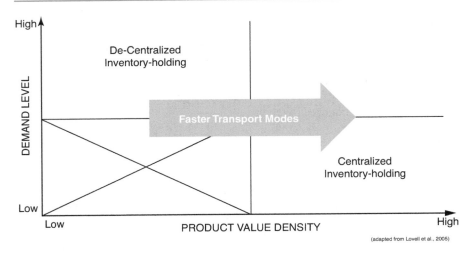

Fig. 9.4 Transport mode selection according to PVD and demand level

centralized inventory can benefit from stock reductions because of risk pooling, and faster transport modes can help reduce the level of safety stock and the stock in-transit too (Lovell et al. 2005).

Figure 9.4 shows the interaction between demand level (throughout) and PVD. As demand level and dispersion increase, a more decentralized inventory holding logistics network design can be justified to meet various customer demands. If the PVD is low, a high demand level provides opportunities for achieving economies of scale in manufacturing, thus a more decentralized approach to holding inventory is possible. By contrast, when PVD is high and demand level is low, a more centralized inventory holding is preferred as high holding costs drive the need to minimize inventory levels, and a faster mode of transport should be selected.

In practice, it is quite common to use more than one mode of transport to ship goods, especially for international trade. This is often referred to as **intermodal** transportation. For example, when importing products from overseas to the UK, goods are first loaded onto trucks using the truck-size intermodal containers, and then delivered via road to some exporting ports where they will be loaded onto container ships. When the goods arrive at the importing ports, possibly at port of Felixstowe—the UK's biggest and busiest container port that handles almost half of Britain's containerized trade (see Fig. 9.5), they will be unloaded onto trucks and then delivered to their final destinations.

The most common intermodal combinations are truck/rail-water-rail/truck and truck-rail-truck, which are facilitated by using the standardized shipping containers. The commonly used two container sizes are 20 ft and 40 ft in length, respectively, but with the same width (8 ft) and height (8.5 ft).

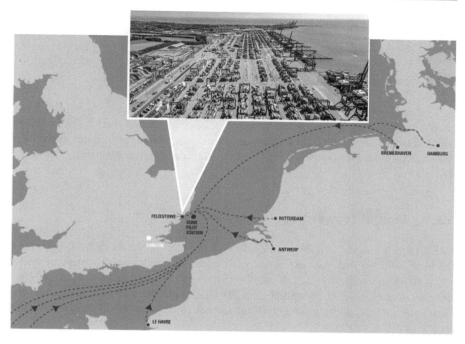

Fig. 9.5 Port of Felixstowe, Suffolk, England. Source: © 2021 Port of Felixstowe. Reproduced with permission

9.3   Logistics Service Providers

Though many firms are still managing their own logistics today, there is a surging level of outsourcing the logistics activities to the specialist logistics service providers. This is usually because the logistics function is not their core business, therefore external service providers would allow companies to focus on their core competences and to potentially reduce cost.

Traditional freight firms normally provide only basic transportation services, however there is a tendency nowadays that these providers are moving towards offering a variety of sophisticated value-adding logistics solutions to other businesses. Based on the services they provide, these logistics providers can largely fall into the following categories:

9.3.1   Freight Companies

This is a broad term used to describe companies that are specialized in the moving of freight from one place to another. Freight companies can handle both international and domestic shipments. They may specialize in one or more types of transport modes, depending on the location and type of freight being shipped.

9.3.2   Freight Carriers

Freight carriers focus on moving goods around the country and the world. They handle freight directly. Examples include trucking companies, rail services, ocean freight carriers, and air freight carriers. In most cases, shipments require intermodal transportation and may thus require more than one carrier to reach their final destinations.

9.3.3   Freight Forwarders

Instead of moving freight themselves, freight forwarders are specialized in finding the most efficient and least expensive ways to move goods, mostly internationally. They act as an agent on behalf of the shippers to arrange and negotiate pricing with freight carriers. Freight forwarders usually deal with all documentation, customs clearance, rate negotiation, and consolidation and coordination of freight from the source to the customer.

9.3.4   Third Party Logistics (3PL) providers

3PL companies provide outsourced logistics services for a business. The range of services they provide and depth of integration into a firm's supply chain can vary significantly from business to business. In general, 3PL providers will tailor their services to meet the specific needs of their customers. Some may only handle transportation and storage, while others may take over the complete supply chain management for a large organization. The main logistics services that a 3PL provides can include but are not limited to the following:

- Transportation
- Warehousing
- Inventory management
- Freight forwarding
- Delivery and order fulfilment
- Order management
- Logistics optimization
- Returns processing

9.3.5   Fourth Party Logistics (4PL) Companies

In recent years, there is another emerging term that has been used to define the complete and comprehensive supply chain solutions that a logistics provider can offer— i.e., 4th Party Logistics (4PL) . Different from 3PL, the 4PL providers integrate all the members of a supply chain in order to design, source, plan, and control all logistics activities to meet the specific customers long-term performance objectives. These providers develop their own capabilities and technologies, and usually have their own complex distribution networks to offer globally consistent and value-adding logistics solutions. The 4PL providers are often those lead logistics providers (LLP) such as DHL and UPS.

Figure 9.6 depicts some of the differences between 3PL and 4PL logistics services. However, note that in practice it is often hard to draw a clear line between 3PL and 4PL companies, as more and more 3PL providers tend to expand their services offering by providing more integrated and comprehensive logistics solutions to their customers.

9.4   Global Logistics Management

Due to the increased level of overseas outsourcing and international business, many organizations are either directly or indirectly involved in global trade and logistics operations. According to the World Trade Organization (WTO) (2020), the volume of global container shipping has been showing an upward trend from 2007 to 2020,

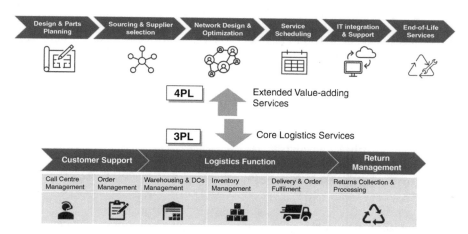

Fig. 9.6   Differences between 3PL and 4PL

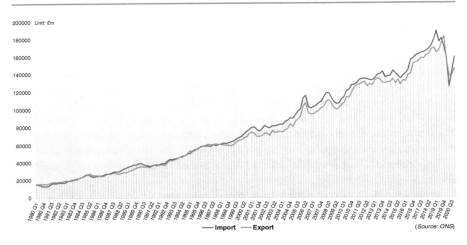

Fig. 9.7   UK total import and export data since 1980

though experiencing some percentage drop during the financial crisis of 2008–2009 and the COVID-19 pandemic.

The UK is ranked the fourth largest global trader in 2019 (WTO 2020), with a total trade about £1,406 billion according to the ONS, following the USA, China, and Germany. The top five UK trading partners by total trade in goods were the USA, Germany, China, the Netherlands, and France, which accounted for 46.0% of UK total trade in goods, excluding unspecified goods in the first half of 2020 (ONS 2020).

Figure 9.7 illustrates the total trade (incl. imports and exports) of UK from 1980 to 2020.

For businesses involved in global trade and logistics, one important thing they need to make sure in their contract is who are responsible for shipping and delivery of goods. As a supply chain manager, you would probably need to discuss and negotiate the following issues with your suppliers:

- Where will the goods be delivered to?
- How will the goods be shipped?
- Who arranges the shipment?
- Who is responsible for insurance?
- Who deals with customs clearance?
- Who pays any tariffs and taxes?

For instance, you might agree with your suppliers that they will deliver the goods, at their own expense, to a destination port in your country. They might also agree to arrange insurance for the goods until they reach the destination port; however, they will pass this cost to you. You will then take over responsibility for the goods from the port, paying for customs clearance and duties, and arrange delivery to your warehouse.

9.4.1 Incoterms

The International Chamber of Commerce (ICC) has published an International Commercial Terms (commonly known as **Incoterms**) in 1936, with the ninth version, i.e., Incoterms 2020, having been published in 2019 (International Chamber of Commerce 2020). Incoterms contains a series of pre-defined three-letter trade terms, which set out the obligations, costs, and risks between sellers and buyers participating in the import and export of global trade.

There are 11 incoterms in Incoterms 2020. Here, we introduce the most commonly used ones with respect to the mode of transport they are intended for.

- **Rules for any mode or modes of transport**
    - **EXW (Ex Works)**

        The seller makes the goods available at the seller's premises. The buyer bears all the transportation costs and the risks of bringing the goods to their final destination.
    - **FCA (Free Carrier)**

        The seller is only responsible for delivery of the goods to a carrier nominated by the buyer. Responsibility for cost and risk is then transferred to the buyer.
    - **CIP (Carrier and Insurance Paid to)**

        The seller arranges and pays for the transportation and insurance to the named overseas place of destination, but risk is transferred to the buyer once the goods are delivered at the first carrier. Under CIP, the seller is required to obtain insurance cover complying with Institute Cargo Clauses (A) or similar clause in the buyer's name.
    - **DPU (Delivered at Place Unloaded)**

        The seller is responsible for delivery of goods and take all the costs and risks until the goods are unloaded at the named place at destination. The buyer is then responsible for customs clearance at their own cost and risk.
    - **DDP (Delivered Duty Paid)**

        The seller delivers the goods to the named place at destination and is responsible for all the costs in bringing the goods to the destination, including customs duties and taxes. The risks pass to the buyer once the goods are delivered at the named place of destination. The seller is not responsible for unloading under DDP.

- **Rules for sea and inland waterway transport**
    - **FAS (Free Alongside Ship)**

        The seller delivers the goods at the loading port alongside the ship. From this point onward, the buyer bears all the costs and risks.
    - **FOB (Free On Board)**

        The seller is responsible for delivery of the goods loaded onboard a vessel at the loading port. As soon as the goods have been loaded, any costs and risks are transferred to the buyer.
    - **CFR (Cost and Freight)**

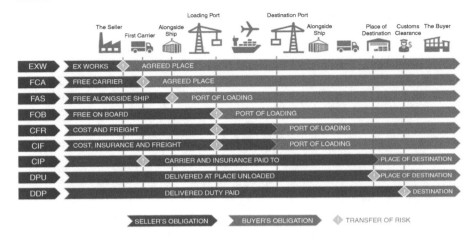

Fig. 9.8 Commonly used incoterms 2020

The seller covers all the costs in bringing the goods to the overseas destination port. However, risk is transferred to the buyer once the goods have been loaded onboard a vessel at the loading port. If the buyer requires the seller to obtain insurance, CIF should be used instead.

– **CIF (Cost, Insurance, and Freight)**
This is the same as CFR except that the seller must also obtain and pay for the insurance. Risk is still transferred to the buyer at the loading port. The seller is required to obtain the minimum insurance cover complying with Institute Cargo Clauses (C).

A summery and graphical representation of these different incoterms can be found in Fig. 9.8. For more information about incoterms, visit the International Chamber of Commerce website.

9.5   Logistics Network Design

Logistics network design is a broad and important subject for effective supply chain management. An optimized logistics network can bring down costs, improve smooth material flows, and enhance customer service.

There are different logistics network design decisions, including:

* **Facility role**: what role and processes should each facility have in the network?
* **Facility location**: where to build facilities?
* **Number of facilities**: how many facilities to build?
* **Capacity allocation**: how much capacity should be allocated to each facility?
* **Market allocation**: what markets should each facility serve?
* **Route choice**: What delivery routes to choose in an optimized way?

In this section, we cover some of the essential topics in logistics network design.

9.5.1 Location Decisions

In logistics network design, location choice perhaps is one of the most important decisions to make facing logistics and supply chain managers. For instance, when selecting suppliers, a critical factor to consider is where they are located and if it is required, whether the suppliers are willing to build factories/warehouses close to your premises. For instance, when Jaguar Land Rover (JLR) built its first plant in China, many key suppliers also moved over and built their factories close to JLR's manufacturing base there.

In addition to supplier selection in the upstream, location decisions can also include downstream decisions from choosing manufacturing sites, DCs, warehouses, to retail stores. Organizations often need to consider where to build new facilities if demand surges or to shut down facilities in one location and move to another if demand changes. Obviously, these are strategic location decisions that may have a long-term effect on firm performance.

There are many factors that impact location decisions such as costs, regional demands level, and regulations. Below we list some key factors to consider:

- **Cost**—Cost can be a major factor influencing the decision. The costs may include some fixed costs such as the direct cost of acquiring land and building new facilities, and variable costs such as transportation cost (e.g., depending on the total distance a delivery truck travels).
- **Proximity to source**—Some raw materials may be rare to gain, and thus getting close to the supply can be advantageous in the competition.
- **Proximity to market**—Getting closer to the customers can make fast and flexible deliveries, thus satisfying customers and occupying the market.
- **Accessibility**—when making location decision, another important factor to consider is whether the site has easy access to other facilities, such as airports, shipping ports, railways, and motorways, etc. Good accessibility can mean speed and efficiency, as well as reduced cost.
- **Demand level**—when there is a surging demand in some area, firms may need to consider either expanding their existing facilities or building new ones to cover the demand there. In addition, as depicted in Fig. 9.4, demand level can also influence the decision of using either centralized or decentralized warehouses.
- **Service level**—this is related to proximity to market and demand level. To achieve a high service level, companies need to consider not only where to build but also the number and size of facilities to build, as well as a good alignment with different transport modes.
- **Risk factor**—this may relate to the wider political, cultural, economic, and environmental uncertainties, as well as the risk of competition, demand variation, and potential loss of customers due to, for example, lack of stock availability, delays, and the return process.

Centre of Gravity Method

The centre of gravity (COG) method is a traditional approach used to identify a suitable geographic location for a new facility that minimizes the total transportation cost.

Assume that (x, y) is the coordinates for the new facility location, given n customer locations, $i = 1, ..., n$, the distance d_i between the new facility and the customer location i (x_i, y_i) can be expressed as follows:

$$d_i(x,y) = \sqrt{\left(x - x_i\right)^2 + \left(y - y_i\right)^2} \tag{9.2}$$

Then, the objective of the centre of gravity method can be written as:

$$\min \mathrm{TC} = \sum_{i=1}^{n} D_i C_i d_i \tag{9.3}$$

$$= \min \sum_{i=1}^{n} D_i C_i \sqrt{\left(x - x_i\right)^2 + \left(y - y_i\right)^2} \tag{9.4}$$

where

- TC is the total transportation cost,
- D_i is the quantity of demand at customer location i,
- C_i is the shipping rate to customer location i.

The new facility location (x, y) can be given by

$$x = \frac{\sum_{i=1}^{n} D_i C_i x_i}{\sum_{i=1}^{n} D_i C_i} \text{ and } y = \frac{\sum_{i=1}^{n} D_i C_i y_i}{\sum_{i=1}^{n} D_i C_i} \tag{9.5}$$

Albeit the COG is a useful method for identifying a reasonable area to locate new facilities, in practice, the selection of locations can be more complicated than simply considering the transportation cost as other factors must be taken into account too. For example, as discussed earlier, the accessibility issues, i.e., whether the chosen location has good transport links. The land cost and availability of space can be important factors to consider as well.

In addition to the above factors, when making location decisions, organization should also consider its business objectives, performance target, and strategic orientations. This is because the location, size, number, and capacity of new facilities can have long-term effects on the success of the business operations. Often location decision making can be challenging especially when there is a high volatile market and demand uncertainties prevail, therefore the ability to make good location decisions can be regarded as a firm's strategic supply chain capabilities that other competitors are difficult to imitate.

9.5.2 Centralization vs De-centralization

In logistics network design, the location and number of warehouses can have major implications for successful logistics operations within a supply chain. When all inventories are held in one central location, it is often referred to as a **centralized warehouse**, whereas when inventories are held in many locations close to the customers, it is referred to as **decentralized warehouses** (see Fig. 9.9).

As discussed previously, demand level can affect the decision on how inventories should be held. Generally, increasing the number of warehouses can improve customer service level because of the reduction of average delivery time to the customers; however, it can also increase the overall inventory costs due to increased level of safety stocks in each warehouse against uncertainties in demand. Total transportation cost may decrease to certain extent as the number of warehouses increases, however it may start to increase again as the transportation costs from suppliers and/or manufacturers to the warehouses can increase when the distribution networks get more complicated.

Thus, the centralization vs. de-centralization logistics network design is often a trade-off decision between cost and responsiveness as depicted in Fig. 9.10. In essence, an organization must decide a balance between the total costs and the desired customer service level, depending on its competition strategies and performance objectives.

Square Root Law

The Square Root Law (SRL) that was initially proposed by Maister (1976) in 1976 provides a theoretical framework for centralization vs. de-centralization decision

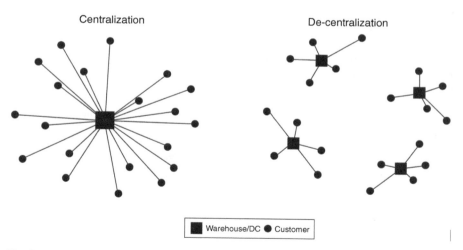

Fig. 9.9 Centralized vs. decentralized warehouses

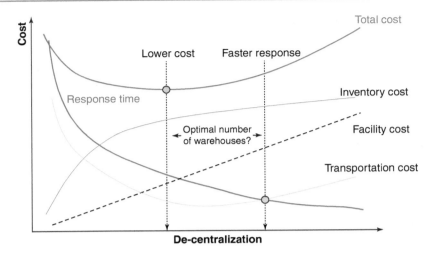

Fig. 9.10   Cost vs. responsiveness trade-off

making as it can be used to predict inventory levels based on the degree of de-centralization. Basically, according to the SRL, total future inventory can be approx-imated by multiplying the current inventory by the square root of the number of future warehouses divided by the current number of warehouses.

$$S_2 = S_1 \times \sqrt{\frac{n_2}{n_1}} \qquad (9.6)$$

where

- S_2 is the total inventory in future warehouses,
- S_1 is the total inventory in existing warehouses,
- n_2 is the number of future warehouse (s),
- n_1 is the number of existing warehouse (s).

Example

Current inventory level is 5000 units; one centralized warehouse expands to nine to cover the same level of total demand in different regions.

$$\text{Using the SRL, the future inventory} = 5,000 \times \sqrt{\frac{9}{1}} = 15,000 \text{ units.}$$

Under the assumptions of SRL, centralization automatically reduces inventory level. Though in practices its application is debatable (Oeser and Romano 2016), the SRL explains the relationship between inventories in centralized and decen-tralized warehouses, which provides useful insights into managerial decision making in logistics network design.

Table 9.3 Centralized vs. decentralized warehouse comparison

	Advantages	Disadvantages
Centralized warehouse	• Integrated planning and control • Reduced overall level of inventory • Efficient warehousing and capacity utilization • Centralized routing optimization and scheduling • Potentially reduce operating costs (e.g. overheads, insurance, etc.) • Possible economies of scale	• Slow response to local customer needs • Customer service and support can be relatively poor • High transportation cost • High risks of warehousing operations (e.g. flood, fire, natural disasters, etc.) • Centralized decision-making may not reflect different market needs
De-centralized warehouses	• Fast and flexible response to local customer demand • Improved after-sale customer services and support • Reliable and resilient inventory control (e.g. more safety stock held locally) • Low risks (e.g. in the event that one warehouse is temporarily inaccessible)	• Excessive total inventory holding • Difficult to ensure consistent practices across all locations • Potential diseconomies of scale • High operating costs overall • Decisions-making may not always align well with company's strategic objectives

In addition to the total cost perspective, centralized and decentralized warehousing have their respective advantages and disadvantages as listed in Table 9.3. For instance, in a centralized warehouse network design, companies can have integrated planning and control of inventory and warehouse operations, and thus improved capacity utilization and efficiency. However, in such a design, companies may have relatively slow response to local customer requests, and the customer support can be relatively poor. ◄

9.5.3 Logistics Network Design Example with PuLP

Now let us look at a simplified logistics network design problem. In this example, a pizza franchise business decides to open additional stores to cover the demand in five different areas subject to certain constraints.

Example

Assume the example data is from a pizza store trying to optimize its logistics network across five regions, i.e., R1, R2, R3, R4, and R5. The pizza store is considering opening additional stores to cover the demand in each region. You, as the logistics manager, are given the daily total demand from each region, the average delivery costs between every two regions, the fixed costs of opening each store in each region. The additional stores will have the same design with two capacity options (i.e., High capacity vs. Low capacity). The objective of this problem is to minimize the total costs while satisfying all the demand in five regions.

Region	Demand	Fixed cost		Capacity options		Delivery cost				
		Low_fix	High_fix	Low_cap	High_cap	R1	R2	R3	R4	R5
R1	5000	800	1200	2000	6000	5	12	17	8	7
R2	1800	1250	1650	2000	6000	12	4	10	7	8
R3	800	900	1450	2000	6000	17	10	3	11	8
R4	630	650	800	2000	6000	8	7	11	7	18
R5	490	666	950	2000	6000	7	8	10	18	6

Task:

- Your task is to analyse where to open the stores and with what sizes for each opening store to meet all the requirements as set out above. ◄

This is a cost minimization problem, which can be formulated as the following:

$$\min \sum_{i=1}^{n} f_i y_i + \sum_{i=1}^{n} \sum_{j=1}^{m} d_{ij} x_{ij} \tag{9.7}$$

where

- f_i is the fixed cost of keeping store i open,
- y_i is binary variable, $y_i = 1$ if store i is open, 0 otherwise,
- d_{ij} is the average delivery cost per unit from store i to region j,
- x_{ij} is the quantity shipped from store i to region j,
- n is the potential number of new stores,
- m is the number of regions.

subject to the following conditions,

$$\sum_{i=1}^{n} x_{ij} = D_j \quad \text{for } j = 1, \ldots, m \tag{9.8}$$

$$\sum_{j=1}^{n} x_{ij} = C_i y_i \quad \text{for } i = 1, \ldots, n \tag{9.9}$$

where

- D_j is the total demand from region j,
- C_i is the potential capacity of store i.

Specifically, the constraint in Eq. (9.8) requires that the total quantity delivered from potential stores meet the total demand from each region. The constraint in Eq. (9.9) requires that the total quantity delivered out of each store cannot exceed its potential capacity (either large or small).

Next, let us solve the minimization problem with PuLP in Python. To use the package, we need to import it in our notebook, consider below:

Ex. 9.1

```
# Import PuLP modeler functions
from pulp import *
```

Then, we load the data from the 'PizzaStoreLocation.csv' file:

Ex. 9.2

```
import pandas as pd
Data = pd.read_csv("PizzaStoreLocation.csv", index_col='Region')
Data
```

Region	Demand	Low_fix	High_fix	Low_cap	High_cap	R1	R2	R3	R4	R5
R1	5000	800	1200	2000	6000	5	12	17	8	7
R2	1800	1250	1650	2000	6000	12	4	10	7	8
R3	800	900	1450	2000	6000	17	10	3	11	8
R4	630	650	800	2000	6000	8	7	11	7	18
R5	490	666	950	2000	6000	7	8	10	18	6

We can copy specific parts of the DataFrame for easy access when building our model with PuLP. Consider below:

Ex. 9.3

```
fix_cost = Data[['Low_fix', 'High_fix']]
fix_cost.columns=['Low_cap','High_cap']
capacity = Data[['Low_cap', 'High_cap']]
ship_cost = Data[['R1', 'R2', 'R3','R4', 'R5']]
```

Recall that we can initialize the problem model with LpProblem function in PuLP. For this example, let us give it a name 'Pizza_Store_Network_Design' and select LpMinimize as the objective. A list of location and size have also been created for looping purpose later.

Ex. 9.4

```
# Initialize model
model = LpProblem("Pizza_Store_Network_Design", LpMinimize)
loc = ['R1', 'R2', 'R3', 'R4', 'R5']
size = ['Low_cap','High_cap']
```

Next, we move onto creating decision variables x and y using LpVariable. dicts(). x contains a dictionary of all potentially shipped quantity from each store to each region, whilst y contains a dictionary of all possible stores with either low or high capacities. Note that the category type is set to `Binary` here, so $y = 1$ if store is open, 0 otherwise.

Ex. 9.5

```
# Define variables
x = LpVariable.dicts("quantity_", [(i,j) for i in loc for j in loc],
                lowBound=0, upBound=None, cat='Integer')
y = LpVariable.dicts("store_",[(i,s) for s in size for i in loc],
                cat='Binary')
```

As the objective of this example is to select the new pizza stores that can minimize the total fixed and variable costs (i.e., the delivery cost in this case). Thus, we define our objective function as follows:

Ex. 9.6

```
# Define objective function
model += (lpSum([fix_cost.loc[i,s] * y[(i,s)]
                for s in size for i in loc])
        + lpSum([ship_cost.loc[i,j] * x[(i,j)]
                for i in loc for j in loc]))
```

The first part of this objective function represents the total fixed cost, depending on whether to open the store at region i and the size (i.e., capacity) of the opening store. The second part represents the total delivery cost shipping from store i to region j. However, the objective function is subject to the two constraints set out in Eqs. (9.8) and (9.9), which can be coded as below:

Ex. 9.7

```
# Define the constraints
for j in loc:
    model += lpSum([x[(i, j)] for i in loc]) == Data.loc[j,'Demand']
for i in loc:
    model += lpSum([x[(i, j)] for j in loc]) <= \
                lpSum([capacity.loc[i,s] * y[(i,s)] for s in size])
```

Now we have defined everything needed to build our optimization model in PuLP. Let us solve it and print out the model status to check if an optimal solution can be found:

Ex. 9.8

```
# Solve
model.solve()
# Print model status
print(LpStatus[model.status])
```

```
Optimal
```

Great! An optimal solution has been found for our model. We can examine the
optimized delivery routes, the capacity options of the opening stores, and the total
costs using the following code:

Ex. 9.9

```
# Print Solved Store Delivery Options
Sol = [{'Delivery':"{} to {}".format(i,j), 'Amount':x[(i,j)].varValue}
for i in loc for j in loc]
print(pd.DataFrame(Sol))

# Print Solved Store Openning Options
Sol = [{'loc':i, 'Low_cap':y[(i,size[0])].varValue,
        'High_cap':y[(i,size[1])].varValue} for i in loc]
print(pd.DataFrame(Sol))

# Print Total Optimized Costs
print("Total Optimized Costs = £{}".format(value(model.objective)))
```

	Delivery	Amount
0	R1 to R1	5000.0
1	R1 to R2	0.0
2	R1 to R3	0.0
3	R1 to R4	0.0
4	R1 to R5	490.0
5	R2 to R1	0.0
6	R2 to R2	1800.0
7	R2 to R3	0.0
8	R2 to R4	630.0
9	R2 to R5	0.0
10	R3 to R1	0.0
11	R3 to R2	0.0
12	R3 to R3	800.0
13	R3 to R4	0.0
14	R3 to R5	0.0
15	R4 to R1	0.0
16	R4 to R2	0.0
17	R4 to R3	0.0
18	R4 to R4	0.0
19	R4 to R5	0.0
20	R5 to R1	0.0
21	R5 to R2	0.0
22	R5 to R3	0.0
23	R5 to R4	0.0
24	R5 to R5	0.0

	loc	Low_cap	High_cap
0	R1	0.0	1.0
1	R2	0.0	1.0
2	R3	1.0	0.0
3	R4	0.0	0.0
4	R5	0.0	0.0

Total Optimized Costs = £46190.0

From the output we can see that the new pizza stores should be opened in regions
R1, R2, and R3 only. And stores in R1 and R2 should have the high-capacity design
though there will be slack capacities, whilst store in R3 can have the low-
capacity option.

Specifically, store in R1 should cover both R1 and R5 regions, and store in R2
should cover both R2 and R4 regions. Store in R3 only serves the region itself.
Based on the optimized solution, the total costs can be £46,190.

In this simplified example, we have learnt how to optimize a logistics network design from the total cost perspective while meeting certain conditions using mixed integer programming in PuLP. In practice, however, more advanced approaches are often used, and there can be more constraints when making location decisions such as meeting delivery time window. Certain machine learning algorithms such as K-means method can also be applied to solve location problems. However, they are beyond the scope of the book and thus will not be covered here.

9.6   Route Optimization

Imagine you are driving a truck and trying to deliver the goods to the customers in different locations, what would be the best delivery route that can reduce the total cost (e.g., travelling distance)? This question brings another import topic in logistics network design, i.e., delivery route optimization. Given a list of customers and their locations, one might be able to work out the best route to travel to meet customer demands whilst reducing the total travelling distance. In this section, we will cover some commonly used approaches and algorithms for route optimization problems.

9.6.1   Travelling Salesman Problem

The travelling salesman problem (TSP) is the most well-known route optimization problem which has been introduced a few decades ago, and still attracts researchers from various fields today. In TSP, a salesman, starting from his home, must visit all the other cities and then return home. Each city is to be visited only once. Taking into account the locations and distances between each pair of cities, the TSP aims to find the total distance travelled as short as possible.

Though TSP may seem to be a simple problem to solve, it turns out that the optimization is quite complex and difficult to achieve. In the simplest version of TSP, the distance between two cities (or nodes) is symmetric, i.e., the distance is the same both ways, and there is a single vehicle without capacity constraint. In practice, TSP can be more challenging to solve as it may involve many constraints such as capacity, traffic, and different distance (time) in each direction. Therefore, some extension of the TSP research has emerged in the past, which adds more variants and complexity to the traditional TSP problem. For example, the asymmetric TSP (ATSP), TSP with time windows (TSPTW), and the multiple TSP (M-TSP).

In addition to the various constraints, as the number (N) of cities (or nodes) increases ($N!$ possible routes), the computing time grows exponentially to find the true optimal tour, making the TSP more difficult to solve (see Fig. 9.11). Prior research has applied various approaches to solving this problem including, for example, linear programming, Monte Carlo estimation, Tabu searchers, genetic algorithms, ant colony algorithms, particle swam optimization, and bat algorithm (Osaba et al. 2020), etc. In this book however, we only look at some of the fundamental methods for TSP.

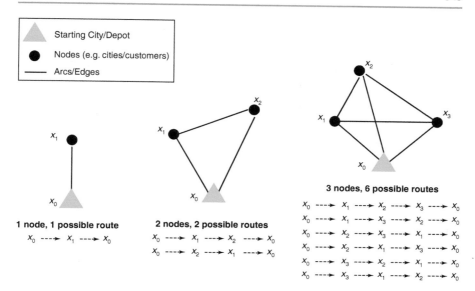

Fig. 9.11 Possible routes as nodes grows

First, the TSP can be solved using linear programming. One of the notable formulations is the Miller–Tucker–Zemlin (MTZ) formulation (Miller et al. 1960). Given a network of n nodes, a salesman begins trip in node 1 (which is the depot) and must visit each node only once and then return to node 1. The MTZ formulation can be expressed as follows:

$$\min \sum_{i=1}^{n} \sum_{j \neq i, j=1}^{n} c_{ij} x_{ij} \tag{9.10}$$

subject to

$$\sum_{j=1, j \neq i}^{n} x_{ij} = 1 \quad (i = 1, \dots, n), \tag{9.11}$$

$$\sum_{i=1, i \neq j}^{n} x_{ij} = 1 \quad (j = 1, \dots, n), \tag{9.12}$$

$$u_i - u_j + n x_{ij} \leq n - 1 \quad (2 \leq i \neq j \leq n), \tag{9.13}$$

where, $x_{ij} = \begin{cases} 1, & \text{if arc}(i,j) \text{ is in the tour} \\ 0, & \text{otherwise} \end{cases}$, $(i, j = 1, \dots, n; i \neq j)$

c_{ij} is the associated cost (e.g., distance) with each arc (i, j),

u_i is the additional free variable used to give an ordering to all nodes to prevent subtours. Since the tour starts from the depot node $i = 1$, we can set the following constraints:

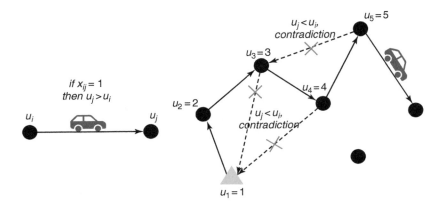

Fig. 9.12 Subtour elimination constraint

$$u_1 = 1, \tag{9.14}$$

$$2 \le u_i \le n \quad (i = 2,\ldots,n), \tag{9.15}$$

Constraint in Eqs. (9.11) and (9.12) represent that each node must be visited exactly once. The inequalities in Eqs. (9.13), (9.14), and (9.15) are subtour elimination constraints.

When $x_{ij} = 1$ (i.e., the arc is in the tour), the inequality in Eq. (9.13) becomes $u_j \ge u_i + 1$, suggesting that the next node order value is greater than its previous one. To better illustrate this, consider the diagram in Fig. 9.12.

As shown in Fig. 9.12, the constraint enforces that there is only one tour that can cover all nodes, than having two more disjointed tours that collectively cover all nodes. For instance, if the salesman travelled from u_3 to u_1 or from u_5 to u_3, it would certainly violate the condition in Eq. (9.13). Therefore, satisfying the constraints can avoid the creation of subtours and ensure that the feasible solution contains only one closed circle of nodes.

Linear programming can be useful for solving some simple TSP problems. In practice however, it may take months or even years to solve some real-life problems. Therefore, instead of finding optimal solutions, efforts have been placed on the development of heuristic algorithms that aim to find the close-to-optimum routes.

TSP Heuristics

The heuristic technique is often based on the past experience or a rule of thumb that is usually effective in dealing with a given situation. Heuristics can guide the search for best possible solutions, though not optimal, and are extremely effective to problem solving processes.

For TSP, there are different construction heuristics that can be applied to determine a tour based on certain construction rules. Note however that a construction heuristic does not attempt to improve upon the tour once built and parts already built remain unchanged throughout the algorithm. Three common construction heuristics are as follows:

- Nearest Neighbour Heuristic
- Insertion Heuristics
- Savings Heuristic

Nearest Neighbour

The nearest neighbour (NN) heuristic selects the nearest unvisited node as the next move until all nodes are visited and the salesman returns to the depot. This algorithm probably represents the real salesman's approach as shown in Fig. 9.13 below.

The NN algorithm is one of the earliest algorithms used to solve the TSP problems. It is easy to execute and can efficiently create a short route. Though the algorithm often misses shorter routes, the resulting tours can serve as a good starting point for the application of improvement methods.

Nearest Insertion

One of the popular insertion heuristics is the nearest insertion algorithm, in which a tour starts with a small subset of nodes (e.g., two or three), and then a new node that is closest to any node in the subtour is inserted into the tour. An example of the insertion process can be seen in Fig. 9.14 below.

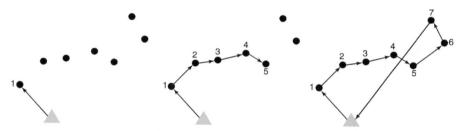

Fig. 9.13 Nearest neighbour heuristic

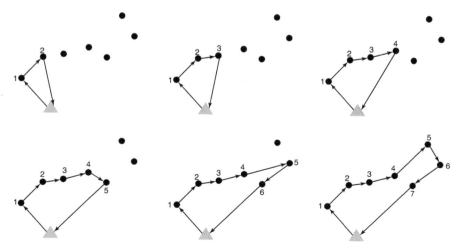

Fig. 9.14 Nearest insertion heuristic

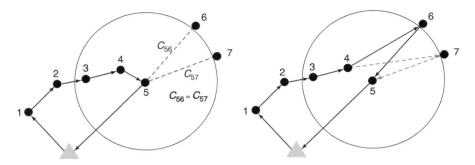

Fig. 9.15 Cheapest insertion heuristic

Cheapest Insertion

A similar insertion algorithm is the cheapest insertion. However, instead of inserting new node that is closest to any nodes in the existing subtour, the cheapest insertion selects the unvisited node whose insertion causes the minimum increase in total tour length.

As shown in Fig. 9.15, node 6 and node 7 have the same distance to node 5 (i.e., $c_{56} = c_{57}$), in such a case, node 6 is inserted first as it causes the lowest increase in the total tour length.

Savings Method

The savings method was initially proposed by Clarke and Wright (1964). The idea behind this algorithm is simple. Imagine the salesman must visit two cities, instead of having two separate trips from home to each city, the salesman can leave home and visit the two cities on a single trip and then return home. By combining the trips, the total distance travelled can thus be reduced.

The algorithm works this way. First, select any node as the depot and index it as 0. Then, form individual routes from the depot to each node. Next, calculate all savings by joining two nodes and eliminating a trip back to the depot with the following equation:

$$S_{ij} = C_{0i} + C_{0j} - C_{ij} \text{ for } i, j = 1, 2, \ldots, n \qquad (9.16)$$

Once the savings are all calculated, order them from largest to smallest. Then, start forming larger subtours by linking appropriate nodes i and j according to the savings ranking. Finally, repeat until a tour is formed covering all the nodes.

Figure 9.16 demonstrates the process of using the savings method to solve a simple symmetric TSP problem.

Note that the example is a symmetric problem, i.e., $C_{ij} = C_{ji}$, for $i, j = (0, 1, \ldots, n)$, so that $S_{ij} = S_{ji}$. There are $(n - 1)(n - 2)/2$ savings to calculate if the problem is symmetric. In our example, there are six nodes in total, i.e., $n = 6$, then $(6 - 1)(6 - 2)/2 = 10$ savings to calculate. If the problem is asymmetric, then there are $(n - 1)(n - 2)$ savings to calculate.

C_{ij} \ S_{ij}	0	1	2	3	4	5
0		-	-	-	-	-
1	5		10	9	5	1
2	7	2		13	9	4
3	10	6	4		15	8
4	9	9	7	4		11
5	6	10	9	8	4	

Note: $S_{ij} = S_{ji}$ since the problem is symmetric

Ranking: S_{34}, S_{23}, S_{45}, S_{13}/S_{24}, S_{35}, S_{14}, S_{25}, S_{15}

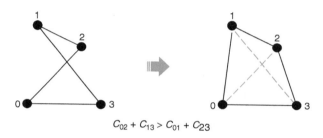

Fig. 9.16 Savings method

Fig. 9.17 2-opt exchange

$$C_{02} + C_{13} > C_{01} + C_{23}$$

Improvement Methods for TSP

The three common construction heuristics introduced above can help efficiently find a short route for TSP, however the solutions are often not optimal. Various approaches have been proposed to improve the tours such as Lin–Kernighan heuristic (or k-opt heuristic) (Lin and Kernighan 1973) and V-opt heuristic. Here we introduce two improvement heuristics: 2-opt and 3-opt, which are special cases of k-opt heuristic.

2-opt, or 2-optimal, is a heuristic that was first proposed by Croes (1958) in 1958. This technique originated from the idea that tours with cross-cover edges are not optimal as shown in Fig. 9.17. 2-opt attempts to swap every possible two edges when it results in a shorter tour.

The 2-opt algorithm keeps iterating until no further improving step is found and ends in the local optimum. Thus, it is regarded as a local search algorithm for solving the TSP problems.

3-opt heuristic works in the similar fashion; however, instead of swapping two edges, it breaks three edges and then reconnect the nodes in different possible ways. In the following example (t_1) as illustrated in Fig. 9.18, there are seven alternative ways to reconnect though not all these cases are considered (Helsgaun 2009).

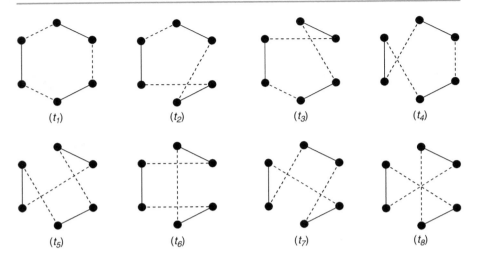

Fig. 9.18 3-opt exchange example

Note here that t_2 to t_4 in the diagram are equivalent to a single 2-opt exchange as one of the three broken edges remains unchanged. Likewise, t_5 to t_7 are equivalent to two subsequent 2-opt exchanges.

The 3-opt algorithm repeats for a different set of three edges until all possible combinations are tested and no further improvement can be made.

9.6.2   Vehicle Routing Problem

A similar routing problem that has been widely studied is the vehicle routing problem (VRP) in which there are multiple vehicles to serve customers. When there is only a single vehicle, it is no different from a TSP problem. However, if a fleet of vehicles exist, the VRP becomes more complex and challenging to solve as a set of optimal routes is required to serve all customers at minimum cost.

In addition, the complexity of a VRP may also arise from various restrictions that are placed on the problem, including, for example:

- Vehicle constraints (e.g., different sizes/capacities of vehicles)
- Different time windows (e.g., 10 am–11 am or 1 pm–2 pm time slots)
- Deliveries combined with pickups
- Profits (e.g., not all customers need to be visited/some must be visited)

The objective function of a VRP can be different too. For example, a common objective is to minimize total cost (e.g., total distance travelled). Others may include minimizing the number of vehicles required to serve all customers, profits maximization, least variation in travel time, to name a few.

Because of these different requirements and objectives, several variants of the VRP have emerged, for example:

- CVRP—capacitated vehicle routing problem
- VRPTW—vehicle routing problem with time windows
- VRPP—vehicle routing problem with profits
- VRPPD—vehicle routing problem with pickup and delivery
- MDVRP—multi-depot vehicle routing problem

There are a number of studies available for more details on these different VRP variants and results. In this section however, we focus only on the simplest form of the VRP problem.

Sweep Algorithm

Sweep algorithm is one of the classical heuristics for solving the VRP problems. It is simple, yet effective and is a good example of the 'cluster first, route second' approach. In other words, customers (or nodes) are included into a cluster as they are swept, until a vehicle cannot accommodate the next node due to some constraints such as its maximum capacity. Then, within each cluster, a TSP algorithm (e.g., nearest neighbour) can be used to optimize the route for each vehicle.

As illustrated in Fig. 9.19, the sweeping process can be described as follows:

- Start with a ray from the depot (at a random angle)
- Sweep ray in one direction and assign nodes to a cluster until some constraints are reached for each vehicle (e.g., max capacity, distance limit, time windows)
- Continue sweeping until all nodes are covered.

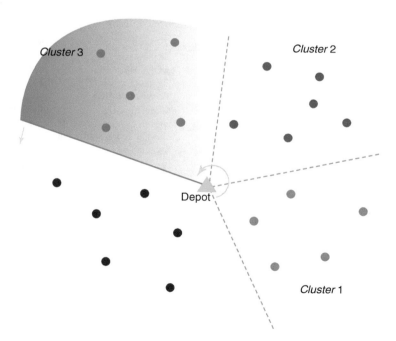

Fig. 9.19 Sweep method for clustering

Note that the full fleet of vehicles are not always required if all the constraints and objectives functions are satisfied. For instance, if two trucks can make deliveries to all the customers without delays, a third vehicle might not be required due to cost considerations, unless a higher customer service level is desired. In addition, since the sweep direction is arbitrary at a random angle, there is no guarantee that optimal routing solutions can be realized.

Clustering Algorithm

Instead of using the arbitrary sweep method, we can also apply the clustering algorithms introduced in early chapter (e.g., K-means and DBSCAN) to group customers. These algorithms are powerful in clustering date points based on geometry such as distances between points or graph distance. The outcomes of the clustering can potentially lead to better routing solutions that minimize the total travelling distances.

We will not go through a particular clustering algorithm here, for more details see **scikit-learn documentation on clustering**. Table 9.4 below provides a comparison among some popular clustering algorithms.

9.6.3   Route Optimization Example: The Cambridge Pizza Store

After learning the basics of the TSP and VRP problems, let us work on two simplified routing problems for a pizza store located at central Cambridge, United Kingdom.

Table 9.4 A comparison of the clustering algorithms in Scikit-learn

Method	Parameters	Scalability	Use case	Metric used
K-Means	Number of clusters	Very large samples, medium clusters	General-purpose, even cluster size, flat geometry, not too many clusters	Distances between points
Affinity propagation	Damping, sample preference	Not scalable with samples	Many clusters, uneven cluster size, non-flat geometry	Graph distance (e.g., nearest neighbour graph)
Mean-shift	Bandwidth	Not scalable with samples	Many clusters, uneven cluster size, non-flat geometry	Distances between points
Spectral clustering	Number of clusters	Medium samples, small clusters	Few clusters, even cluster size, non-flat geometry	Graph distance
DBSCAN	Neighbourhood size	Very large samples, medium clusters	Non-flat geometry, uneven cluster sizes	Distances between nearest points
Gaussian mixtures	Many	Not scalable	Flat geometry, good for density estimation	Mahalanobis distances to centres

(*Source: Scikit-learn*)

In the first example, the pizza store tries to distribute promotional flyers to the 31 colleges of Cambridge University, as historical data indicate that there is a strong correlation between the promotion and sales. The delivery will be made by one staff cycling around the colleges, which is identical to a TSP problem.

To solve the problem in Python, we need to import necessary packages into the notebook first:

Ex. 9.10

```
from pulp import *
import pandas as pd
import matplotlib.pyplot as plt
import seaborn as sns; sns.set()
```

Next, let us import the data that contains the latitude and longitude information of each college and the pizza store (i.e., the nodes), as well as the distances between each pair of nodes. The output has been truncated for brevity, see below:

Ex. 9.11

```
Cambridge = pd.read_excel('Cambridge.xlsx', index_col="College" )
Cambridge
```

College	Latitude	Longitude	The Pizza Store	Wolfson College	Christ's College	Churchill College	Clare College	Clare Hall	Corpus Christi College	Darwin College	...
The Pizza Store	52.203982	0.118100	0.0000	1.2850	0.3906	1.6080	0.23540	0.9359	0.11630	0.4828	...
Wolfson College	52.199085	0.101017	1.2850	0.0000	1.6650	1.5660	1.17400	0.6183	1.22800	0.8741	...
Christ's College	52.206260	0.122464	0.3906	1.6650	0.0000	1.7200	0.51320	1.2530	0.48250	0.8702	...
Churchill College	52.213150	0.099859	1.6080	1.5660	1.7200	0.0000	1.37400	1.0360	1.67300	1.6770	...
Clare College	52.205106	0.115172	0.2354	1.1740	0.5132	1.3740	0.00000	0.7420	0.30390	0.5090	...
Clare Hall	52.204251	0.104373	0.9359	0.6183	1.2530	1.0360	0.74200	0.0000	0.93320	0.7461	...
Corpus Christi College	52.202943	0.117899	0.1163	1.2280	0.4825	1.6730	0.30390	0.9332	0.00000	0.3901	...
Darwin College	52.200632	0.113592	0.4828	0.8741	0.8702	1.6770	0.50900	0.7461	0.39010	0.0000	...
Downing College	52.200948	0.125807	0.6242	1.7020	0.6331	2.2290	0.85970	1.5060	0.58280	0.8332	...

To have a better visualization of the locations of nodes, we can plot them onto a map. Consider below:

Ex. 9.12

```
# Plotting Cambridge colleges on map
cam = plt.imread('Cam.JPG')
fig, ax = plt.subplots(figsize=(10, 6))
ax.scatter(Cambridge.Longitude, Cambridge.Latitude,
           zorder=1, c='#0072ce', s=50)
# Plot the pizza store
ax.scatter(Cambridge.iloc[-1].Longitude,
           Cambridge.iloc[-1].Latitude,  marker="*", c='r', s=300)
# Set x,y limits
ax.set_xlim(0.0728, 0.1509)
ax.set_ylim(52.18, 52.2324)
ax.imshow(cam,extent=(0.0728,0.1509,52.18,52.2324),aspect='equal')
ax.grid(False)
```

Linear Programming with PuLP

First, let us try to solve the routing problem using MTZ formulation. We set the number of vehicle $v = 1$ since there is only one person to delivery all the flyers to the 31 colleges. Consider below:

Ex. 9.13

```
# Initialise the VRP model
VRP = LpProblem("VRP", sense=LpMinimize)

# Define Decision Variables
X = LpVariable.dicts('X', [(i, j)
                           for i in colleges for j in colleges],
                     cat='Binary')

# Auxiliary variables for subtours elimination
U = LpVariable.dicts('U', [i for i in colleges],
          lowBound=1, upBound=len(colleges), cat='Integer')

# Define Objective
VRP += lpSum([Cambridge.loc[i, j] * X[(i, j)]
              for i in colleges for j in colleges])
```

The constraints can be set according to Eqs. (9.11), (9.12), and (9.13). See below:

Ex. 9.14

```
# Define Constraints
for i in colleges:
    cap = v
    # Sum of departure cities
    VRP += lpSum([X[(i, j)] for j in colleges if i != j]) == cap
    # Sum of arrival cities
    VRP += lpSum([X[(j, i)] for j in colleges if i != j]) == cap

# Eliminate Subtours
N = len(colleges)/v
for i in colleges:
    for j in colleges:
        if i != j and (i != 'The Pizza Store' and j != 'The Pizza Store'):
            VRP += U[i] - U[j] <= (N)*(1-X[(i, j)]) - 1
```

The model is now ready to be solved. We can simply use the `solve()` method and check the status of the output with the following code:

Ex. 9.15

```
# Solve Model
VRP.solve()
print(LpStatus[VRP.status])
Optimal
```

Great! Our model has found an optimal solution. To get the delivery route, we can define a helper function, consider below:

Ex. 9.16

```
# Define a function to get the sequence of the route
def get_route (start):
    route = [start]
    edge = edges.copy()
    found = True
    while found:
        found = False
        for (i, j) in edge:
            if i == route[-1]:
                route.append(j)
                edge.remove((i,j))
                found = True

    return route
```

We can get the `edges` in the function by the listing the selected (i, j) link from the model output:

Ex. 9.17

```
edges = [(i, j) for (i, j) in X if value(X[(i, j)])
        != 0 and value(X[(i, j)]) != None]
```

Then, the delivery route can be printed out with the code below:

Ex. 9.18

```
route = get_route('The Pizza Store')
print(' -> '.join([r for r in route]))
```

```
The Pizza Store -> Gonville & Caius College -> Sidney Sussex Co
llege -> Jesus College -> Christ's College -> Emmanuel College
-> Downing College -> Hughes Hall -> Homerton College -> Peterh
ouse -> Pembroke College -> Corpus Christi College -> St Cathar
ine's College -> Queens' College -> Darwin College -> Newnham C
ollege -> Wolfson College -> Selwyn College -> Clare Hall -> Ro
binson College -> Churchill College -> Girton College -> Fitzwi
lliam College -> Murray Edwards College -> St Edmund's College
-> Lucy Cavendish -> Magdalene College -> St John's College ->
Trinity College -> Trinity Hall -> Clare College -> King's Coll
ege -> The Pizza Store
```

The optimized total travelling distance can be obtained using the model's objective function:

Ex. 9.19

```
# Print the optimized solution
print("The minimized travel distance is {0:.3f} km".\
       format(value(VRP.objective)))
The minimised travel distance is 15.477 km
```

Finally, we can plot and visualize the optimized route, consider below:

Ex. 9.20

```
# Plot colleges
fig, ax = plt.subplots(figsize=(15, 10))
ax.scatter(Cambridge.Longitude, Cambridge.Latitude,
           zorder=1, c='g', s=80)

# Plot the pizza store
ax.scatter(Cambridge.iloc[0].Longitude,
           Cambridge.iloc[0].Latitude,
           marker="*", c='r', s=300)

# Set x,y limits
ax.set_xlim(0.080, 0.145)
ax.set_ylim(52.185, 52.230)

# Set annotation
for txt in route:
    ax.annotate(txt, xy=(Cambridge.loc[txt].Longitude,
                         Cambridge.loc[txt].Latitude),size=9)

# Plot the route
position = Cambridge[['Longitude', 'Latitude']]
for (i, j) in edges:
    p1, p2 = position.loc[i], position.loc[j]
    ax.annotate("", p1, p2, arrowprops=dict(arrowstyle="<-",
                                    color='blue', lw=2))
```

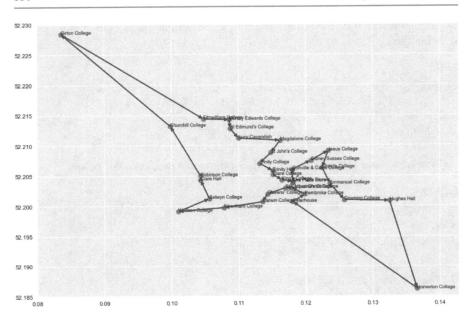

We have successfully solved a simple TSP problem using linear programming with PuLP. However, when the number of nodes is large and more vehicles are involved, linear programming can take extremely long time to solve the problem. In the following section, we will consider using some heuristics to solve the same problem.

Nearest Neighbour with Python

Recall that the NN heuristic inserts the next closest node to the tour. To use the NN heuristic, we can simply define a function using the `while` loop, consider below:

Ex. 9.21

```
def get_nearest_neighbour(unvisited):
    current = 'The Pizza Store'  # starting point
    NN_path = []
    while True:
        NN_path.append(current)
        unvisited.remove(current)
        if not unvisited:
            break

#idxmin() returns the index of the minimum value of the dataframe
        current = Cambridge.loc[unvisited, current].idxmin()
    NN_path.append('The Pizza Store')
    return NN_path
```

Then, we can call the function on the index of the Cambridge data that contains all the nodes:

Ex. 9.22

```
route = get_nearest_neighbour(list(Cambridge.index))
```

Once the route is obtained, we can apply the same code as in *Ex. 9.20* to plot the route:

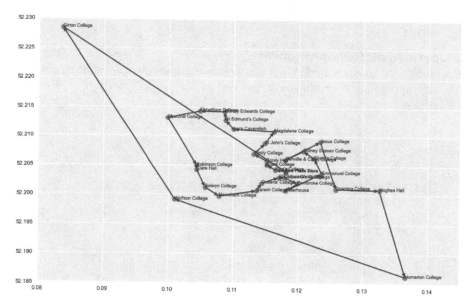

As can be seen, the route seems longer than the one created by linear programming. Let us create a helper function to get the total travelling distance created by the NN algorithm, consider below:

Ex. 9.23

```
# Helper function
travel_distance = lambda route: sum(Cambridge.loc[i, j]
                        for i, j in zip(route, route[1:]))

print('Total travel distance is {0:.3f} km'.\
    format(travel_distance(route)))
Total travel distance is 19.852 km
```

As the result suggests, the total travelling distance has increased to 19.852 km compared to 15.477 km generated by linear programming.

2-Opt Heuristic for Improvement

Apparently, the route created by NN is not optimal. To improve upon the new route, we can apply the 2-opt heuristic by defining a helper function in Python. Consider below:

Ex. 9.24

```python
def two_opt(route):
    best = route
    found = True
    while found:
        found = False
        # i starts at index location 1, as 0 is where the trip begins
        for i in range(1, len(route)-2):
            for j in range(i+1, len(route)):
                if j-i == 1: continue
                new_route = route.copy()
                new_route[i:j] = route[j-1:i-1:-1]   # 2-opt swap
                # compare the total travel distance
                if travel_distance(new_route) < travel_distance(best):
                    best = new_route
                    found = True
        route = best
    return best
```

The function takes the existing route and then keeps swapping edges until no further improvement can be made and eventually returns the best-found route. We can call the function on the route generated by the NN algorithm:

Ex. 9.25

```python
two_opt_route = two_opt(route)
```

Once we get the new improved route, we can use the same code to plot it:

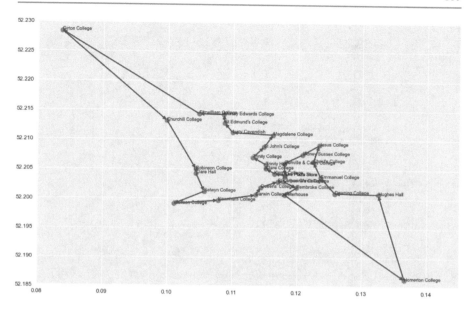

The improved route looks the same as the one generated by linear programming except the direction of the arrows as indicated above. We can double check the total travelling distance:

Ex. 9.26

```
print('The improved travel distance with 2-opt heuristic is {0:.3f} km'.\
      format(travel_distance(two_opt_route)))
The improved travel distance with 2-opt heuristic is 15.477 km
```

After applying 2-opt swap, we have obtained the same result as the one created by linear programming but the direction of the route. In short, using the NN algorithm first followed by the 2-opt heuristic can certainly help to improve the route. This approach can make a big difference when dealing with a large routing problem as computing efficiency can be significantly improved with heuristics.

The Cambridge Pizza Store with Four Vehicles

In the second example, the pizza store delivers pizza with four drivers. Assume each vehicle must cover certain number of colleges without capacity and time window constraints. When demand arrives from all 31 colleges, what would be the best routes to deliver pizza with four vehicles that minimize the total travelling distance? This is a simplified VRP problem, in which the number of vehicle $V = 4$.

Since there are no other constraints on this VRP, we can first use the NN heuristic to generate four separate routes and then improve them using 2-opt heuristic. We need to define a new NN function that considers multi-vehicles:

Ex. 9.27

```
# Define a sequential nearest neighbour function
def get_seq_NN(unvisited, v):
    current = {} # starting point for all vehicles
    seq_path = {}

    for vehicle_id in range(v):
        seq_path[vehicle_id]= []
        current[vehicle_id] = ['The Pizza Store']
        seq_path[vehicle_id].append(current[vehicle_id][0])

    unvisited.remove('The Pizza Store')

    while True:
        for vehicle_id in range(v):
            current[vehicle_id][0] = Cambridge.\
            loc[unvisited, current[vehicle_id][0]].idxmin()
            seq_path[vehicle_id].append(current[vehicle_id][0])
            unvisited.remove(current[vehicle_id][0])
        # break the for loop if all colleges have been visited
            if not unvisited:
                break
    # break the while loop if all colleges have been visited
        if not unvisited:
            break

    for vehicle_id in range(v):
        seq_path[vehicle_id].append('The Pizza Store')

    return seq_path
```

Note that the routes are generated arbitrarily so that optimal routes are not guaranteed. We can call the function on the Cambridge data and create the routes:

Ex. 9.28

```
route = get_seq_NN(list(Cambridge.index), 4)  # with 4 vehicles
```

Next, we can visualize the routes using the same code as in *Ex.* 9.20 with slight modification as indicated below:

Ex. 9.29

```
# Plot the route
for routes in route.values():
    position = list(zip(*[(Cambridge.loc[i].Longitude,
                        Cambridge.loc[i].Latitude) for i in routes]))
    plt.plot(position[0], position[1], linewidth=3)

    total_travel_distance += travel_distance(routes)

print("The total travel distance using NN algorithm is {0:.3f}km".\
    format(total_travel_distance))
The total travel distance using NN algorithm is 25.255km
```

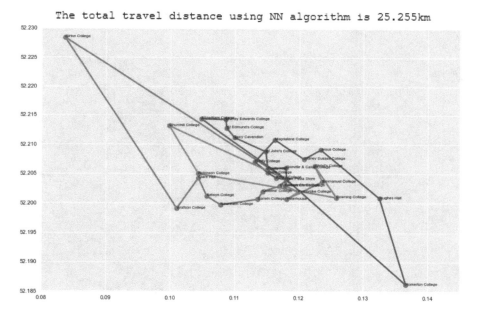

The total travel distance using NN algorithm is 25.255km

Using the NN algorithm, we have obtained four routes with a total travelling distance of 25.255 km. Obviously, this is not the optimal result as we can see cross-over edges on the plot.

Let us try to improve the result with 2-opt heuristic and then re-plot the routes. Consider below:

Ex. 9.30

```
# Initialise total travel distance value
total_travel_distance = 0

# Plot improved routes with 2-opt
for vehicle_id, routes in route.items():
    improved_NN_route = two_opt(routes)
    position = list(zip(*[(Cambridge.loc[i].Longitude,
                          Cambridge.loc[i].Latitude)
                         for i in improved_NN_route]))
    plt.plot(position[0], position[1], linewidth=3)
    total_travel_distance += travel_distance(improved_NN_route)

print("The total travel distance with 2-opt heuristic is {0:.3f}km".\
      format(total_travel_distance))
The total travel distance with 2-opt heuristic is 23.909km
```

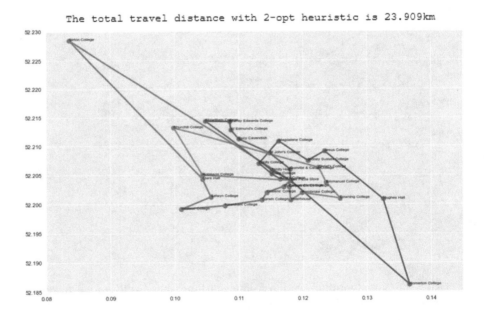

The total travel distance with 2-opt heuristic is 23.909km

As can be seen, the total travelling distance has improved when the cross-over edges are eliminated for each delivery route.

Spectral Clustering

Lastly, we can apply certain clustering algorithms to group the colleges into four clusters first and then use NN algorithm within each cluster to get the route. Here, the spectral clustering algorithm will be used for our VRP problem.

Spectral clustering algorithm is rooted in graph theory and can be very useful for identifying communities of nodes in a graph based on the edges connecting them. The resulting clusters by spectral clustering often outperform the traditional approaches (von Luxburg 2007).

To use the algorithm in Python, simply import it from scikit-learn implementation:

Ex. 9.31

```
from sklearn.cluster import SpectralClustering
```

Next, let us set the number of clusters equal to the number of vehicles, i.e., $V = 4$, and fit the model on the colleges data that contain the distances between each pair of nodes. Consider below:

Ex. 9.32

```
# Initialize the model
v = 4 # number of delievery vehicles
clt = SpectralClustering(n_clusters=v, random_state=42,
                         affinity='nearest_neighbors')
clt.fit_predict(colleges)
array([2, 3, 1, 0, 2, 0, 2, 3, 3, 1, 1, 0, 3, 3, 3, 0, 1, 1, 1, 2, 3, 3,
       0, 2, 2, 0, 0, 1, 0, 0, 0])
```

We can then plot the clusters according to the labels of each node:

Ex. 9.33

```
# Plot colleges
fig, ax = plt.subplots(figsize=(15, 10))
ax.scatter(location.Longitude, location.Latitude,
           c=clt.labels_, cmap='viridis',s=150)

# Annotation
for txt in Cambridge.index:
    ax.annotate(txt, xy=(Cambridge.loc[txt].Longitude+0.0002,
                Cambridge.loc[txt].Latitude+0.0005), size=9)
# Plot the pizza store
ax.scatter(Cambridge.iloc[0].Longitude,
           Cambridge.iloc[0].Latitude, marker="*", c='r', s=300);

# Set x,y limits
ax.set_xlim(0.080, 0.145)
ax.set_ylim(52.185, 52.230);
```

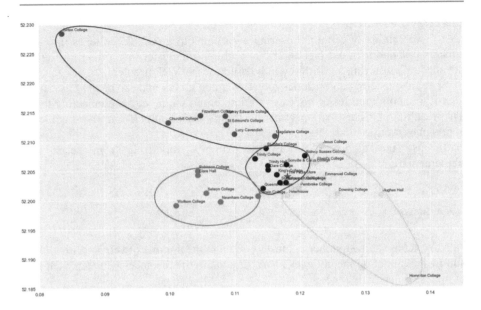

After the clustering, we can use the NN algorithm to get the delivery routes for each cluster and visualize the result. Consider the code below:

Ex. 9.34

```
# Initialise total travel distance value
total_travel_distance = 0

# Get the routes
for i in range(v):
    unvisited = colleges[clt.labels_ == i].index.tolist()
    current = 'The Pizza Store'  # starting point
    unvisited.append(current)
    route = get_nearest_neighbour(unvisited)

    position = list(zip(*[(Cambridge.loc[j].Longitude,
                Cambridge.loc[j].Latitude) for j in route]))
    plt.plot(position[0], position[1], linewidth=3)
    total_travel_distance += travel_distance(route)

    print('Vehicle No.{} Route:'.format(i+1))
    print('{}\n'.format(route))

print("The total travel distance using NN algorithm is\
    {0:.3f}km".format(total_travel_distance))
The total travel distance using NN algorithm is 20.778km
```

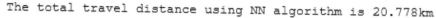

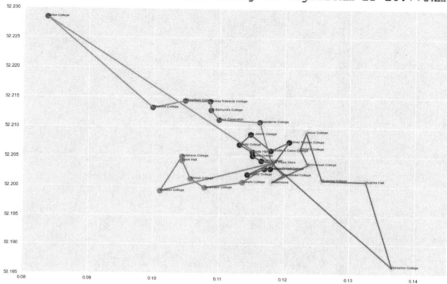

The total travelling distance has significantly improved with the clustering approach. Since there are still cross-over edges in the routes, we can further improve the result by applying 2-opt heuristic. See the code below (truncated for brevity):

Ex. 9.35

```
# Plot improved routes with 2-opt
    improved_NN_route = two_opt(route)
    position = list(zip(*[(Cambridge.loc[i].Longitude,
                           Cambridge.loc[i].Latitude)
                          for i in improved_NN_route]))
    plt.plot(position[0], position[1], linewidth=3)
    total_travel_distance += travel_distance(improved_NN_route)

print("The total travel distance with 2-opt heuristic is\
      {0:.3f}km".format(total_travel_distance))
```

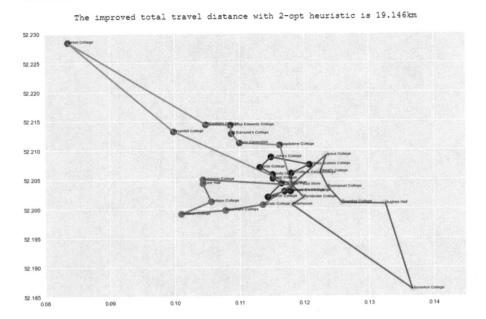

The improved total travel distance with 2-opt heuristic is 19.146km

After the 2-opt swapping, the total travelling distance has reduced to 19.146 km—more than 4 km savings, which is a big improvement! It is obvious that using clustering algorithm can significantly improve the route optimization for our VRP problem.

In summary, we have gone through two simplified routing problems in this section. Linear programming can usually produce a good result; however, it is not feasible for solving large routing problems as computing time grows exponentially. Hence, construction heuristics such as NN algorithm can be applied to efficiently produce less-than-optimal routes that can be improved later using heuristics like 2-opt swap. A better approach to solving the VRP is the application of clustering algorithms to first group customers into similar clusters, then use heuristics to build and improve the resulting routes.

In real-world, VRP can be more challenging to solve due to various constraints and uncertainties such as different travel time, traffic conditions, weather conditions, etc. For interested students, there are a number of studies that focus on developing more complex and effective algorithms for VRP problems, however they are beyond the scope of this book.

Summary of Learning Objectives

1. **Describe the importance of logistics management and its major management activities.**

   Logistics is considered a part of supply chain processes, which mainly deals with the physical movement and distribution of goods and services along a company's supply chain. Logistics management is important for effective supply chain management as it can ensures the smooth and timely delivery of the material flows throughout a supply chain to fulfil customer request. Logistics management is also closely related to a firm's performance objectives as demonstrated in Table 9.1. The main activities involved in logistics activities include inbound and outbound logistics, which can be broken further down into warehousing, storage, materials handling, packing and transportation as well as the associated information and security management. Location decision and route optimization are considered two major tasks in logistics network design, which is also considered a critical component of logistics management.

2. **Understand different modes of transport, their respective advantages and disadvantages, and how to select appropriate transport modes.**

   There are essentially five major modes of transport, including road, rail, water, air, and pipeline. Each mode has its own purpose of usage and associated pros and cons. A comparison of different transport modes is illustrated in Table 9.2. For instance, road transport has the advantages of high accessibility and flexibility, however it has low carrying capacity and may experience frequent delays due to traffic conditions. By contrast, rail has a high carrying capacity but is constrained by restricted routes and networks, hence reduced accessibility, especially for door-to-door access. Selecting appropriate transport mode can depend on many factors such as cost, service availability, speed, flexibility, risk and security considerations. In freight and cargo shipping, chargeable weight is often used to estimate the cost of shipping. Another useful metric is called product value density (PVD), which can be used to determine the appropriate mode of transport for shipping a particular product based on its value density.

3. **Learn different logistics service providers, their roles and differences in terms of the services and value-adding activities they provide.**

   As introduced in Sect. 9.3, there are five common types of logistics service providers, including freight companies, freight carriers, freight forwarders, 3PL and 4PL. In addition to the basic transportation services, freight forwarders usually also deal with all documentation, customs clearance, rate negotiation, consolidation, and coordination of freight from the source to the customer. 3PL generally provide a wider range of services and a deeper integration with a firm's supply chain than freight forwarders. 4PL is a relatively new term, which has been used to describe the complete and comprehensive supply chain solutions the logistics providers can offer. The 4PL providers develop their own capabilities and technologies, and usually have their own complex distribution networks to offer globally consistent and value-adding logistics solutions. The 4PL providers are often those lead logistics providers (LLP) such as DHL and UPS. Figure 9.6 compares some differences between 3PL and 4PL logistics services.

4. **Grasp the meaning of commonly used INCOTERMS in global trade.**

   The ICC publishes Incoterms which contains a series of pre-defined three-letter trade terms that set out the obligations, costs, and risks between sellers and buyers participating in the import and export of global trade. There are a total of 11 incoterms in the 2020 version. In this chapter, we focus on nine commonly used ones. A summary and graphical representation of these different incoterms can be found in Fig. 9.8. For more information about incoterms, visit the International Chamber of Commerce website.

5. **Understand different location decisions and the approaches to making effective location selection.**

   Location choice can be one of the most important decisions to make facing logistics and supply chain managers. It can involve supplier selection and facility location choice such as determining manufacturing sites, DCs, warehouses, and retail stores. Making effective location selection can have a long-term effect on firm performance. There are several factors to consider when making location decisions, including cost, proximity to source, proximity to market, accessibility, demand level, service level, and risk factor. There are different approaches that can be used to identify suitable locations for a new facility such as the centre of gravity method and the square root law for centralization or de-centralization in warehouse location choices.

6. **Learn different route optimization algorithms and be able to use them to solve basic routing problems.**

   In this chapter, we focus on only the basic route optimization problems such as TSP and VRP without adding variants and complexity to them. The algorithms introduced for solving the TSP problem include nearest neighbour heuristic, nearest insertion, cheapest insertion, and savings method. These algorithms can be useful in finding a short route; however, their solutions are often not optimal. Thus, the k-opt heuristic can help improve the solutions found by these algorithms. In this chapter, we mainly introduce 2-opt and 3-opt. Figures 9.17 and 9.18 illustrate how these two heuristics work. For VRP, sweep algorithm can be effective which 'cluster first and route second'. Last but not least, clustering algorithms can be useful for solving the VRP problems as demonstrated in the Cambridge Pizza Store example. Make sure you learn and understand these algorithms and be able to use them to solve some basic routing problems.

Discussion Questions

1. Choose a company and discuss how it manages its logistics operations, by either itself or a logistics provider? What are the key modes of transport, and what are the main logistics decisions to make for your chosen company?
2. XYZ company is going to ship some cargo from Auckland, New Zealand to Birmingham, UK via air. The shipment has a gross weight of 420 kg, with dimensions 120 cm(L) × 80 cm(W) × 100(H), what is the chargeable weight? What about via sea?
3. If your company is going to import two containers of goods from China, you want to insure your goods once they leave the loading port, what Incoterms you could negotiate with the supplier?
4. If you are a supply chain manager for a supermarket chain, and your company wants to build an additional regional DC to cover the increasing demand and cut down costs, what factors do you need to consider for this location decision of the new DC? Should you use centralized or decentralized warehouses? Explain the reason for your choice.
5. What are the major differences between Nearest Neighbour algorithm and Cheapest Insertion algorithm?

Keyboard Exercises

1. In your notebook, import necessary packages, re-run all the exercises in this chapter. You can select your own algorithms and fine-tune the estimator of your choice. Can you find an even better route for the Cambridge Pizza Store example?
2. Download the TSP exercise data 'p01_d.txt' and 'p01_xy.txt' from our online repository and try to solve the problem by yourself. What is the shortest total travel distance that can you find?
3. In the Cambridge Pizza Store example, what if the number of delivery cars has increased to five?
4. Try to develop your own 3-opt algorithm in Python, and see whether it can used to improve the Cambridge Pizza Store routing result?

References

Clarke, G. & Wright, J.W. 1964. "Scheduling of vehicles from a central depot to a number of delivery points", Operations Research, Vol. 12 No. 4, 568-581.

Croes, G. A. 1958. "A method for solving traveling-salesman problems", Operations Research, Vol. 6 No. 6, 791-812.

Freight Transport Association. 2019. "Logistics Report 2019".

Helsgaun, K. 2009. "General k-opt submoves for the Lin–Kernighan TSP heuristic", Math. Prog. Comp. Vol 1, pp. 119–163.

International Chamber of Commerce. "Incoterms 2020". Retrieved at https://iccwbo.org/resources-for-business/incoterms-rules/incoterms-2020/, on 5th April 2021.

Lin, S. & Kernighan, B.W. 1973. "An Effective Heuristic Algorithm for the Traveling-Salesman Problem", Operations Research, Vol. 21 No. 2, pp. 498–516.

Lovell, A., Saw, R. & Stimson, J. 2005, "Product value-density: managing diversity through supply chain segmentation", The International Journal of Logistics Management, Vol. 16 No. 1, pp. 142-158.

Maister, D.H. 1976. "Centralisation of Inventories and the "Square Root Law"", International Journal of Physical Distribution, Vol. 6 No. 3, pp. 124-134.

Miller, C.E., Tucker, A.W. & Zemlin, R.A. 1960. "Integer Programming Formulation of Traveling Salesman Problems". J. ACM, Vol. 7 No. 4 pp. 326–329.

Oeser, G. & Romano, P. 2016. "An empirical examination of the assumptions of the Square Root Law for inventory centralisation and decentralization", International Journal of Production Research, Vol. 54 No. 8, pp. 2298-2319.

Office for National Statistics. 2020. "UK trading partners and trade relationships: 2020".

Osaba, E., Yang, X.S. & Ser, J.D. 2020. "Chapter 9 - Traveling salesman problem: a perspective review of recent research and new results with bio-inspired metaheuristics, in Nature-Inspired Computation and Swarm Intelligence, Academic Press, pp. 135-164.

von Luxburg, U. 2007. "A tutorial on spectral clustering", Stat Comput Vol. 17, pp. 395–416.

World Trade Organization. 2020. "World Trade Statistical Review 2020".

Worstall, T. 2013. "Why Apple Sends All iPhones And iPads By Air: It's Cheaper", Forbes.

Index